Honoré M. Catudal

Soviet Nuclear Strategy from Stalin to Gorbachev

Honoré M. Catudal

Soviet Nuclear Strategy from Stalin to Gorbachev

A Revolution in Soviet Military and Political Thinking

Foreword by
Ambassador Martin J. Hillenbrand

HUMANITIES PRESS INTERNATIONAL, INC.
Atlantic Highlands, NJ

Originally published 1988 in Germany by Berlin Verlag

This edition published 1989 by
Humanities Press International, Inc.
Atlantic Highlands, NJ 07716

Library of Congress Cataloging-in-Publication Data

Catudal, Honoré Marc. 1944 –

Soviet nuclear strategy from Stalin to Gorbachev: a revolution in Soviet military and political thinking/Honoré M. Catudal; foreword by Martin J. Hillenbrand.

p. cm.

Sequel to: Nuclear deterrence.

Bibliography: p.

Includes index.

ISBN 0-391-03611-4. ISBN 0-391-03612-2 (pbk.)

1. Soviet Union—Military policy. 2. Strategic forces—Soviet Union. 3. Nuclear warfare. 4. Deterrence (Strategy) 5. United States—Military relations—Soviet Union. 6. Soviet Union—Military relations—United States. I. Title.

UA770.C37 1989

355'.0335'47—dc19 88-13668

CIP

Printed in the United States of America

In order to establish the strategic thought and doctrine of alien military culture, it is first necessary to escape the confines of one's own implicit and unconscious strategic concept.

Raymond Garthoff

To my love, Carol

Previous publications by Honoré (Marc) Catudal:

Steinstuecken: A Study in Cold War Politics (New York: Vintage Press, 1971), Foreword by General Lucius D. Clay

The Exclave Problem of Western Europe (Alabama: University of Alabama Press, 1979). Foreword by Eleanor L. Dulles

The Diplomacy of the Quadripartite Agreement on Berlin (West Berlin: Berlin Verlag Arno Spitz, 1977). Foreword by Ambassador Kenneth Rush 335 p.

A Balance Sheet of the Quadripartite Agreement on Berlin (West Berlin: Berlin Verlag Arno Spitz, 1978). Foreword by Ambassador Kenneth Rush 303 p.

Kennedy and the Berlin Wall Crisis: A Case Study in U.S. Decision-Making (West Berlin: Berlin Verlag Arno Spitz, 1980). Foreword by Ambassador Martin J. Hillenbrand 360 p.

Nuclear Deterrence: Does it Deter? (ATLANTIC HIGHLANDS, N.J.: HUMANITIES PRESS INTERNATIONAL, INC., 1986). Foreword by Ambassador Martin J. Hillenbrand 528 p.

CONTENTS

Preface

This study of Soviet nuclear strategy is a sequel to my book *Nuclear Deterrence: Does it Deter?*, in which I argue that there is a growing body of evidence which suggests that nuclear deterrence does not deter – at least not as we think it does... . In the main, the investigation of nuclear deterrence consisted of in-depth studies of the Cold War conflict and a detailed analysis of the structural weaknesses of the various nuclear deterrent strategies adopted by the United States.

In applying deterrence theory, U.S. policymakers were shown to have erred in a number of ways. First, they tended to take an oversimplified view of the world. Second, policymakers erred in relying too heavily on vaguely constructed nuclear deterrent strategies in situations more suited to conventional approaches. Finally, they have tended to assume for too long that the Soviets thought like U.S. policymakers did on the crucial matter of issuing threats and counterthreats.

This last mistake was especially serious, as this second volume shows. For the Soviet political leadership does not subscribe to many American doctrinal innovations. Soviet nuclear strategy is singularly Soviet. And it must be seen in its own special context, less the fallacy of mirror imaging occur.

Since U.S. policymakers tend in the last analysis to base their decisions in the area of nuclear strategy on what they believe Soviet policy is, it is extremely worthwhile to examine closely Soviet military doctrine as it has evolved over time and scrutinize carefully the basic underlying assumptions of Soviet nuclear policy. To be sure, there is no guarantee that Soviet doctrine will predetermine Soviet behavior in a crisis. Nevertheless, it is an important indicator of general strategic dispositions that will affect Soviet military actions in a confrontation.

During the early days of the Reagan Administration, there has been a lot of talk about nuclear war-fighting strategies and limited nuclear war. The debate over the question whether the Soviets think they can fight and win a nuclear war is still being waged. But this study has noted a number of important refinements in Soviet nuclear policy that are not generally taken into account when the issue is disputed today.

The idea of nuclear deterrence is central to the American defense posture. And many proponents of deterrence seem to assume that the Soviet leadership has accepted nuclear deterrence in the same way as the United States. But do the political and military leaders in the U.S.S.R. embrace nuclear deterrence? The continuing Soviet military buildup and repeated expressions in published Soviet military writings of a war-fighting doctrine have convinced some – and troubled others – as to Soviet views on this important and controversial matter.

This book attempts to illuminate Soviet thinking – which is not as monolithic as often assumed – on these – and other – major subjects relating to Soviet nuclear strategy. In particular, this inquiry considers the interrelationship of Soviet ideological beliefs, political imperatives and calculation, military views and doctrine and their reconciliation in Soviet policy. Finally, it points up some important fundamental differences between Soviet and American strategic thinking which is still evolving – both at the level of value and the level of methods. It is hoped that a recognition of these basic differences can have a favorable impact on the highly contentious U.S.-Soviet strategic relationship.

Collegeville, Minn. Honoré (Marc) Catudal
February, 1988

Acknowledgements

This book is the product of the efforts of many people. I am especially indebted to numerous middle-level officials in the Department of State, Defense and the U.S. Arms Control and Disarmament Agency who screened my drafts for errors of fact. For those remaining errors, the author bears full responsibility.

Those individuals to whom I owe a special debt and who may be named include: Abbot Jerome Theisen, O.S.B., who took a personal interest in this two-volume project;

President Hilary Thimmesh, O.S.B., St. John's University, who supported my research;

Dean Robert L. Spaeth, the author of an important book on nuclear weapons, who funded my extensive photocopying efforts, diligently scrutinized various draft chapters and warned me about my enthusiasms;

Professor Joe Farry, my department head, colleague and good friend, whose repeated kindness, perceptive advice and general guidance have been instrumental in my career;

My other colleagues at St. John's University, who read copy, engaged me in continuous dialogue and brought much important material to my attention, especially Ernie Diedrich, Marty Andrews, Sy Theisen, Otmar Drekonja, Bob Joyce and Bob Weber.

Ambassador Martin J. Hillenbrand, who critiqued several drafts of the text, astutely guiding me away from shoals and keeping me within the limits of the evidence at hand, and who above all contributed a valuable foreword;

General Andrew Goodpaster, President of the Institute for Defense Analyses, for his detailed criticism of various chapters;

John C. Ausland, formerly Secretary to the American delegation in the SALT I negotiations, whose valuable advice and detailed comments saved me from many a pitfall and oversimplification.

Professor Robert M. Slusser of Michigan State University, for his review of some draft chapters and long-time scholarly advice and assistance;

Professor Carl Anthon of American University, a long-time mentor who encouraged my best efforts;

My right arm Shirley Zipoy, who selflessly typed various drafts of the manuscript with an energy and enthusiasm that knew no bounds;

My special assistants, Nancy Hutchinson, Sherman Marek, Kevin Osterbauer and Randy Divinski, who sacrificed many hours reading drafts, checking details, suggesting alternative language and challenging my arguments;

Finally my students, Lynn Rausch, Greg Friederichs, Kim Davis, Jayme Trusty, Wende Varsoke, and Susan Lawyer who contributed many hours of their time xeroxing materials and otherwise providing me with important assistance and who once again showed the validity of the wisdom that "by one's students one will be taught."

For any merit in this study, these men and women deserve a large share of the credit. The errors are my own.

Foreword

A reasonably correct assessment of Soviet strategic thinking in the nuclear age should obviously be an integral part of any sound American military and political strategy. Yet the numerous books and articles written over the years on various aspects of the subject do not add up to any clear consensus, nor indeed even agreement on the most basic questions. On the one hand there are those who maintain that Soviet strategy assumes that one can fight and win a nuclear war, provided only that the elements of surprise or clear superiority can be achieved. On the other hand, some competent experts argue that an evolving Soviet strategy has come to accept that the enormous mutual destructiveness of a major nuclear exchange between the two superpowers precludes victory in any rational definition of the term.

One of the problems frequently facing the Western analyst is the difficulty in distinguishing between genuine views and deliberate attempts at disinformation on the part of Soviet spokesmen. Nikita Khrushchev was a master of bluster and bluff, he also sometimes said precisely what he meant. Other Soviet writers and speakers may use more sophisticated language in efforts to mislead, but the interplay of truth and calculated falsehood has provided a continuing problem of decipherment for those seeking to obtain a coherent picture of what the Soviet Union's real strategy is. Last spring's Soviet nuclear disaster at Chernobyl provided a classic example both of Soviet reticence in providing accurate information about developments that might reflect unfavorably on the U.S.S.R. and, in the face of this, of Western difficulties in trying to ascertain precisely what had happened. Similar barriers obviously exist as far as Soviet weapons development, deployment and potential use are concerned.

One approach, overly simplistic to its critics, is to deduce Soviet strategy from observable deployments of weapons systems. This is just another variant of the old tendency of military men to equate capabilities and intentions, but it would be foolish to argue that the kinds of weapons one favors throw no light on strategic intentions. If Soviet emphasis on heavy, land-based missiles may have been partly a function of available technology and of choices made two decades ago, it may also reflect a certain confidence that the boost power of delivery systems may be the ultimate determinant of a nuclear engagement.

These are obviously important questions within the framework of continuing mutual deterrence. Unfortunately, clear and unchangeable answers are not available about Soviet strategy any more than even the closest observer of the Washington scene could expect to come up with conclusions about American strategic thinking that would be unmistakable and without contradiction within the strategic establishment. A consistent reader of the annual reports of the Secretary of Defense will note certain underlying assumptions about Soviet strategy that are believed to have major implications for American weapons policy. Much of the debate during the early Reagan years about a so-called window of vulnerability obviously involved assumptions about possible Soviet intentions that, fortunately, were never put to the test. One of the great merits of the Scowcroft Commission Report of 1983 was its persuasive argument that the American deterrent still remained a reality.

Professor Catudal's book attempts to deal with all of the important aspects of Soviet strategic thinking, including reactions in Moscow to American rhetoric and actual weapons policies. Given the difficulties, he has come up with a balanced, thoughtful and scholarly appraisal from which much can be learned. His account in Chapter 10 of the Soviet reaction to President Reagan's Strategic Defense Initiative is concise and suggestive; it obviously could not, given the exigencies of publishing deadlines, hope to describe the developing Soviet position as revealed in the ongoing Geneva arms reduction talks and the accompanying propaganda battle between Gorbachev and Washington.

It is particularly difficult to ascertain what the Soviets really think about the internal debates in the United States on various aspects of strategy. They can read about these in major American newspapers and specialized publications, and there is no reason to suppose that their Embassy in Washington cannot report more or less accurately what they can easily observe in the American strategic community. They must surely be aware, for example, of the strong criticism to which the Strategic Defense Initiative has been subjected. The problem lies in the inability of Soviet leaders to comprehend the role of public debate in democratic societies. To them, ultimate decisions rest in the hand of the capitalist power structure, and public discussion of issues is essentially camouflage for this basic reality. Actual interpretations in Moscow of what Soviet leaders think they see happening in the United States are bound to be distorted by such ideological lenses.

Conversely, American leaders – no matter how sound the advice they get from the community of Sovietologists – inevitably find it difficult to fathom the thinking in Moscow. This fact has undoubtedly affected American strategy in important ways. Any book such as this that makes a real contribution to our understanding of Soviet strategic thinking must be welcome. A careful study of its contents in Washington can only be beneficial even if it does not lead to that unanimity of view based on clear agreement with respect to facts that ideally would make the devising of American strategy, weapons systems and arms control position have maximum rationality and relevance. We live in too dangerous a world to accept that there is any merit in tolerated ignorance or misapprehension. It would be tragic if a few surviving historians twenty or thirty years from now were to conclude that a dialogue of the deaf between the United States and the Soviet Union was the continuing characteristic of the last years of the twentieth century.

Martin J. Hillenbrand

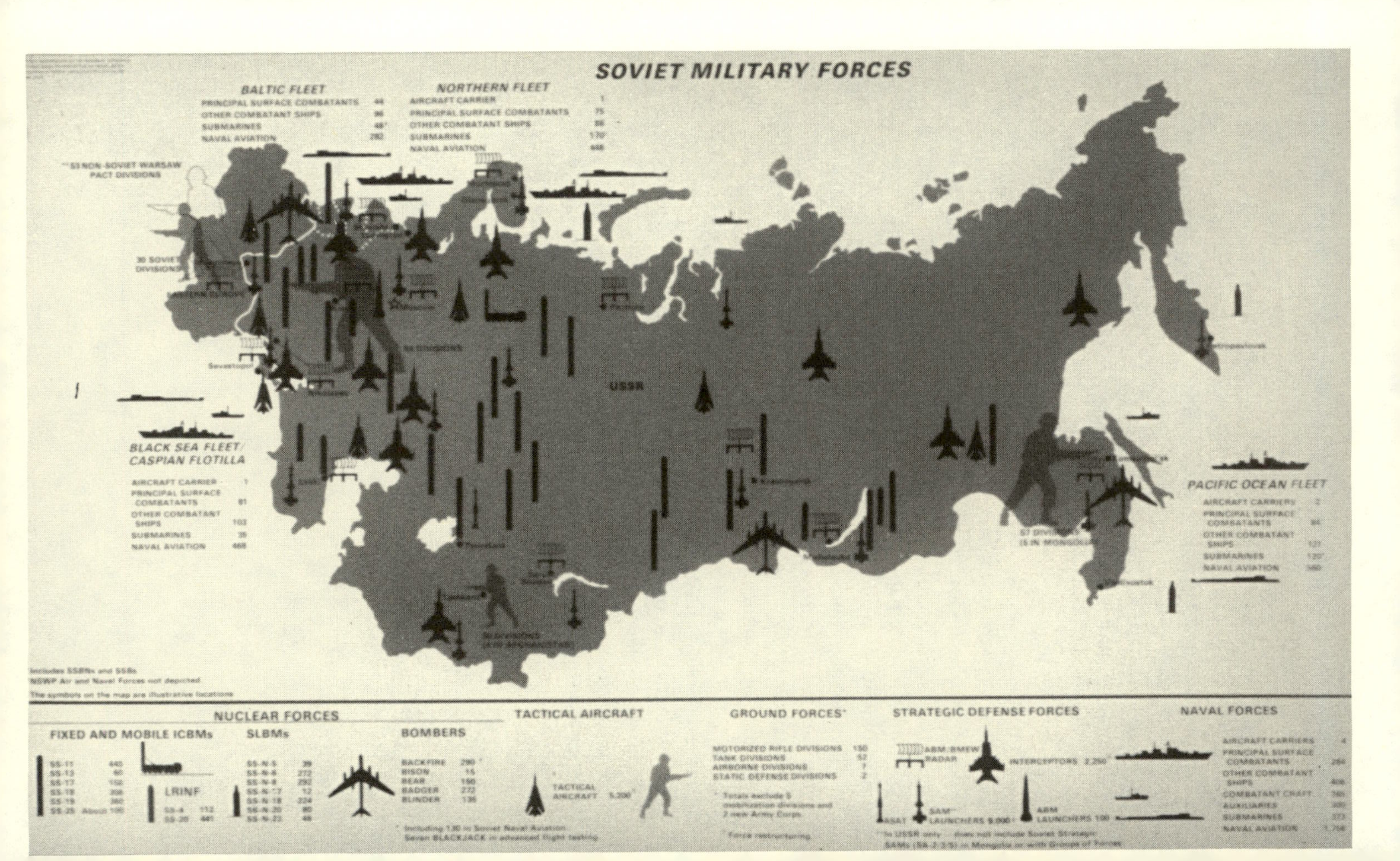
SOVIET MILITARY FORCES
BALTIC FLEET
PRINCIPAL SURFACE COMBATANTS 44
OTHER COMBATANT SHIPS 96
SUBMARINES 48
NAVAL AVIATION 282
NORTHERN FLEET
AIRCRAFT CARRIER 1
PRINCIPAL SURFACE COMBATANTS 75
OTHER COMBATANT SHIPS 86
SUBMARINES 170
NAVAL AVIATION 448
53 NON-SOVIET WARSAW PACT DIVISIONS
30 SOVIET DIVISIONS
Sevastopol
USSR
Petropavlovsk
Vladivostok
57 DIVISIONS (5 IN MONGOLIA)
BLACK SEA FLEET/ CASPIAN FLOTILLA
AIRCRAFT CARRIER 1
PRINCIPAL SURFACE COMBATANTS 81
OTHER COMBATANT SHIPS 103
SUBMARINES 35
NAVAL AVIATION 468
PACIFIC OCEAN FLEET
AIRCRAFT CARRIERS 2
PRINCIPAL SURFACE COMBATANTS 84
OTHER COMBATANT SHIPS 127
SUBMARINES 120
NAVAL AVIATION 560
NUCLEAR FORCES
FIXED AND MOBILE ICBMs
LRINF
SLBMs
BOMBERS
BACKFIRE 290
BISON 15
BEAR 150
BADGER 272
BLINDER 135
TACTICAL AIRCRAFT
TACTICAL AIRCRAFT 5,200
GROUND FORCES
MOTORIZED RIFLE DIVISIONS 150
TANK DIVISIONS 52
AIRBORNE DIVISIONS 7
STATIC DEFENSE DIVISIONS 2
Force restructuring
STRATEGIC DEFENSE FORCES
ABM/BMEW RADAR
INTERCEPTORS 2,250
ASAT
SAM LAUNCHERS 9,000
ABM LAUNCHERS 100
NAVAL FORCES
AIRCRAFT CARRIERS 4
PRINCIPAL SURFACE COMBATANTS
OTHER COMBATANT SHIPS
COMBATANT CRAFT
AUXILIARIES
SUBMARINES
NAVAL AVIATION

History has taught the Soviet Union to depend mainly on itself in ensuring its security and that of its friends ... After all, when the security of a state is based only on mutual deterrence with the aid of powerful nuclear rockets it is directly dependent on the good will and designs of the other side, which is a highly subjective and indefinite factor.

Major General Nikolai A. Talensky, U.S.S.R. (Deceased)

I. PROBLEMS OF STUDYING SOVIET NUCLEAR STRATEGY

The process of evaluating Soviet nuclear strategy, particularly as it fits into the broader framework of Soviet military doctrine, is a much more elusive task than is commonly realized in the West.[1] In part, this is because we know surprisingly little about the individuals and institutions whose responsibility it is to formulate policy in this crucial area. The matter is handled with the utmost secrecy, which conceals from outsiders many of the controversies that undoubtedly surround it.

1 One should distinguish here between Soviet "doctrine" and Soviet "strategy." Soviet doctrine, according to definition, is a system of scientifically based views, accepted by the government on the nature of modern war. In Soviet parlance, strategy is subordinate to doctrine. Soviet strategists work out and investigate the concrete questions concerning the character of a future war, the preparation of the country for war, the organization of the armed forces and the methods for waging war. See *Slovar' Osnovnykh Voyennykh Terminov* (Moscow: Voenizdat, 1965). John J. Dziak, Chief of the Political-Military Affairs Branch in the U.S. Defense Intelligence Agency, observes: "At the intersection where political strategy and military considerations converge, *military doctrine* ... begins. In Party terms, military doctrine is Party writ in the realm of military programs. It is the policy of the Party-State – worked out by the political leadership – on the nature of future war, the methods for waging it, and the preparation and organization of the armed forces and the country for such warfare. Finding a U.S. counterpart for the term (military doctrine) is difficult, though an analogy might comprise a blend of 'grand strategy' and 'national security policy' ..." See his *Soviet Perception of Military Power: The Interaction of Theory and Practice* (New York: Crane, Russak & Co., 1981), p. 21.

Soviet strategic policymaking occurs in a far more vertical and closed system than in the case of the United States. Expertise tends to be monopolized by the military establishment and a subset of the top political leadership. To be sure, elites external to the group do bid for its scarce resources. But they have great difficulty challenging its values and judgments. Issues of doctrine, force acquisition and war planning are much more intimately connected within this decision group than in the U.S. Policy arguments do take place,[2] but the identification of issues, alternatives and parameters in these debates must always be somewhat speculative.[3]

Problems of Sources

In addition to the problem of identifying with precision the Soviet decision-making process on matters of nuclear strategy, there is the problem of sources. Many of the difficulties in understanding the nature and purposes of Soviet nuclear strategy stem from determining which statements are authoritative (i.e., indicative of actual policy at the highest level). Unfortunately, too many Western military analysts today still tend to rely on outdated sources for their evaluation of a strategic doctrine that is not static but gradually

2 There is evidence that the Soviet political leadership has been more influenced by the views of the military than has the political leadership of the United States. Moreover, on those clearly technical issues the Soviet leadership has tended to defer to the military. See John Newhouse, *Cold Dawn: The Story of SALT* (New York: Holt, Rinehart & Winston, 1973), p. 105. This insider's account was compiled with the considerable help of such actors as Henry Kissinger and his staff. See also, Carnegie Panel on U.S. Security and the Future of Arms Control, *Challenges for U.S. National Security: The Soviet Approach to Arms Control; Verification; Problems and Prospects; Conclusions* (Washington, D.C.: Carnegie Endowment for International Peace, 1983), p.8.

3 The use of public source materials to identify these issues raises an important question regarding their accuracy as expressions of Soviet thought. Here we might defer to Raymond L. Garthoff, a leading American student of Soviet military affairs. He exhaustively surveyed both classified and open sources on Soviet strategy between 1945 and 1960 and offers this judgment: "These [classified] sources go further into some sensitive matters but in no case did the open materials display any discrepancy or divergence from the secret ones. This confirms and underlines the conclusion that open sources are, to the extent that they do treat strategic matters, a generally reliable source." See Garthoff, *Soviet Strategy and the Nuclear Age* (New York: Praeger, 1958), p.288.

evolving as Soviet military power has increased.[4] This practice of relying on old and cherished source materials has given rise to a number of myths regarding Soviet military intentions, strengths and weaknesses. As the eminent British student of Soviet military policy John Erickson has observed: "The convenient myth of Soviet nuclear troglodytes seemingly died hard, only to be replaced by the equally distorted simulacrum of Soviet nuclear supermen."[5]

In reality, of course, there is no absolutely clear and detailed statement of Soviet nuclear doctrine binding for all purposes. In the main, Western analysts rely for their understanding of "Soviet doctrine" on a careful study of the extensive public and semi-private literature written by professional military officers and civilian strategists. From these writings, Western analysts attempt to distill what they believe is a cohesive *interpretation* of Soviet military doctrine. Whether it is correct or not is another matter.[6]

The main problem with this kind of speculative analysis can best be demonstrated when the tables are reversed, and we try to see how the leaders in the Kremlin perceive American military (nuclear) policy. The most comprehensive official presentation of the Soviet side of the arms race came in January 1982, when the Ministry of Defense in Moscow published a glossy booklet entitled *Whence the Threat to Peace.*[7] In 78 pages this pamphlet details the size of the U.S. armed forces and their location, the number of U.S.

4 See the interview with Lt. General M. Milshtein, "Moscow Expert says U.S. is Mistaken on Soviet War Strategy," *International Herald Tribune*, August 28, 1980. Also important here is the study of Henry Trofimenko, *Changing Attitudes towards Deterrence* (University of California ACIS Working Paper No. 25, July, 1980), p. 54, which recommends the works by former Defense Minister Ustinov and the former Chief of the Soviet General Staff Ogarkov, among others.

5 John Erickson, "The Soviet View of Deterrence: A General Survey," *Survival*, Vol. 24, No. 6 (November-December 1982), p. 243.

6 It is often asserted that little or nothing on Soviet military affairs appears in print in the U.S.S.R. without at least tacit party approval. (See for instance John J. Dziak, *Soviet Perceptions of Military Power: The Interaction of Theory and Practice* [New York: Crane, Russak & Co., 1981], p. 66.) However, although the party does run the whole Soviet media, including the military press, this statement does not tell the whole story. "Clues," as Donald S. Zagoria calls them, do exist as to certain differences of opinion within open Soviet communications, but one must look with a well trained eye for them. See Zagoria, *The Sino-Soviet Conflict 1956-61* (Princeton University Press, 1962), pp. 30-34.

7 USSR Ministry of Defense, *Whence the Threat to Peace* (Moscow, 1982).

bases overseas, the size of the U.S. military-industrial complex, and the planned expansion of U.S. forces. It emphatically declares: "The United States of America is developing and widely advertising various military-strategic concepts of an undisguisedly aggressive nature ... their main idea invariably centers on unrestricted use of the U.S. strategic offensive forces in a pre-emptive strike against the U.S.S.R. *The notion that a nuclear war is winnable recurs in all U.S. strategic concepts ever since the 1950s."* (Italics mine)

Propaganda? Undoubtedly. But such a bleak view of U.S. intentions cannot be dismissed so easily because it is supported by the "evidence" of handbooks issued by the Pentagon itself. For example, U.S. Army Field Manual FM-287, *The Tank and Mechanized Infantry Company Team,* published in 1980, states categorically: "The U.S. Army must be prepared to fight and win when nuclear weapons are used."[8] Similar statements can be found in many other American military publications for perusal by U.S. troops. Are they authoritative?

An intriguing aspect of the Soviet pamphlet on the "threat posed by the West" and its propagandistic summation of the military balance is that all the illustrations are from either U.S. Department of Defense sources or the Western press. All the "facts" are taken from unclassified documents released as a matter of course by the Pentagon or through the Congress. As Andrew Cockburn has noted in his controversial book *The Threat: Inside the Soviet Military Machine,* this raises an important point: "the Soviet picture of U.S.

8 Quoted in Andrew Cockburn, *The Threat: Inside the Soviet Military Machine* (New York: Random House, 1983). A Defense Department official who reviewed this chapter says here: "Our publications index shows no manual by this number. The manual with this name is FM 71-1, dated 30 June 1977." This manual reads: "With the advance of nuclear technology, many armies will soon be able to use nuclear weapons. It is the policy of the United States not to employ nuclear weapons unless the enemy uses them first, or unless conventional defenses become inadequate. However, the U.S. Army *must be ready to fight and win when nuclear weapons are used."* (Italics mine). In his important study done for the RAND Corporation, J. Michael Legge states: " ... if one attempted to describe NATO theater nuclear policy on the basis of unclassified U.S. Army operational manuals, NATO training exercises, and the statements of senior military officers, the resulting picture would differ considerably from the doctrine developed within the political councils of the Alliance ..." See Legge, *Theater Nuclear Weapons and the NATO Strategy of Flexible Response* (Santa Monica: Rand Corporation, 1983), p.46.

military power differs only in its conclusions from the picture the Pentagon likes to present of itself."[9]

The upshot of this analysis is that "Soviet strategic doctrine" often exists in the minds of Western war planners in the abstract. There is a broad diversity of opinion on the subject. Thus, we must view with the appropriate skepticism those statements by Western officials that interpret Soviet strategic policy in such a way as to promote an image of the adversary that has the effect of furthering their own policies.

Until recently, many Western analysts would have questioned the utility of Soviet public pronouncements in ascertaining actual Soviet attitudes, intentions and expectations regarding the role of nuclear weapons in current Soviet strategy. Now, however, many of those concerned with Soviet affairs assume that the public utterances of the ruling hierarchy of the U.S.S.R. often provide a substantially accurate account of the attitudes of the Soviet leadership – even if one has to be able to read between the lines and understand the full context of what is being said and why as well as the special "code words."[10] Thus, the approach used by this writer, while it is not without risks, conforms in practice to that adopted by many students of Soviet military matters today.[11]

9 Andrew Cockburn, *The Threat: Inside the Soviet Military Machine* (New York: Random House, 1983, p.11. This provocative book is being embraced by many skeptics of the defense policies proclaimed by the Reagan Administration, but it should be handled very cautiously. Its thesis seems to be that U.S. officials, particularly those in the Reagan Administration, have gravely overstated the "threat" posed by the Soviet Union. It takes a critical look at the "numbers game", but unfortunately some of the analysis is marred by sloppiness with the "facts." For instance, it gives 900,000 soldiers as the number of Soviet forces stationed in East Germany. A more realistic figure is less than half that.

10 Leon Gouré *et al., The Role of Nuclear Forces in Current Soviet Strategy* (Coral Gables: University of Miami, 1974), p. IX.

11 Ambassador Raymond L. Garthoff lists ten fallacies common to Western analysis of Soviet intentions. These fallacies may be extended to apply to Western efforts to determine Soviet strategic aims. These are: (1) when in doubt, assume the worst; (2) never estimate intentions, only capabilities; (3) the mirror image; i.e., the strategic perceptions and intentions of the Soviet leaders are the same as those of the United States; (4) the double mirror image, i.e., the strategic perceptions and intentions of Soviet leaders are necessarily different from those of the United States; (5) the Soviets never mean what they say, or always mean what they say; (6) U.S. national security means military security against the Soviet Union; (7) Soviet capabilities are larger than needed for deterrence; (8) the Kremlin seeks military superiority; (9) reliance on irrelevant, misleading or

Role of Soviet Military Doctrine

If there is what William G. Hyland, a long-time U.S. student of Soviet affairs, calls "a studied ambiguity" surrounding Soviet nuclear policy,[12] then three assertions can be made with confidence.. First, Soviet nuclear policy, to be fully understood, must be seen in the context of overall Soviet military doctrine. Second, Soviet military planning is carried out under the close supervision of the country's highest political body – the Politburo. Thus, Soviet military strategy is regarded as an intrinsic element of "grand strategy", whose arsenal also includes a variety of non-military instrumentalities. Third, the Soviets generally regard warfare as a science. Military instruction is offered at an extensive network of university-level institutions in the U.S.S.R., and several hundred specialists, most of them officers on active duty, have been granted the Soviet equivalent of the Ph.D. in military science. The effect of this is that Soviet military doctrine is formulated by fulltime specialists. This is not to say, as one noted American historian of the Soviet Union has, that Soviet military doctrine "is as much the exclusive province of the certified military professional as medicine is that of the licensed physician."[13] However, it is true that the civilian strategic theorist, who since World War II has played a decisive role in the formulation of U.S. strategic doctrine, is not much in evidence in the Soviet Union, and probably plays mostly a secondary consultative function.[14]

Although most Soviet comment on military issues is made by the military, this does not mean that the views are identified with

overly selective quantitative indicators: and (10) "bad news" is public news, i.e., only alarming developments or estimates should be brought to light. See Raymond L. Garthoff, "On Estimating and Imputing Intentions," *International Security* (Winter, 1978), pp.22-32.

12 William G. Hyland, "The USSR and Nuclear War," in Barry M. Blechman (ed.), *Rethinking the U.S. Strategic Posture* (Cambridge: Ballinger Publishing Co., 1982), pp.47-75.

13 Richard Pipes, "Why the Soviet Union Thinks It Could Fight and Win a Nuclear War," *Commentary,* Vol.64 (July, 1977), p.27.

14 It is noteworthy that published criticisms of current U.S. strategy have come for the most part from civilian commentators, not professional Soviet military officers, and have appeared in media that have substantial propaganda functions. See Benjamin S. Lambeth, *Selective Nuclear Options in American and Soviet Strategic Policy* (Santa Monica: The Rand Corporation, 1976), p.47.

policy. In fact, Soviet military writing has a specific exhortive function, among other things. To some extent, it reflects the conservatism among the military in general. This is the tendency to worry about – even to downplay one's capabilities. Given this situation, and the frequent lack of hard facts, Soviet military commentary must be read with caution.

Technically, military doctrine in the Soviet Union is defined as the system of views that a state holds at a given time on "the purposes and character of a possible war, on the preparation of the country and the armed forces for it, and also on the methods of waging it."[15] Generally, military doctrine from the Soviet viewpoint has two closely related sides. These are the political (which dominates) and the military-technical. "The former sets out the political purposes and character of war and their implications for defense policy; the latter deals with the methods of waging war and the organization, equipment, and combat readiness of the armed forces."[16] In practice, of course, these two sides are not only directly related; they overlap as well.

It is important to note here that Soviet use of the term "doctrine" is narrower than the American one. One does not find, for instance, any reference to "naval doctrine." At the same time, however, the term is more general: One discovers that it merges with the principles that underlie Soviet foreign policy.

Doctrine itself flows from a number of different sources. Among the most important are Marxist-Leninist thought, Russian nationalism and changing military requirements. Military doctrine is determined in the Defense Council, which functions as a kind of subcommittee of the Kremlin leadership. Though frequently viewed as empirical and "scientific," doctrine is not static and unchangeable. Modifications of doctrine reflect not only changes in military strategy and technology, but political decisions as well.

If Soviet nuclear strategy must be seen in the context of overall Soviet military doctrine, several students of Soviet affairs warn against interpreting military doctrine as the key to Soviet strategic policy. To do so, Matthew Gallagher says, "would be both to mis-

15 *Sovyetskaya Voennaya Entsiklopedia,* Vol. 3 (Moscow: Voenizdat, 1977), p. 225.

16 David Holloway, "Military Power and Political Purpose in Soviet Policy," *Daedalus* (Fall, 1980), p. 19.

read the doctrine and to underestimate the dynamics of the Soviet decision-making process." Gallagher argues that Soviet military doctrine is a "highly generalized and ambiguous set of guidelines," in which each proposition is counterbalanced by a contradictory one. He points out, for example, that according to Soviet doctrine a general nuclear war might be either short or long, that while strategic missiles would provide the main striking power, all forces would be required for victory; and that war with NATO, while possibly nuclear, might also take a conventional form. Since Soviet doctrine is so flexible, it can hardly serve – in Gallagher's view – to provide detailed guidance for Soviet military policy.[17]

Another student of Soviet military affairs takes a similar view. In his study of Soviet procurement decision-making, Arthur Alexander argues that doctrine is a "poor predictor of future capabilities." This is because doctrine is so "elastic" that many different – and even contradictory – decisions could be compatible with it. Consequently, one cannot say from a study of doctrine which decisions will in fact be taken. Moreover, doctrine may merely serve as a basis for rationalizing decisions which have already been made for other reasons.[18]

These caveats notwithstanding, a study of Soviet military doctrine, particularly as it has evolved in the nuclear era, can still be useful in providing outsiders with important insights into Soviet strategic policy. It should, however, be supplemented with other information, including the role of Soviet political leaders.

Conclusions

American policymakers must in the last analysis make their own decisions in the area of nuclear strategy. But they tend to base them on what they believe Soviet policy is. In particular, they are concerned with the problem of how doctrinal asymmetry might affect

17 Matthew P. Gallagher, "The Military Role in Soviet Decision-Making," in M. McCGwire *et. al.* (eds.), *Soviet Naval Policy: Objectives and Constraints* (New York: Praeger, 1975), p.56.

18 Arthur J. Alexander, *Decision-Making in Soviet Weapons Procurement* (London: International Institute for Strategic Studies, 1978-79), p.54.

– and possibly limit – U.S. options in a crisis. Thus, it is extremely worthwhile to examine closely Soviet military doctrine as it has evolved over time and to scrutinize carefully the basic underlying assumptions of Soviet nuclear policy. Although there is no guarantee that Soviet doctrine will predetermine Soviet behavior, it is nevertheless an important indicator of general strategic dispositions that will affect Soviet military actions in a crisis.

Military doctrine is viewed as very important by the Soviet military. But in actual practice, doctrine is not regarded by policymakers as the key to specific decisions. To be sure, doctrine does provide a framework for the formulation of policy. But it does not determine the outcome of the policymaking process.

It should be noted that the framework for doctrine has evolved over the years in response to changes in the military-political context. Military doctrine, for instance, was reformulated for the nuclear age, and it has been adapted since then to exploit the opportunities of changing military realities in the world. But more important, doctrine is not monolithic. As David Holloway observes: "Within its framework, substantial ambiguities, crosscurrents, and differences of emphasis may be found. Stress can be put on the preparation for war or on the pursuit of political measures to prevent it; on the possibility of victory or on the destructiveness of nuclear war; on the offensive political uses of military power or on the need for accomodation with the West. Variation can be found in Soviet writings, and this presumably reflects divergences of opinion inside the Soviet Union."[19] In short, outside observers should be careful about imputing to Soviet leaders a single undifferentiated view on what are in reality very important and complicated matters.

19 David Holloway, "Military Power and Political Purpose in Soviet Policy, *Daedalus* (Fall, 1980), p. 24.

Stalin was frightened to the point of cowardice. He ordered that all our technological efforts be directed toward developing atomic weapons of our own.

Nikita Khrushchev

II. THE ORIGINS OF SOVIET NUCLEAR STRATEGY

As is the case with American nuclear doctrine, Soviet nuclear policy has undergone (and continues to undergo) searching review and modification. For the most part, it has reflected the shifting views of Soviet political leaders, developing first under the particular biases of Stalin and then adjusting to those of Khrushchev and his successors. This chapter will focus on Stalin's contribution to Soviet nuclear thought.

The basis for understanding Soviet strategic thinking during the period 1945-53 is Stalin's total dominance over the political and military institutions of the U.S.S.R. "The memory of the purges which had decimated the ranks of the Party cadres and the military officer corps destroyed any prospect of their independent assertiveness." Moreover, "the 'cult of personality' that enveloped the image of Stalin in the aftermath of the Soviet triumph over Nazi Germany made his judgment unassailable."[1]

In order to legitimize his own strategic doctrines and policies, the Soviet leader found it necessary to disparage the claims of Lenin and Trotsky to military genius.[2] Until his death in 1953, the Soviet

1 Stephen M. Meyer, "Soviet Theatre Nuclear Forces: Part I: Development of Doctrine and Objectives," *Adelphi Paper No. 187* (London: The International Institute for Strategic Studies, 1984), p.7.

2 "One may think that Lenin ... left us a heritage of guiding theses on the military question," wrote Stalin in 1947. But such "a statement is incorrect, since in reality

dictator encouraged people to call him the "greatest military genius of modern times".

After Stalin's death, Soviet military writers admitted that[3]
the development of Soviet military science in that period was hampered by the personality cult. The development of military theory and its separate problems were insufficiently pursued. An attempt was made to fit everything new in military affairs into one or another saying of Stalin.

Khrushchev himself later chose to debunk Stalin's claims to military expertise by severely criticizing the dead dictator in 1956. "The nervousness and hysteria of Stalin", he said, "demonstrated that interfering with actual military questions caused our army serious damage."[4]

The "Permanently Operating Factors"

At the end of World War II the U.S.S.R. emerged as a member of the winning coalition. But with the onset of the "cold war" the international situation changed drastically for the Soviet Union.[5] Given the enmity of the capitalist powers, and the possibility that they might revert to war, the following course seemed prudent: The U.S.S.R. must again seek to industrialize as rapidly as possible and once again seek to avoid war. To be sure, as Herbert S. Dinerstein

no such 'theses' of Lenin exist." See J.V. Stalin, "Comrade Stalin's Answer to a Letter from Comrade Razin," *Bolshevik,* Vol. 3 (February, 1947)

3 S.N. Kozlov *et al., On Soviet Military Science* (Moscow: Military Publishing House), partial translation in Harriet F. Scott and Wilson F. Scott, *The Soviet Art of War* (Boulder, Colo.: Westview Press, 1982), pp. 91-4.

4 From Khrushchev's secret speech at the 20th Party Congress, February, 1956.

5 A Soviet reviewer of John Gaddis, *The United States and the Cold War 1941-1947* made the following observation: "Gaddis' research is sufficiently convincing to lead the reader to the conclusion that during the war years and immediately after the war there existed objective preconditions for the broad development of Soviet-American relations. However, writes the author, 'subjective factors' – the views of some people, the ignorance and inexperience of others, the fear and hatred of still others, etc., together with what Senator Fulbright later described as 'the arrogance of power' – have for a long time hindered and reversed the positive development of Soviet-American relations." Quoted in Morton Schwartz, *Soviet Perceptions of the United States* (Los Angeles, Calif.: University of California Press, 1978), p. 191.

has pointed out, the "problem of preparing to fight another war a generation or two hence, still lagging far in industrial strength, was not inviting (to Stalin), but there was no real alternative." Stalin could only hope that "once again the imperialist states would be divided among themselves, but he could not count on that."[6]

Soviet military policy from 1945 to 1953 was characterized by a basic reliance on massive conventional forces deployed in an active posture of defense with a narrow continental mission.[7] This military policy stemmed from Stalin's principles of warfare, which were based for the most part on his experiences during World War II. To be sure, modern military weapons and equipment were introduced into the Soviet military establishment during this period. But Stalin continued to exhort his strategists to "look back" to the "great patriotic war" and to draw both theoretical and practical lessons of warfare from it. As one student of Soviet military policy has written, Stalin "allowed scope for little more than repetition of the military precepts developed in World War II."[8] These were summed up in his own formulation of the "permanently operating factors" of war. Briefly, these were:

- the stability of the rear;
- the morale of the troops;
- the quality and quantity of divisions;
- the armaments of the army; and
- the organizational ability of the command personnel of the army.

Once articulated by Stalin, these permanently operating factors could not be openly challenged. Subsequently, they became the centerpiece of Soviet military science until Stalin's death.[9]

6 Herbert S. Dinerstein, *The Making of a Missile Crisis, October 1962* (Baltimore: Johns Hopkins University Press, 1976), p.153.

7 During the Stalinist era, Soviet ground forces were supplemented by the national armies of "allied" countries. These national armies were closely controlled by Moscow through a Byzantine network of Soviet advisors, Soviet commanders, communist commanders, elaborate party structures within the armies and political officers as well as military and state security services. As Richard C. Martin writes, "The Soviets enjoyed a degree of control over the national forces in those days that they have not been able to match since." See his "Warsaw Pact Modernization: A Closer Look," *Parameters,* Vol.XV, No.2 (Summer, 1985), p.3.

8 Raymond L. Garthoff, "Introduction: (Soviet) Military Strategy in Perspective," in Marshal V.D. Sokolovsky (ed.), *Military Strategy: Soviet Doctrine and Concepts* (New York: Praeger, 1967), p.VII.

9 Occasionally, a sixth factor was added – adequate reserves.

Development of Soviet Atomic Bomb

Despite the important role Stalin assigned the permanently operating factors, he did not disregard the development of nuclear weapons. In fact, he pushed Soviet programs aimed at acquiring nuclear weapons – rockets as they came to be called.

For a long time, Western analysts were left in the dark as to when precisely the Soviet leadership decided to embark on a nuclear weapons program, as distinct from earlier work pursued by Soviet scientists in the general field of nuclear physics. The first painstaking examination published in the West of the Soviet atomic program was by Arnold Kramish of the RAND Corporation. His study, which was entitled *Atomic Energy in the Soviet Union,*[10] placed this decision not later than the fall of 1943.

According to some new research,[11] the Soviet Union could have developed the first nuclear chain reactor and also the first atomic bomb.[12]During World War II the Soviets had an atomic laboratory under nuclear physicist Igor Kurchatov. In August 1940, Kurchatov presented a proposal for additional funds to develop nuclear fission, stressing its "military significance" and the prospect that "a uranium bomb could be built." But the project was turned down by the Soviet Academy in 1940 because, according to David Holloway, the prospects for success seemed so far in the future. Then, in June 1941, the German invasion halted all Soviet nuclear fission research, and Kurchatov turned his attention to work on navy ships.

Since the Soviets were fighting for their lives at this time, Soviet

10 Arnold Kramish, *Atomic Energy in the Soviet Union* (Stanford: Stanford University Press, 1959).

11 This research was conducted by David Holloway. His findings were presented in a paper entitled *Entering the Nuclear Arms Race: The Soviet Decision to Build the Atomic Bomb, 1939-1945,* Working Paper No.9, International Security Studies Program, Woodrow Wilson International Center for Scholars, Washington, D.C., July 1979. Holloway's findings were based on an extensive review of Soviet and American documents.

12 One Soviet physicist who, together with a colleague, was responsible for discovering spontaneous fission maintains that "Had it not been for the war ... we would in no way have lagged behind the U.S., and it is quite probable that we would have had a chain reaction before 1942. After all, in 1939 in Leningrad we were discussing all of the things that Fermi did in the U.S. in 1942." See P. Astashenkov, *Kurchatov* (Moscow, 1968), p.102.

efforts were postponed. In fact, it was not until the end of 1944 when the tide of the war had turned that Kurchatov had some 100 researchers back at work in his nuclear fission lab.[13]

At that point the Soviets decided to obtain some outside help for their project. "As the Red Army moved into Germany, strenuous efforts were made to recruit German scientists to work for the Soviet Union," Holloway states. There was even a list of scientists, like Manfred Von Ardenne, who were considered the most desirable.

On May 6, 1945, the Second White Russian Army under General Konstantin Rokossovsky, occupied Peenemünde, salvaging what they could of the bomb-damaged installation. Rounding up the dispersed rocket specialists, they implemented the equivalent of America's Operation Paperclip.

The Russian search was not in vain. Among other things, they found the V-2, the blueprints for the ocean-spanning A-9/A-10 rocket and the surface-to-surface *Rheinbote*. In the category of surface-to-air missiles, they obtained the *Rheintochter, Wasserfall, Taifun* and the series known as the *Henschel* missiles in various stages of development.

In addition to Peenemünde, the Soviets found other rocket centers partially or completely destroyed.

Reportedly, Stalin was not satisfied with the progress of recruiting and rebuilding the German rocket complexes and rockets, so he ordered General Ivan Serov of the secret police to ship the entire operation to the U.S.S.R. Consequently, in October 1946, more than six thousand German technical specialists of all kinds and about twenty thousand members of their families were carted off to the Soviet Union without prior notice.[14]

After a close scrutiny of Soviet and American documents, Holloway cannot be certain whether or not Stalin knew Truman was talking about the atomic bomb when he told the Soviet dictator after one meeting at Potsdam in July-August, 1945 that "we have a

13 For a study of the impact of World War II on the Soviet Union see Susan J. Linz, *The Impact of World War II on the Soviet Union* (Totowa, N.J.: Rowman & Allanheld, 1985). Western research on the Soviet Union is perhaps weakest for the period of World War II and its immediate aftermath. This collaborative volume fills in some of the gaps for this period.

14 See Michael Stoiko, *Soviet Rocketry: Past, Present and Future* (New York: Holt, Rinehart and Winston, 1970), pp.71-72.

new weapon of unusual destructive power." The Soviet Minister of Defense at the meeting, Marshal Georgi K. Zhukov, wrote in his memoirs that "we'll have to have a talk with Kurchatov today about speeding up our work."[15] Another Soviet memoir from a participant at Potsdam conflicts with this interpretation. It records the Truman statement, but adds that "Stalin ... did not get from the conversation with Truman the impression that what was mentioned was a weapon that was new in principle." In any case, the Soviet program was not speeded up until August 1945 after the U.S. atomic bombs were dropped on Japan.[16]

Relying on an unpublished biography of the then head of Soviet munitions who had been called to the Kremlin in mid-August 1945 to confer with Stalin, Holloway says that Stalin decided at that time to "launch an all-out effort to develop the atomic bomb." Kurchatov reportedly joined the session and the Soviet leader allegedly declared: "A single demand of you, comrades: provide us with atomic weapons in the shortest possible time. You know that Hiroshima has shaken the whole world. The equilibrium has been destroyed. Provide the bomb – it will remove a great danger from us.[17]

15 See Marshal G.K. Zhukov, *Vospominanie i razmyshlenie* (Moscow: Novosti Press Agency, 1969), p.713.

16 In his excellent book, *Russia at War,* Alexander Werth notes that "Although the Russian press played down the Hiroshima bomb, and did not even mention the Nagasaki bomb until much later, the significance of Hiroshima was not lost on the Russian people. The news had an acutely depressing effect on everybody. It was clearly realized that this was a New Fact in the world's power politics, that the bomb constituted a threat to Russia, and some Russian pessimists I talked to that day dismally remarked that Russia's desperately hard victory over Germany was now "as good as wasted." Alexander Werth, *Russia at War* (New York: Avon Books, 1965), p.934. See also, General of the Army V. Tolubko, *Nedelin* (Moscow, 1979), p.174.

17 According to one authority, Stalin put his secret police chief Lavrenti P. Beria in charge of the administration of the Soviet atomic program. See John Prados, *The Soviet Estimate* (New York: Dial Press, 1982), p.16. Beria remained in overall charge of the nuclear weapons program until he was arrested in 1953. Following his removal, the Ministry of Medium Machine Building was created to run the nuclear weapons program. See Mark E. Miller, *Soviet Power and Doctrine: The Quest for Superiority* (Washington, D.C.: Advanced International Studies Institute, 1982), p.8.

Developing a Delivery Capability

Exploiting the opportunity offered by Soviet spies who managed to steal plans for the building of the American atomic bomb, the Soviets exploded their first nuclear device in August 1949 – a number of years earlier than expected in the West. (Four years later, Moscow concluded the second, and militarily more significant, phase of its nuclear weapons program: This was the successful test of a thermonuclear device on August 12, 1953. Soviet authorities claim that this was the first test of a hydrogen bomb, since the November 1952 U.S. test of a 60-ton thermonuclear device was not a deliverable weapon.)[18]

But the acquisition of the atomic bomb alone did not hold out the prospect for parity with the United States.[19] For the U.S. possessed a fleet of strategic bombers that could deliver this weapon to distant targets, whereas the Soviet Union lacked adequate means of delivering it across continents. However, even the Soviet possession of a strategic air force comparable to that of SAC would not by itself have overcome this disparity.

At the time, aircraft did not have the range to make round trips between the Soviet Union and the United States. Only staging bases between the two states made strategic bombing feasible. Without such bases, only suicide missions could gain one access to the territory of the adversary, and this was hardly a credible basis for war planning. In the case of the United States, it had access to bases in Western Europe, the Western Pacific and the Eastern Mediterranean. These bases brought the major urban and industrial centers of the U.S.S.R. within reach of American bombers. By way of contrast, the Soviet presence in Central Europe brought only Western Europe and the United Kingdom within effective bomber range.[20]

18 For a first-rate account of early Soviet thermonuclear tests and their implications for the arms race, see David Holloway, "Research Note: Soviet Thermonuclear Development," *International Security* (Winter 1979/80), pp.192-197

19 Early U.S. intelligence reports estimated that the Soviet Union had between ten and twenty atomic weapons in 1950 and between 100 and 200 in 1953. Today, however, the evidence suggests that no Soviet nuclear weapons were available for military use until late 1953 or early 1954. See Stephen M. Meyer, "Soviet Theatre Nuclear Forces: Part II: Capabilities and Implications," *Adelphi Paper No. 188* (London: The International Institute for Strategic Studies, 1984), p.4.

20 The first Soviet aircraft capable of carrying an atomic bomb was the Tu-4 Bull.

In view of this lack of bases, Stalin decided around 1945 or 1946 to push forward with the development of ballistic missiles that could reach the United States.[21] This decision was not very prudent if one assumed that nuclear weapons would continue to be fission weapons (which were too heavy for a missile to carry).[22] But the development of the H-bomb in the early 1950s by the Soviet Union proved Stalin's decision to be the correct one. For the H-bomb was much lighter than the atomic bomb and could be carried by a missile. At one stroke, this technological innovation opened up the possibility of a symmetrical relationship between the Soviet Union and the United States.[23]

Three American B-29 Superfortresses had landed in Siberia in 1944 after bombing raids against Manchuria and Japan. These aircraft were copied by the Soviets very quickly. The first Tu-4 Bull flew late in 1946, and soon the aircraft was in serious production. Some 1,200 Bulls were delivered during the next few years. This was how the Soviet Union obtained a "strategic" bomber. In May 1948, Western intelligence agents sighted the first Soviet Tu-4. Other sightings, together with testimony from a defector from the Soviet Long Range Air Force, led the American intelligence community by the spring of 1950 to ascribe to the Soviets a large and rapidly growing operational force of Tu-4s. (See John Prados, *The Soviet Estimate: U.S. Intelligence Analysis and Russian Military Strength* [New York: Dial, 1982], pp.38-39). With a bombload of five and half tons, the Bull could fly 3,000 miles at a cruising speed of some 225 m.p.h. This meant that by taking off from bases in northern Russia and Siberia, the planes could reach some targets in the northern U.S. on a 13-hour flight. As things turned out Soviet planners, for a number of reasons, found it much more efficient and credible to aim their planes at Europe than to tackle the problem of reaching targets in the United States. These would make more demands on aircraft, require refueling in flight and call for different types of pilot training. See Norman Polmar, *Strategic Weapons,* rev. ed. (New York: Crane, Russak, 1982), p.19 and Thomas W. Wolfe, *Soviet Power and Europe 1945-1970* (Baltimore: Johns Hopkins Press, 1970), p.40.

21 According to Soviet sources, the first Soviet ballistic missile unit was formed in 1946 from two Guards Katusha regiments of World War II fame. See Army General V. Tolubko, "Raketnyye voyske startegicheskogo naznacheniya," *Voyenno-Istoricheskii Zhurnal,* Vol.10 (1976), pp.19-20. Experimental testing of short-range land-and-sea launched missiles was undertaken at the end of the war. By 1950 the design plans for developing medium- and intercontinental-range ballistic missiles had been established. In 1950-51, the first Soviet Rocket Division was formed and armed with V-2s and Pobedas.

22 In Soviet military writings the long-range ballistic missile was portrayed as far superior to the bomber for fulfilling military requirements. For one thing, the missile's high speed and ability to reach its target (there were no effective defenses) were compared to the strategic bomber's low speed and vulnerability to enemy air defenses. For details see V.D. Skolovskiy, *Soviet Military Strategy,* 3rd ed. (London: Crane, Russak, 1975), pp.193, 252.

23 During the 1940s there was a tendency in the U.S. to dismiss ICBMs as delivery

Major Military Changes

By 1948, air defense forces were withdrawn from the command of the Soviet Army. They were recognized into an independent service, the National Air Defense Forces. As Robert P. Berman and John C. Baker write, their "increasing autonomy signaled the USSR's first recognition that its security in the postwar world could no longer be based solely on the Ground Forces."[24]

At the beginning of the postwar period, the Soviet air defenses comprised only approximately one thousand World War II vintage fighters. However, by 1953, these forces were equipped with about two thousand modern jet aircraft, large numbers of anti-aircraft artillery and electronic early-detection systems for long-range enemy bombers.[25]

To counter the possibility of amphibious assaults by Western naval powers, the Soviets began a massive construction program after World War II to create a naval force capable of defeating a Western seaborne invasion. This program foresaw the deployment of many surface ships, diesel submarines and torpedo bombers for intercepting and destroying enemy amphibious forces at sea. Later this program was modified somewhat, but countering a direct naval threat to the Soviet motherland continued to be a major feature of Soviet strategic planning.[26]

vehicles on the grounds that they compared very poorly with bombers in terms of cost and accuracy. Many in government assumed that the Soviets would reach a similar conclusion. According to Lawrence Freedman, "When the news of the first atomic test was made public in 1949 it was reported that the Pentagon was not anticipating Soviet ICBMs for another 25 years." See his *U.S. Intelligence and the Soviet Strategic Threat* (London: The Macmillan Press, 1977), p.68.

24 Robert P. Berman *et al., Soviet Strategic Forces: Requirements and Responses* (Washington, D.C.: The Brookings Institution, 1982), p.39.

25 According to a Soviet technical officer who defected in 1948, Stalin and Malenkov had taken a personal interest in pushing plans for the development of long-range bombers. See G.A. Tokaev, *Stalin Means War* (London: George Weidenfeld & Nicolson, Ltd., 1951), pp.93-95.

26 Robert P. Berman et al., opus cit., p.40.

Conclusions

The Soviet decision to build the atomic bomb was one of the most fateful weapons decisions of this century. It led ultimately to the formation of Soviet strategic forces which are such a major factor in international tensions today.

The decision to develop the bomb was largely Stalin's. It was the product of his intuitive political judgment and his penchant for intervening in scientific and technological developments. As David Holloway writes:[27]

The military rationale for the atomic bomb was simple ... The military appear to have played absolutely no part in the decision. This was not surprising since Stalin was Supreme Commander-in-Chief during the war and the final authority on all military matters, whether doctrinal or technological ... The political rationale for the atomic bomb was more important: in order to safeguard its own political gains and to restrain the United States from offensive military or political moves, the Soviet Union would have to have the atomic bomb.

In the first phase of Soviet postwar military policy (1945-1953), the Soviets attempted to come to grips with the significance of nuclear weapons. Given Soviet success in World War II, however, Stalin remained convinced that the conventional superiority of the Soviet armed forces would remain the key to victory in a future war.

This is not to say, as many have,[28] that Stalin did not understand some of the implications of nuclear weapons technology or that he chose to ignore them in his formulation. Clearly, Stalin was well aware of the general importance of these new weapons. Their potential role was examined, although in a rather incomplete fashion.

During the Stalin era nuclear weapons were not the principal means of military combat. Their major role was to play a supportive

27 Quoted in Jiri Valenta *et al.*, eds., *Soviet Decision-Making for National Security* (London: George Allen & Unwin, 1984), p.58.

28 As Stephen M. Meyer points out: "Among the most widely held misperceptions in the West is the belief that Stalin either did not understand the military implications of nuclear weapons technology, or that he chose to ignore them in his formulation of Soviet military power." See his "Theatre Nuclear Forces: Part I: Development of Doctrine and Objectives," *Adelphi Paper No. 187* (London: The International Institute for Strategic Studies, 1984), p.8.

function in military operations. The main operational arm of the military establishment continued to be the Ground Forces.

Nuclear weapons came to be viewed generally in the Stalin period as an important new form of massive fire-power. However, they were not regarded as decisive weapons of warfare.[29] That is, their use or lack of use would *not* importantly alter the course and outcome of war. Traditionally, Soviet military doctrine had denied the possibility of *absolute* weapons, and nuclear weapons were no exception.[30]

29 In this connection, Stalin stated in an interview with *Pravda* on September 25, 1946: "I do not believe the atomic bomb to be so serious a force as certain politicians are inclined to consider it. Atomic bombs are intended to frighten the weak-nerved, but they cannot decide the outcome of a war, since they are by no means adequate for this purpose." See also J.V. Stalin, *Works* (in Russian) Stanford, 1967, Vol. III, p. 56. The reasoning behind Stalin's refusal to attribute decisive influence to nuclear weapons was largely political: So long as the Soviet Union dit not possess such weapons of her own, her leader could not admit that no defense against them was yet possible. See Curt Gasteyger, "Modern Warfare and Soviet Strategy," *Survey* (October, 1965), p. 46.

30 The reason for this was that technology could not be seen to change the progressive course of history. As one military analyst in the U.S.S.R. put it in 1964: "Stalin did not consider the atomic bomb as a radically different weapon ..." He continued to view his military problems from the perspective of his past experiences. See Colonel I. Korotkow, "O razvitii sovetskoi voennoi teorii v poslevonnye gody," *Venno-istoricheskii zhurnal,* Vol. 4 (April, 1964).

> Yet it would be wrong to try to discover permanent rules of Soviet behavior, because the context in which the Soviet Union exercises its military power is changing.
>
> *David Holloway*

III. THE SOVIET NUCLEAR BUILDUP

The foundations for the modern Soviet build-up in nuclear weapons were laid by Nikita Khrushchev. He also raised crucial questions about the nature of nuclear war and its utility as a political instrument, sometimes coming down on both sides of an issue! Among other things, he compelled the Party to confront the very notion of the inevitability of war in the nuclear era and its compatibility with the teachings of Marxism-Leninism.

A Period of Transition

Beginning shortly after Stalin died in 1953, a number of efforts (largely by the military) were made to cut the restrictive bonds of "Stalinist military science" and, somewhat belatedly, to adapt to the world of nuclear weapons. Between 1953 and 1957 a debate took place in the pages of Soviet publications which, for all its textural obscurity, indicated to some Kremlinologists that a new school of Soviet strategic thinking had arisen to challenge the conventional wisdom.[1] One of the most articulate spokesmen of this "new

1 Herbert Dinerstein has sought to explain the doctrinal discussions of the 1950s as reflection of internal infighting over the adequacy of Soviet strategic expenditures and the influence of this issue on the struggle for power within the Politburo. See his *War and the Soviet Union: Nuclear Weapons and the Revolution in Soviet Military and Political Thinking* (New York: Praeger, 1959), p.91.

school" was the late Major General Nikolai Talensky, editor of the influential military journal *Military Thought.* He argued that the advent of nuclear weapons, particularly the hydrogen bomb which had just appeared on the Soviet scene, had fundamentally altered the nature of warfare. The sheer destructiveness of these weapons was such that one could no longer talk of a socialist strategy automatically overcoming the strategy of the capitalist countries. In the oblique way in which Soviet debates on issues of great import are invariably conducted, General Talensky was saying in effect that perhaps, after all, war had ceased to represent a viable instrument of state policy.[2]

But more important than Talensky's controversial utterances were the speeches delivered by leading Soviet politicians in the winter of 1953-54. These seemed to support the thesis advanced by President Eisenhower in his address before the United Nations of December 1953 – namely, that nuclear war could spell the demise of civilization. In his address delivered on March 12, 1954, Stalin's immediate successor, Georgi Malenkov, echoed the sentiments earlier expressed by Eisenhower. Malenkov said that a new world war would unleash a holocaust which "with the present means of warfare, means the destruction of world civilization."[3]

This attack on the traditional thinking of the Soviet military

2 Talensky's "heresy" brought an immediate and vehement response from serving Soviet officers, who rushed into the military press to criticize him by name – a move that rarely happens to Soviet general officers. They did not, however, take issue with Talensky's views so much as they did to his having stated them in public. Such loose talk, his opponents made clear, was tactless in the extreme because it dangerously undermined the case for a strong and prosperous military establishment in the U.S.S.R. For instance, General K. Bochkarev, Deputy Commandant of the Soviet General Staff Academy, argued that if ideas like those expressed by Talensky took hold, "the armed forces of the socialist states ... will not be able to set for themselves the goal of defeating imperialism and the global nuclear war which it unleashes and the mission of attaining victory in it, and our military science should not even work out a strategy for the conduct of war since the latter has lost its meaning and its significance ... *In this case, the very call to raise the combat readiness of our armed forces and improve their capability to defeat any aggressor is senseless.*" (Italics mine). See Andrew Cockburn, *opus cit.,* p.214.

3 *Pravda,* March 13, 1954. It is important to note here that Malenkov reversed himself in April 1954, with the statement that a new world war would lead to the "collapse of the whole capitalist system." *Pravda,* April 27, 1954. One can only conclude that he was forced to retract his original views in the face of stiff opposition in the military (but also the party).

establishment triggered a furious reaction. The military leaders of the Red Army were not about to let the Soviet armed forces be relegated to the status of a militia whose principal task was averting war rather than winning it. In the view of several historians of the period, Malenkov's unorthodox views on war may well have contributed to his downfall.[4] In any case, his dismissal in February 1955 as party leader was accompanied by a barrage of press denunciations of the idea that war had suddenly become unfeasible.

The Khrushchev Era

There are some indications that the chief rival of Malenkov – Khrushchev – capitalized on the discontent within the military establishment to form with it an alliance with whose help he eventually rose to power. The successful military counter-attack appears to have been led by the World War II hero Marshall Georgi Zhukov, whom Khrushchev made his Minister of Defense and brought into the Praesidium (as the Politburo was then called).

The guidelines of Soviet nuclear strategy during the period of Khrushchev's tenure were formulated during 1955-57 under the leadership of Zhukov himself. They resulted in the rejection of the notion of the "absolute weapon" and many of the theories that U.S. strategists deduced from it. At the same time, the stultifying notion of "permanent operating factors" was discarded, and Soviet leaders came to recognize the increased importance of surprise.[5]

During the Khrushchev period, military theory also began to place a great deal of emphasis on the concept of the "offensive." In both strategic and theater operations, the offensive came to have fundamental importance. Under specific situations, room was left for other such methods as "strategic defense", "holding operations" and "strategic withdrawal." But, according to one Soviet source, "Only a decisive offensive with massive use of all forces, involving both mutual cooperation and the exploitation of their specific indi-

4 See for instance Leon Gouré *et al.*, *opus cit.*, p.xv.

5 See Harriet F. Scott, *Soviet Military Doctrine: Its Continuity 1960-1970* (Stanford: Stanford Research Institute, 1971), p.68.

vidual capabilities and taking into account the decisive role of missile-nuclear weapons, can bring victory."[6]

Soviet military writers in the mid-1950s acknowledged the "possibility" of nuclear weapons use in some future war. But they were quick to point out that once nuclear weapons had been used such a war would "inevitably" become an all-out nuclear war. In the words of Major General G. Pokrovskii, "atomic and thermonuclear weapons at their present stage of development only supplement the firepower of the old forms of armament." Although nuclear strikes could exert a "significant" influence on the "course" of the war, they could not exert a "decisive" influence. The decisive influence in the war would be played by the ground forces.[7]

Despite this debate, really serious reform of Soviet strategic doctrines and policies did not begin until the struggle for political succession in the Communist Party was settled. This occurred after Khrushchev managed to oust Malenkov from his positions in the party and government and effectively demolished the myth of the infallibility of Stalin. After a period of vacillation, Soviet military posture and strategic doctrine were formalized in 1960.

Changes in the Soviet Strategic Posture

During the mid-to-late 1950s the Soviet Union undertook a number of major changes in its strategic position. No doubt, changes in Western strategic forces at this time had an important impact on Soviet strategic thinking. For the Eisenhower Administration had begun a world-wide military buildup, which significantly included the stationing of tactical nuclear weapons in regions close to the U.S.S.R. This last development in particular led to an increased emphasis on Soviet Air Defense Forces.

As early as 1954, nuclear weapons came to be integrated into the Soviet armed forces and were taken into account in military

6 Kozlov *et al.*, *O Sovetskoi voennoi nauke*, p.249, quoted in Thomas W. Wolfe, *Soviet Power and Europe 1945-1970* (Baltimore: The Johns Hopkins University Press, 1970), p.199.

7 Quoted in Raymond L. Garthoff, *Soviet Strategy in the Nuclear Age* (New York: Praeger, 1958), pp.78-79, 102-03.

training. Among these first nuclear weapons systems was a series of tactical missiles – the SS-1 and SS-2. They were specifically developed for the Ground Forces. By 1955, an operation-tactical missile, the SS-3, was assigned to support Ground Force operations. Given the limited range of these missiles and their command under Ground Forces, it is probable that these weapons were seen as modern equivalents of traditional Soviet artillery in providing fire support for the Ground Forces.[8]

During this period, the U.S.S.R. upgraded its ground-based warning-and-control system. It also deployed surface-to-air missiles for the first time and introduced high speed interceptor aircraft capable of all weather operations. At the same time, circles of SA-1 missile launchers were deployed around the Soviet capital, while SA-2 missiles provided a high altitude defense of other vital targets. Finally, efforts began to integrate the Warsaw Pact allies into the Soviet strategic air defense system.[9]

About this time, Stalin's plans to build a large navy of surface ships were temporarily abandoned. This was done in large part because it was becoming apparent that the primary naval threat to the Soviet homeland was not amphibious in nature but nuclear-armed aircraft launched from aircraft carriers. As a consequence, the Soviet leadership turned its attention to cruise missile-firing submarines and land-based aviation as a much more effective solution to the current naval problems of the Soviet Union. Also, in this regard, submarines capable of firing nuclear torpedoes began to be built and were among the first Soviet nuclear delivery systems.[10]

For the U.S.S.R. at this time, the primary means for delivering nuclear weapons over long distances was the manned bomber. Therefore, Long Range Aviation obtained great importance in Soviet defense planning. In the eyes of some Soviet leaders, the ability of the bomber to deliver nuclear attacks against enemy targets gave

8 For details see Joseph D. Douglass, Jr., *The Soviet Theater Nuclear Offensive*, Studies in Communist Affairs, Vol. 1, prepared for the Office of Director of Defense Research and Engineering and the Defense Nuclear Agency (Washington, D.C.: U.S. Government Printing Office, 1976).

9 See William F. Scott, "Troops of National Air Defense," *Air Force Magazine* (March, 1978).

10 See Raymond L. Garthoff, *Soviet Strategy in the Nuclear Age* (New York: Praeger, 1958), pp. 203-04.

the Soviet Union certain political and military benefits it had once lacked. This enhanced the sense of threat in the Soviet position as far as the United States and its NATO allies were concerned, particularly during the 1958-61 Berlin crisis.

One might have thought that with the Soviet headstart in missile technology, the U.S.S.R. would have decided to forgo a significant bomber-building program altogether. But this was not to be. As senior RAND analyst Thomas Wolfe suggests, if Khrushchev had done this, "he would have exposed the Soviet Union to the risk of a lengthy hiatus in which it would have possessed no modern strategic delivery capability at all." Indeed, there "was a longer delay in converting Soviet missile technology into operational forces than Khrushchev himself had evidently expected." In a sense, then "his decision to procure large numbers of strategic bombers, even if basically a stopgap measure rather than one founded on serious expectations of overcoming the US bomber lead, proved to be prudent."[11]

Consequently, in 1956, the Soviet Union began to deploy long-range bombers – the Tu-20 Bear and the Mya-4 Bison. The end of American invulnerability to significant nuclear attack was at hand.[12] The U.S.S.R., however, did not build up such a large strategic bombing force as the U.S. did. (At its peak, SAC was flying about 2,000 bombers.)

As Khrushchev later explained: "Our potential enemy – our most dangerous enemy – was so far away from us that we couldn't have reached him with our air force. Only by building up a nuclear missile force could we keep the enemy from unleashing war against us."[13]

More dramatically, in August 1957, the Soviets flight-tested an intercontinental ballistic missile – the SS-6 – at full range. (It was not until 1961 that the U.S.S.R. began deploying a "handful" of soft-site,

11 Thomas W. Wolfe, *Soviet Power and Europe, 1945-1970* (Baltimore: The Johns Hopkins University Press, 1970), p.179.

12 Even before the Bear and the Bison appeared, the Soviet Union had deployed the Tu-Badger, a swept-wing bomber comparable in size, role and performance to the American B-47. First flown in 1952, the Badger began entering service in 1954-55. It could carry a bomb load of three and half tons for a distance of 3,800 miles. This meant that Badgers could reach many cities in the U.S. on one-way flights from northern Soviet bases. See Norman Polmar, *opus cit.*, p.28.

13 *Khrushchev Remembers* (Boston: Little, Brown, 1970).

nonstorable liquid-fuel ICBMs.) A couple of months later, they dramatically launched the first space satellite, Sputnik I. This unprecedented space achievement was quickly followed by Sputnik II.[14]

Taking advantage of these Soviet successes, Khrushchev began to play on Western fears of an alleged "missile gap". Shrewdly exploiting Western miscalculations of the number of deployed Soviet ICBMs, the Soviet leader seized upon the so-called "missile gap" as a golden opportunity to wrest political concessions, to maintain the initiative in international relations and to make negotiations on disarmament seem less desirable.[15]

With the recognition of the mythical "missile gap" in 1961, Western leaders began to make more realistic estimates of Soviet strategic capabilities. At the same time the United States began substantially to increase its missile production, leaving no doubt as to where the strategic balance of power lay.[16]

Khrushchev's Military Program

On January 14, 1960, Chairman Khrushchev, shortly after returning from the United States, delivered an important policy address to the Supreme Soviet.[17] (The Supreme Soviet acts as the national parliament which endorses programs already agreed upon by the party leadership.) Basically, Khrushchev's program represented a compromise between existing doctrinal views and force structures desired by the military and Khrushchev's own desire to retrench by reducing the size of the armed forces by one third (from 3.6 to 2.4 million men) by the end of 1961. The First Secretary justified this drastic reduction on the grounds that the development of modern weapon-

14 For details see William H. Schauer, *The Politics of Space: A Comparison of the Soviet and American Space Programs* (New York: Holmes & Meiers, 1976).

15 Regardless of how one tends to view the so-called "missile gap" in retrospect, it is probably true that the Soviet Union began intensive long-range ballistic missile research and development six or seven years before the United States. See Mark E. Miller, *Soviet Strategic Power and Doctrine: The Quest for Superiority* (Washington, D.C.: Advanced International Studies Institute, 1982), p.13.

16 See Desmond Ball, *Politics and Force Levels: The Strategic Missile Program of the Kennedy Administration* (Berkeley: University of California Press, 1980), pp.107-26.

17 See N.S. Khrushchev in *Pravda,* January 15, 1960.

ry had rendered traditional military forces, especially large standing armies, obsolete.[18] The power of the U.S.S.R., he maintained, would not be determined by the numbers of men that it outfitted in "army greatcoats" but by the amount of "firepower" it could employ.[19] Thus, Khrushchev announced as part of his new defense policy the creation of a new service within the Soviet military. This was the Strategic Rocket Forces, SRF (*Raketnye Voiska Strategicheskogo Nazacheniya),* which would now be responsible for deploying strategic missiles. In line with Khrushchev's view that nuclear missile forces would dominate future wars, the SRF was elevated to the rank of a separate service on May 7, 1960 and then to the position of senior armed service.[20]

Today the SRF is responsible for all land-based ballistic missiles with ranges greater than 1,000 kilometers (about 620 miles). It is believed to have close to 400,000 active-duty military personnel, 50,000 civilians and a ready reserve of approximately 520,000.[21]

One of the main reasons for this shift in policy was to reduce military expenditures by relying more heavily on strategic nuclear missiles and cutting back on the more expensive traditional forms of Soviet military strength. But the "new look" trend (which reminded observers of Dulles' "more bang for the buck" strategy of the early 1950s) was opposed by at least some of the military leaders. (Several, including Marshal Sokolovsky, one of the foremost military

18 There has been some speculation that one reason for this deemphasis on military manpower was the serious Soviet military manpower problem at the time. Fewer babies had been conceived in the U.S.S.R. between 1941 and 1945. The number of youths reaching military service each year declined from over 2,380,000 in 1957 to a low of 917,000 in 1962. See Murray Feshbach, "Population," *Economic Performance and the Military Burden of the Soviet Union,* Joint Economic Committee of the Congress of the United States (Washington, D.C.: U.S. Government Printing Office, 1970), p.68. The problem is recurring today with respect to the Slavic population (not Asian) in the U.S.S.R. As a consequence, women may now volunteer for the Soviet armed forces.

19 Morton Schwartz, "The Cuban Missile Venture," in James B. Christoph *et al., Cases in Comparative Politics,* 3rd ed (Boston: Little, Brown & Co., 1976), p.342.

20 The establishment of the SRF as an independent service was foreshadowed by an earlier organizational development. This was the creation in 1948 of a special section within the Ministry of Defense to oversee the military aspects of the Soviet missile development program. For details see Edward L. Warner, *The Military in Contemporary Soviet Politics* (New York: Praeger, 1977), p.27.

21 *Air Force Magazine* of December 1984 credits the Strategic Rocket Forces with 415,000 personnel.

theoreticians, were retired in the spring of 1960). Their lack of confidence in the strategic potential of missile forces is perhaps best evidenced in the fact that "until 1960, no branch of the Soviet military establishment had strategic rockets as its primary mission."[22] Rather, as Graham Allison points out, Soviet missiles heretofore "belonged to the artillery section of the Soviet Ground Forces," the main purpose of which was to support Soviet ground forces in Europe.

The traditional military leaders must have been doubly upset with Khrushchev's sweeping plans. In the first place he was relying on nuclear armed missiles as the state's first line of defense when he had just a few years before decided not to deploy more than a handful of such weapons. In the second place, he was now asking the military to reduce substantially the size of Soviet ground forces *before* the second-generation ICBMs had been deployed. Undoubtedly, some in the military (particularly the older, more conservative leaders) saw this program as a threat to Soviet security and to their very jobs. With significant cuts in the size of the standing forces, career officers would have smaller armies to lead.[23]

New Soviet strategic doctrine and posture reflected the views of Khrushchev about the nature of war, particularly nuclear war. These views stressed that a war, no matter how initiated, would rapidly escalate into an all-out nuclear exchange. In view of this situation, reliable strategic deployment capabilities and only marginal conventional forces were necessary. An underlying premise of the new doctrine was Khrushchev's solemn conviction that nuclear war had become politically useless, since there would be no victors and the damage would be so vast and devastating that organized society would cease to exist.

To be sure, Khrushchev only arrived at this position gradually. For instance, he maintained in 1954 that in the event of a nuclear war the "imperialists will choke on it" and it "will end up in a catastrophe for the imperialist world." In 1956, he appeared to begin to hedge, declaring that "war is not fatalistically inevitable."[24] And by

22 Graham T. Allison, *Essence of Decision: Explaining the Cuban Missile Crisis* (Boston: Little, Brown & Co., 1971), pp. 114-15.

23 See Roman Kolkowicz, "Strategic Parity and Beyond: Soviet Perspectives," *World Politics* (April, 1971), p. 433.

24 *Pravda,* February 14, 1956.

1958 he reversed himself, now asserting that a "future war would cause immeasurable harm to all mankind."[25]

Missile Deployments[26]

With the shift in strategic doctrine under Khrushchev, an important decision was made in connection with the establishment in December 1959 of the Strategic Rocket Forces. The SRF was given responsibility for both theater and intercontinental missile forces and was declared in Soviet military writings to be the preeminent service in wartime, a position formerly occupied by the Ground Forces. Soviet industrial resources were now shifted from strategic bomber to missile production.

Khrushchev's internal policy position revision compelled basic changes in Soviet defense concepts. For one thing, the Soviet leader's belief that nuclear missiles reduced the need for large numbers of conventional forces and such weapons as strategic bombers was instrumental in orienting the Soviet military posture increasingly toward nuclear missiles. At the same time, the party leadership was given an important role in modernizing the Soviet strategic posture. Although many in the military resisted these trends, their efforts did not prevail.[27]

For a number of years after the establishment of the Strategic Rocket Forces, they were armed predominantly with regional-range strategic missiles. Partly this development occurred because of the technical difficulties associated with the early Soviet ICBM program. But it also reflected the importance the Soviets continued to give to political and military objectives in the regional theaters surrounding the U.S.S.R.

The strategic missiles deployed during the late 1950s and early 1960s were generally seen as the means for meeting Soviet regional

25 Radio Budapest, April 3, 1958.

26 This section draws heavily on the work done by Robert P. Berman and John C. Baker, *Soviet Strategic Forces: Requirements and Responses* (Washington, D.C.: The Brookings Institution, 1982).

27 Consult Carl A. Linden, *Khrushchev and the Soviet Leadership, 1957-1964* (Baltimore: Johns Hopkins Press, 1966), pp.72-81.

military requirements. The SS-4, a medium-range ballistic missile, was first deployed in late 1958. By 1965, there were nearly 600 SS-4 launchers deployed. These SS-4s were eventually supplemented by about 100 SS-5 intermediate-range ballistic missiles which became operational in 1961. Together, the SS-4s and SS-5s could attack a wide range of military and industrial targets throughout Western Europe and the Far East.[28]

Early Soviet missiles did not compare well with American missiles. For one thing, the famous SS-6 ICBM was never deployed in more than token numbers.[29] There were just too many bugs in the system. (For instance, the missile's nonstorable, liquid propellant hampered its launching, and its radio guidance could be disrupted by electronic interference.) However, as the main booster for the early Soviet space program, it performed reasonably well.

By the late 1950s, several new strategic missiles were in the process of development.[30] These included the SS-7, SS-8, and SS-9 – all large ICBMs suitable for covering area targets such as bomber bases and early missile sites in the U.S. Design plans for other missiles were also being set. Some of these were for the smaller SS-11, which was probably intended for use against maritime targets, and the Soviet Union's first solid-fuel ICBM, the SS-13.[31] Submarine-launched missiles were also under consideration.

28 The first Soviet strategic missiles – the regional SS-4s and SS-5s – were deployed above ground in the early 1960s in clusters of three or four relatively soft launchers. Each came with a reload missile. From 1963 to 1966, 135 of these missiles were placed in hardened shelters. Then the hardening program ceased, perhaps because of the priority placed on the construction of silos for the SS-9 and SS-11. See Graham T. Allison, *The Essence of Decision: Explaining the Cuban Missile Crisis* (Boston: Little, Brown, 1971), p.104.

29 The SS-6 passed its static trials in August 1957, but only four missiles were ever deployed. See Karl F. Spielmann, *Analyzing Soviet Strategic Decisions* (Boulder, Colo.: Westview Press, 1979).

30 Early deployments of the SS-6 were at above ground launch pads which were extremely vulnerable. Given the awkwardness and volatility of the missile's nonstorable liquid fuel, both launch areas and support facilities had to be exposed in this fashion. With the deployment of the second-generation SS-7s and SS-8s, greater attention was paid to their protection and concealment. Nevertheless, like the SS-4s and SS-5s, most of them were deployed in soft, concentrated clusters with two launchers per site. See *The New York Times*, July 26, 1962.

31 The SS-13 seems to have been intended to serve as a strategic reserve force for Soviet land-based missiles. As Robert P. Berman and John C. Baker point out, "Its propulsion system made it feasible to be deployed as a mobile missile, difficult

With the abrupt resumption of nuclear testing in the fall of 1961, the escalation of the Soviet strategic effort began. In part, this was no doubt due to the perception by the Soviet leadership that the United States was outdistancing the Soviets in strategic competition.

During this period a number of changes took place in the Soviet force posture. Particularly important here was the reorientation of the SS-11 ballistic missile from an antinaval role[32] to that of a system flexible enough to perform both regional and intercontinental strategic missions.

It was at this time also that the Soviets suddenly faced a serious threat from American forces that could not be countered by either its growing regional forces or its strategic forces. Consequently, the initial burden of responding to the American ICBM force fell on the second-generation Soviet ICBMs. These were the SS-7 and SS-8, which were not available for deployment until 1962-63. Their poor accuracy and high vulnerability to counterattack, however, made them an inadequate counter to the new U.S. missiles.[33] Moreover, the low production rate of these large Soviet missiles permitted the U.S. to soon open up an expanding lead in numbers of missiles deployed. So it was not long before the Soviet leadership came to the realization that its planned strategic posture was inadequate to meet the evolving U.S. strategic threat.[34]

to locate and destroy in wartime." However, serious "technical problems associated with the SS-13's guidance system and solid-fuel motor apparently hampered its development. Only sixty of the ICBMs were deployed, all of them in silos." See their *Soviet Strategic Forces: Requirements and Responses* (Washington, D.C.: The Brookings Institution, 1982), p.54.

32 One U.S. government "insider" observes here: "Soviet intelligence capabilities in 1960-65 were not able to target U.S. naval forces in a timely fashion."

33 See Lawrence Freedman, *US Intelligence and the Soviet Strategic Threat* (Boulder, Colo.: Westview Press, 1977), p.99.

34 During the early 1960s the U.S. changed its policy of massive retaliation to flexible response. No longer would the United States threaten to launch an immediate, all-out nuclear attack on an adversary guilty of encroaching on America's vital interests. Instead the enemy would be faced with a wide range of military responses on the part of the U.S., including the possible use of nuclear weapons.
The Soviets remained skeptical of this change in strategy, however. Standard Soviet analysts depicted the strategy of flexible response as part of a continuing attempt by the United States to achieve a capability to conduct all-out nuclear war. See, for example, V.D. Sokolovsky (ed., *Soviet Military Strategy*, 3rd ed. (New York: Crane, Russak, 1968), p.58.

Conclusions

According to one Soviet account of postwar development of the Soviet armed forces near the end of the Khrushchev period, the main characteristic of the years between 1945 und 1954 was the effort to develop and master the new technology of the nuclear missile gap. By way of contrast, the main feature of the subsequent decade was the process of incorporating the new weapons into the armed forces along with the appropriate doctrine for their use.[35] To be sure, there was some overlap between these two phases of development. But in the main it remained for Khrushchev to preside over the second phase of operations, namely, the introduction of new weapons and concepts of modern warfare into the Soviet armed forces.

The changes that Khrushchev introduced were basically threefold. In the first place, military technology and weaponry were modernized. In the second place, the massive conventional forces were gradually reduced by more than half. At the same time, Soviet strategic doctrine and policy were sharply modified. All this occurred in a time period when the Soviet Union's political influence and international role were expanding considerably.

To begin with, the production and deployment of strategic nuclear weapons under Khrushchev's tenure was relatively modest.[36] Between 1957 and 1962 the Soviets decided to forgo the creation of a large, long-range bomber force and to give priority to medium-range missiles aimed at Europe rather than at the United States. For reasons cited earlier, the Soviets chose at this time not to deploy in large numbers their first ICBM (the SS-6).[37] Instead, they waited for

35 See Colonel I. Korotkov, "The Development of Soviet Military Theory in the Postwar Years," *Voenno-istoricheskii zhurnal,* No. 4 (April, 1964).

36 From public reports it appears that the first U.S. intelligence estimates of Soviet ICBM strength during 1962 put it at 50-75 missiles, increasing after July 1962 to 75-100. The figure for mid-1963 was 91 missiles in place. By mid-1964 the Soviets had built 188-191 ICBMs, and by mid-1965, 224. The limited pace of Soviet ICBM deployment did not give much support to assertions that the U.S.S.R. was keenly interested at this time in obtaining parity with the U.S. See Lawrence Freedman, *opus cit.,* p. 101. "What they wanted to do and what they could do are not the same thing," argues one U.S. official.

37 Some studies blame the slow pace of ICBM development on technical difficulties. See P. Joubert, "Long Range Air Attack," in A. Lee (ed.), *The Soviet Air and Rocket Forces* (New York: Praeger, 1959). Other investigators have focused on

the more advanced and more reliable SS-7s and SS-8s. But even then the deployment level was not massive; only about 200 of these second-generation ICBMs were fielded. Importantly, Khrushchev chose to install most of these long-range missiles in more secure underground silos – even though he could have achieved a much faster buildup through the deployment of the more vulnerable, above-ground launchers.

When compared to the situation in the U.S. during this period, the early deployment of Soviet missile-launching submarines seems especially moderate. The first generation "G-class" was crude and minimally effective. It was diesel powered, and its missiles had a limited range (approximately 350 nautical miles).[38] Moreoever, Soviet submarines had to rise to the surface in order to fire. In the end, only some seventy launchers were actually deployed.

In the second class of Russian subs (the "H-class"), significant improvements were noted by the American intelligence community. Of the eight submarines of this type that were actually assigned a duty station, all were nuclear powered. They carried about 30 missiles, and enjoyed a longer range (approximately 700 nautical miles).

More or less the same pattern prevailed in the case of Soviet heavy bombers. The Bison (MYA-2) and the Bear (Tu-95) were never manufactured in any great number. And for a long time, these models were never replaced.[39] (Only in 1984 did the U.S.S.R. begin adding the Bear-H-bomber, an entirely new Bear variant, to carry a new long-range air launched cruise missile. At this writing, the Blackjack, which is larger than the American B-1B, is in the flight stage of production.)

economic constraints as being responsible. See, for example, L. Bloomfield *et al., Khrushchev and the Arms Race* (Cambridge: MIT Press, 1966), pp.106-115. Still others attribute the gap between Khrushchev's rhetoric about strategic power and reality to the resistance of conservative elements in the military. See, for instance, M.P. Gallagher *et al., Soviet Decision-Making for Defense: A Critique of U.S. Perspectives on the Arms Race* (New York: Praeger, 1972), pp.35-37. Finally, Horelick and Rush suggest that the Soviet leadership made a carefully calculated decision to leap to the second generation of nuclear weapons. See A.L. Horelick and M. Rush, *Strategic Power and Soviet Foreign Policy* (Chicago: University of Chicago Press, 1965), p.37.

38 "Yes," says one U.S. arms control expert, "but fifty percent of U.S. industry and population was in range of these missiles."

39 For background here see Robert P. Berman, *Soviet Air Power in Transition* (Washington, D.C.: The Brookings Institution, 1978), p.8.

Under Khrushchev, the Soviet armed forces underwent a "revolution in military affairs" (to use the Soviet phrase). Military doctrine and organization were completely overhauled in response to the development of nuclear weapons.

Khrushchev himself came down on both sides of the nuclear issue. But in the end he came to reject outright the notion of the political utility of nuclear conflict. At the same time, he rejected the idea of limited nuclear war.[40] In his view, such a war would rapidly become a general nuclear war.

During the 1950s and early 1960s, Khrushchev placed increasing stress on strategic weapons as measures of Soviet power. As a whole, the Soviet leadership did not view the function of Soviet strategic power in the narrow terms of deterring nuclear attack. To be sure, Soviet rockets were viewed as the principal means of devastating aggressors and resisting nuclear blackmail by the United States. But more importantly the status of the U.S.S.R. as a nuclear power was associated with the prospects of the broader struggle between socialism and capitalism in international relations.[41]

For ideological and tactical reasons, Khrushchev repeatedly stressed the importance of "wars of national liberation." Moreover, he called for support of these wars. However, given the rather inadequate quantity and quality of his conventional forces,[42] it is improbable that the Soviet Chairman ever seriously contemplated direct Soviet involvement in these wars.[43]

40 The following is a typical expression of Khrushchev's view on limited war: "Should such wars break out, they could soon (escalate) into a world war." *Tass*, December 5, 1957.

41 See Khrushchev's remarks in, for instance, *Pravda*, March 27, 1958 and *Pravda*, January 28, 1959. William D. Jackson has a similar view. See his "The Soviets and Strategic Arms: Toward an Evaluation of the Record," *Political Science Quarterly*, Vol. 94, No. 2 (Summer, 1979), p. 246.

42 "What the Soviet lacked at this time," states one U.S. official, "was the ability to project these forces overseas to support 'national wars of liberation.'"

43 Ambassador Martin Hillenbrand would insert the following observation here: "Whatever Khrushchev's reliance on nuclear armed missiles with only a marginal role for conventional forces in actual war-fighting, he was certainly aware of the need to maintain large numbers of conventional forces in Eastern Europe, both to maintain the Soviet grip over Warsaw Pact countries and to offset NATO conventional forces. His threats to take unilateral action against the Allied position in West Berlin during 1958-1963 would not have made much sense without enormous conventional superiority in and about Berlin." Letter to this writer, May 2, 1985.

If Khrushchev recognized the basic political changes caused by the emergence of weapons of mass destruction, he nevertheless pursued a very vigorous, frequently militant policy during the latter half of the 1950s. At the same time he sought to avoid war or a major confrontation with the United States he was not above making bombastic threats to frighten Western publics. This form of "saber rattling" was most frequent during the Suez crisis of 1956 and during the tense period of the Berlin crisis, beginning in 1958.

After 1961 Khrushchev followed a policy of gradually ascending risks and costs. On the one hand, the Soviets still boasted of the powerful might of Soviet missiles. However, Khrushchev viewed a full-scale arms race with the West as the least desirable alternative and so he did not attempt to match American strategic capabilities. This decision was due to a number of factors, but not unimportant was the fact that Khrushchev's ambitious Seven-Year Plan, aimed at the domestic sector of the economy, was running into major difficulties.

Khrushchev's nadir came one year later, in October 1962.[44] At the time the United States enjoyed an overwhelming advantage in strategic nuclear missiles. And the Soviet leader may have been hoping to change the perception of the strategic balance by stationing medium and intermediate range ballistic missiles ninety miles off the coast of the United States.[45] Whatever the case,[46] the

44 The Cuban Missile Crisis had a profound effect on the relations between party and military. Much about that period remains vague. But the substance of their dialogue after the crisis suggests that certain military circles opposed Khrushchev's handling of the matter. See Roman Kolkowicz, *The Soviet Military and the Communist Party* (Princeton University Press, 1967), p.210.

45 So far as one can judge, the decision for the Cuban venture was not Khrushchev's alone. Other leaders, both civilian and military, partook in it. In his memoirs Khrushchev states: "When I was the head of the government and also held the highest post in the central committee, I never made a decision on my own ..." See *Khrushchev Remembers: The Last Testament* (New York: Bantam Books, 1976), p.618.

46 Khrushchev later argued on a number of occasions (his most definitive exposition being his December 12, 1962 speech before the Supreme Soviet) that the U.S.S.R. had placed missiles in Cuba in order to discourage the United States from attacking Cuba. See *Pravda,* December 13, 1962.
Castro gave the following explanation as to why he accepted the Soviet missiles: "We had discussed among ourselves the possibility of asking the U.S.S.R. to provide us with rockets. But we had not reached any decision when Moscow offered them to us. It was explained that by accepting them we would strength-

unprecedented Soviet decision to deploy nuclear missiles outside the borders of the U.S.S.R. quickly led to a dangerous military confrontation with the Kennedy Administration. Everything was in combat readiness in the U.S., and the danger of nuclear war was fully realized. As the American President himself said later, the odds that the Soviets would go all the way were "somewhere between one out of three and even."[47]

But in the end both sides showed restraint,[48] and a nuclear holocaust was avoided. Khrushchev's dangerous gamble was rebuffed, and the Soviet leader was persuaded to withdraw his missiles from Cuba.[49] Two years later Khrushchev was overthrown in a bloodless *coup d'état.*

en the socialist camp on the world scale. And since we were already receiving a large amount of help from the socialist camp, we decided that we could not refuse. That is why we accepted them. *It was not in order to ensure our own defense, but primarily to strengthen socialism on the international scale.* That is the truth, even if different explanations are given elsewhere." (Italics mine.) *Le Monde,* March 22, 1963.

47 Quoted in Theodore C. Sorensen, *Kennedy* (New York: Bantam Books, 1966), p. 705.

48 After the crisis, Khrushchev attempted to paint the fiasco in Cuba not as a failure but rather as a mutual accomodation of interests by the U.S. and the U.S.S.R. But these arguments are not entirely convincing: "There are people who claim that Cuba and the Soviet Union suffered defeat in the Caribbean conflict. But such people have a strange logic: How can it be that we suffered defeat, when revolutionary Cuba exists and is growing stronger? Who really retreated and who won in this conflict?"
"We are told: If you removed the missiles from Cuba, you retreated ... Yes, this was our concession in exchange for a concession by the other side; this was a mutual concession The imperialists were compelled to make a concession and renounce invasion of Cuba. And it was to protect Cuba from invasion by the imperialists that we installed the missiles. Consequently, our missiles performed their role." *Pravda,* January 17, 1963.

49 For an excellent analysis of Soviet policy and behavior pertaining to the Cuban Missile Crisis, see A. Horelick, "The Cuban Missile Crisis: An Analysis of Soviet Calculations and Behavior," *World Politics,* No. 3 (April, 1964).

A nightingale to one is an owl to another.
Soviet Ambassador S.K. Tsarapkin

IV. THE BREZHNEV LEGACY: A NUCLEAR BALANCE SHEET

Following the unprecedented removal of the First Secretary of the Communist Party in 1964, the "collective leadership" consisting of Party Leader Leonid Brezhnev, prime Minister Aleksei Kosygin, and President Nikolai Podgorny (who succeeded as head of state in December 1965), emerged. They were immediately faced with a serious situation brought on by Khrushchev's erratic and sometimes bombastic foreign policy. To the new regime, the best antidote to the past failures of Khrushchev appeared to be sobriety, pragmatism and the attainment of credibility in international affairs through the acquisition of conspicuous capabilities to match specific Soviet national objectives.

This chapter attempts to come to grips with some of those conspicuous capabilities, particularly as they affect nuclear weapons policies and developments. Special attention will be paid to developments in ICBMs, SLBMs and strategic bombers. In the end, a balance sheet will be drawn to determine whether or not the Soviets have achieved nuclear superiority.

Speak Softly While You Carry A Big Stick

The strategic policy of the new regime has been described as a "speak-softly-while-you-are-carrying-a-big-stick" policy.[1] In the words of Party Secretary Brezhnev: "We are striving to make our

1 Roman Kolkowicz, *opus cit.*, p. 437.

diplomacy vigorous and active, and at the same time we exhibit flexibility and caution."[2] A "mere bookish knowledge of Marxism does not supply the confidence possible for working policy." Although the new regime significantly transformed the method and style of Soviet policy, it did retain a central assumption of Khrushchev's policy regarding the political and strategic environment of the Soviet state. This was that a nuclear war would be a catastrophe for both the East and West.[3]

The new attitude of prudence and pragmatism notwithstanding, the new Soviet leaders were very much concerned with the marked strategic inferiority of the Soviet Union. They also were troubled by the inadequacy of their predecessor's strategic policy, which rested on an "all-or-nothing" proposition regarding nuclear war. Such a rigid nuclear doctrine had effectively deprived the U.S.S.R. of military flexibility and the necessary range of options for dealing with sub-nuclear conflicts.[4]

2 *Pravda,* September 30, 1965.

3 Roman Kolkowicz, *opus cit.,* p. 437. One Soviet expert in the government would disagree here with what he sees is the implication that the Soviets never have sought war-winning, war-fighting, war survival capabilities or any form of superiority. This person argues that "there is virtually no authoritative indication of official rejection or questioning of the nuclear war theses put forth so regularly by all military commentators from Sokolovsky to Ogarkov. The only contrary views were the occasional generalities on the catastrophe expressed by some political leaders and many foreign-propaganda flacks (the Arbatovs *et al.*) when addressing Western audiences or promoting the Soviet version of arms control. Kolkowicz's assertion has an element of truth – at all times Soviet leadership, including the military, has recognized that nuclear war would exact extremely high prices, even if somehow won.
"This has equally and clearly been translated into a set of policies and strategies which had as one primary objective the avoidance of such a war. However, in the context clearly implied in this chapter, that of whether Soviet official strategy sought superiorities, etc., the Kolkowicz quote is either inaccurate or taken out of context. It is not until the official line of no victors and no present escape from mutual assured destruction began to come into official military writings, Ustinov's speeches and articles, etc. (in the late 1970's) that a good case can be made for this (and even then, there is a disquieting congruence with the needs of a Soviet world-wide peace campaign against INF, space weapons, etc.)."

4 According to Benjamin S. Lambeth, a former CIA official, Soviet "military professionals began to exert sustained pressures on their party superiors to replace rhetoric with actions, and the stage was gradually set for a sweeping departure from the pre-established mold of Soviet strategic policy." See his *The Politics of the Soviet Military Under Brezhnev and Kosygin* (Washington, D.C.: Georgetown University, unpublished M.A. thesis, 1968). See also Roman Kolkowicz, *The Di-*

Consequently, the new regime decided to embark on a concentrated build-up of military forces across the board. Programs for the production of offensive as well as defensive strategic nuclear weapons were accelerated. Beginning in 1965, there was a small increase in the official defense budget. But increases continued over the next five years for a total increase of almost forty percent.

The new Soviet military program called for a long-term build-up of strategic nuclear forces.[5] But it also called for substantial increases in conventional strength, particularly along the long boundary with China in the Far East. In fact, the bulk of Soviet defense spending during this period was not poured into an expansion of its nuclear arsenal. Rather, it went to reequipping the Soviet Army (especially in European Russia and Central Europe) creating a new, tactical air force and developing for the first time a "blue water" navy. Roughly 10 to 15 percent of the overall total of Soviet defense spending during this period was directed at the threat posed by China. (It should not be forgotten that China's explosion of a nuclear device in late 1964 added a new potential threat to Soviet interests.)[6]

But Brezhnev's contribution should not be exaggerated.[7] In the

lemma of Superpower: Soviet Policy and Strategy in Transition (Institute for Defense Analysis, 1967).

5 At least three explanations have been offered to cover the Soviet buildup from 1965-71. John Erickson outlines their basic points: "The first general explanation is inclined to see this as an effort to recover from the strategic inferiority which the Soviet leadership inherited in 1964 ... the second view is at pains to stress that Soviet formulations about superiority should be taken at their face value and that the Soviet Union is aiming for a definite strategic advantage as part of a 'master-plan' concept: a third view holds that the build-up proceeded without a defined single objective – rather this pragmatism was made up of a number of elements, in which 'parity' and possible 'superiority' were intermingled and where the notion of sufficiency or 'adequacy' had differing military and political connotations." See John Erickson, *Soviet Military Power* (London: Royal United Services Institute for Defense Studies, 1972).

6 By the mid-1960s Sino-Soviet relations had fully deteriorated, and the Soviet military received new instruction to cover Chinese targets. By 1969, additional Soviet nuclear forces (including some SS-14s and SS-15s) were deployed close to the border with the PRC. See *The New York Times*, May 24, 1969.

7 Under Brezhnev, the Politburo possessed ultimate authority. As Dimitri K. Simes, a well-known Soviet expert, writes, "From a primarily pro forma group of Stalin's handpicked loyal lieutenants, the Politburo had turned under Khrushchev, into an advisory body filled with personal allies and protégés of the leader. Brezhnev's Politburo resembled more a supreme legislative-executive committee of a

eyes of many U.S. military analysts of the Soviet Union, his major contribution was to decide on the final size of the force. The weaponry that was deployed was, for the most part, constructed on the basis of technology that was already developed. Thus, the new Soviet ICBMs (the SS-9, the SS-10, which eventually floundered, and the SS-11) and the Y-class submarine were known by the West as being in an early stage of development in late 1964.

Soviet ICBM Buildup

Soviet strategic forces[8] are composed of substantial regional forces directed against adjoining areas such as the People's Republic of China und West Europe as well as intercontinental-range nuclear forces capable of striking targets in the United States. For most of the Soviet Union's history, the most vital interests and greatest threats to Moscow have been in neighboring areas. Thus, the Soviets tend to attribute – in a matter not fully appreciated in the U.S. – a strategic importance to their regional nuclear forces. In the

chairman of the board who had great personal authority but who could not, and did not want to, monopolize the formation of policy." In several cases, Brezhnev at the very least tried to involve his colleagues in determining responses to important questions. "In the course of discussing ICBM limitations with Kissinger during the secretary of state's visit to Moscow, Brezhnev went so far as to claim that, 'If I agree to this, this will be my last meeting with Dr. Kissinger because I will be destroyed.' While the Secretary General was probably exaggerating, and the Soviets made some concessions the next day, the shift in Moscow's position occurred only after a six-hour Politburo session which delayed a scheduled meeting between Kissinger and Brezhnev. See Dimitri K. Simes, "Soviet Policy toward the United States," in Joseph S. Nye, Jr., *The Making of America's Soviet Policy* (New Haven: Yale University Press, 1985), pp.298-99.

8 Soviet officials and their American counterparts in START have been unable to agree on a definition for the word "strategic." The Soviets maintain that any weapon that can hit the Soviet homeland is strategic, but that their SS-20 missiles do not fit that category because they can only reach Europe and Asia and not the mainland United States.
This position represents a change from earlier times. Previously, in Soviet usage, "strategic missiles" included missiles of intercontinental (ICBM), intermediate (IRBM) and medium-range (MRBM). These were under the control of the strategic missile forces. Other missiles of lesser range, designated as "operational-tactical missiles" in Soviet usage, were to be found in the armament of the ground, air and naval forces. See Marshal V.D. Sokolovskii *et al.*, *Soviet Military Strategy* (Englewood Cliffs: Prentice-Hall, 1963), pp.51, 521.

words of one author, "The Soviet need for intercontinental strategic forces became critical by the early 1960s when the United States began to deploy large numbers of intercontinental weapons that could not be effectively offset by Soviet defenses or regional forces."[9] As a consequence, the Soviets undertook a series of measures and long term programs that shaped the nature and extent of their missile programs into the 1980s.

The Soviet ICBM build-up is sometimes portrayed in the West as a rapid one.[10] But some U.S. Kremlinologists dispute this. They have identified two major stages of development. The first took place between 1959 and 1965; the second occurred between 1966 and 1971.[11] (Some would add a third stage for MRVs, 1972-1979, a

9 Robert P. Berman *et al., Soviet Strategic Forces: Requirements and Responses* (Washington, D.C.: The Brookings Institution, 1982), p. 2. This assertion is, in the view of one student of Soviet military policy, a serious oversimplification. "Certainly, this was a factor, but other things also undoubtedly played a part. *Inter alia* these include:

1. "Simple technological and production lags.
2. "Khrushchev had attempted to bluff an overwhelming strategic capability from the late 1950s. Ironically, the partial success of this bluff greatly contributed to the development of the U.S. offensive strategic buildup in the early and mid-1960s.
3. "Starting in the latter part of the 1950's, the Soviets began to try to play a truly global role. Much of this was focused on economic levers, but always against the backdrop of military capabilities and the claim of also being one of two superpowers.
4. "The seriousness of the Sino-Soviet dispute, the strategic implications of which was undoubtedly more evident, earlier, to the Soviet leadership than the West, probably also contributed.

"In sum, given the consistency of serious Soviet strategic writing, as well as the lead time in strategic weapons development programs (years in the R & D phase when [especially then] its detection by Western intelligence generally lags its initiation), followed by years of T & E before initial IOC, and then years before deployment is complete, it simply strains credibility to imply that the 1960s Soviet strategic buildup was simply a response to the U.S. programs."

10 In the words of U.S. Ambassador Martin Hillenbrand: "The U.S. nuclear buildup has been described as one of fits and starts and that of the Soviet Union as one of steady progression upwards. Not all U.S. Kremlinologists would dispute that the Soviet ICBM buildup has been steady and at times rapid. The only source you cite is Bellamy, which dates back to 1974 before the deployment of SS-18s had taken place. Moreover, the 'final total of Soviet ICBMs for that period' (1963-1972) which you give as 1030 is misleading since, as you point out later, the SALT I Interim Agreement accepted a considerable Soviet superiority in total ICBM and SLBM launchers (including some 1618 ICBM launchers)." Letter to this writer, May 2, 1985.

11 One critic would take issue with this analysis. He argues that this breakdown

fourth stage, 1979-1985 with the MIRV, and a fifth stage, 1985-88, with mobile missiles.) During the first two stages, the pace of the development of land-based strategic nuclear weapons conformed strikingly to a pattern that could be found in American rates of deployment.[12] This essential point is often obscured by the fact that the actual deployment of new Soviet ICBMs greatly exceeded the original projections of the American intelligence community.

Frequently, the total number of Soviet ICBMs is compared with the American level in order to show that the Russians are determined to achieve nuclear superiority. However, as William Hyland, a long-time student of Soviet affairs, points out, the actual comparison of separate ICBM systems "raises some questions about this interpretation."[13] While numerous Western sources contain conflict-

"doesn't hold water." He says that it is striking that the two phases "are without a gap" – illustrating a continuous effort at least until 1971. The point that the build-up was not really very rapid compared to the U.S. buildup phases is accurate, but hardly surprising. It is not surprising because the U.S.S.R. simply cannot technologically match the U.S. when the U.S. is making a real effort. It begs the point because the serious claims of concerted and continuing Soviet efforts to achieve superiorities charge that the Soviets have consistently pursued a long term effort at about the maximum pace that actual technical and production capabilities, resources and political realities and tactics would allow.

"More seriously, it is difficult to accept that there were no major stages of development after 1971 as implied here. Throughout the 1970s new models, incorporating often major improvements in accuracy, MIRVing, etc. appeared in IOCs which argue for extensive and consistent concerted Research and Development. U.S. Department of Defense annual reports regularly reported that other systems were in the R & D stages. The SS-20 (and the possible continuation of the SS-16 program under SS-20 guise) was basically part of a post-1971 buildup phase.

"New strategic weapons made IOC in the late 1970s, reflecting an earlier development phase. The SS-N-17, for all of its problems, made IOC in 1977, the SS-N-18 (without similar problems) in 1978 and the SS-NX-20 (IOC, 1981) and the Oscar submarine with its relatively long range cruise missiles (1982) both reflected long R & D and production during the latter 1970s. Even the later BLACKJACK aircraft (new long range strategic bomber) undoubtedly started R & D well before the advent of any U.S. buildup.

"All of this argues strongly that the so-called phases of Soviet strategic buildup continued virtually unabated through the 1970s and into the 1980s."

12 See Ian Bellany, "Strategic Arms Competition and the Logistic Curve," *Survival* (September-October, 1974), p.228 *Passim.*

13 William G. Hyland, "The USSR and Nuclear War," in Barry M. Blechman (ed.), *Rethinking the U.S. Strategic Posture* (Cambridge: Ballinger Publishing Co., 1982), p.52. Hyland worked on the Soviet desk in the Bureau of Intelligence and Research in the State Department before moving over to the White House during the Nixon years.

ing figures for the Soviet missile buildup, the most authoritative official U.S. figures are found in the annual Department of Defense *Reports,* which have been declassified for the years 1963-72. These figures reveal that the final total of Soviet ICBMs for that period, 1030, only slightly exceeded the American program. (The bulk of these ICBMs consisted of the SS-11, which is very roughly comparable to the U.S. Minuteman III ICBM, which reached the arbitrary level of 1,000 deployed.)[14]

Those analysts who maintained that the Soviet leadership was striving for military superiority over the United States tended to focus on increases in the large Soviet ICBM – the SS-9 – and today its strategic replacement, the formidable SS-18, as constituting proof of the Soviet drive for a clear strategic advantage. During the late 1960s the Soviets increased the number of SS-9s, and this development was singled out by some U.S. analysts as evidence of Soviet intentions to acquire a capability to cripple the hardened silcs in which American Minuteman launchers are located.

Actually, U.S. officials could only speculate as to the ultimate objective of the Soviet leadership in this area. But it is important to note that the then favored scenario in American government circles for the Soviets obtaining this alleged strategic advantage proved to be wrong. As one former U.S. intelligence official recalls: "In this scenario, the SS-9 was singled out as early as 1967 in the United States as the candidate to be the first Soviet missile to be equipped with multiple independently targetable reentry vehicles (MIRVs)." Such a capability, which has the effect of multiplying the number of warheads deliverable by a single booster to separate aiming points, was predicted to be operational by 1971-72. "Confirmation seemed to have been provided by the testing of a multiple warhead (but

14 One Soviet expert would make the following point here: "Catudal notes that Soviet final totals of deployed ICBMs for 1963-1972 only slightly exceeded the American program. The implied conclusion that they had no longer range goals of numerical (or other) advantage simply doesn't follow; nor were there any appreciable number of Western observers who thought so then. This is precisely the period that the prevailing U.S. assumption (upon which SALT I was based) was that the Soviets would build until they reached parity. Those who noted that this didn't seem consistent with stated and published military writings were few and far between at that time. What the figures did show was probably more the rates of development and deployment that the Soviets could sustain in this period."

not a true MIRV) that began in the USSR in August 1968." In 1969, American officials "were predicting a Soviet objective of at least 400 SS-9s, each probably armed with three warheads." (This would be the required combination in order to attack American silos with one warhead targeted against one silo.) By 1970, some U.S. officials even went so far as to claim that "the Soviets had already acquired a true MIRV capability."

"In fact," as this source discloses, "the SS-9 program had been a logical progression from the previous generation (SS-7) and was probably designed by the same team." While its size and throw-weight were larger than its predecessor, this was "not because of its MIRV potential, because the SS-9 was never developed to be equipped with MIRVs." The first Soviet MIRVed missile, the SS-18, "was still another generation of technology away."[15] And testing of this missile with MIRVs "did not begin until 1974, and deployments of the SS-18 were not completed until 1980-81" – about ten years after the initial U.S. intelligence prediction.[16]

As Raymond Garthoff has observed, politics – rather than strategic doctrine or military strategy – appears to account for the hesitation (even confusion) in the final phase of Soviet strategic nuclear deployments in the early 1970s.[17] The major political context was the SALT I negotiations. And here the Soviet decision to adjust its

15 One U.S. missile expert would point out that "the SS-18 is identified as the first Soviet MIRVed missile. Not so. The first SS-18 mod reached IOC in 1975 and the first MIRVed SS-18 mod in 1977, both after years of Research and Development T & E. But the first MIRVed SS-19 has a listed IOC of 1974. Moreover, the SALT II treaty which identifies Soviet nomenclature lists the SS-18 as the RS-20 and the SS-19 as the RS-18. This clearly suggests that the US numerology is chronologically inaccurate. This, of course, also relates to the well documented story of the Soviets concealing aspects of the SS-19 until after SALT I was signed in order to insure that it didn't qualify as a heavy missile."

16 William Hyland, *opus cit.,* p. 52. One critic would comment here that "the true statement that SS-18 deployment was not completed until the end of the decade is quite misleading. The deployment was continuous over half that decade following earlier RD T & E. Soviet capabilities (or for that matter American) do not allow instantaneous deployment of such numbers – especially when the deployments not only replace entirely different earlier systems but at the same time replace earlier models of the new system with more advanced, more capable versions."

17 Two important articles here are Garthoff's "SALT and the Soviet Military," *Problems of Communism* (January-February, 1975), and "Negotiating with the Russians: Some Lessons from SALT," *International Security* (Spring, 1977).

ICBM deployment before a final SALT agreement could be achieved seems decisive. Thus, as the original SS-9 deployment was almost completed at 306 silos, the Soviets built twenty additional silos of a completely different kind. These turned out to be for the formidable SS-18 ICBM. The precise reason for this move is conjectural, but apparently the Soviets were interested in establishing a precedent for the new ICBM launchers for MIRVed missiles that Moscow wanted deployed during the five-year interim period of the Salt I agreement. As things turned out, the Soviets eventually refitted all their SS-9 silos to accomodate the SS-18 missiles, changing the threat from 924 MIRVs to at least 3080 MIRVs.

The crucial point of this historical treatment is that the bulk of the building programs associated with the early Soviet ICBM force was halted in 1971, short of the level anticipated by the United States in the late 1960s.[18] This development occurred in the context of the negotiations over SALT I and surprised a number of U.S. government officials who were operating on a "worst-case" basis in the late 1960s.[19]

18 See William G. Hyland, *opus cit.,* p.53.

19 The idea of SALT originated not in the arms control bureaucracy in Washington but with Secretary of Defense Robert McNamara, who was supported by Secretary of State Dean Rusk. The U.S. Ambassador to the Soviet Union privately proposed to the Soviet leadership bilateral talks on the matter in December 1966. This proposal, which emphasized the limiting of ABM systems, led to further exchanges in 1967. The Soviets asked that talks on strategic arms limitations cover not only ABMs but also strategic offensive arms. The U.S. promptly agreed. There was some delay until the Soviet Union was finally prepared to start negotiating in mid-1968. One reason for the delay may well have been the disparity in strategic strength at the time of SALT. In 1967, the strategic force levels of the U.S.S.R were considerably inferior to those of the U.S. (In January 1967, the United States had 1,630 operational ICBMs and SLBMs while the Soviet Union had only about 600). The Russians only agreed to begin talks when it appeared that they were in reach of numerical parity in strategic intercontinental systems in mid-1968. And U.S. policy was to allow them to catch up. For details see John Newhouse, *Cold Dawn: The Story of SALT* (New York: Holt, Rinehart & Winston, 1973) and the book by the SALT I negotiator Gerard Smith, *Doubletalk: The Story of SALT I* (New York: Doubleday, 1980).

The SALT I Agreements

The SALT I negotiations culminated in the signing of two major arms agreements in Moscow on May 26, 1972. One treaty limited strategic missile defensive systems; another agreement restricted offensive nuclear weapons launchers. The SALT I interim accord expired in 1977, whereas the ABM treaty remains in effect. Until recently both sides continued to abide by the interim accord.[20]

The first agreement took the form of a treaty limiting both the United States and the Soviet Union to two ABM (anti-ballistic missile) sites. One of these sites was to be for the defense of the national capital of each side and another for the defense of an ICBM field in each country.

The second pact was a five-year interim agreement which limited offensive missile launchers – land-based silos and submarine missile tubes – to those under construction or deployed at the time of the signing.[21] For its part, the U.S. had a total of 1,710 launchers, including 1,054 ICBMs and 656 SLBMs (submarine launched ballistic missiles).

The U.S.S.R. was estimated to have a total strategic missile launcher strength of 2,358 – 1,618 ICBM launchers and 740 SLBM launchers.

In addition to the numerical edge, the Soviets also had the advantage in throw-weight. (Throw-weight is the total weight of what can be carried by a missile over a particular distance and is a measure of its destructive capability.) This was estimated at several times that of the United States. For its part, the U.S, had a numerical advantage in warheads, as well as superiority in strategic bombers – 460 at that time compared to a total of 140 for the U.S.S.R. – and aircraft that could strike the Soviet Union on one-way missions from Western Europe.

If the SALT I agreement froze the numbers of strategic launchers

20 It should be noted that the SALT I Interim Agreement has been superceded by SALT II ceilings to which both sides say they are still adhering. For the text see U.S. Arms Control and Disarmament Agency, *Arms Control and Disarmament Agreements* (Washington, D.C., 1982).

21 The SALT I agreement provides no numbers for ICBMs. It refers only in terms of those ICBM sites constructed as of July 1, 1972. The numbers provided are for those given by the U.S. government.

possessed by the two superpowers, it also left a gaping loophole in the area of *qualitative* improvements.[22] Most important here was the lack of restraint on such controversial and destabilizing technologies as the MIRV and now the MARV systems. (MARV is an acronym for maneuverable re-entry vehicles). There is some evidence which suggests that President Nixon[23] and Henry Kissinger were under some pressure during the SALT I talks not to close this loophole in order to placate the American military (which was ahead in this technology) and to gain its acquiescence in the final SALT accord, which by law had to be ratified by the U.S. Senate.[24]

One U.S. "insider" to the SALT talks has written that a "ban on MIRV's may well have been a victim of the Soviet occupation of Czechoslovakia, which aborted the beginning of SALT."[25] In August 1968, the very month of the Soviet invasion, "the first American

22 "Verification capabilities left no choice," says one U.S. arms control expert.

23 Largely as a result of SALT I, which was concluded during the Nixon period, Soviet analysts have described President Nixon as "the first President since Franklin Roosevelt to have recognized the legitimate interests of the USSR." See Morton Schwartz, *Soviet Perceptions of the United States* (Los Angeles, Calif.: University of California Press, 1978), p.45.

24 In a "backgrounder" in December 1974, Kissinger said: "I would say in retrospect that I wish I had thought through the implications of a MIRVed world more thoughtfully in 1969 and 1970 than I did." Transcript of press backgrounder, December 3, 1974. Soviet analysts tended to view Kissinger as "the President's man, that is, the one who does not represent narrow departmental interests." In Soviet eyes, he became in effect "deputy President on foreign policy matters." See Morton Schwartz, *opus cit.,* p.72.

25 A former planner in the State Department's Office of Political and Military Affairs recalls the period when the MIRV issue was first raised in the State Department. "When Leon Sloss pointed out to me the implications of the MIRVs, I suggested to Phil Farley that we send a memo to Secretary of State Rusk. In this, we suggested that we hold up on testing until we could see if we could work out an agreement with the Soviets not to MIRV. I believe this was in 1968, before Czechoslovakia, but I am not sure. In any event, Rusk declined to intervene, saying this was McNamara's problem. I have since seen that he has told the press that this was a mistake.
"It certainly was. It was clear to anyone who thought about it for even a minute that the MIRVs would lead to a terrible increase in the number of warheads. Since retiring, I have read that there were others in Congress and in the Pentagon who were trying to do the same thing, with similar results.
"In retrospect, I think it regrettable that we did not join forces at that time and make more of a fuss. I might add that we got no help from the scientific community, which was preoccupied with ABMS. I think most people today would be glad to trade the MIRV missiles for a few ABMs. It is, however, too late to undo this error, for which both the US and Soviet leaders must bear the responsibility."

MIRV flight tests took place." By the time "a MIRV ban was tepidly advanced by both sides in April 1970, the multi-headed cat was out of the bag; the United States had developed a deployable MIRV – and within weeks began to deploy it."[26]

Contrary to the general impression of the U.S. public, both the history of the SALT II deliberations and the parallel history of the continuing Soviet military build-up indicate that the rough guidelines laid down by SALT I were followed for the most part.[27] Thus, the build-up of nuclear weapons systems in those areas not constrained by SALT I (namely, qualitative improvements of both ICBMs and SLBMs) proceeded along virtually predetermined technical lines with some adjustments being made in the bargaining process over SALT II.[28]

Accordingly, the Soviet phased replacement of its older SS-9s and SS-11s with the new fourth generation of ICBMs (SS-18s, SS-19s and SS-17s) was completed at approximately the same rate as the earlier American conversion to MIRVed missiles.[29] From 1974 through 1980, the Soviets converted 288 SS-9 silos to accomodate the heavier, more lethal SS-18s. At the same time, the Kremlin proceeded to convert some SS-11 silos to SS-19 silos (excluding sixty silos for the SS-19 already built in 1971). The Soviet conversion average during this period was about 120 per year. This figure compared favorably with the U.S. MIRV conversion rate of approximately 130 per year.[30]

26 See Raymond L. Garthoff, "SALT II: An Evaluation," *World Politics* (October, 1978), p.14.

27 The Soviet Union was required to dismantle its 209 older SS-7 and SS-8 ICBMs in order to be allowed to continue to build up the number of SLBM launchers to a total of 950. Nevertheless, the public perception of a larger number of launchers for the U.S.S.R. than the U.S., played up in some circles, proved troublesome to succeeding Administrations – American advantages not limited by SALT I notwithstanding.

28 One of the most important books on SALT II is that by Strobe Talbott, *Endgame: The Inside Story of SALT II* (New York: Harper Colophon Books, 1980). One U.S. official would insert here: "We showed restraint; the Soviets did not, e.g. MIRVing their ICBMs."

29 An official from the U.S. Arms Control and Disarmament Agency would add: "But the Soviets have since exchanged 1, 4 and 6 MIRV capable ICBMs for all ten (SS-18) and all 6 (SS-19). The U.S. has not. Moreover, the Soviets have exchanged MRV ICBMs (SS-11) for MIRV ICBMs (SS-19). The U.S. has not."

30 For an authoritative source regarding the conversion statistics during this period see William G. Hyland, *opus cit.*, p.55.

According to William Hyland, the above rate "was probably envisaged when the Soviet Union first proposed a MIRV ceiling of 1,000 [ICBMs] to last through 1980."[31] Later, at the Ford-Brezhnev summit in Vladivostok in 1974, the Russians agreed to a limit of 1,320 MIRVs through 1985. This, in Hyland's estimation, presumably reflected "a decision to split their MIRVed forces between 900 ICBMs and 420 SLBMs." However, during the SALT II negotiating, when the bargaining became more intense, the Soviets proved willing to adjust to an overall ceiling of 820 for landbased MIRVed launchers (instead of insisting on their own proposal for 850). The overall total of permissible MIRVs for one side was eventually set at 1,200, as the Soviets had proposed in late 1977.

The SALT II Agreements

The SALT II negotiations culminated in the signing of an agreement in Vienna on June 18, 1979. This agreement was originally sent to the U.S. Senate for approval, but in the wake of the Soviet invasion of Afghanistan the Carter Administration decided to shelve the accord. Although strongly opposed to the treaty during the presidential campaign of 1980, Ronald Reagan upon taking office indicated to the Soviets that the U.S. would not undercut the agreement if the U.S.S.R. would not.[32] The treaty was never ratified by the U.S. Senate.[33]

In summary, the unratified document provides that each coun-

31 *Ibid.*

32 One U.S. official notes here: "Actually, Richard Burt [head of the Bureau of Politico-Military Affairs in the State Department] made a public statement to this effect which then became policy." One of the few Soviet public statements referring to this understanding was made by L. Zamyatin, a member of the Soviet Central Committee, who said on June 21, 1982: "If the United States will observe SALT I and SALT II, then the Soviet Union, to the same degree, will abide by the provisions of these agreements." Cited in *The Arms Control Reporter*, July, 1982, p.807. B. 7.

33 As might be expected, party leaders and the Soviet press greeted the signing of SALT II as an important step forward in U.S.-Soviet relations. However, in contrast with the period following SALT I, enthusiasm was limited. In general, the press warned that reactionary forces would put up stiff resistance to the ratification of SALT II. Even stronger expressions of anxiety appeared in the military press. See for instance, *Pravda*, June 20, 1979 and *Krasnaya Zvezda*, July 14, 1979.

How SALT II affects the Soviet arsenal

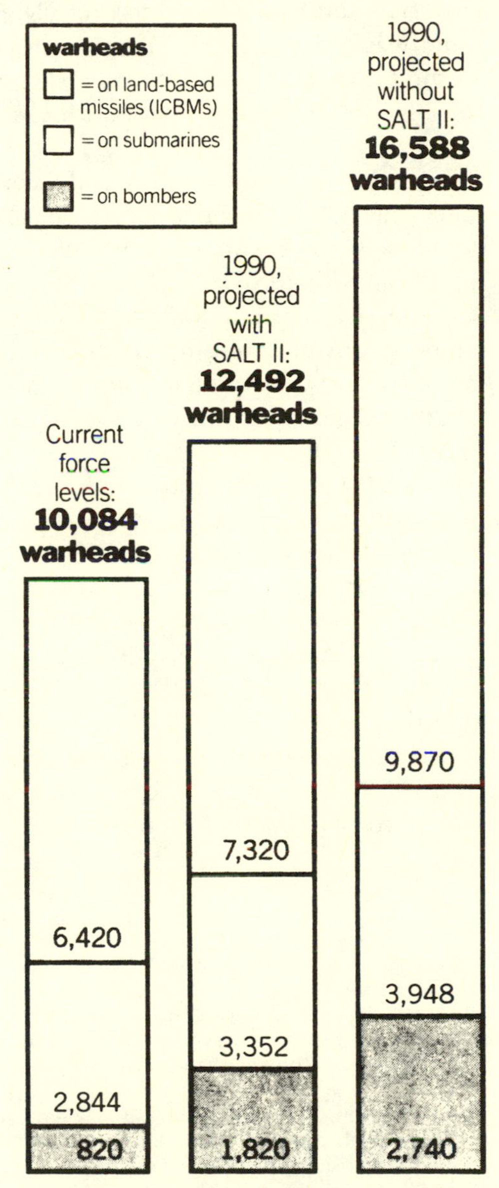

The warhead numbers assume the Soviets will use as many warheads per weapon as possible, within the SALT guidelines.

Source: Central Intelligence Agency

try is restricted to 2,400 strategic nuclear delivery vehicles (long-range ballistic missiles and heavy bombers) initially. By the end of 1981 that number was to be reduced to 2,250. At the time of the signing in 1979 the U.S. had 2,283 and the U.S.S.R. 2,504. (The U.S. figure does not include a couple of hundred B-52s in deep storage.)[34]

Of the total number of strategic nuclear delivery vehicles allowed each state, only 1,320 can be MIRVed missiles or bombers carrying cruise missiles. (The United States had 1,049 and the U.S.S.R. 752 at the time of the signing.)

Of the 1,320, only 1,200 can be MIRVed strategic missiles. (This leaves 120 bombers carrying cruise missiles a number which can be increased if the number of MIRVed missiles is decreased accordingly.) Of the 1,200 maximum of MIRVed missiles, not more than 820 can be ICBMs.

Critics of the SALT process have pointed out that the Soviet MIRV program permitted under SALT is not greatly different than it probably would have been without any limits.[35] Thus, from this perspective, all the arms controllers did was to legitimize the arms race. In response, those at a high level who negotiated with the Soviets over SALT maintain that such an observation fails to take into account the favorable impact the talks had on the overall Soviet-American relationship. Without these discussions with the Soviets, which produced tangible restraints on strategic nuclear weapons, they argue, the political environment might have been very different with unknown consequences for Soviet force planning.

34 A U.S. government expert adds: "SALT II would have required the Soviets to destroy 250 operational launchers – the U.S. none. (Our 2283 included many mothballed B-52s.) This sounds like a good deal to me. By not ratifying the treaty, we did not receive this benefit, however; instead we chose to abide by other provisions which Reagan and company had criticized. This never made sense to me."

35 Ambassador Martin Hillenbrand would point out here: "A very important U.S. advantage from SALT II which you do not mention is the ceiling on MIRV's per missile – 10 – for those already tested with 10 as of the date of signing; and similarly with other MIRVed missiles. As has long been observed, this prevents the Soviets from putting some 27 to 30 MIRVs on their SS-18s." Letter to this writer, May 2, 1985.

SALT Criticisms

George F. Will, an articulate critic of the arms control process, makes the following observation: "Americans see arms control as a way of freezing the status quo; the Soviets see it as one arena in a comprehensive, unending competition."[36]

A knowledgeable insider, Seymour Weiss, takes a different tack. In a recent paper presented at the Lehrman Institute, the retired Ambassador and State Department planner in the Office of Political and Military Affairs from 1960-67 argued that enthusiasm for the whole arms control process – a process said to be barren of achievements – reflected a misapprehension about the usefulness of that process in slowing down the arms race, saving money and "taming" the Soviet Union.

In addition to promoting discord among U.S. allies and paralyzing U.S. procurements, Soviet negotiators have, Weiss argues, five aims. First, they want to limit the "wrong" things (e.g. launchers – basically holes in the ground). Second, they want to make sure that the limits on important things are ambiguous. (SALT I limited but did not end up defining "heavy" missiles). Third, the Soviets want to accept specific limits only if they are unverifiable (for example, the ban on biological weapons or the SALT II limits on the range of cruise missiles). Fourth, the Soviets are said to desire to evade even strict, verifiable limits by claiming that they do not apply to this or that program. (In this connection, the Soviets claim that their limited ABM system is just a defense against bombers.) Lastly, the Soviets want to get the treaty to legitimize violations of the treaty. (N.B. The SALT II flimsy verification terms forbid encryption of data from missile tests – except when encryption is not intended to evade arms-control limits. However, given that it is encrypted, how are outsiders to tell?)[37]

36 See *Newsweek*, June 18, 1984.

37 As one U.S. official points out, "the Soviets determine what information is necessary for U.S. to verify compliance."

Current-Land-Based Systems

At present, Soviet land-based strategic forces consist of some 1,398 ICBMs allowed under SALT II. Of this total, 550 are SS-11s; 60 are SS-13s; 150 are SS-17s; 308 are SS-18s; and 360 are SS-19s.[38] All but 60 of these ICBMs are propelled by liquid fuel. The vast majority of the SS-17s, all SS-18s and SS-19s are armed with multiple independently targeted reentry vehicles (MIRVs). This means that the 1,398 Soviet ICBMs carry more than 6,250 warheads or approximately 70 percent of the total Soviet strategic missile warhead inventory of 9,208.[39]

The SS-17 is outfitted with four MIRVed warheads, each of which is in the 200 kiloton range. This land-based ICBM employs what is known technically as a "cold-launch" technique. This is a technique that delays main engine ignition until the missile has exited its hardened silo. Not only does this technique minimize launch damage to the silo, but it is consistent with the development of a capability to reload and refire during a protracted nuclear conflict. Or at least this is the theory.

The SS-18 is the largest of the current Soviet ICBMs. It forms the backbone of the U.S.S.R.'s alleged, and highly publicized, "first-strike" capability which, the Pentagon says, could destroy a high percentage (80-95 percent) of the U.S. landbased missile force.[40] It

38 Joint Chiefs of Staff, *United States Military Posture FY 1985*, p.21.

39 Burns H. Weston (ed.), *Toward Nuclear Disarmament and Global Security: A Search for Alternatives* (Boulder, Colo: Westview Press, 1984), p.8.

40 U.S. Ambassador Raymond Garthoff would make the following observation here: "while a theoretical ability to destroy 90 percent of U.S. ICBM silos alarms many Americans, the Soviet leaders understand full well that even if they could have confidence in achieving such an outcome, it would not amount to a 'disarming' strike. Moreover, there is no evidence or even indication that the Soviet leaders have regarded their ICBM capability as providing a military advantage translatable into a political 'option' for their own policy." See his *Detente and Confrontation: Soviet-American Relations from Nixon to Reagan* (Washington, D.C.: Brookings Institution, 1985), p.797.
Another point needs to be made in this connection. This is that little attention has been paid to the current greater American capability to destroy a larger proportion of the Soviet strategic force. With no MX or Trident II missiles, in a preemptive strike, the United States, using only its 550 Minuteman IIIs with their 1,650 warheads and concentrating fire on the 800 or so Soviet SS-17s, SS-18s and SS-19s would threaten to destroy some 4,300 warheads, or 39 percent of the Soviet strategic force. By way of contrast, even if 90 percent of U.S. land-

is now deployed in ten multiple warhead versions which utilize a cold-launch technique.[41] The yield of a SS-18 is believed by U.S. intelligence officials to be in the 25 to 50 megaton range.[42] This weapon is said to possess the accuracy necessary to destroy any known fixed target with high probability. The MIRVed versions of the SS-18 carry 10 warheads with yields estimated at one or two megatons apiece.[43] Some 3,000 Soviet warheads are carried by the SS-18 missiles.[44]

The SS-19 uses a "hot-launch" technique with engine ignition taking place while the missile is in its silo. Like the SS-18, this ICBM has all multiple-warheads. The yield of this strategic weapon is estimated to be between 10 and 25 megatons.[45] U.S. intelligence

based ICBMs could be destroyed by the Soviet SS-18 force, the loss would represent only 1,900 warheads or 18 percent of the U.S. strategic force.

41 Some experts believe that the SS-18 is already equipped to carry 14 warheads. Actually, no more than 10 reentry vehicles have been observed to be released in a flight-test, but on several occasions the missile carried out maneuvers that could have simulated the release of additional RVs. This took place before the SALT II Treaty was signed. At American inistence, a provision was included in the treaty to count such "simulated releases" as though they were RVs.

42 Revised estimates of the yield of the SS-18 have been lowered considerably to 600 kilotons.

43 U.S. monitoring of Soviet missile tests has been more difficult by some questionable and possibly illegal encryption practices. According to U.S. intelligence sources, the Soviets continue to encrypt – making it impossible for American electronic intelligence collectors to understand – the radio messages on performance data sent from their test missiles as they travel through space to their targets.
Under SALT II, President Brezhnev agreed that neither nation was to interfere with the other's collection of information on these missile tests. When the U.S. complained at the special Geneva commission set up to handle such arms control problems, the Soviets asked what information the U.S. was unable to collect. Rather than give away interception capabilities, U.S. officials have been pressing the Soviets to stop encoding *all* their telemetry data, something they refuse to do.

44 According to the Pentagon a new ICBM to replace the SS-18 is nearing the flight test stage of development. See U.S. Department of Defense, *Soviet Military Power* (Washington, D.C.: U.S. Government Printing Office, 1985), p.31.

45 During the SALT I negotiations, the American side thought it had frozen the Soviet monopoly in heavy ICBM launchers at 308. But it failed to achieve a definition of the word "heavy." This failure allowed the Soviets to proceed with the development and deployment of the SS-19, an extremely powerful new missile. Technically the SS-19 was smaller than the SS-18, but it was more advanced technologically. For details see Strobe Talbott, *Deadly Gambits: The Reagan Administration and the Stalemate in Nuclear Arms Control* (New York: Knopf, 1984), pp.214-15. Revised estimates of the yield of the SS-19 have been lowered to 550 kilotons.

sources believe the MIRVed version of this missile to be capable of delivering six warheads, with yields estimated to vary between 200 kilotons and one megaton per warhead. The Pentagon estimates that by 1985 the Soviet Union had deployed 360 SS-19 missiles.[46]

For some time, the Soviets have been testing two new mobile strategic intercontinental ballistic missiles. These are the ten-warhead SS-X-24, which is expected to go into silos in 1986 and onto rail-mobile launchers in 1987,[47] and the single-warhead SS-X-25, which has begun deployment on road-mobile launchers and launched from garages with sliding roofs. Both new missiles are solid fuel and are said to enjoy greater accuracy.[48] The SS-X-25 has a range of some 10,500 miles, whereas the SS-X-24 has a range of 10,000 miles.[49]

46 According to a revised assessment of the SS-19 by U.S. intelligence officials, the Soviet missile is now believed to be too inaccurate to pose a threat to American missile silos. The new appraisal, which differs from Defense Department assessments, is contained in a highly secret report, the National Intelligence Estimate. The importance of the new report can not be underestimated since the alleged capacity of the SS-19 to destroy U.S. missile silos has been an important political factor in American arms control considerations and in the campaign to build an American counterpart – the MX. The previous estimate was central to the view that the U.S. faced a "window of vulnerability." For details see *The New York Times,* July 19, 1985.

47 According to Pentagon sources, a solid-propellant missile that may be larger then the SS-X-24 will begin flight testing in the next few years. This missile is expected to possess better accuracy and greater throw weight than its precedessor.

48 According to one U.S. Arms Control and Disarmament Agency official, these new mobile missiles are not as accurate as the SS-18. They may not have a hard target kill capability.

49 The Reagan Administration has taken a dim view of these new mobile missiles. For instance, on March 17, 1985 Secretary of State George Shultz remarked that the two new Soviet ICBMs "raise considerable questions about [verification]." His reasoning was that because these missiles are mobile, verification of where they are and how many there are will be difficult.
The interesting point in this, as Admiral Stansfield Turner, former Director of the CIA, points out, "is that we have been urging the Soviets for years to rely less on large, nonmobile ICBMs and, yet, these two new mobile missiles may be a sign that they are doing just that ...
"We have been intent on reductions in the number of their large ICBMs because such a force can be kept in readiness for a surprise attack at the push of button; because a nonmobile missile force must be viewed as vulnerable to today's accurate weapons and there is always a risk that a vulnerable force will be launched unwisely out of concern that it would otherwise soon be destroyed; and because the large size of Soviet fixed ICBMs permits them to be loaded with up to 30 warheads, many more than ours ..." See *Christian Science Monitor,* April 10. 1985.

Beginning in October 1985, the Soviet Union started to deploy its mobile, single-warhead SS-25 nuclear missile. U.S. Defense officials declined to say how many SS-25s had become operational or where they were deployed, but they did indicate that they were being deployed in violation of the SALT II Treaty.[50] (This treaty allows the U.S. and the U.S.S.R. only one new intercontinental missile each, and Moscow already said it was testing the larger SS-X-24.) Moscow contends that the SS-25 is not a new missile, but is a modification of the older, two war-head SS-13.[51]

Toward the end of 1985 the CIA reported that the Soviet Union was getting ready for the initial flight testing of two new intercontinental ballistic missiles in 1986. U.S. intelligence had been tracking the development of both missiles – dubbed the SS-X-26 and SS-X-27 since open-air test firing of their engines was observed and publicized several years earlier. One of the untested ICBMs would replace the giant, liquid-fueled SS-18. The other appears to be a smaller, solid-fueled missile about the size of the MX missile being built

50 According to the Pentagon's annual publication *Soviet Military Power* (Washington, D.C., 1986), the Soviet Union over the last year brought its deployment of the mobile SS-25 to 70 in number.

51 The dispute over the legitimacy of the SS-25 is unlikely to be resolved, since data on SS-13 flight tests are sketchy. "We do not know," U.S. Air Force Chief of Staff General Charles A. Gabriel testified last year. "They say that it is within parameters. We do not think it is. But it is on the margins whether or not that is a new missile." Quoted in *The Defense Monitor* (1985), Vol XIV, No. 6.
In a briefing to NATO allies in October 1985, Defense Secretary Caspar Weinberger used up-to-date satellite photographs to show the SS-25 to be 10 percent longer, 11 percent wider and possessing 92 percent more throw weight than the SS-13. Under the terms of SALT II, a modernized missile cannot exceed its predecessor's length, diameter, launch weight and throw-weight by more than 5 percent. See *The Washington Post*, October 30, 1985.
The SS-25, if deployed within treaty limits, will not increase total warhead numbers. Although there are allegations that the SS-25 carries three warheads, neither the CIA nor the Defense Intelligence Agency believes that is the case. Moreover, the CIA now says that SS-11s are being retired to accomodate new SS-25s under the SALT treaty.
It is important to note here that it was the Soviet Union that during the SALT II talks proposed a ban on *any* new ICBM for the duration of the treaty. But the U.S. government considered the MX essential, so this sweeping language was not included in the final text.
According to new forecasts by the CIA, the SS-25 and SS-24 represent part of a new discernible trend in Soviet missile developments. By the mid-1990s it is expected that the U.S.S.R. will have missiles that can travel by rail or road, with nearly a fourth of its warheads projected to be deployed in this less vulnerable way. For details see *The New York Times*, June 26, 1985.

by the U.S. In the eyes of U.S. intelligence officials, steady progress on these two missiles, as the SS-24 and SS-25 are being deployed, illustrates the Kremlin's determination to continue modernizing Soviet strategic forces.[52]

The United States does not have a land-based mobile intercontinental missile. However, studies are being conducted on a single-warhead, mobile small ICBM (SICBM), or "Midgetman" missile which would begin flight testing in 1988. The first of from 250 to 1,000 SICBMs would enter service in 1992. The rationale for moving in this direction is belated recognition of the fact that MIRVed missiles are destabilizing.

How Does the Soviet ICBM Force Compare with That of the U.S.?

The number of Soviet ICBMs has declined but there has been a dramatic rise in the number of warheads. Ten years ago (1977) the U.S.S.R. had 1,600 ICBMs. Today (1987) it has but 1,398. Generally Soviet missiles are larger than those of the United States, with greater throw-weight. U.S. strategic missiles are smaller because they have miniaturized, computerized guidance packages, more efficient rocket engines, thinner but more effective heat shields, greater accuracy and more compact, efficient hydrogen weapons.

Approximately ninety-five percent of the Soviet strategic missiles are liquid-propelled ICBMs. Recently the Soviets have shifted to more modern ICBMs, with relatively smaller yield warheads – following the American lead. Since 1979, the Soviet Union has completely modernized its ICBM force; the U.S. has not.

Soviet missiles carry large warheads to compensate for their inaccuracy. Overall, Soviet ICBMs are less reliable and less accurate than U.S. intercontinental ballistic missiles. Nevertheless, they are

52 For details see *The Washington Post*, December 21, 1985. "These may or may not be new missiles that would violate SALT II limits," one former Air Force officer says, "but it is clear the Soviets are not going to help us make that decision." This last statement refers to Soviet concealment by camouflage of the size of the new ICBM test silos. These measures prevent U.S. satellites from photographing the silos.

still sufficient *theoretically* to threaten destruction of eighty percent of U.S. land-based forces.

The United States now maintains a level of 1,024 ICBMs. (This total will drop to 1,000 in 1987 when the last of the big liquid-fuel Titan IIs are retired.) But it has modernized its missiles by withdrawing old types such as Minuteman I and adding types such as Minuteman II and Minuteman III. The United States has also completed hardening of some 550 Minuteman III silos and installed an improved guidance system which doubles their accuracy.[53]

The U.S. has MIRVed 550 of its 1,000 Minuteman ICBMs, whereas the Soviets have MIRVed at least 900 of their ICBMs. The United States has completed retrofitting 300 of these 550 nuclear weapons with the Mk-12A warhead. This will double each weapon's explosive power and increase lethality.[54] According to one CIA insider, the U.S.' 500 three-warhead Minuteman IIIs are more accurate than the most modern Soviet weapons.

The United States will soon replace fifty of its Minuteman IIs with MIRVed Minuteman IIIs. This will add a net increase of 150 highly accurate weapons to the total ICBM warhead force.

Generally, American ICBMs maintain a 98 percent alert rate. It is believed that the alert rate of Soviet ICBMs is much lower.[55] (Until recently, the U.S.S.R. was known to keep only a small portion of its land-based missiles on full alert.)[56]

53 One critic would point out here that "U.S. silo hardening and improved accuracy are mentioned without mention of the fact that the Soviets are estimated to have greater hardening than the U.S. and that the Soviets have made great strides in increasing their accuracy."

54 According to one U.S. official, "against the newly hardened Soviet silos, there is no net increase in effectiveness."

55 One military expert would insert the following observation: "You simply note the much higher U.S. alert rate for ICBMs but ignore the context. [Soviet] liquid fuelled ICBMs simply cannot be maintained at the same continuous state of alert, but in any crisis (which the Soviets continuously say will precede any hostilities) they can be raised to full readiness rather rapidly.

"Moreover, this undoubtedly reflects real (as opposed to stated) perceptions of the two powers. Realistically or not, fear of a sudden Soviet attack has been real in U.S. strategic circles. It is probably not true for the Soviets. In addition, close to full readiness for immediate response (the high U.S. alert rates) are the logical corollary of a strategy of mutual assured destruction based on retaliation. It has been argued that the lack of such a posture is one more indicator that the Soviet strategic approach is different."

56 *Allocation of Resources in the Soviet Union and China – 1978.* Hearings before

Especially important is the ability of the U.S. to order a launch of its ICBMs from airborne command posts should ground command centers be destroyed in a surprise attack. (Of course, electromagnetic pulse – EMP – effects could prevent this. The Soviets face the same problem, although it is sometimes argued that their capabilities are less susceptible to EMP.)[57]

The fact that about seventy percent of Soviet strategic weapons are on stationary, land-based ICBMs (compared to less than twenty percent for the U.S.) poses an acute problem for Soviet planners. General Lew Allen, Air Force Chief of Staff, has identified the danger for the Soviet Union by its great reliance on land-based missiles. "This poses a terrible problem, because we at that point, particularly with the MX, would have a clear first-strike capability [sic] against their ICBMs, which would be devastating to them. They have to consider a U.S. first-strike whether we think we would do that or not."[58]

Moreover, while the United States faces only one nuclear-armed opponent, the Soviets have to take into account four – the U.S., France, Britain (with an additional 420 warheads) and China (with 80 warheads). Only the U.S. could possibly pose a potential "first-strike" threat, a threat which the United States has purposely avoided developing. But Soviet military planners undoubtedly envisage the possibility of a combined attack.

Development of Sea-Based Systems

Let us now turn to the development of Soviet submarine-launched ballistic missiles. The Russians pioneered in naval missiles.[59] However, once the Western states realized their poten-

the Subcommittee on Priorities and Economy in Government of the Joint Economic Committee, 95th Congress, 2nd session (Washington, D.C.: U.S. Government Printing Office, 1978) part 4, pp.67-68, 117-18.

57 One student of Soviet nuclear policy states: "You note the U.S. ability to launch from airborne command posts, but you ignore the ability of the U.S.S.R., implying a U.S. advantage where none exists. The only real difference in the two powers' airborne launch command capabilities is a much more regular and higher U.S. rate of maintaining such airborne command posts in the air."

58 Quoted in *The Defense Monitor,* Vol.11, No.1 (1982), p.6.

59 Among the German war material that fell into Soviet hands in 1945 were several

tial, they quickly overwhelmed the Soviet Union with superior technology.

The first experimental launch of a ballistic missile from a Soviet submarine occurred in September 1955. This was four and a half years before the first launchings of American Polaris SLBM test missiles.[60]

The Soviet Union's first-generation sea-launched ballistic missile – the SS-N-4 Sark – was deployed in 1958 on six medium-range, diesel-powered patrol submarines converted to carry two missile launchers in their conning towers. The missiles had a limited range of 350 nautical miles and could only be launched while the submarines were on the surface.[61]

This conversion was followed by 23 GOLF diesel submarines and eight HOTEL nuclear submarines completed between 1958 and 1962. Both types of submarines were originally deployed with the surface-launched SS-N-4 ballistic missile. However, in 1963, they were refitted with the more advanced SS-N-5 missile that could be launched from a submerged submarine.[62] In the meantime, the first Soviet nuclear submarine went to sea in 1959 – not quite five years after the USS Nautilus, which was not armed with missiles.

The American SLBM program was far advanced when the first modern (third generation) Soviet YANKEE-class-submarines appeared in the late 1960s and early 1970s. By that time the U.S. had already

submarine-towed containers for V-2 missiles. As Norman Polmar writes: "After being towed underwater to within striking range of an enemy coast, the container was to be ballasted to the vertical position, the missile fueled and checked out, and the missile then fired against the enemy's coastal cities. Although none of these V-2 containers is believed to have become operational in the Soviet Navy, the concept of the Submarine-launched Ballistic Missile (SLBM) was clearly recognized by Soviet 'technocrats,' and by the early 1950s a major effort was clearly underway to provide the Soviet Navy with an SLBM capability." See his *Strategic Weapons,* rev. ed. (New York: Crane, Russak, 1982), pp. 31-32.

60 The first ballistic-missile submarine, the *George Washington,* became operational in November, 1960. It was armed with 16 solid-fuel Polaris A-1 missiles, which could be fired at a rate of about one per minute.

61 *Fiscal Year 1972 Authorization for Military Procurement, Research and Development, Construction and Real Estate Acquisition for the Safeguard ABM, and Reserve Strengths,* Hearings before the Senate Armed Services Committee, 92nd Congress, 1st Session (Washington, D.C.: U.S. Government Printing Office, 1971), part 4, p. 3447.

62 *United States Military Posture for FY 1979* (Washington, D.C.: U.S. Office of the Joint Chiefs of Staff, 1978), p. 28.

completed its deployment of forty-one missile-firing submarines capable of carrying a total of 656 SLBMs.

The YANKEE submarines represented a significant improvement over their predecessors. They carried the SS-N-6 missile, which some analysts contend was actually a "quick fix" substitute for the tactical SS-NX-13 which was tested but never deployed. Altogether, thirty-four YANKEE-class submarines were deployed between 1966 and 1974. However, they began to be dismantled in accordance with the SALT I Treaty as newer DELTA-class submarines became available.[63]

Apparently, the YANKEE-class submarines were assigned only a limited role in intercontinental strike missions. These were against targets located in American coastal areas. The reason for this may have been, in part, because the survivability of these submarines in wartime was questionable. In any case, the deployment of these subs signaled the beginning of a period in which the role of Soviet sea-based SLBM forces would increase – especially in the intercontinental theaters of operations.[64]

By 1970, patrol areas were established for the YANKEE submarines off both U.S. coasts. This deployment gave the Soviet Union sea-based coverage of a wide range of targets.

If the Soviets were able to terminate one phase of their land-based missile program neatly with the conclusion of SALT I, this was not the case with Moscow's submarine-launched missile program. To reach a force level comparable with that of the United States, the Soviet Union would have had to deploy by 1972 a force of about sixty ballistic missile submarines.[65]

There is widespread belief in the United States that the various

63 *United States Military Posture for FY 1978* (Washington, D.C.: Office of the Joint Chiefs of Staff, 1977).

64 For details see Claude R. Thorpe, "Mission Priorities of the Soviet Navy," in Paul J. Murphy (ed.), *Naval Power in Soviet Policy* (Washington, D.C.: U.S. Government Printing Office, 1978), pp. 163-64.

65 Since 1965 the total number of Soviet submarines (excluding those carrying strategic nuclear missiles) has been allowed to decline, whereas the total number of major surface ships has risen. Thus, despite a recent upturn in all building, by 1980 the number of Soviet submarines had fallen by about 30 percent, whereas the number of major surface vessels had gone up about 25 percent. See Ian Bellany, "Sea Power and the Soviet Submarine Forces," *Survival,* Vol. 24, Nos. 1-2 (January-April, 1982), p. 3.

strategic armaments agreements reached with the Soviet Union since 1979 have had the effect of conferring a one-sided advantage in the ability of the Soviets to carry out a "first strike". However this may be, it is certainly true that these same agreements have not removed a one-sided advantage to the U.S. in the area of submarine-launched missiles, which are not yet accurate enough to destroy ICBM silos. SALT II, for instance, restricts the U.S. and the U.S.S.R. to the development of only one new ICBM model (and the Soviet Union has developed two) but it places few restrictions on new submarine-launched missile developments (it forces trade-offs if SALT limits are to be met). As Ian Bellany writes: "The ballistic missile technology race is restricted in the one area where the USSR suffers from no particular handicaps, but is left wholly uncontrolled in the area where she is most disadvantaged – temporarily, no doubt, by technological weakness, but more fundamentally also, through geography and the nature of Soviet society."[66]

Today the Soviet Union has sixty-two ballistic missile submarines and 924 submarine-launched ballistic missiles (SLBMs) counted under SALT.[67] Of these, only about 300 missiles currently are MIRVed, for a total of some 2,178 SLBM warheads. All but 72 Soviet SLBMs use liquid fuel. By way of contrast, the U.S. today has about 37 missile submarines, carrying 640 solidfuel missiles. All American submarine-launched ballistic missiles are heavily MIRVed giving the U.S. 5,728 sea-based warheads. This is almost three times the amount of those the USSR posesses. (Most of Soviet submarine-launched missiles are still one-warhead weapons.)

It should be noted that U.S. missile firing submarines are the on-

66 Ian Bellany, "Sea Power and the Soviet Submarine Forces," *Survival*, Vol. 24, Nos. 1-2 (January-April, 1982), p. 6. It should be noted that Soviet SLBM warheads are increasing in numbers, whereas US submarine-launched ballistic missile warheads are coming down with each new SLBM deployed, e.g. Trident I vs the Poseidon.

67 Under the SALT agreements the Soviets are allowed 62 modern missile firing submarines. In actuality, they have 65, however. The three not covered in the 62 limit are not considered "modern" under the Interim Agreement since they were commissioned prior to 1965. According to the U.S. Arms Control and Disarmament Agency, the launchers on these older submarines do count toward the 950 SLBM launcher limit under SALT since they are used for modern ballistic missiles or are built into submarines that are nuclear powered. See U.S. Arms Control and Disarmament Agency, *Fiscal Year 1986 Arms Control Impact Statements* Washington, D.C.: U.S. Government Printing Office, 1985), p. 176.

ly strategic weapons in the U.S. arsenal that are not equipped with a safeguard system known as "permissive action links" (PAL). Unlike the PAL-configured bombers and ICBMs, the missile submarines are physically capable of launching nuclear weapons without top-level authority.

In 1984, the following nuclear-powered ballistic missile submarines were included in the Soviet fleet. They were 24 YANKEE-class submarines (first deployed in two versions in the late 1960s and early 1970s), 38 DELTA-class submarines (which first appeared in 1972),[68] 8 HOTEL-class submarines (first deployed in the early 1960s) and 2 TYPHOON-class submarines (which first appeared on station in 1980).

Of all the Soviet submarines, the new and very large strategic submarine known as the TYPHOON is the most important. Five TYPHOON submarines are now (1987) commissioned;[69] each carries twenty solid-fuel SS-N-20 SLBMs with six-to-nine warheads apiece. The TYPHOON is substantially larger than the U.S. Trident, seven subs of which are in the American fleet.

Today the Soviets maintain day and night more than 300 nuclear weapons at sea targeted against the U.S. However, the Soviets maintain a much smaller percentage of their strategic subs at sea than the U.S.[70]

68 One milestone which the U.S.S.R. passed before the United States was the ultra-long-range SLBM. The 4,300 nautical mile, single warhead SS-N-8 carried by the DELTA-class submarines first appeared eight years ahead of the MIRVed Trident C-4. See Ian Bellany, *opus cit.,* p.5. The extended range of the DELTA submarines means that they can strike their targets virtually from closeby coastal water – and in some cases from their home ports.

69 According to the Pentagon, three or four additional TYPHOONS are probably now under construction. By the early 1990s, the Soviets could have as many as eight of these weapons systems in their operational force. See Department of Defense, *Soviet Military Power* (Washington, D.C.: U.S. Government Printing Office, 1985), p.31.

70 This ratio is improving for Soviet subs, according to one U.S. insider. This person would also point out that now over two-thirds of Soviet ballistic missile submarines, including those equipped with MIRVed missiles, are fitted with long-range SLBMs that enable the submarines to patrol in waters close to the Soviet Union. This gives them considerable protection from NATO antisubmarine warfare operations.

How Soviet Strategic Submarines Compare with Those of the United States

The United States has recently completed the retrofitting of Trident I missiles on 12 of 31 Poseidon submarines. The weapons on these new missiles have 60 percent longer range, are two and one-half times more powerful and are more accurate than the weapons on the Poseidon missiles they are replacing. The Trident I missiles, which will also be deployed on new Trident subs, will provide 3,000 new nuclear weapons for the American strategic arsenal in the 1980s.

The Navy wishes to build at least twenty Trident subs, while retiring all of its Poseidons by 1998. If 20 Trident submarines are built, the cost will be about $92 billion. Beginning in 1989, the United States will field the first Trident II D-5 missiles. Most of these heavy SLBMs will carry eight 475-kiloton warheads. Others will carry up to 14 of the 100-kiloton warheads currently on Trident I missiles.

Traditionally, submarine-launched ballistic missiles have lacked the accuracy to destroy missile silos. But Trident II will represent the world's first true silo-busting SLBM.[71] By the mid-1990s, the U.S. will have enough Trident IIs to destroy the entire Soviet silo-based missile force with little warning time.

The U.S. submarine force is considered virtually invulnerable by Washington.[72] (And that is why more than fifty percent of U.S. nuclear warheads are carried by submarines.) The same may not be true for Moscow. Although the Soviet Union has the world's longest coastline, it is actually all but landlocked as far as its submarine fleet is concerned. By acquiring very long-range submarine missiles the Soviets have attempted to overcome this disadvantage, but the basic limits on Soviet naval deployment remain.[73]

71 According to one U.S. official, the Trident I has more counter-silo punch than is generally known. A 1982 Pentagon document says Trident I has the accuracy of Minuteman III and can be targeted on Soviet silos. The Soviet Union is not thought to possess similarly accurate ballistic missile-firing submarines.

72 From time to time there have been reports of "breakthroughs" in Soviet anti-submarine warfare, but the CIA denies them. In its view "we do not believe there is a realistic possibility that the Soviets will be able to deploy in the 1990s a system that could pose any significant threat to U.S. SSBNs on patrol."

73 In the spring of 1984 the Soviets announced that the number of cruise missile-

Another crucial element in assessing the SLBM balance is the number of submarines a state can keep routinely on station. Currently, only about fifteen percent of the Russian force is at sea on any normal day.[74] (By way of contrast, the United States maintains about two-thirds of its 37 ballistic missile submarines at sea at all times.) The remaining eighty-five percent of the Soviet ballistic-missile submarines are in port without adequate shelter.[75] Even during periods of international crisis, the Soviets usually maintain more or less the same deployment rate, unlike the United States which increases the number of submarines at sea to almost 100 percent.[76] (In 1941, the U.S.S.R. had the most numerous submarine force in the world, but the vast majority of these units were designed to defend home fleet areas against naval incursions.)

The low rate of Soviet submarine deployment is due to a number of factors. One technological reason may be primitive nuclear engineering that forces Soviet submarines into port for long intervals while their nuclear reactors are being refueled. But the more

firing submarines stationed off the east and west coasts of the United States had been significantly increased. This was allegedly done to balance the threat posed by U.S. intermediate range missiles in Europe. The Soviet Defense Minister said at the time that the nuclear missiles carried by the submarines could reach their targets in 10 minutes. The American reaction was to downplay the Soviet move. "There has been no essential change in the strategic situation," the White House spokesman, Larry Speakes, said. "The numbers don't change much." See *The New York Times,* May 22, 1984.

74 Soviet missile-firing submarines spend most of their time in port, primarily assigned to four main bases in the Northern and Pacific Fleets: Petropavlovsk and Vladivostok in the Pacific and Polyarny and Severomorsk in the North. "Submarine tunnels" have reportedly been built for them. See William M. Arkin *et al., Nuclear Battlefields* (Cambridge, Mass.: Ballinger Publishing Co., 1985), p. 47.

75 Those Soviet submarines in port are highly vulnerable not only to nuclear attack from Western strategic nuclear forces, but, since many of them are riding at anchor at Polyarny, they will also be "sitting ducks" for the new generation of NATO Long Range Theater Nuclear Forces, particularly for the Pershing II, should these missiles be retargeted.

76 See Joel S. Wit, "Advances in Antisubmarine Warfare," *Scientific American,* Vol. 244, No. 2 (February, 1981), p. 37. The Soviet Union and its allies could send as many as 200 submarines of all kinds out to sea, but there they would face an almost equal number of enemy submarines plus thousands of anti-submarine aircraft and helicopters. A U.S. official would insert here: "You fail to point out that U.S. ballistic missile submarines go on patrol alone; many Soviet SSBMs would be defended by surface, air and other submarines. We could *not* destroy these before they launched their missiles."

important reasons are the shortage of trained crews and inadequate maintenance facilities. Unlike the U.S.S.R., the U.S. maintains two crews for each submarine.[77] In view of American advantages in this crucial area, the Russians insisted during the SALT I negotiations that the total number of Soviet submarines for SALT-counting purposes should be sixty-two modern submarines with 950 missile launchers. The U.S. agreed, but it was not until 1981 that the Soviets were able to attain this goal.[78]

A third factor that must be taken into consideration is the "noisiness" of Soviet submarines. Soviet subs are much noisier than their American counterparts. This is particularly significant since a capability to build quiet vessels appears to go hand in hand with a good capability for detecting and analyzing the underwater sounds made by enemy submarines. The United States, which is generally acknowledged to be ahead of the U.S.S.R. in anti-submarine warfare (ASW),[79] is presumably able to track most of the Soviet subs. In a war, American Navy commanders are confident of being able to destroy them fairly quickly.

A fourth factor that must be taken into consideration in assessing the importance of the 62 Soviet strategic missile-firing submarines is that the vast majority of these subs are still outfitted with liquid-fuel missiles.[80] These missiles are very unstable, given the ten-

77 Trident submarines, for instance, are manned by two alternating crews of 160 persons (15 officers and 145 enlisted). The 95-day operating cycle consists of a 25-day refit period followed by a 70-day at sea period. Crew endurance is the dominant factor limiting the Trident's ability to stay at sea.

78 "Maybe we are paying for the high number of missiles permitted, as the Soviets are MIRVing them," says one U.S. official.

79 According to one authority "it scarcely makes much sense to speak of a mid-ocean Soviet ASW capability." See Ian Bellany, *opus cit.,* p. 5. One high level U.S. intelligence official would make the following comments here: "The impression you give is somewhat misleading. U.S. ability to track Soviet SSBNs is good in peacetime when they follow routines (although even then there are frequent uncertainties and surprises about locations). Whether the U.S. capability would be as effective in war is much more questionable (unless the U.S. initiated the war almost "out of the blue").
Incidentally, the statement that U.S. Navy commanders are confident of being able to destroy them fairly quickly is both highly scenario dependent and, to my knowledge, not universally held (it may not even be a majority view).

80 According to one U.S. Defense expert, "The Soviets are generally viewed as ahead of us in liquid-fuel technology. Perhaps they are more satisfied with liquid fuel than Western analysts think."

dency of the fuel to corrode its containers and explode. The Soviets would like to replace these liquid-fuel missiles with all solid-fuel missiles as the U.S. Navy did years before, but the limitation of Soviet rocket technology has hampered their efforts. In 1978, the Soviets developed a solid-fuel naval missile, the SS-N-17, and they even armed a submarine with it – which was duly hailed by U.S. officials as having "increased range" and "greater accuracy." Hardly had these pronouncements been made, however, then the twelve operational SS-N-17s were withdrawn. Recently, the Soviets tried again – this time with the SS-N-20 TYPHOON Missile. But their efforts were set back because this missile displayed an unfortunate tendency to explode in flight.[81] Now the Soviets have deployed the SS-N-20 on their TYPHOON submarine.

One last factor is that Soviet contingency planners must take into account the submarine threat posed by other countries. Although both the United States and the U.S.S.R. must be wary of the Chinese submarine force,[82] the threat to Soviet interests is more direct. Indeed, as one authority, Michael MccGwire, put it, a Soviet planner who is planning aggression "has to allow that, with few exceptions, all the significant navies in the world are at best neutral and most of them must be included in the list of potential adversaries."[83]

81 See Andrew Cockburn, *The Threat: Inside the Soviet Military Machine* (New York: Random House, 1983), p. 256. According to one submarine missile expert, the "discussion of the drawbacks of Soviet liquid-fueled SSBMs is an important point, but its implications are overstated. Comparison with U.S. Titan missiles is very misleading due to the extreme age of the Titans and their relatively very low priority in U.S. force maintenance. No mention is made of the SS-N-18 Soviet solid-fueled SSBM (on 14 submarines in 1983). It is true that there have been problems with the SS-N-17 but, contrary to you, they have not disappeared right after IOC. And there are no known similar problems with the SS-N-18."

82 According to one U.S. insider, the Chinese submarine force consists of two SSBNs, one older diesel SSB (GOLF intermediate range) on trial and a large number of diesel attack subs but which are (contrary to the Soviet submarine fleet) almost all obsolescent coastal defense types.

83 See Michael MccGwire, "Soviet Naval Doctrine and Strategy," in Derek Leebaer (ed.), *Soviet Military Thinking* (London: Allen & Unwin, 1981), p. 171.

Strategic Bombers

Unlike the United States, the Soviet Union does not maintain a large contingent of manned strategic bombers. In large part this situation is due to Soviet tradition. During World War II the Russians used their air force mainly in support of their ground troops. There were few Soviet attacks against targets in the interior of the enemy. And there was no articulated doctrine of "strategic bombing" such as that which underlay the rear-area bombing carried out by the United States and Great Britain.

Now the situation may be changing. According to the Pentagon, the Soviet Union is building a new long-range bomber that is codenamed the Blackjack. The Blackjack, which is larger than the American B-1B, is in the flight stage of production and is scheduled to be in service in 1988 or 1989. When it does finally fly, the Blackjack can be expected to carry air-launched cruise missiles and nuclear bombs.

At present, the Soviet strategic bomber force consists of some 170 obsolescent bombers (codenamed the M-4 Bison and the TU-95 Bear). Approximately 100 of these planes are old, slow, propeller driven aircraft. (In 1984, the U.S.S.R. began adding Bear-H bombers, an entirely new Bear variant, to carry a new long-range air-launched cruise missile, the AS-15.) The aged Soviet bomber force carries only about five percent of Soviet strategic weapons and is considered at least partially vulnerable to attacks on Soviet airfields.

Backfire Bomber

The most famous bomber the Soviets have deployed is the medium-range TU-26 Backfire. This bomber, which first became operational in 1974, is effective against both land and sea targets because it can fly at low altitudes as well as at high speeds, thus reducing the amount of time enemy air defense systems have to react.[84] The

84 Recently, the Defense Intelligence Agency significantly lowered its estimate of the range of the Soviet bomber. Administration sources said in September 1985 that the new estimate reinforced the contention by some arms-control proponents that the bomber was designed to attack ships and targets in Europe and

Backfire has the flexibility to perform both nuclear and nonnuclear missions.[85]

U.S. defense planners tend to regard the Backfire bomber as "intercontinental". However, without in-flight refueling, it is mainly capable of one-way nuclear attack on North America.[86] So far, the Soviets have deployed 250 copies of this bomber. 130 Backfire jet bombers have been assigned to bombing missions, whereas 120 others have an anti-ship role.

In each of the past years, the U.S.S.R. has built 32 or 33 Backfire bombers despite an American claim that then-Soviet President Leonid Brezhnev pledged in 1979 not to increase the production rate above thirty a year. Or at least this is the position taken by U.S. intelligence sources who have studied the matter.

The Brezhnev pledge, which was made orally, was given as a side agreement to the SALT II Treaty.[87] Therefore, the Reagan Ad-

Asia, not in the United States. Previously, the Pentagon's position was that the Backfire had a unrefueled combat range of 3,000 miles. With the revision, "the Defense Intelligence Agency has moved substantially in the direction of the C.I.A.," an Administration official stated. For details see *The New York Times*, October 1, 1985.

85 Philip A. Peterson, "Flexibility: A Driving Force in Soviet Strategy," *Air Force Magazine* (March, 1980), p. 96.

86 One U.S. official would take issue here with this analysis. "The dismissal of the BACKFIRE is incomplete and therefore possibly misleading," he says. "Some U.S. targets can be reached without refuel on a two-way mission. Moreover, there are solid indications of a refuel capability for BACKFIRE, and even without refuel, missions could be flown to recover in Cuba, potentially Nicaragua and formerly potentially in Grenada.

"In connection with refueling, your discussion is incomplete. The picture is modified somewhat when it is realized that much of the U.S. tanker fleet would be fully occupied in non-strategic nuclear operations (airlift) and that the Soviets do not have a similar need in any European conflict."

In rebuttal, one is tempted here to refer to Khrushchev's memoirs. There the story is told of one aircraft designer Vladmir Myasishchev who was commissioned by Stalin to build him a bomber that could fly to the United States and back. As things turned out, the plane was not completed until after Stalin had died, which was perhaps fortunate for Myasishchev since his plane did not perform as required. "This plane failed to satisfy our requirements. It could reach the United States, but it couldn't come back. Myasishchev said it could bomb the United States and then land in Mexico.

"We replied to that idea with a joke: 'What do you think Mexico is – our mother-in-law? You think we can go calling any time we want? The Mexicans would never let us have the plane back.'"

87 At the time of the signing of the SALT II Treaty, Edward Rowny went before the U.S. Senate and testified against the treaty. Here is what he said regarding the

ministration has considered including the Backfire bomber issue in a list of new Soviet violations of arms control agreements. However, a detailed review of the Backfire question shows a disagreement between the U.S. and Soviet governments on the production number.

According to one intelligence report, the Soviet Backfire production rate in 1978 and 1979 – before the SALT II declaration – was 31 bombers a year. But at the 1979 Vienna summit and thereafter the U.S. position was that "President Brezhnev confirmed that Soviet Backfire production rate would not exceed 30 per year."[88]

When the Backfire production rate was brought up to the Soviets at Geneva, they said that they were following Brezhnev's promise not to increase production "as compared to the present rate." But the Soviets took issue with the American 30-a-year figure.

U.S. government sources maintain that the Kremlin is consciously breaching the Backfire limit of building 30 a year. But there is little agreement as to why Moscow is doing it. The additional bombers do not give the Soviets any serious military advantage. But the extra production illustrates what one former Defense Department official called a tendency to "thumb their noses at limitations they don't think necessary." This official would point out that Soviet military men did not want to include the Backfire, which they considered a medium-range bomber, in the SALT II agreement and were unhappy when Brezhnev agreed to the oral arrangement under pressure from President Carter.[89]

Backfire bomber: "The 'assurance' that the Soviet Union will not increase the production rate of the Backfire beyond 30 a year is ... meaningless. The Soviets could not build more than 30 Backfires a year without considerable effort – nor do they need to do so. The 375 Backfires that the Soviets will possess by 1985 is greater than the number of B-52s the United States will possess in its active inventory at that time. Importantly, by not counting the Backfires in their inventory, the Soviets will not have to reduce their ICBM and SLBM forces by some 375 launchers ..." See *Military Implications of the Treaty on the Limitation of Strategic Offensive Arms and Protocol Thereto,* Hearings before the Committee on Armed Services, 96th Congress, 1st Session (Washington, D.C.: Government Printing Office, 1979), pp. 982-89.

88 The Soviet-American agreement took the form of a letter handed by the Soviets to President Carter at Vienna. It stated only that the Backfire production rate would not be increased above its current value. But the figure 30 per year was confirmed orally by Leonid Brezhnev.

89 For background see *The Washington Post,* December 22, 1984.

How do U.S. Strategic Bombers Compare with Those of the Soviet Union?

The United States possesses a fleet of 264 B-52 and 61 FB-111 bombers, all of which are assigned to the Strategic Air Command (SAC). The U.S. also has over 40 long-range bombers in active reserve and over 230 in storage. (These latter bombers would take about a year to become operational.) Over 100 U.S. bombers would be on airborne alert prior to a Soviet missile attack against the U.S.[90]

It is sometimes argued that the American B-52s lack the capability to penetrate adequately extensive Soviet air defenses. But the U.S. Arms Control and Disarmament Agency takes issue with this point. According to its latest publications on the subject, it reports[91]

Although the aging B-52s are losing their ability to penetrate the most modern Soviet air defenses, studies have shown that the bomber force can best realize its mission objectives by presenting a multiplicity of delivery modes and weapons, to include gravity bombs, SRAM, and ALCM. The combination of B-1B high penetration speed, low-altitude terrain-clearing flight, reduced radar cross-section, and advanced electronic countermeasures will provide a flexible, large-payload delivery aircraft capable of penetrating Soviet defenses well into the 1990s.

In addition to strategic bombers, the U.S. has over 400 short-range aircraft which are equipped with nuclear weapons aboard its aircraft carriers. These are for force projection against naval targets at sea.

The United States is in the process of adding about 4,350 nuclear-tipped air-launched cruise missiles (ALCMs) to enhance the capability of its strategic bomber force. About 100 B-52Gs are now outfitted with ALCMs, improving considerably their penetration capability against increasingly dense and sophisticated Soviet air de-

90 One high-ranking Defense Department official interjects here: "I think you should say something about the extreme age of the B-52 bomber. Most are older than the pilots who fly them. Are these aircraft reliable? I think not."

91 See U.S. Arms Control and Disarmament Agency, *Fiscal Year 1986 Arms Control Impact Statements* (Washington, D.C.: U.S. Government Printing Office, 1985), p. 93.

fenses.[92] Among the new cruise missiles to be deployed inside each B-52 will be a new type, the Advanced Cruise Missile (ACB), which enters production in 1986.

One of the biggest advantages the U.S. has over the Soviet Union is air refueling capability. The U.S. has 615 KC-135 tankers to extend the ranges of its long-range bombers and other aircraft. The Soviets have only a little over 30 long-range tankers.(According to one U.S. official, the U.S. would be hard pressed to meet the needs of its B-52 force with the tankers it has now.)

Conclusions

The expansion of Soviet strategic forces since the mid-1960s, if difficult to explain, is in fact a harsh reality. Some relatively unsophisticated observers espouse what has been termed "the blueprint hypothesis" when explaining this phenomenon. This theory assumes that long-term Soviet goals are fixed and force procurements reflect "an irrevocable commitment to the pursuit of regional or global domination and strategic 'superiority.'" However, as this chapter tries to show, this is much to simple a view of the Soviet buildup.

Perhaps one of the best arguments against the "blueprint hypothesis" is that made by Thomas W. Wolfe in his testimony to the U.S. Senate Subcomittee on Strategic Arms Limitation Talks. Although now dated, his analysis is quite relevant:[93]

... The Soviet leaders probably embarked on the build-up without a fixed blueprint for the future and without having settled among themselves precisely what sort of strategic posture *vis-à-vis* the United States would prove satisfactory to Soviet policy needs during the next decade. Some segments of the leadership, for example, may have preferred to seek a stable and low-cost strategic relationship with the United States in order to channel more re-

92 Joint Chiefs of Staff, *United States Military Posture for FY 1985,* p. 25. According to one U.S. insider, there will be no penetration role for the B-52 after 1986.

93 See U.S. Senate, Armed Services Committee, *Hearings before the Subcommittee on Strategic Arms Limitations Talks* (Washington, D.C.: Government Printing Office, 1970), pp. 61-2.

sources to domestic purposes; others perhaps favored parity pegged at a high level in order to keep third parties like Germany and China in their place and to sustain a duopoly of Soviet-American power in international politics; still others may have set their sights on attaining general strategic superiority over the United States in the belief that only thus could military and political freedom of action requisite to Soviet needs be assured...

Wolfe's analysis leaves some questions unanswered. But it does seem to conform to the variegated nature of the evidence, at least for the early Brezhnev period. This is the period in which the Soviet "crash program" in nuclear weaponry took place. Since 1969, when rough equilibrium was achieved by the Soviets, both sides have been jockeying for positional advantages.

When President Reagan came into office in 1981, he was convinced that the Soviets had obtained a margin of superiority by their military buildup. To combat this perceived military imbalance, Reagan initiated the largest peacetime expansion of U.S. military forces since World War II. The massive military build-up of the Reagan Administration, which was originally projected to cost approximately $1.5 trillion over five years, embraced a number of major new weapon systems. As of late 1984, the Administration had increased U.S. defense spending in real terms by nearly thirty percent over the budgets of the last two years.[94] By early 1986, however, Congressional pressure was on to keep a lid on military spending, and there was considerable sentiment for a no-growth ceiling.

Among the most important nuclear weapons systems that the Reagan Administration is emphasizing is the MX (Missile Experimental). Originally, the U.S. government had hoped to place 200 of these multiwarhead missiles in Minuteman silos. But Congress capped the number at 50 because of concern that the silos would be vulnerable to Soviet attack.

The small, mobile Midgetman missile designed to complicate Soviet targeting is being developed, but the high cost of deploying the single-warhead weapon has raised concerns in Congress. (The GAO has estimated that it could cost $44 billion for a force of 500

94 See Caspar W. Weinberger, *Annual Report to Congress, FY 1984* (Washington, D.C.: U.S. Government Printing Office, 19837, pp.61-66.

mobile missiles and said there were other technical problems confronting the program, such as developing an affordable guidance system that would remain accurate while the missile was moving.[95]

At the same time, the U.S. is moving forward with the Trident II (D-5) missile. This long-range missile will give submarine-launched missiles the ability to destroy hardened missile silos for the first time.[96]

The U.S. is building a fleet of at least one hundred B-1B bombers. The first B-1Bs entered service in 1985.[97] Moreover, it is planning to build an advanced technology "Stealth" bomber to replace the B-1. The "Stealth" Technology Bomber (ATB) will come on-line about 1992. Some 132 of these small, radar-evading bombers are said to be planned by 1996.

The United States is also now deploying modern, highly accurate, highly lethal ground, air and sea launched cruise missiles. Over 9,000 will be deployed. And all are nuclear.

The U.S. is substantially increasing spending on ballistic missile defense. It could begin the first phase of deployment of such a new system in the early 1990s.

The U.S.S.R. has tested and already deployed a crude, rocket-launched anti-satellite weapon system. But the U.S. is now testing and, if Congress agrees, will soon deploy a much more sophisticated anti-satellite weapon which can be launched from modified modern aircraft.

The Soviet leadership has stated that it will match any U.S. nuclear advance.[98] And U.S. authorities have acknowledged that the

95 *The Minneapolis Star and Tribune,* November 8, 1985.

96 J.S. Wit, "American SLBM: Counterforce Options and Strategic Implications," *Survival,* Vol. 24, Nos. 4-5 (July-October, 1982), pp. 163-174. These deadly accurate weapons pose a grave danger to Soviet land-based missiles, which represent the bulk of Soviet strategic capabilities. They may force the Soviets to adopt a launch-on-warning policy if they have not already done so. This is a policy that the United States officially deems too dangerous for itself.

97 According to the U.S. Arms Control and Disarmament Agency, "the first production model of the B-1B began flying on October 18, 1984, and the program is ahead of schedule and within budget." See U.S. Arms Control and Disarmament Agency, *Fiscal Year 1986 Arms Control Impact Statements* (Washington, D.C.: U.S. Government Printing Office, 1985), p. 93.

98 In the view of one critik "to talk about Soviet capabilities to match any U.S. nuclear advantage is very misleading. It implies that they are *capable of* developing a new manned bomber, advanced cruise missiles, etc. as if this would only be *in*

Soviets are capable in the next decade of developing a new manned bomber, advanced cruise missiles, improved submarine-based missiles, more accurate ICBMs and new ABM systems.[99]

In short, the Soviets "do not have," as former Defense Secretary Harold Brown said on April 30, 1982, "anything like strategic superiority in the sense of a military or politically usable advantage in strategic nuclear forces."[100]

When asked by Senator Charles Percy on April 29, 1982, "Would you rather have at your disposal the U.S. nuclear arsenal or the Soviet nuclear arsenal?" Defense Secretary Weinberger stated: "I would not for a moment exchange anything, because we have an immense edge in technology."[101]

In short, the highly touted nuclear superiority of the Soviet Union does not exist when a close look is taken at the individual strengths and weaknesses of both sides nuclear arsenals. In some areas, the U.S.S.R. is ahead, but an overall balance shows that the United States remains ahead in other crucial areas.

response to the Reagan program. This ignores the fact that testing on many of these programs has been reported well under way already. This testing could only follow a relatively lengthy R & D phase – one which began before the current U.S. buildup plans were announced."

99 According to a recent CIA report, the Soviet Union is in the midst of a nuclear weapons building boom that could double its arsenal of nuclear warheads by the mid-1990s if treaty restrictions are removed. The report, presented to the U.S. Senate in June 1985 says that the Soviet Union has made "major strides" in developing missiles that can travel by rail or road, with nearly a fourth of its warheads expected to be deployed in this less vulnerable way by the mid-1990s. The report also predicts that Soviet military spending will increase by four percentage points more than the inflation rate over the next several years. This is more than double the intelligence agency estimate of Soviet spending in recent years.
In a statement that goes beyond prévious estimates, the report says that "By the mid-1990s, nearly all of the Soviets' currently deployed intercontinental nuclear attack forces – land and sea-based ballistic missiles and heavy bombers – will be replaced by new and improved systems."

100 Quoted in *The Defense Monitor,* Vol.11, No.6 (1982), p.1.

101 *Ibid,* p.2. For a less optimistic view see the interview with General John Vessey, Jr., Chairman of the Joint Chiefs of Staff, *U.S. News and World Report,* March 28, 1983.

The atomic bomb does not adhere to the class principle.
Official Soviet Communist Party statement, 1963

V. SOVIET "WAR FIGHTING" STRATEGY

Few aspects of Soviet nuclear policy are as hotly debated in the West as the U.S.S.R.'s war-fighting strategy. At the present time, U.S. policymakers, who are convinced that the Soviets believe they can fight and win a nuclear war, are in ascendance in the Reagan Administration. But there are many informed students of Soviet nuclear affairs who strongly disagree with the interpretation of these strategic thinkers. This chapter takes a detailed look at the positions of both sides in this dabate. It analyzes critically some of the key elements making up Soviet nuclear war-fighting strategy.

The Decisive Nature of Nuclear War

During the 1960s, we are told by one longtime U.S. analyst of Soviet military policy, Soviet "strategic doctrine was probably significantly in advance of operational policy."[1] This was because only a handful of military and political leaders in the Soviet Union "were trying to think through the various aspects of the military build-up that was evolving in conventional and nuclear weaponry."[2] In this

1 William Hyland, "The USSR and Nuclear War," in Barry M. Blechman (ed.), *Rethinking the U.S. Strategic Postue* (Cambridge:Ballinger Publishing Co., 1982), pp. 56-57. According to one U.S. arms control insider, the Soviet situation here is "like the U.S. doctrine-capability gap today."

2 Raymond L. Garthoff put it a little differently. In 1966, he wrote that "Soviet military *theory,* written by military men, bore little relation to ... government statements of Soviet military *policy.*" See his "Khrushchev and the Military," in Alexander Dallin (ed.), *Politics in the Soviet Union* (New York: Brace and World, 1966), p. 257.

view, two propositions seem to have had an impact on the development of Soviet forces. The first emphasized the decisive nature of nuclear war, whereas the second stressed the crucial importance of its initial phase.

Following this general thinking, Robert McNamara writes, for "much of the postwar period, Soviet military doctrine appears to have assumed that war between the great powers would include the use of nuclear weapons."[3] Soviet publications "stressed the use of both long and intermediate-range nuclear weapons in the initial hours of conflict, to destroy concentrations of enemy forces and the ports, airfields, and other facilities necessary to support military operations." And these publications "emphasized as well the use of tactical nuclear weapons on the battlefield."[4]

Until the mid-1960s, the writings of a number of Soviet military officials consistently argued that the only conflict possible between the great powers was all-out nuclear war. Furthermore, they asserted that the Soviet Union could possibly prevail in such a conflict. And they argued the military and social preparations necessary to ensure that the Soviet Union emerged triumphantly from any nuclear conflict. In fact, it was these writings that were used so devastatingly in the late 1970s by opponents of nuclear arms control in the debate on the SALT II Treaty.[5] However, by 1979, this portrayal of Soviet military doctrine was becoming badly out of date – if it ever were reflective of actual Soviet intentions.[6]

Official Soviet military doctrine appeared to change slightly in the mid-1960s as more and more Soviet writers began to admit the

3 "This was because Soviet conventional forces so greatly outnumbered those of NATO," asserts one U.S. military official familiar with this subject.

4 Robert McNamara, "The Military Role of Nuclear Weapons: Perceptions and Misperceptions," *Foreign Affairs,* Vol. 62, No. 1 (Fall, 1983), p.65.

5 See Richard Pipes, "Militarism and the Soviet State," *Daedalus* (Fall, 1980), pp.1-12.

6 Richard T. Ackley argued in 1974 that a careful examination of the Soviet strategic literature indicated a Russian belief in a "war-winning" strategy through nuclear superiority as the best possible deterrent. Although there was fundamental uncertainty in Soviet military writings as to who would actually start a nuclear war, Ackley said, there was every indication that the Russians would launch a pre-emptive strike if they were convinced the United States seriously endangered them. See "What's Left of SALT?" *Naval War College Review* (May-June, 1974), pp.43-44.

possibility of a "war by stages" in Europe. The first stage of such a conflict, it was asserted, could be a conventional one and very short. However, Soviet writers maintained that the conflict would "inevitably" escalate to allout nuclear war, thus they broke only slightly from the doctrinal rigidity of the past.

Through the 1960s and 1970s, Soviet experts and military officials debated the inevitability of nuclear escalation. For many of these people the question was settled by the time of a famous speech of General Secretary Leonid Brezhnev at Tula in 1977. Soviet strategic thinkers then admitted the possibility of a major protracted war between the East and West, in which nuclear weapons would not be used.

Indeed, Soviet policymakers now officially insisted that they would not be the first to make use of nuclear weapons. In the words of D.F. Ustinov, then Minister of Defense of the U.S.S.R., "Only extraordinary circumstances – a direct nuclear aggression against the Soviet state or its allies – can compel us to resort to a retaliatory nuclear strike as a last means of self-defense."[7]

This position was not new for the Soviet Union, although it was first stated by Brezhnev at the United Nations in June of 1982.[8-9] Previously, Soviet spokesmen had mostly been willing to declare that they would not use nuclear weapons against non-nuclear powers. (For some time before this they had sought a joint promise with Washington not to be the first to use nuclear weapons, but U.S. officials had always rebuffed the idea.)

Most importantly, this shift was accompanied by the explicit and often stated renunciation of what some Soviet officials had argued for more than two decades, namely, that it was possible to fight and win a nuclear war. Now, all Soviet officials and political leaders addressing this question solemnly declare that "there will be no victors in a nuclear war."

After Yuri Andropov came to power in 1982, the official Soviet position regarding nuclear weapons use did not change. In fact, just a few weeks after he was named to succeed Brezhnev, the Secre-

7 D.F. Ustinov, "We Serve the Homeland and the Cause of Communism," *Izvestia,* May 27, 1982.

8 For details see *The New York Times*, June 16, 1982.

9 See No. 8

tary General of the Communist Party proclaimed that a "nuclear war, whether big or small, whether limited or total, must not be allowed to break out." As might be expected, when Andropov died in early 1984, Konstantin Chernenko, a protegé of Brezhnev (and by some accounts even his designated successor in 1982), moved quickly to affirm this policy. The new Communist Party leader even publicized a proposal calling for a nuclear freeze, an old idea of Brezhnev.[10] When Chernenko died in March 1985, Mikhail Gorbachev did not hesitate to reiterate Soviet emphasis here.[11]

Changes in Doctrine

Does this major shift in policy suggest that the Soviet leadership is no longer prepared to fight a nuclear war? Certainly not. The Soviet leadership is obviously prepared to respond if the U.S. decides to initiate nuclear war.

In the event of such a war, Soviet military strategy calls for a policy that is very different from that of the United States. It stresses optimistically quick victory – not deterrence.[12] And it stresses offensive action – not retaliation.[13] There are some signs of a Soviet

10 *The Christian Science Monitor*, March 14, 1984. As early as April 21, 1981, Konstantin Chernenko once and for all exempted nuclear conflicts from the cloak of rationality implied by Clausewitz's dictum that war was simply a tool of foreign policy.

11 See for instance the joint communiqué, released at the end of the Geneva Summit Conference, and published in *The New York Times*, November 22, 1985. At that time both Soviet and American leaders stated unequivocably: The sides ... have agreed that a nuclear war cannot be won and must never be fought."

12 Contrary to the impression of many Westners, the Soviet Union is not obsessed with the notion of *Blitzkrieg*. From the early days of the Soviet regime right down to the Second World War, Soviet military doctrine has postulated that a future conflict would be protracted. See, for instance, General of the Army S.P. Ivanov (ed.), *Nachal'nyy period voyny* (Moscow, 1974), pp.72, 203.

13 In this regard see Marshal N.V. Ogarkov's article "Military Strategy" in the authoritative *Soviet Military Encyclopedia (Sovetskaya Voyennaya Entsiklopediay)*, Vol. 7 (Moscow: Voyenizdat, 1979), p.564. A key section reads: "It is considered that, with the contemporary means of destruction, world nuclear war will be comparatively short. However, considering the enormous potential military and economic resources of the coalitions of belligerent states, it cannot be excluded that it may also be prolonged. *Soviet military strategy proceeds from the view that should the Soviet Union be thrust into a nuclear war then the Soviet people and their Armed Forces need to be prepared for the most severe and protracted trial.*" (Italics mine.)

shift to a concept of prolonged war, reflected in the writing of the former Chief of the General Staff, Marshal N.V. Ogarkov.[14] In any case, Soviet military doctrine seems to suggest that *any* U.S. use of nuclear weapons – whatever its form or purpose – would relieve the Soviet Union of its obligation to observe restraints on the use of nuclear weapons within the theater of war.[15]

Preemption. One of the costliest lessons of World War II was the importance of not being caught by surprise. Stalin's failure to mobilize in face of the impending Nazi attack in 1941 led to frightful losses for Soviet forces and, as a result, the U.S.S.R. was nearly defeated.[16] This experience etched itself deeply in the minds of Soviet political and military leaders. Consequently, probably no point is emphasized more consistently in Soviet military writings today than the resolve never again to be caught in a surprise attack.[17] As elaborated by the late Leonid Brezhnev, "we are taking into consideration the lessons of the past and we are doing everything so that nobody takes us by surprise."[18]

Soviet strategic thinkers draw an important distinction, which is not always understood in the West, between a "preventive" and "pre-emptive" attack. They claim that the Soviet Union will never start a war. That is, the U.S.S.R. will never launch a preventive attack. However, once Soviet leaders have concluded that an attack upon the Soviet Union is imminent, they might not hesitate to pre-empt –

14 See Marshal N.V. Ogarkov, *Kommunist*, No. 10 (July, 1981).

15 One U.S. government insider would observe here: "This is a good psychological ploy on their part, one which is aimed at the West Europeans."

16 As the Western Allies celebrated the 40th anniversary of the D-Day landings in Normandy, the Soviet Union prepared a counter-offensive to show that the invasion was of relatively minor significance when compared with the Red Army's battles against the Germans and the Soviet drive to Berlin. The Soviets noted that the first 15 days of fighting after June 6, 1944, cost the Western forces 122,000 soldiers killed and the Germans 113,000. These figures were compared with the outcome of a single tank battle, at Prokhorovka during the Kursk battle of 1943. They said that 150,000 Germans died in that one battle. The Soviets went on to point out that they lost some 20 million in the war, whereas the total of American dead in World War II was 505,000 and the total of British dead was 370,000. See *The New York Times*, June 2, 1984.

17 See Jiri Valenta, "Soviet Use of Surprise and Deception," *Survival*, Vol. 24, No. 2 (January-April, 1982), pp. 50-59.

18 Quoted in Arthur D. Nicholson, Jr., *The Soviet Union and Strategic Nuclear War* (Monterey: Naval Postgraduate School, 1980). Some scholars maintain that the U.S. also has a "surprise attack" phobia as a result of Pearl Harbor.

or, to use Malcolm Mackintosh's succinct phrase, "to strike first in the last resort."[19]

The Soviet approach to nuclear war-fighting tends to stress that whichever side can deliver the greatest blow first is likely to remain in a better position thereafter.[20] This approach, in part, explains the Soviet preoccupation with land-based, highly controlled, large ICBMs rather than bombers.[21] Hence a Soviet objective in arms control negotiations has been to retain these forces and to ensure their modernization.

It is important to note here that there is no evidence in Soviet doctrinal writings that Soviet military leaders believe they could pre-empt against the United States with impunity.[22] Moreover, the

19 Quoted in John Erickson, "Soviet Theatre-Warfare Capability: Doctrines, Deployments, and Capabilities," in Lawrence L. Whetten (ed.), *The Future of Soviet Military Power* (New York: Crane, Russak & Co., 1976), p.135.

20 As stated before, official Soviet policy now renounces the notion of "victory" in a nuclear war. Thus, Brezhnev said that "anyone who starts a nuclear war in the hope of winning it has thereby decided to commit suicide." (*Pravda*, October 21, 1981). Nevertheless, victory is still alluded to in authoritative Soviet military writing (including that of the former Chief of Staff, Marshal Ogarkov). "Victory" is defined in Soviet writings as "crushing" the enemy's forces and destroying the opponent's economic and political potential. (See Joseph D. Douglass and Amoretta M. Hoeber, *Soviet Strategy for Nuclear War*, Palo Alto, Calif., The Hoover Institution, 1979, pp.14-15.) Soviet military writings, however, do not elaborate on how this is to be achieved and hardly mention concomitant devastation of the Soviet Union or the cost of such a victory.

21 There are a number of reasons to explain why the Russians continue to resist diversifying their strategic forces to any substantial degree. Explanations range from the bureaucratic dominance of the land-based strategic missile forces to the qualitative inferiority of the Soviet sea-based nuclear forces compared with those of the U.S. Another factor has probably been the American advantage in anti-submarine warfare forces, and the potential threat this capability presents to Russian sea-based forces. In an oped piece in *The New York Times* on April, 11, 1982, Nobel physicist Hans Bethe and Kurt Gottfried of Cornell University wrote: The Russians were forced to put most of their nuclear eggs into one basket "because of their technological backwardness and geographical position. Their submarines are inferior to ours; they have no bomber bases close to us, while ours encircle the Soviet Union; and they have not been able to develop cruise missiles (sic), which are now revitalizing our bomber fleet. Their ICBM force is so large because that is all they can do well."

22 Unfortunately, there has been a great deal of confusion – even misrepresentation – of the Soviet concept of pre-emption in many U.S. writings. In this connection, it may be relevant to recall that the United States, too, once articulated a confidential national policy of pre-emption, but not preventive war. This occurred in the 1950s. NSC-68, adopted in 1950 as the basic U.S. political and military guidance, while rejecting "preventive war" went on to state: "The military

rationale behind their emphasis on pre-emption is certainly not to pursue the key to a quick and easy victory – or the illusion that such a victory might even be possible. Rather, as former CIA analyst Benjamin S. Lambeth points out, "it seems to reflect a conviction that the least miserable option at the brink of a hopelessly unavoidable nuclear catastrophe would be to strike first and decisively so as to secure a measure of initiative and control, without which even a Pyrrhic victory would remain beyond reach."[23]

If one had to pick the one single event that just might act as the trigger for Soviet pre-emption, it would be the dispersal of NATO nuclear warheads from their storage facilities in a crisis. For this reason, in the view of one scholar, "internal fights within NATO would be likely to break out over this decision."[24]

John Erickson, Director of Defense Studies at the University of Edinburgh, for one, is somewhat uneasy with this characterization of the Soviet nuclear outlook. He states that it is easy enough to label the established Soviet orthodoxy in linking military principles – speed, surprise, shock, firepower and the winning of the initiative – after Western styles such as pre-emption. But he thinks this strategy is "better described as a preference for a strategic 'disruptive strike.'" This is not "unlike Soviet artillery practice in World War II

advantages of landing the first blow become increasingly important with modern weapons, and this is a fact which requires us to be on the alert in order to strike without full weight as soon as we are attacked, *and, if possible, before the Soviet blow* is actually delivered." See *Foreign Relations of the United States, 1950; National Security Affairs; Foreign Economic Policy,* Vol. I., H. Doc. 82-264, 82 Cong., 1st session (Washington, D.C.: Government Printing Office, 1977), p. 282. (Italics mine.)

23 Benjamin S. Lambeth, "How to Think About Soviet Military Doctrine," paper sponsored by the Program for Science and International Affairs, the Center for International Affairs, and the Russian Research Center, Harvard University, February 13, 1978.

24 See Paul Bracken, *The Command and Control of Nuclear Forces* (New Haven: Yale University Press, 1983), p. 175. According to Bracken, the "political fighting might lead to outright disruption of the alerting process to forestall Soviet retaliation. As the Anglo-French Alliance of 1940 became unglued, this is what happened." (In June 1940, French military units physically blocked a British bomber force from using an airfield in Marseilles as it was about to launch an attack on Italy. British officers on the scene requested permission from Prime Minister Winston Churchill to clear the runway with machine gun fire. But this permission was refused and the air strike never took place. See Noel Barber, *The Week France Fell,* New York: Stein & Day, 1976, pp. 93-95.)

when the artillery *kontrpodgotovka* fired off its delicately timed fire blow designed to disrupt enemy preparations for attack." Here, he says, it "is worth noting that the Soviet missile forces were first developed by officers who had an artillery background."[25]

Despite Soviet emphasis on the importance of initiative and anticipation of surprise, they do not envisage *their* initiation of war as a "bolt from the blue" or a "standing start" charge from garrison to the border with no preparation. Strategic surprise is almost ruled out since the Soviet Union anticipates that a major international crisis would precede hostilities. In fact, the attainment of even operational surprise would be unlikely because as Soviet theorists have observed, modern technical reconnaissance would make it very difficult to deny information about one's activity to the adversary.[26]

Surprise must instead be obtained through the manipulation of the adversary's interpretation of the activity he observes. For instance, major exercises and deployments ostensibly intended to suppress political unrest (in Poland, for example) might be one means of justifying to NATO partial mobilization of Warsaw forces. Another device might be incremental upgrades of low-readiness divisions carried out at a rate too slow for the West to detect or interpret as especially important. Finally, at a time of political crisis, the Soviet Union might succeed in deceiving NATO into thinking the crisis had passed its most acute phase when in fact the Soviets were preparing to attack.[27]

High State of Combat Readiness

Related to the notion of "pre-emption" in the Soviet military literature is the point that the armed forces must always be in a high state of combat readiness.[28] Emphasis on the maintenance of a

25 John Erickson, *opus cit.,* p.247. Interestingly, Khrushchev, in his memoirs, makes a point of singling out Soviet artillerymen as opponents of missiles. See his *Khrushchev Remembers: The Last Testament* (Boston:Little, Brown, 1974), p.52.

26 Marshal of Tank Troops, O.A. Losik, "Lokalni valky a vojenskeumeni," *Lidova Armada,* Vol. 16 (1982), pp.746-7.

27 For details see Philip A. Peterson *et al.,* "The Conventional Offensive in Soviet Theater Strategy," *Orbis* (Fall, 1983), p.734.

28 Despite the Soviet emphasis on maintaining a high state of combat readiness,

large ready force is one of the constant themes of Soviet military literature. Such a high level of readiness should allow Soviet forces to convert to active operations with the least possible delay. Nuclear warfare grants no time for mobilization. This emphasis on readiness helps explain the huge land forces which the Soviets maintain at all times and outfit with the latest weapons as they roll off the assembly lines.[29]

But this is only the appearance. Reality is quite different. As one student of Soviet military affairs writes: "In the Russian Army, appearance as opposed to reality is carried to an extreme."[30] Much equipment is not only unused, it is not even in running condition. In regular units, this equipment is brought out once or twice a year for large-scale exercises. Otherwise, training is conducted with what little equipment is not in storage or with crude simulators.

Individual training is stressed in the Red Army. For approximately seventy-five percent of the Army consists of two-year conscripts. Most of the non-commissioned officers are appointed conscripts. To be sure, Soviet officers are all voluntary and professional, but they are required to perform much of the supervision done by NCOs in Western armies.

As is the case with many armies in less affluent states, the Red Army is often called out to perform nonmilitary duties. For instance, bringing in the annual crops for several weeks is a regular activity. Helping out during natural disasters is also standard. Moreover, the thousands of trucks of the active divisions are a unique transportation resource in a country where over 80 percent of the transportation system consists of waterways and trains.

Because of the relatively strict discipline, the leaders of the Red Army can get their units in shape and on the road quickly, in spite of drugs, drunkenness, poor morale, missing supplies and spotty training. However, fighting is another matter. The authors of articles in Soviet military journals are constantly complaining that training has

Soviet strategic forces are still kept at lower levels of alert than American strategic forces. See Albeter Carnesale *et al.*, *Living with Nuclear Weapons* (New York: Bantam Books, 1983), p.137.

29 Ellen Jones, "Soviet Military Manpower: Prospects in the 1980s," *Strategic Review* (Fall, 1981), p.66.

30 See James F. Dunnigan, *How to Make War* (New York: Quill, 1983), p.245.

become mostly form with little substance. At best, units deploy and go through the motions of rigid adherence to regulations. At worst, even the simplest maneuvers are botched. With little combat experience since World War II, the Soviet armed forces has few veterans who are able to warn of the perils of peacetime soldiering.[31] The recent Soviet experience in Afghanistan may shake up things somewhat, but many problems will still remain, the experts say.

Combined-Arms Operations. Soviet theoretical writings unequivocably reject reliance on any one strategy (e.g. the *Blitzkrieg*) or on any one weapon to fight a war. The Soviets believe that if a nuclear war occurs, it will require the employment of all arms.

The Soviet Army has recognized the importance of combined-arms operations since the 1930s. But Soviet tactics and weapons frequently did not permit them to translate their ideas into effective action. Today the Soviets have refined their operational and tactical thought and equipped themselves with adequate weapons, so that all operations and all tactics down to company level or below are carried out by combined-arms forces.[32]

The standard formulation on balanced forces and combined arms operations (though now dated) was provided in a major article by former Defense Minister Marshal A.A. Grechko:[33]

War may begin with the use of nuclear weapons or by conventional forces and means. Various versions of the combined utilization of all types of weapons in the enemy's possession are also possible...

Therefore, all types of armed forces and branches are being developed by us and are being perfected and equipped for combat utilization in modern battle, in operations, and in war as a whole.

31 It should be noted here that there is less rather than more Soviet reliance on Eastern Europe military forces. The military reality of this situation was perhaps best shown by the major Soviet exercises at the end of June and the beginning of July, 1984. As John Erickson writes, "for all practical purposes, the Pact members were ignored, evidently taking no part in this exercise in the coordination of Soviet theater forces." Realistically, the Soviets would be hard pressed to attack West Europe without the full participation of some of the non-Soviet forces. See "The Warsaw Pact: From Here to Eternity?," *Current History*, Vol. 184, No. 505 (November, 1985), p.360.

32 See David C. Isby, *Weapons and Tactics of the Soviet Army* (New York: Jares, 1981), p.21.

33 A.A. Grechko, "V.I. Lenin and the Building of the Soviet Armed Forces," *Kommunist*, No. 3 (February, 1969), p.23.

Although the Soviets place great emphasis on combined arms operations in the fighting of a war, the obvious should be noted: This will be very difficult in the context of the unprecedented levels of destruction associated with the use of nuclear weapons.

Should nuclear war erupt, both the military and political leaders of the U.S.S.R. believe it will invariably escalate to all-out war.[34] Thus, the idea of an extended nuclear war is deeply embedded in Soviet military planning. Limited nuclear war, controlled escalation, and many of the numerous refinements of U.S. deterrent doctrine find no place in Soviet military strategy (although one assumes that they are taken into consideration in Soviet operational planning).

Renunciation of Military Superiority

One of the most notable changes in Soviet military doctrine in the last decade and half has been in the area of military superiority. During the 1950s and 1960s it became commonplace for high-level military (and even political) leaders to make calls for military superiority. In fact, if one were to judge solely by the volume of utterances on the subject, then the Soviet belief in the need to achieve military superiority over the West would seem unshakable.[35] But beginning in the period from 1969 to the Twenty-fourth Party Congress (1971), there was a discernible trend leading to a cessation of such calls by the top political and military authorities. From that time on there was gradually an adoption of calls for military parity and equality, particularly in the context of the SALT I negotiations.

To be sure, during the early and mid-1970s the standard military discussion of doctrine – as distinct from official pronouncements by top political leaders – continued from time to time to call routinely for military superiority. One of the last references of this kind was an unsigned article in 1976 on "Military-Technical Superiority"

34 See Joseph D. Douglass, Jr. *et al., Conventional War and Escalation: The Soviet View* (New York: Crane, Russak & Co., 1981), p.25.

35 See, for instance, the statement by Chairman Nikita Khrushchev, in which he stated that the policy of peaceful coexistence rested on the premise that the East European countries and the Soviet Union "have a rapidly growing economy and surpass the imperialist camp in armaments and armed forces." Election speech in Kalinin District, *Pravda*, February 28, 1963.

in the Soviet Military Encyclopedia. This article stated military-technical superiority as an aim of the Soviet armed forces. Interestingly, the encyclopedia, which contained an article on "Superiority over the Enemy," carefully referred only to military operations in the field and not to the overall military posture. In a major signed article on "Military Strategy," Marshal N.V. Ogarkov, formerly First Deputy Minister of Defense and Chief of the General Staff, argued for not permitting "the probable enemy" to acquire military-technical superiority. But he continued to affirm that "Soviet military strategy... does not have as its own objective the attainment of military-technical superiority over other countries."[36]

As for the important (confidential) General Staff organ *Military Thought*, this publication continued in the latter 1970s to contain occasional references to "victory" as a theoretical objective of war. For instance, Major General N.G. Popov *et al.* wrote in 1977: "The main decisive fundamental task of military science is to work out theoretical conceptions of the character and strategic content of war that imperialist circles may unleash, and for achieving victory in which our country and its armed forces must be ready."[37]

These exceptions not withstanding, the Soviets began in the early 1970s to formulate a new positive military doctrine explicitly renouncing military superiority as an aim of Soviet policy. Brezhnev himself unveiled the new doctrine in a major speech at Tula on the eve of the Carter Administration's assumption of office. Disavowing any goal of military superiority aimed at a "first strike," he proclaimed:[38]

Of course, comrades, we are improving our defenses. It cannot be otherwise. We have never neglected and will never neglect the security of our country and the security of our allies. But the allegations that the Soviet Union is going beyond what is sufficient for defense, that it is striving for superiority in arms, with the aim of delivering a 'first strike,' are absurd and utterly unfounded ... Our efforts are

36 *Sovetskaja voyennaya entsiklopediya,* Vol. 7 (Moscow: Voyenizdat, 1979), p. 564.

37 Major General N.G. Popov and Colonel M.I. Galkin, "Basic and Applied Military Science Research," *Voyennaya mysl'*, No. 9 (September, 1977), p. 43.

38 L.I. Brezhnev, "Outstanding Exploit of the Defenders of Tula," *Pravda*, January 19, 1977. Official acceptance of parity was stressed in early 1977 in military and political journals even before Brezhnev's speech.

aimed at preventing both first and second strikes and at preventing nuclear war altogether...

The official Soviet position was spelled out in detail by Georgi Arbatov, Director of the Institute of USA and Canada Studies, in *Pravda* shortly after the Tula speech. He attempted to refute arguments that the U.S.S.R. was seeking superiority and accurately described areas of the arms race in which the Soviet Union was leading, e.g. the overall numbers of ICBM and SLBM missile launchers and strategic missile throw-weight, and those in which the U.S. was leading, e.g. numbers of strategic bombers and bomber throw-weight, numbers of missile warheads and forward submarine bases. Therefore, he pointed out, "while enjoying an approximate equality (parity) in general, the two countries have within this parity considerable differences (asymmetries) in various components of their armed forces, connected with differences in geographic situations, the nature of possible threats to their security, technical characteristics of individual weapons systems, and even in traditions of military organization." The main thing, however, is "the existence of an approximate balance, that is, a parity in the correlation of forces about which the USSR and the United States came to agreement with the signing of the principle of equal rights to security."[39]

Since Brezhnev's Tula speech in 1977 there have been many authoritative statements by military and political leaders which have echoed the theme of the nonpursuit of superiority. For example, in August, 1979, Marshal Ogarkov, now operational commander of the Soviet Union's western front, specifically cited Brezhnev's statement from the Tula speech as Soviet doctrine. ("We have no other doctrine," Ogarkov wrote.)[40] The same subject has been addressed in the concurrent regimes of Andropov, Chernenko and Gorbachev.

Throughout the 1950s and 1960s, the United States maintained a clear strategic nuclear superiority. But in the latter half of the 1970s as the U.S.S.R. consolidated its strategic parity new fears

39 *Pravda*, February 5, 1977.

40 *Pravda*, August 2, 1979. Later Marshal Ogarkov exclaimed: "One does not have to be a military man or a scholar to know that a further increase of strategic forces is already becoming senseless." Quoted by Jerry F. Hough in *The Washington Post*, November 4, 1985.

arose in the United States. Officials began to point to what they called a "relentless" military buildup on the part of the Soviet Union leading to nuclear superiority. This point was made decidedly by the Carter Administration,[41] but the Reagan Administration gave it even more emphasis.

In short, U.S. Ambassador Raymond Garthoff writes, "during the entire period from 1977 into the early 1980s, considerable weight was placed on the trend in Soviet defense spending, especially for the procurement of weapons and other investment, as a reflection – and indicator – of a growing Soviet threat." In the SALT II debate in 1979, "this issue was given particular prominence, as Kissinger and a number of other earlier supporters of SALT conditioned their support for ratification of the SALT II Treaty on a commitment to an increase in the rate of U.S. defense expenditures to deal with the spending gap and its consequences." Others charged "that the relentless continued increase in Soviet military spending showed that the Soviet Union was taking advantage of detente."[42]

As it turned out, these confident estimates of a steady acceleration in Soviet military spending were wrong. To be sure, Soviet defense spending continues to be estimated as having grown at a rate of some four to five percent a year during the first half of the 1970s. But revised CIA and NATO estimates since 1983, based on new and better information, show only a two percent increase a year for the period since 1976. In addition, investment and especially procurement of military hardware have leveled off since 1976. In other words, there was virtually no increase in rate of growth. "New information indicates," says the CIA, "that the Soviets did not field weapons as rapidly after 1976 as before. Practically all major categories of Soviet weapons were affected – missiles, aircraft, and ships."[43]

41 See U.S. Defense Department, *Annual Report, Fiscal Year 1982* (Washington D.C.:U.S. Government Printing Office, 1982), p.3.

42 Raymond Garthoff, *Detente and Confrontation: American-Soviet Relations from Nixon to Reagan* (Washington, D.C.: Brookings Institution, 1985), p.795.

43 For details see "CIA Briefing Paper Entitled 'USSR: Economic Trends and Policy Developments,'" in *Allocation of Resources in the Soviet Union and China – 1983*, Hearings before the Subcommittee on International Trade, Finance and Security Economics of the Joint Economic Committee, 98th Congress, 1st Session (Washington, D.C.: U.S. Government Printing Office, 1984), p. 306. It should be noted that CIA findings in this regard did not agree with those of the Defense Intelligence Agency. In fact, they caused a major controversy between the two

The reasons for this reduced rate of defense are not entirely known to the CIA. But the "extended nature" of "the slowdown in the growth of military procurement... goes far beyond normal dips in procurement cycles." As the CIA concludes, growth of Soviet GNP has slowed, so much that the share of GNP devoted to defense has remained about the same. The *earlier* estimated growth in that share has simply not occurred.

The slowdown in the rate of growth of defense spending has lasted too long to be plausibly explained as a lull caused by the phasing out of old programs and the introduction of new ones. As D. Holloway observes: "It seems more reasonable to interpret it as resulting from a policy decision on the part of the Soviet leaders. It coincides with the decline in the rate of growth of the economy as a whole." (From 1966 to 1976 the Soviet GNP grew at 2.2 percent a year and defense outlays at 2.0 percent.) Thus, the "slowdown in the rate of defense expenditure can be interpreted ... as a response to the more general slowdown in economic growth, and to the pressures on resource allocation that have followed from this."[44]

During this period, there were, of course, significant real improvements in Soviet – and Western – military capabilities. But as Ambassador Garthoff states, "the spending gap proved no more solid than the gaps – bombers, missiles, ABM, and civil defense – of preceding decades."[45]

In March 1982, President Ronald Reagan stated in an impromptu reply to a question at a press conference that "the truth of the matter is that on balance the Soviet Union does have a definite margin of superiority."[46] But this judgment was not supported by the positions taken earlier and subsequently by the Chairman and

agencies. Some of the differences stemmed, in part, from variations in the two agencies' methods of estimating Soviet expenditures. According to both agencies, the Soviets between 1976 and 1983 purchased 1,100 land-based intercontinental ballistic missiles and 700 submarine-launched ballistic missiles, 5,000 fighter planes, 300 bombers and 15,500 new tanks.

44 David Holloway, *The Soviet Union and the Arms Race*, 2nd ed. (New Haven: Yale University Press, 1984), p.XXII. "It's not what you spend," argues one government expert. "It's what you get with the money you do spend that is important."

45 Raymond Garthoff, *opus cit.*, p.796. For an important analysis see Richard F. Kaufman, "Causes of the Slowdown in Soviet Defense," *Soviet Economy*, Vol. 1 (January-March, 1985), pp.9-41.

46 For the text see *The New York Times*, April 1, 1982.

other members of the Joint Chiefs of Staff. The same was true of Secretary of Defense Caspar W. Weinberger and such purveyors of warnings of a Soviet threat as Senator Henry M. Jackson, James R. Schlesinger and Zbigniew Brzezinski to name but a few.[47] However, whatever its analytic foundation, it was clear that the President was expressing a view that was widely held by Americans.[48]

No First Use

In June 1982, the Soviet Union publicized its nuclear firing position by declaring that it would not be the first to use nuclear weapons. Speaking at the Special Session on Disarmament at the United Nations on June 15, Party Leader Brezhnev affirmed that "the Union of Soviet Socialist Republics assumes an obligation not to be the first to use nuclear weapons." He expected other states with nuclear weapons to "assume an equally precise and clear obligations." That, he declared, would be "tantamount to a ban on the use of nuclear weapons."[49]

In his speech, Brezhnev added an important qualifier that many people have subsequently overlooked. He said that the Soviet Union "will naturally continue to take into account how the other nuclear powers act." This statement was interpreted by most Western analysts as an escape clause that would enable the Soviets to renounce their promise if the United States, Britain and France did

47 See *The New York Times*, April 2, 1982.

48 Former CIA analyst Benjamin S. Lambeth summarizes some of the skepticism of the new Soviet position on superiority: "Several continuing undercurrents in Soviet policy make it particularly hard to swallow Moscow's recent claims that its 'old' doctrine has been discarded. First, senior military figures who have endorsed the Tula principles at one level have repeatedly given voice in other contexts to the continued primacy of all the classic principles of Soviet military thought. Second, even those speeches and publications expressly aimed at promulgating the Tula message have taken care to avoid using formulations that would directly contradict established doctrinal premises. Third, and most revealing, there is nothing in recent Soviet R & D and weapons development that would indicate any substantial departure from the basic doctrinal guidance that has governed Soviet force development since the buildup began two decades ago." See his *The State of Western Research on Soviet Military Strategy and Policy* (Santa Monica: The Rand Corporation, 1984), pp. VII-VIII.

49 See *The New York Times*, June 16, 1982.

not follow suit – which they did not. (China already pledged that it would not use nuclear weapons first after exploding its initial device in 1964.)

Contrary to popular belief, the no first use policy was not completely new for Soviet military doctrine. Just six months earlier, the Ministry of Defense had published a booklet in which it stated categorically: "At the foundation of Soviet military strategy is the principle that the Soviet Union will not be the first to use nuclear weapons."[50]

Privately, Soviet officials indicated that the subject of no first use had in fact been considered at a high level several times since the mid-1970s. In fact, the subject had even been brought up publicly as early as the 1960s. According to U.S. Ambassador Raymond Garthoff, it was broached in SALT in 1970 but not pursued because the United States took a negative position. After further discussions in Moscow, a new series of initiatives began after the Twenty-fifth Party Congress in 1976. And in November of that year the party chiefs of the Warsaw Pact countries, meeting as the Political Consultative Committee of the Pact, formally proposed a draft treaty banning first use of nuclear weapons.[51] Brezhnev subsequently noted in his Tula speech of January 1977 Western rejection of this proposal but reaffirmed Soviet support for a mutual renunciation of first use of nuclear weapons.[52] Since 1978, there have been a number of conditional public pledges not to use nuclear weapons except in "extraordinary circumstances, aggression by another nuclear power against our country or our allies"[53] and not to use nuclear weapons against nonnuclear states that had renounced nuclear arms.[54] In September 1981, Foreign Minister Gromyko proposed a draft resolution in the UN General Assembly to the effect that states who used nuclear weapons first would be committing a very grave crime against humanity.[55] By mid-1982, the Soviet leadership

50 U.S.S.R. Ministry of Defense, *Whence the Threat to Peace* (Moscow: Voyenizdat, Ministerstvo Oborony SSSR, 1982), p.12.

51 For the text see *Pravda*, November 28, 1976.

52 See *Pravda*, January 9, 1977.

53 Speech by Brezhnev, *Pravda*, April 26, 1978.

54 Statement by Gromyko, *Pravda*, May 27, 1978.

55 *Pravda*, September 24, 1981.

decided to go all the way in formally renouncing the first use of nuclear weapons.

The Soviet commitment not to use nuclear weapons first was generally regarded in the West as no more than propaganda. U.S. officials, in particular, could remember back years when Soviet proposals of one kind or another for banning the use of nuclear weapons were a central feature of Soviet efforts to inhibit the United States from deriving political advantage from its superior nuclear position. (Or so they were interpreted.) In particular, a ban on first-use of nuclear weapons was closely linked to the U.S.S.R.'s European diplomacy, for it was viewed as cancelling out the guarantee of American nuclear protection to Western Europe.[56]

It is clear that there is an important element of propaganda in the Soviet proposal. And it is obviously designed to embarrass NATO, which refuses to make a similar pledge.[57] But there is more to the Soviet position than that.

For one thing, it may signal Soviet recognition of the uselessness of nuclear weapons. As Marshal Ogarkov wrote, both before and after he was removed as Chief of the Soviet General Staff, nuclear weapons are almost impossible to use.[58]

For a number of years now, former high-level U.S. government officials have been making this same point. As former U.S. Ambassador to NATO Harland Cleveland has stated: "Nuclear weapons have turned out to be 'ultimate' in an unanticipated sense of the word. No nation's military planners have been able, in 38 years, to think up a way to use such huge explosions with such pervasive aftereffects in ways that are clearly advantageous to their side. This may be the most important thing about nuclear weapons in the 1980s: that they are militarily unusable."[59]

Whatever the case, the Soviet renunciation of the first use of nuclear weapons fits into the pattern of recent organizational chan-

56 See Thomas W. Wolfe, *Soviet Power and Europe, 1945-1970* (Baltimore: Johns Hopkins Press, 1970), p.512.

57 One State Department official with NATO experience would make the following observation here: NATO has pledged no first use of force, which is even broader, but reserves the right to use any available means to repel an attack.

58 Quoted in *The Christian Science Monitor*, January 18, 1984. This view is also shared by Melvin Laird, Secretary of Defense in the Nixon Administration.

59 See Jerry F. Hough, "Gorbachev's Strategy," *Foreign Affairs* (Fall, 1985), p.40.

ges in the armed forces. As David Holloway, a distinguished Soviet scholar, concludes: The Soviet "Ground and Air Forces have gone through a period of reorganization that points to a determination to achieve the goals of war in Europe as quickly as possible by *conventional* arms."[60] (Italics mine.)

To be sure, the constant threat of nuclear attack under the conditions of non-nuclear warfare remains a frequent admonition of Soviet millitary writers. However, there is evidence that the contemporary emphasis on non-nuclear combat has resulted in reduced Soviet troop training for battlefield nuclear combat. Stephen M. Meyer writes, "Increasingly, training has emphasized conventional skills, while nuclear defensive tactics (necessary operations in a nuclear environment) have been neglected."[61] In short, it seems that training to fight in a nuclear environment is no longer accorded the same priority at higher and lower levels of command.

It is hard to know exactly what the commitment not to be the first to use nuclear weapons means in actual practice.[62] For one thing, it does not mean that the U.S.S.R. will refrain from counterforce systems in favor of those that are to be used only in retaliation against

60 David Holloway, *The Soviet Union and the Arms Race*, 2nd ed. (New Haven: Yale University Press, 1984), p.XV.

61 Stephen M. Meyer, "Soviet Theatre Nuclear Forces: Part II: Capabilities and Implications," *Adelphi Paper No. 188* (London: The International Institute for Strategic Studies, 1984), p.35. The first Soviet battlefield exercise under simulated nuclear conditions occurred in 1954. Frequently, thereafter Soviet troop and command post exercises began with large-scale nuclear attacks. Significantly, in 1980, the Soviet armed forces reportedly carried out their first all-conventional exercise since 1960. Only at this time did the Soviets avowedly make the transition to full-fledged conventional warfare the basic option. See Arch Shero and Richard Oden, "Exercise Zapad-81," in *Review of the Soviet Ground Forces* (Washington, D.C.: Defense Intelligence Agency, 1982), p.1.

62 Benjamin Lambeth sizes up the implications of no first use in this way: "The recent Soviet no-first-use vow ... entails less than meets the eye. Not only is it compatible with Soviet doctrine when viewed in an operational context; it makes sense on military as well as political grounds ... So long as Soviet conventional operations in a European war went according to plan, Soviet commanders would have no reason to initiate nuclear war and every incentive to observe nuclear restraint. There is even reason to believe that the Soviets would be prepared to countenance a small number of NATO demonstration nuclear strikes without replying, so long as their conventional offense remained undisrupted. But there is no ground for believing that they have relinquished their traditional determination to land the first *massive* nuclear blow in any situation where they would risk operational defeat by doing anything less." See his *The State of Western Research on Soviet Military Strategy and Policy*, p.VIII.

cities (i.e., countervalue systems.) For another, it does not appear to rule out a preemptive strike against an enemy that is preparing a nuclear attack on the Soviet Union. However, the Soviet pledge does reflect an awareness that nuclear war would certainly have catastrophic consequences. Moreover, it has its roots in the conviction that nuclear war, once started, would be very difficult to limit. Finally, it is consistent with recent Soviet strategic thought that stresses that even in the event of war it makes sense to try to prevent the use of nuclear weapons.[63]

"Counterforce" and "Countervalue" Targeting

Traditionally, American nuclear strategy has distinguished between two types of targeting strategies: "counterforce" and "countervalue" targeting. Soviet strategy, by and large, does not emphasize this distinction.[64] (However, the capabilities of their systems give them the ability to distinguish between the two types of targets.)

Some Western observers argue that Soviet nuclear targeting is counterforce oriented. It targets for destruction – in the initial strike at least – not the cities of the enemy but his military forces and their command and control facilities. Its primary aim is seen by these persons as destroying not civilians but soldiers and their leaders and undermining not so much the will to resist as the capability to do so.

In making this argument, the following statement made in 1971 by former Soviet Minister of Defense Andrei Grechko is usually cited:[65]

The Strategic Rocket Forces, which constitute the basis of the military might of our armed forces, are designed to annihilate the means of the enemy's nuclear attack, large groupings of his armies, and his

63 See Philip A. Peterson *et al.*, "The Conventional Offensive in Soviet Theater Strategy," *Orbis* (Fall, 1983), pp. 695-739. It is important to reiterate in this context that the Soviets have a full panoply of nuclear weapons and will use them if they feel it necessary. Moreover, there are extensive propaganda benefits to be derived from publicly foistering off an adversary the odium of escalating the cost of war.

64 See Leon Goure *et al.*, p. 17.

65 A.A. Grechko, *Na Strazhe mira i stroitel'stva Kommunizma* (Moscow, 1971), p. 41.

military bases; to destroy his military industries; (and) to disorganize the political and military administration of the aggressor as well as his rear and transport.

If the Soviets do employ "counterforce" targeting, this is not to say, however, that they subscribe to the American counterforce deterrent strategy. The Soviet leadership remains adamantly opposed to the kind of limited war scenarios which are part and parcel of much of American strategic thinking today. As the Soviets generally see things, there are some important reasons for not playing the American strategic game at the level of counterforce doctrine. Perhaps most important here is the concern that the kind of nuclear "war fighting" doctrine that animates current American military strategy serves to legitimize nuclear war. But doctrinal matters aside, the Soviet leadership is very much aware that acknowledgment of limited war scenarios would mean conceding the results of American nuclear advantages, thereby subjecting themselves to nuclear blackmail. Consequently, they have backed up their rejection of limited war options with deployments of strategic forces that complicate any effort by American war planners to plan a disarming first strike.[66]

66 Some Western observers find the Soviet position on this issue suspect because of the considerable propaganda value they have obtained from it. As Fritz Ermarth writes: "There are several reasons why Soviet public pronouncements should not be taken as entirely reflecting the content of operative Soviet strategic thinking and planning regarding limited nuclear war." For one thing, "qualified acceptance in doctrine and posture of a non-nuclear scenario, or at least a non-nuclear phase, in theater conflict displays some Soviet willingness to embrace conflict limitation notions previously rejected." In addition, "Soviet strategic nuclear force growth and modernization ... have given Soviet operational planners a broader array of employment options than they had in the 1960s and may have imparted some confidence in Soviet ability to *enforce* conflict limitations." It would "not be surprising, therefore, to find some Soviet contingency planning for various kinds of limited nuclear options at the theater and, perhaps, at the strategic level." Having said this, Ermarth goes on to acknowledge that one "may seriously doubt, however, whether Soviet planners would approach the problem of contingency planning for limited nuclear options with the conceptual baggage the U.S. system carries. *It would seem contrary to the style of Soviet doctrinal thinking to emphasize bargaining and risk management.*" See Fritz W. Ermarth, *opus cit.*, p.149.

Pipes and His Critics

Much of the foregoing analysis is challenged by Richard Pipes. Pipes is a Professor of Russian history at Harvard and was, until just a couple of years ago, the senior expert on the Soviet Union on President Reagan's National Security Council. Pipes is convinced that "the Soviet Union thinks it can fight and win a nuclear war." His study of Soviet military journals and Russian military writing in traditional sources convinces him that the Soviets believe they can accomplish political objectives by threatening and, if necessary, fighting a nuclear war. In his view, the Soviets, because they have a better civil defense program, will suffer less damage, and therefore they will win.[67]

In making his case, Pipes gives special credence to the apparent enthusiasm shown by present Soviet military leaders for Lenin's endorsement of Clausewitz, the nineteenth century philosopher – warrior whose masterpiece *On War* proclaimed that "war is the continuation of policy by other means." Taking up the classic work, *Military Strategy,* Pipes points to the words of the late Marshal Sokolovsky, who said that "the essential nature of war as a continuation of politics does not change with changing technology and armaments."[68]

The argument made by Pipes has been criticized on several important grounds. Regarding the point on Clausewitz, John Erickson had this to say: "While it is frequently said that the Soviet view is 'Clausewitzian,' in fact, Lenin modified Clausewitz's dictum to read '*imperialist* wars are a violent extension of the politics of impe-

67 See for instance, Richard Pipes, "Why the Soviet Union Thinks it Could Fight and Win a Nuclear War," *Commentary* (July, 1977), p. 21-34. A U.S. official with experience in civil defense, says: "There are a handful of people, like Pipes and T.K. Jones, who push the civil defense superiority theory. I participated in an extensive governmental CD study in the late 70s, and I think this theory is borderline crackpotism."

68 For a more detailed presentation of Pipes view, see his edited publication *Soviet Strategy in Europe* (New York: Crane, Russak, 1976). Ambassador Martin Hillenbrand would make the following point here: "Brodie has argued that Clausewitz's dictum cannot be interpreted as justifying nuclear war, since this would be incompatible with the realization of those political goals that in the dictum are the only justification for war. In any event, Clausewitz lived and wrote in the pre-nuclear war." Letter to this writer, July 9, 1985.

rialism,' where the essence of imperialism must generate chronic conflict." In this search for the "laws of armed conflict," Erickson says, "Soviet theory also departs from Clausewitz in refusing to regard wars as isolated phenomena."[69]

Other students of Soviet military affairs criticize Pipes for ignoring much of what Soviet theorists traditionally have had to say on the matter of the specific context in which nuclear weapons might be used. This is spelled out in the standard political-military text, *Marxism-Leninism on War and Army,* a publication compiled by a committee of Soviet political officers.[70] It says in part:

Politics will determine when the armed struggle is to be started and what means are to be employed. Nuclear war cannot emerge from nowhere, out of a vacuum, by itself... war cannot be understood without first understanding its connection with the policies preceding it ... The political interest of the classes at war [and of their conditions determine the war] aims, while armed struggle is the means of achieving these aims ... [W]ar is the continuation of the politics of definite classes and conditions by violent means.

In the opinion of Ambassador George Kennan, it is precisely because Soviet leaders do see war as an extension of politics that gives us hope of avoiding it. While Soviet leaders are hardly pacifists, they do not normally go to war without good reason. And what "limited objective," what "limited danger," what "special fear," what "ambition," what "local situation," could "conceivably justify" a nuclear war – for the Soviets no less than ourselves?

Recently, the debate took on a new dimension with the publi-

69 John Erickson, "The Soviet View of Deterrence: A General Survey," *Survival,* Vol. 24, No. 6 (November-December, 1982), p. 243. While it is true that Lenin embraced the observation of Clausewitz that "war is a continuation of politics by other means," a number of Soviet writers (mainly but not exclusively civilians) have over the years been so impressed by the enormous danger of any nuclear world war and any war that could escalate into such a war that they have challenged this view. One civilian commentator on political-military subjects even went so far as to paraphrase Clausewitz (and Lenin) to say "War can only be the continuation of madness." See Boris Dmitriyev, "Brass Hats: Peking and Clausewitz," *Izvestiya,* September 25, 1963. To be sure, some of these commentators have been criticized for their statements and have responded accordingly.

70 Colonel G. Fedorov *et al., Marxism-Leninism on War and Army,* 5th ed. (Moscow: Progress Publishers, 1972). The first edition of this publication was produced by political officers of the Lenin Military-Political Academy and appeared in early 1961.

cation in 1980 of the updated *Soviet Military Encyclopedia*. Writing in that important work, Marshal Nikolai Ogarkov said: "If a nuclear war is foisted upon the Soviet Union," the Soviets "will have definite advantages stemming from the just goals of the war and the advanced nature of their social and state system." This, Ogarkov maintained, "creates objective possibilities for them to achieve victory." When some American military analysts began to interpret this article (which others tended to downplay as another example of "ideological breastbeating") as representing tangible new evidence of a Soviet plan for nuclear victory, the official press in Moscow took pains to discredit such a view.

According to Richard J. Barnet, a former consultant to the Defense Department, one very realistic way of looking at such statements by Soviet military leaders emphasizes a common problem faced by the Russians as well as the American military establishment. Year after year both need to maintain the readiness of forces that are designed not to be used and yet offer the hope of victory. To construct an armed forces on the prospect of either permanent inaction or annihilation is virtually impossible. This reality causes military men on both sides to develop "war-winning" fantasies and to write for themselves documents which alarm their opposite numbers. As Barnet argues, anyone who knows anything about the Pentagon and the way it works knows that "U.S. military officers have written bloodcurdling scenarios about a successful first strike on the Soviet Union."[71]

Those Western experts, who believe the Soviet leadership is committed to using its nuclear arsenal, point to the way Soviet soldiers have been trained, the kind of protective clothing and decontamination equipment they have been issued and the nature of their military exercises. For years these exercises (like those of their American counterparts) have included a simulated nuclear phase in which the mock launching of nuclear missiles has occurred. These

71 Richard J. Barnet, *Real Security: Restoring American Power in a Dangerous Decade* (New York: Touchstone Books, 1981), p.36. "This is baloney," exclaims one high-level Pentagon official consulted by this writer. Whatever the case, Barnet's remarks should be tempered by the observation that it is a myth that "the Pentagon always exaggerates the threat." While there is obviously a strong tendency in this regard, the tendency in the mid-1960s, for instance, was to underestimate Soviet strategic capabilities.

demonstrations of military preparedness appear to these observers to offer concrete evidence of Soviet willingness to wage nuclear war.[72]

However, the Russians strongly disagree. They have suffered surprise attacks in the past. Of particular importance here was the Nazi invasion of June 1941. And Marxist ideology tells them that they will be attacked again.

The present Soviet military posture might be compared with the German predicament at the turn of the century. The German army, as Alfred Vagts says, was "non-aggressive before 1914 except in its strategy." That strategy was designed to cope with what the military tended to see as the nightmare situation of a two-front war which would require a quick and decisive victory on one front. As the General Staff declared in a confidential statement in 1902:[73]

We want to conquer nothing, we merely want to defend what we own. We shall probably never be attackers but rather always be the attacked. The necessary quick success can be brought us with certainty only by the offensive.

Commenting on this situation, the distinguished American student of the military, Samuel P. Huntington of Harvard University, had this to say: "The German military indeed manifested an almost pathological concern for national security. Far from advocating war, the military leaders generally viewed it as the last resort of policy and looked forward to it with gloomy forebodings and feverish preparations."[74]

Conclusions

The debate over the view that the Soviets think they can fight and win a nuclear war is still being waged. But this study has noted a number of important refinements in Soviet doctrine that are not generally taken into account when the issue is disputed today.

72 See Richard S. Soll, "The Soviet Union and Protracted Nuclear War," *Strategic Review* (Fall, 1980), pp.15-28.

73 Quoted in Alfred Vagts, "Land and Sea Power in the Second German Reich," *Journal of the American Military Institute,* Vol. 3 (Winter, 1939), p.213.

74 Samuel P. Huntington, *The Soldier and the State: The Theory and Politics of Civil-Military Relations* (Cambridge, Mass.: Harvard University Press, 1981), p.101.

The key to the whole affair seems to be the notion of a Soviet "pre-emptive strike." Many have misinterpreted this concept as a euphemism for a preventive or deliberate "first strike." Actually, the concept of a preventive strike is expressly rejected in Soviet military writings (even in the most confidential pages of the General Staff journal).

The Soviets have a special meaning when they talk about the concept of a pre-emptive (literally, "forestalling"; in Russian, *uprezhdaiushchyi*) strike. Implicitly, they mean – *if* the United States were to attack – denying the enemy the fruits of successful surprise by unleashing Soviet offensive forces before the Soviet Union is struck. Thus, for the Soviets preemption has clearly been a contingent concept, a way of acting in a given situation, rather than something to which their whole strategic doctrine and posture would be tailored.

If the Soviets incorporate a policy of pre-emption in their nuclear strategy, they do not appear at all optimistic about the outcome of a nuclear conflict. (This viewpoint is particularly true of the political leadership which controls nuclear release.) This changed attitude represents a major turn-around from earlier years when the strategic emphasis was clearly on victory in war and how to achieve it.

The new Soviet policy that there can be no victors in a nuclear war was reiterated by Mikhail Gorbachev at his summit meeting with President Reagan in November 1985. At that time, the Soviet news agency TASS was authorized to state the following: "A nuclear war is impermissible. There can be no victors. Mutual understanding on this question has been recorded on the summit level. Practical conclusions should be drawn from it."

Critics who scoff at such pronouncements fail often to take into account their impact on the internal dialogue in the Soviet Union. Previously, Soviet statements on the possibility of victory in a nuclear war were considered important, among other things, for maintaining the morale of the military and the civilian population. One Soviet military writer states this point explicitly:[75]

... the dubious theoretical concepts whose adherents deny the possibility of a victory in armed struggle involving the use of nuclear

75 Lt. Colonel N. Tabunov, "New Weapons and the Moral Factor," *Kommunist Vooruzhennykh sil,* No. 2 (January, 1969), pp. 25-32.

missiles are capable of sowing seeds of pessimism among the fighting men and weakening the combat abilities of the armed forces.

More importantly, perhaps, is the following concern: To deny the possibility of a Soviet victory in any war, including a nuclear war, is to challenge, even if not intentionally, Marxist-Leninist ideology and the "laws of history" which are expressed in that ideology.[76]

It is most unfortunate, but it has happened. Those who argue that the Soviets are convinced that they can fight and win a nuclear war have overlooked the obvious. As Gregory Flynn, who is Deputy Director of the Atlantic Institute in Paris, states: "The most important thing that we always overlook is that everything the Soviets have ever said or written has as its starting point that we started the war."[77] In short, the preponderance of evidence is that the Soviets just do not want to fight a war. However, the U.S.S.R. is obviously prepared to respond should the United States choose to initiate nuclear war.

76 See Robert L. Arnett, "Soviet Attitudes Towards Nuclear War: Do They Really Think They Can Win?" *Journal of Strategic Studies*, Vol. 2, No. 2 (1979), p.176. This article gives a good view of Soviet attitudes on nuclear war *before* Brezhnev's 1977 Tula speech.

77 Quoted in *Time*, January 2, 1984. Soviet sources seldom advance beyond the simple assertion that the sole purpose of the Soviet armed forces is to defend the territorial and political integrity of the Soviet Union against all adversaries and to protect the whole "socialist camp" from imperialist aggression. "Only occassionally do Soviet commentators write analytically about the political utility of military power," Robert F. Byrnes (editor) explains. When they do, "it is most often to criticize American concepts and policies." – See his *After Brezhnev* (Bloomington: Indiana University Press, 1983), p.166.

> Policy-making officials in the United States, the United Kingdom and other Western countries can often be heard saying that the best guarantee against a new war is the "balance of fear." Means of destruction and annihilation have become so powerful, argue the proponents of this view, that no state will run the risk of starting a nuclear war since it will inevitably sustain a retaliatory nuclear blow ...
> But to base the policy of states on a feeling of universal fear would be tantamount to keeping the world in a permanent state of feverish tension and eve-of-war hysteria. In such an atmosphere, each state would fear that the other side would lose its nerve and fire the first shot. Would not this create the temptation to prevent the opponent from gaining a lead?
>
> *Soviet Foreign Minister Andrei Gromyko,*
> *Speech to the U.N. General Assembly*
> *September 21, 1962.*

VI. SOVIET VIEWS OF DETERRENCE*

Many proponents of deterrence seem to assume that the Soviet leadership has accepted nuclear deterrence in the same way as the United States. But do the political and military leaders in the Soviet Union accept mutual deterrence? The continuing Soviet military buildup and the continued expressions in published Soviet military writings of a war-fighting doctrine have convinced some – and troubled others – as to Soviet views on this important – and controversial – question.

This chapter attempts to illuminate Soviet thinking on the subject of deterrence. In particular, it will consider the interrelationship of Soviet ideological beliefs, political imperatives and calculation, military views and doctrine and their reconciliation in Soviet policy.

* This chapter draws heavily on the contributions to the literature by John Erickson, Roman Kolkowicz and Benjamin Lambeth. Their research on the subject is highly regarded by students of Soviet nuclear strategy.

An American View of the Soviet Mind

American officials often describe deterrence as the means to influence the Soviet mentality. Thus, in formulating its definition of deterrence, the Joint Chiefs of Staff *Dictionary of Military and Associated Terms* (JCS Pub. 1) refers to "a state of mind." In view of this situation, one would think that if the United States were seriously attempting to implement a policy of deterrence *vis-à-vis* the Soviet Union, high Administration officials would pay close attention to the evidence of how Soviet leaders and military officials think on this crucial matter. While some obviously do, the following statement by former Defense Secretary Caspar Weinberger is not very encouraging: "It's very hard to get inside the Soviet mind. I have not attempted to do that."[1]

Of course, there is no such thing as the "Soviet mind," just as the notion of the "American mind" is a myth.[2] However, Soviet military and political leaders do hold certain strategic views, although differences of opinion obviously exist in the U.S.S.R. as they do anywhere else. In the past, public references by U.S. officials to "the Soviet mind" were frequently made for contriving the most simplistic and self-serving assumptions about Soviet intentions. Only recently are more and more observers coming belatedly to realize that Western leaders may have made a major mistake in assuming that Soviet officials think like them on the crucial issue of deterrence.

John Erickson, Director of Defense Studies at the University of Edinburgh, puts it this way: For a long time, the Americans took a "markedly condescending" attitude towards the Russians, whom they generally assumed thought as they do. This "disdain shown towards the quality (or lack of quality) in Soviet strategic thinking was a marked feature of the 1960s." It was "rooted in the supposed intellectual superiority of American sophistication in matters of 'de-

1 Quoted in *The Defense Monitor*, Vol. 12, No. 3 (1983), p. 5. General Andrew J. Goodpaster, President of the Institute for Defense Analyses, adds here: "the Soviet leaders, both military and civilian, are intelligent people, and ... we are not without a lot of evidence of how they view a great many of their problems, and how they act on them ..." Letter to this writer, June 22, 1984.

2 Professor Robert C. Tucker might disagree. See his book *The Soviet Political Mind: Studies in Stalinism and Post Stalin Change* (New York: W.W. Norton & Co., 1971).

terrent theory.'" And this encouraged "the notion that during the SALT I process the U.S. would perforce initiate the Soviet Union into the mysteries of deterrent theory and the complexities of nuclear war."[3]

To general discomfiture, "it soon became apparent that the U.S.S.R. need no tutoring in matters pertaining to war in general and nuclear war in particular." There was "a singular cogency to Soviet strategic thinking and ... [the] Russians did not necessarily think like Americans."[4] Apparently, the impression was not lasting. For Western specialists in strategic theory continued, in Professor Erickson's words, "to refine their concepts of deterrence into ever more complex (and arcane) theorems, a kind of nuclear metaphysics." And the Russians continued to work "much more closely within classically configured military concepts, inducing at once a much greater degree of military and political realism into what, in American parlance, is termed their 'mind-set.'"

To this day, Western preferences in deterrent thinking are frequently superimposed on the Soviet scene.[5] Many Americans not only continue to believe in their ethnocentric fashion that the Soviets think like they do in matters involving deterrence. But they even go so far as to interpret Soviet weapons programs in terms of a *Western* rationale for such programs.

The process of American misunderstanding of Soviet strategic thought is long established, although it is now subject to some limited change. But, as Professor John Erickson points out, it "had had damaging, not to say dangerous results ..."[6] At the very least it has had a deleterious effect on effective arms limitation and arms control. But more importantly, it has led many U.S. officials to exaggerate American "vulnerabilities" and distort Soviet intentions – all

3 John Erickson, "The Soviet View of Deterrence: A General Survey," *Survival*, Vol. 24, No. 6 (November-December, 1982), p.242.

4 *Ibid.*

5 Raymond L. Garthoff, a distinguished American scholar and former U.S. Ambassador to Bulgaria, maintains that the Soviets "seek to stabilize and maintain mutual deterrence." See his article "Mutual Deterrence, Parity and Strategic Arms Limitation in Soviet Policy," in Derek Leebaert (ed.), *Soviet Military Thinking* (London: Allen & Unwin, 1981), pp.92-124. For a critique of Garthoff's view, see Donald G. Brennan, "Commentary," *International Security* (Winter, 1978), pp.193-98.

6 John Erickson, *opus cit.*, p. 242.

within the framework of what Professor Erickson terms a sort of "strategic demonology."

Differing Conceptual Perceptions

To many Western strategic thinkers, Soviet concepts and doctrines of strategic and limited warfare appear strangely simplistic, anecdotal and "soft" in contrast to the "logically impeccable" and "tightly-reasoned" Western theories of deterrence and war-fighting strategies. Generally, they find Soviet military writings to be excessively politicized and historical as well as subordinated to the prevailing values and whims of political elites. In short, their "primitive" and "unsophisticated" approaches tend to exasperate many Western analysts.

Some of this exasperation is reflected in the commentary of the American editors of the classic Soviet work on *Military Strategy* which was put together by Marshal V.D. Sokolovsky. This volume represented the first major work on strategy by Soviet writers since the 1920s,[7] and it was taken by many in the West as defining the new consensus that had emerged through the post-Stalin debate on nuclear strategy and the more recent arguments with Nikita Khrushchev.[8] The editors of this work write: "Nowhere in this book, as in most Soviet literature as well, are there to be found signs of serious professional interests in concepts like controlled response and restrained nuclear targeting, which have been widely discussed in the West." The editors appear frustrated by the persistent "theme of automacity [sic] of global nuclear war," which they interpret not only as serving to reinforce the credibility of Soviet nuclear retaliation "but also to discourage the United States and its allies from entertaining ideas that ground rules of some sort might be adopted for limiting the destructiveness of a war, should one occur."[9]

7 A. Svechin's *Strategy* was published in 1926.

8 See Lawrence Freedman, *The Evolution of Nuclear Strategy* (New York: St. Martin's Press, 1983), p. 264.

9 The first edition of this book was translated with an introduction by Herbert Dinerstein, Leon Goure and Thomas Wolfe of the RAND Corporation. See *Soviet Military Strategy*, Rand edition (Santa Monica, Calif.: Rand Corporation, 1963), pp. 44-45.

This Western exasperation with Soviet strategic thinking is reciprocated. Many Soviet military and political writers dismiss much of Western strategic and limited-war theory as pretentious, pseudoscientific and even metaphysical.[10] The following statement by G.A. Arbatov, Director of the Institute of U.S.A. and Canadian Studies, is not atypical: "The idea of introducing rules and games and artifical restrictions by agreement seems illusory and untenable. It is difficult to visualize that a nuclear war, if unleashed, could be kept within the framework of rules and would not develop into an all-out war. In fact, such proposals are a demagogic trick designed to reassure public opinion."[11] The authoritative publication. *Marxism-Leninism on War and Army,* put it this way: It is a "cynical and deliberate falsehood" that "the prudence of the opponents will make it possible to coordinate their nuclear targets against which these weapons should be aimed."[12] A prominent (now deceased) Soviet military theorist, Major General Nikolai Talensky, summarizes a major Soviet school of thought: "When the security of a state is based on mutual deterrence with the aid of powerful nuclear weapons..., it is directly dependent on the goodwill and designs of the other side, which is a highly subjective and indefinite factor."[13]

10 Jonathan S. Lockwood, *The Soviet View of U.S. Strategic Doctrine* (New Brunswich, N.J.: Transaction Books, 1983).

11 G.A. Arbatov, *Problemy mira i sotsializma,* No. 2 (February, 1974), p.46.

12 *Marxism-Leninism on War and Army* (Moscow: Progress Publishers, 1972), p.100.

13 N. Talensky, "Anti-Missile Systems and Disarmament," in John Erickson (ed.), *The Military Technical Revolution: Its Impact on Strategy and Foreign Policy* (New York: Institute for the Study of the USSR, 1966), pp.225-27. The late Major General Nikolai Talensky was a former editor of the influential military theoretical journal, *Military Thought,* and an outspoken "revisionist." In 1965, he argued: "In our day there is no more dangerous illusion than the idea that thermonuclear war can still serve as an instrument of politics, that it its possible to achieve political aims by using nuclear weapons and still survive." Several Soviet military writers subsequently attacked General Talensky's position. They maintained that while his position was not theoretically wrong, it was practically dangerous because it undercut the rationale for maintaing large military forces. Today, a number of Soviet military writers have made a rather sharp turn toward accepting views like Talensky's which they previously criticized.

The Abstract Nature of Western Military Doctrines

Soviet analysts generally find Western strategic sophistries unacceptable on the grounds that politics is in effect subordinated to more narrow technological and bureaucratic imperatives than to the abstract notions of game theory and formal logic. As Marshal Grechko, the former Soviet Minister of Defense, wrote shortly before his death, the "bourgeois military theorists ... propagate a different viewpoint from that of communists as a mere armed clash between the two sides ..." In other words, "they emasculate the political content of the concept of war."[14]

One student of Soviet military policy, writing on the differing Soviet and American views of deterrence, notes that American strategic thinkers tend to emphasize the belief that "deterrence stability (hence U.S. and Allied security) is best served by a strategic environment of mutual vulnerability.[15] The Soviets reject 'mutual vulnerability' out of hand as an abdication of political responsibility." Benjamin S. Lambeth goes on to point out that Soviet analysts generally dismiss such common Western strategic notions as "demonstration attacks," "limited nuclear operations" and slow-motion "counterforce duels." Soviet military writers, he says, tend to treat such American conceptualizations of strategic issues "with alternating bemusement, perplexity and sarcasm."[16]

The Status Quo Nature of Deterrence Theory

A major problem the Soviets have with Western deterrence strategies is that they tend to reinforce the territorial *status quo*. As Alexander George and Richard Smoke have written: "Deterrence is a policy which, if it succeeds, can only frustrate an opponent who aspires to changing the international status-quo."[17] As the leader-

14 A.A. Grechko, *The Armed Forces of the Soviet Union* (Moscow: Progress Publishers, 1977).

15 This view changed as a result of President Regan's March 1983 speech on SDI.

16 Benjamin S. Lambeth, "The Political Potential of Soviet Equivalence," *International Security* (Fall, 1979), p. 27.

17 Alexander George *et al.*, *Deterrence in American Foreign Policy* (New York: Columbia University Press, 1974), p. 5.

ship of the Soviet Union, a quasi-revolutionary power, sees things, the *status quo* reflects the interests of the imperialistic West. Thus, it should come as little surprise that the Russians should find pernicious the Western attempt to impose its own rules of the political and strategic game upon socialist countries and on countries in the Third World that are trying to emancipate themselves from colonial or imperialistic shackles.

A recent Rand study has observed that the Soviets pay "no homage whatsoever to the abstract concept of stability" assumed in Western strategic thought under the concept of a *mutual* assured destruction relationship.[18] Other studies have revealed likewise that, generally speaking, the concepts of "equivalence" and "balance" are seen as "unnatural" by the Soviets because they imply "the enshrinement of the status quo, something alien to every known tenet of Soviet political, ideological and historical doctrine."[19] Nowhere in the public record of official Soviet utterances is there any indication that the Soviet leadership has endorsed "essential equivalence" – at least as it is understood by U.S. officials – as the desired endpoint of the SALT process or of Soviet weapons acquisition.

The preferred Soviet formulation is "equal security." This is a far more ambiguous and subjective concept that admits considerably broader and more ambitious definitions of Soviet force requirements than faithful adherence to the more restrictive "essential equivalence" construct allows.[20] The Soviets explicitly disavow any intention to seek "superiority" over the United States.[21] But they

18 Jack Snyder, *The Soviet Strategic Culture: Implications for Limited Nuclear Operations* (Santa Monica, Calif.: Rand Corporation, 1977), p. 18.

19 Benjamin S. Lambeth, *opus cit.,* p. 28.

20 One of the more thoughtful Soviet writers on military affairs, retired Army Colonel V.M. Kulish, has stated that the ultimate measure of strategic adequacy "is the result of a complicated opposition of forces which is impossible to express in terms of simple qualitative indices, even though it may prove impossible to analyze the balance of forces in the absense of such indices." See his *Military Force and International Relations* (Moscow: Izdatel'stvo Mezhdunarodyne Otnosheniia, 1972), p. 29.
One critic would point out here: "Remember that political analyses published in the Soviet Union are never 'value free' research efforts aimed at discovering the 'truth.' Rather, they are always positions intimately related to matters of policy. They are designed more to win debates and bolster policy preferences than to set forth individual perceptions."

21 The Reagan Administration appears to believe that the Soviet leadership is inex-

have made it clear in the context of SALT and elsewhere that they believe that their unique "geo-political problems" (namely China and Western Europe) entitle them to compensating forces over and beyond those required for maintaining just "equal security" with the United States.[22] For obvious reasons, such intimations have failed to elicit much sympathy in official Western circles. But they nevertheless do indicate that to Soviet policy makers, acceptable security genuinely entails not merely "equivalence" with the United States, but a significant *de facto* margin of strategic advantage.[23]

orably committed to the permanent achievement of strategic superiority over the United States. In fact, Ronald Reagan stated publicly that "On balance, the Soviet Union does have a definite margin of superiority." However, there is good reason to believe that while the Soviets find themselves comfortably superior to the United States in some categories of power they find themselves distressingly inferior in others. Given the considerable economic resources, technological capabilities and political determination possessed by the U.S. to neutralize any Soviet attempt to acquire a posture of manifest strategic advantage, there is ample cause to doubt whether the Soviet leadership believes it is able to achieve a goal of permanent strategic authority. For an analysis of Soviet respect for American capabilities here see Morton Schwartz, *Soviet Perceptions of the United States* (Berkeley: University of California Press, 1978), p. 165.

22 One U.S. official observes here: "The Soviet claim for equal security against all perceived adversaries combined means they are superior to each one individually." Dimitri K. Simes points out: "Soviet perceptions of their legitimate defense needs may well differ from American views." Many Soviet officials believe that a superpower has and should have the right to act in areas of its perceived national interest. Generally, these officials express a willingness to recognize that the U.S. has this right, but they feel that the United States is unwilling to reciprocate.

The prominent "Americanologist" Georgi Arbatov has elaborated on this point: the arguments about what defense needs are legitimate in another country are dubious. No country has the moral or political right to determine what another country's defense needs really are. Each country must do this for itself. The Soviet Union is forced to think seriously about its security and defense in order to meet the challenge by the military potential of the United States and Western Europe and ... China ... It would be interesting to see how those who criticize the Soviet Union would talk about legitimate defense needs if they were in this country's position.

Quoted in Burns H. Weston (ed.), *Towards Nuclear Disarmament and Global Security: A Search for Alternatives* (Boulder, Colo.: Westview Press, 1984), p. 8.

23 Benjamin S. Lambeth, "The Political Potential of Soviet Equivalence," *International Security*, (Fall, 1979), p. 26. General Goodpaster: "I believe there is evident in Soviet action a desire for stable security in the sense of avoiding nuclear war as well as nuclear disadvantage in the arms race. At the same time, there is no evidence of which I am aware to suggest that they would not be happy to enjoy strategic superiority. Next, although there are numerous Soviet statements expressing views on the inexorability of escalation from any initial nuclear ex-

Soviet acceptance of the Anti-Ballistic Missile Treaty in 1972 is frequently cited as testimony to some acceptance of the principle of stability governing strategic behavior. However, it is much more probable that the agreement was attractive to the Soviet leadership because superior American ABM technology, plus superior U.S. ABM penetrating technology, would have given the United States a major advantage during the mid to late 1970s. Thus, from the Soviet viewpoint, the 1972 ABM accord was most likely seen as "stabilizing" a process of strategic catchup against a serious risk of reversal. But it did not necessarily imply acceptance of the American principle of stability.[24]

For a long time U.S. strategic thinkers have been relatively sensitive to the potential of technology jeopardizing specific deterrent formulae for achieving stability. The Soviets, too, have generally been sensitive to destabilizing technologies. However, they tend to accept the destabilizing dynamism of technology as an intrinsic aspect of the strategic dialectic. For them, the underlying engine of this dialectic is a political competition not susceptible to stabilization.

The Self-Constrained Nature of Western Doctrine of War

Soviet military analysts are especially critical of Western claims concerning the ability to control, limit and "fine tune" the application of force inherent in the "counterforce" deterrent strategy. In fact, they seriously question the whole idea of limited nuclear war. As Jack Snyder points out: "If there is little convergence in Soviet and American writing on deterrence, there is even less complementarity in their standards on limited nuclear war.[25]

change, however limited, to all-out nuclear war, the evidence is by no means conclusive as to just what they think in this regard or just what they would do. There is a strong strain of Soviet concern over the damage to the Soviet people and territory that would occur as a result of such escalation." Letter, June 22, 1984.

24 See Derek Leebaert (ed.), *Soviet Military Thinking* (London: Allen & Unwin, 1981). pp. 58-59.

25 Jack Snyder, *opus cit.,* p. 19.

Generally, Soviet analysts disbelieve claims to omniscience, omnipotence and ubiquity of cool reason and rationality that are implicit in many Western studies on limited war.[26] As one military publication concludes: "To lull the vigilance of the peoples, the U.S. militarists are discussing the possibility of limiting nuclear war."[27] Soviet writers are skeptical of the notion that prudent opponents will coordinate their nuclear strikes, thus keeping material losses and human suffering at a minimum. For they would have to "rely on the chance that the aggressors will be prudent and will impose certain limits on the use of nuclear weapons."[28]

In the writings of Western strategic theorists, the "counterforce" strategy presupposes certain types of cooperation, coordination and self-denial by the opposing sides. Generally, the Soviets find curious and unrealistic the notion that a nuclear war could remain contained, that it would resist pressures to escalate and that it would come to a conclusion through Schelling's idea of "intra-war bargaining" or compellance, which underpins much of the American writing on limited nuclear war. A survey of official Soviet pronouncements and writings on the "controllability" of escalation and the possibility of limitation in nuclear conflict continues to indicate "no Soviet acceptance of restraint once that threshold has been crossed."[29]

Most importantly from the Soviet perspective, American deterrence doctrine with its increased emphasis on nuclear warfighting is designed to give legitimacy to nuclear war. By making limited nuclear war more feasible, U.S. policy has the effect of making it "more acceptable." Assessing the gist of U.S. deterrent doctrine, General Secretary Leonid Brezhnev stated in 1980 that it "actually boils down to making the very idea of nuclear war more acceptable, as it were, to public opinion."[30]

Professor Henry Trofimenko, Head of a Department at the Institute of U.S.A. and Canadian Studies, Academy of Sciences of the

26 Roman Kolkowicz, "U.S. and Soviet Approaches to Military Strategy: Theory vs. Experience," *Orbis* (Summer, 1981), p. 314.

27 *Marxism-Leninism on War and Army* (Moscow: Progress Publishers, 1972), p. 99.

28 *Ibid.,* p. 100.

29 Benjamin S. Lambeth, *Selective Nuclear Operations and Soviet Strategy* (Santa Monica, Calif.: Rand Corporation, 1975).

30 *Pravda,* August 30, 1980.

U.S.S.R., questions the practice of American leaders of ascribing counterforce intentions to the Soviet Union. He says this "now definitely appears to have been a gimmick used by the U.S. strategists to prepare an American public for the announcement of Washington's own counterforce strategy." In this respect, "the American campaign to call attention to the alleged counterforce threat" is nothing more than a "public relations smokescreen." Each time the U.S. Defense Department "intends to strengthen a new component of its forces, or to introduce a new strategy," he says, "it invariably sets about to 'prove' that 'the Soviets have already acquired such a capability,' and hence, that the United States must follow suit ..."[31]

The Soviet Union, Professor Trofimenko argues, "has emphasized repeatedly that it does not advocate [a] counterforce strategy, as it does not support the first-strike concept."[32] It is "indisputable that [a] counterforce strategy – a strategy of strikes against bomber and submarine bases and against military command and control centers – is an offensive, aggressive strategy," he insists. "All of the so-called Soviet counterforce strategies that are discussed in the U.S. press are strategies imputed to the Soviet Union by American theoreticians who fraudulently like to play out their own counterforce war scenarios on the premise of a 'Soviet attack against the U.S.A.'" This scheme "makes them look more innocent, while, at the same time, they manage to frighten the public at large into loosening their purse-strings for the sake of a new offensive arms buildup."

Trofimenko argues that certain U.S. strategists "ascribe to the Soviet Union the intention to deal the first strike and picture the

31 Henry A. Trofimenko, "Counterforce: Illusion of a Panacea," *International Security*, Vol. 5, (Spring, 1981), pp.28-49. If counterforce is not the official *policy* of the Soviet Union, as many U.S. officials maintain, it is nevertheless true that the number of strategic warheads on each side far exceeds the number of significant non-military targets, so that the majority of weapons can be assumed to be aimed at military (i.e., counterforce) targets.

32 Here Trofimenko cites the Declaration adopted by the Summit Anniversary Conference of the Political Consultative Committee of the Warsaw Treaty Member States, which was held in Warsaw in May, 1980. The member states solemnly reaffirmed that they "have never sought and will never seek military supremacy; they have invariably declared for military equivalence being ensured at increasingly lower levels, for lessening and ending military confrontation in Europe. We do not have, never had and will not have a different strategic doctrine, but a defensive one; we did not and will not have any intention to create a first nuclear strike potential." (*Pravda*, May 16, 1980.)

U.S. *counterforce* strike as merely 'retaliatory.'"[33] However, he points out that "if the bulk of the Soviet strategic forces will be used already in the first strike what is the United States planning to retaliate against?"

"Obviously," Soviet strategic forces "also have components capable of precision strikes against hardened point targets," Trofimenko admits. But "the introduction of such systems into the arsenals of nuclear power," he claims, "is an inevitable result of qualitative improvements in strategic armaments ..."[34]

If Soviet writers like Trofimenko would have Americans take at face value their protestations of innocence for their share of responsibility for the arms race and the deterioration of detente, it is nevertheless true that the Soviet leadership rejects the notion of "limited" nuclear war that is implied in the counterforce deterrent strategy. To a large extent, the Soviet position on this controversial matter is based on the political idea that political objectives – not military goals or the performance of certain weapons systems – determine the scope of war.[35] In addition, the Soviets are skeptical of the kind of American strategic thinking that lies behind the so-called "limited" nuclear war. The Soviets point out that whatever the technical aspects of the weapons involved, American objectives are not unlimited. In fact, the Soviets see the U.S. as employing strategies such as "escalation dominance" in order to maximize "some or other – real or only apparent" – American edge over the U.S.S.R. So no nuclear war operation could be limited in this sense.

33 John Spanier, a former U.S. Foreign Service Officer, writes in his book: "The Soviet Union has thus been building a first-strike or counterforce capability, rather than a second-strike, or retaliatory, counter-city (or economy) force. Its leaders had adopted a 'war-fighting' strategy while the United States was thinking only of deterrence. The result is that, instead of war being 'unthinkable,' as Americans proclaimed, it has become 'thinkable' and will be a genuine option for Soviet policy makers by the middle 1980s." See his *Games Nations Play,* 4th ed. (New York: Holt, Rinehart & Winston, 1983), p.191.

34 Henry Trofimenko, *opus cit.,* p.30.

35 Roman Kolkowicz, *opus cit.,* p.314.

The Correlation of Forces versus the Balance of Power

In the United States and most of the West international relations are seen in the context of the central notion of a "balance of power." To be sure, this core concept of interstate behavior is often disparaged by many academics.[36] But as Henry Kissinger's memoirs reveal, for all its obvious problems it is still generally adhered to by U.S. statesmen. As John Spanier writes, a balance of power is seen as desirable because it is "most likely to deter an attack." By contrast, "possession of disproportionate power might tempt a state to undertake aggression by making it far less costly to gain a predominant position and impose its will upon other states."[37]

If the notion of a power balance underlies much of deterrence thinking in the West, this is not the case in the Soviet Union. There a more subtle concept, known as the *correlation of forces,* acts as the driving force behind much of contemporary Soviet analysis of international affairs. From the perspective of the Kremlin, this idea serves as a tool for measuring the relative capabilities of competing forces or groups of forces. Essentially, it is a multifaceted concept. Soviet sources specifically cite numerous socioeconomic, political, ideological, and military factors when the "international correlation of forces" is debated. But other quantitative and qualitative factors are also involved.[38]

Generally, the Soviet leadership undertakes its assessment of the correlation of forces on at least three different levels. These include (1) the global relationship between the capitalist and socialist countries; (2) regional relationships between movements, alliances or other groups of states; and (3) specific relationships between individual countries. Usually when Soviet officials declare that the

36 As Kenneth N. Waltz writes, the "balance of power is the hoariest concept in the field of international relations. Elaborated in a variety of analyses and loaded with different meanings, it has often been praised or condemned, but has seldom been wholly rejected." See his "International Structure, National Force, and the Balance of World Power," *Journal of World Affairs,* Vol. 21, No. 2 (1967), pp.215-231.

37 John Spanier, *American Foreign Policy Since World War II,* 9th ed. (New York: Holt, Rinehart and Winston, 1983), p.2.

38 For a detailed discussion of the correlation of forces see Michael J. Deane, "The Soviet Assessment of the 'Correlation of World Forces': Implications for American Foreign Policy," *Orbis* (Fall, 1976), pp.625-36.

correlation of forces is shifting in favor of the socialist states, they are stating their view of the long-term trend of the aggregate of global quantitative and qualitative factors. As the Soviets see things, national or regional correlations may *temporarily* move against the Marxist-Leninist tide. However, the overall correlation of forces cannot. This is taken as an article of faith in the U.S.S.R.

Many Soviet commentators maintain that a significant shift in the correlation of forces took place during the Brezhnev era (1964-1982). In the main this shift is linked to the growth of Soviet military capabilities, especially the attainment of strategic nuclear parity with the U.S. According to this view, the attainment by the Soviet Union of strategic parity forced the United States leadership to accept the U.S.S.R. as its military equal. Consequently, these Soviet spokesmen contend that intersystemic competition shifted from the military to socioeconomic, political and ideological planes.

As Brezhnev's close associate – and former General Secretary – Konstantin Chernenko recently put it: "the times of imperialism's omnipotence in international relations, when it could unceremoniously and with impunity throw its weight around in the world ... have receded irretrievably."[39] As "imperialism" has been tamed, the sense of threat and alienation experienced for decades by the Soviet leadership has lessened somewhat.

From the Soviet perspective, public acknowledgment by the United States of the existence of strategic parity and American recognition of the constraining influence exercised by parity on U.S. foreign policy are as important as parity itself. As G.A. Arbatov, the head of the Institute of the United States and Canada in the Soviet Union, wrote as early as 1972: only in conditions of nuclear parity will American policymakers be compelled to "adapt to reality" and curb their instinctive resort to military force.[40]

If the Soviets realize that they are no longer number two in the world, this does not mean that they subscribe to the "parity principle" either as a touchstone of their weapons acquisition program or

39 Konstantin Chernenko, "Constantly Strengthening the Ties with the Masses," *Sovetskaia Moldaviia,* February 27, 1979, pp.1-3, in Foreign Broadcast Information Service, *Daily Report: Soviet Union,* Supplement, March 20, 1979, p.71.

40 G.A. Arbatov, "Sobytie Vazhnogo mezhdunarodnogo znacheniya" ("An Event of Important International Significance"), *SSHA,* No. 8, August, 1972, pp.3-12.

as a preferred basis for nuclear deterrence. As Benjamin S. Lambeth wrote recently: For the Soviets, "parity is less an ultimate goal than a transitory and permissive springboard for testing Western resolve and pursuing whatever additional accretions of strategic power the structures of SALT and American tolerance will allow."[41]

In the view of some Western analysts, the shift in what the Soviets term the correlation of forces has ideological consequences. Most importantly, it is said to have "lessened" the relevance of Leninism and the "Bolshevik" image of the world."[42] Traditionally, many students of Soviet behavior have operated on the assumption that "the views of the Soviet leaders are so rooted in an unchanging ideology and 'national character' that they are entirely resistant to change.[43] But as important studies by William Zimmerman[44] and Jan Triska and David Finley[45] have documented in detail, the *Weltanschauungen* of Soviet officials – particularly those who have carried major occupational responsibilities for the conduct of foreign policy – have been modified. As Zimmerman concludes from his ten-year study of Soviet scholars' work in the major foreign policy institutes, these experts "no longer let Lenin do their thinking," *though they continue to use Lenin to legitimize their arguments.*[46]

41 Benjamin S. Lambeth, "The Political Potential of Soviet Equivalence," *International Security* (Fall, 1979), p.25.

42 See Robert H. Donaldson, "Soviet Conceptions of 'Security,'" in Burns H. Weston (ed.), *Toward Nuclear Disarmament and Global Security: A Search for Alternatives* (Boulder, Colo.: Westview Press, 1984), p.293.

43 See for instance Nathan Leites, *A Study of Bolshevism,* pp.25, 29 and Richard Pipes, "Detente: Moscow's View" in Pipes (ed.), *Soviet Strategy in Europe.*

44 William Zimmermann, *Soviet Perspectives on International Relations, 1956-1967.*

45 Jan Triska and David Finley, *Soviet Foreign Policy,* especially Chapters 3-4.

46 William Zimmerman, *opus cit.,* p.287.
"It is a very tricky thing," states Ambassador Martin Hillenbrand, "to calculate the role of Marxist-Leninist ideology in Soviet strategic thinking, or to factor in the Soviet proclivity for disinformation in writings directed to the West. Nor does there seem to be much coherence in what one can describe as Soviet views on deterrence and their actual deployment of weapons. The Soviets are surely not so unsophisticated as to suppose that the kinds of weapons they have deployed are not liable to be taken by the U.S. as related to intentions, no matter how much they protest to the contrary. Both sides protest that they have not war-initiating intentions with respect to the other, but neither side apparently believes this in the case of the putative opponent."

Soviet Emphasis on Deterrence by Denial

Theorists have explained the general American deterrence doctrine in an oversimplified way as *deterrence by punishment.* In Soviet eyes, it reflects an offensive posture and commitment that is both military and political. Moreover, it is directly related to "escalation dominance," which relies on U.S. military superiority. Thus, as the Soviets see it, the U.S.S.R. is to be "deterred" into accepting a situation that basically implies political and global dominance by the United States.

If the American deterrence posture may be explained as deterrence by punishment, by way of contrast the Soviet position is sometimes explained as *deterrence by denial.*[47] Obviously, this is a somewhat oversimplified description. But it does help to distinguish the two policies.[48]

Deterrence by denial is essentially the policy of traditional defense. It is based on the ability of the defender to convince a potential aggressor that his attack will be met by a military response sufficient to prevent him from gaining his objectives. By way of contrast, deterrence by punishment, which hopes to influence an adversary's estimate of possible costs, does not postulate a direct link between the original defense and the response, and might have little effect on his chances for territorial gain.[49]

It should be noted that the terminology used in the Soviet Union to discuss "deterrence" tends to reflect this dichotomy. Thus, in the 1960s and at present, the Western deterrent concept has been defined as *ustrashenie,* which has a clear hint of threatening intimidation. On the other hand, the Soviet stance has been indicated by the word *sderzhivanie,* which conveys a sense of con-

47 U.S. Secretary of Defense Caspar Weinberger's latest posture statements may be taken as an indication that the U!S. is seriously considering moving in this direction.

48 General Goodpaster states here: "Denial of gain has for a long time been an important part of my own view regarding deterrence, and I believe I have seen it reflected (as your chapter indicates) on the Soviet side ... I would add a reminder, as I put it, that the Soviets seek the fruits of war without the costs of war." Letter, June 22, 1984.

49 For more on this distinction see Glenn Snyder, *Deterrence and Defense* (Princeton: Princeton University Press, 1961).

straining a foe. Frequently, the word "defense" (*oborona*) is used in the context of official Soviet "deterrent" doctrine. On the face of it, this may seem like mere semantic hair-splitting, but this is not the case at all.[50]

Some authorities have explained the origins of the Soviet view of deterrence on the basis of its experience during the Great Patriotic War (World War II). As a result of the near catastrophe of June 1941, when German armies steamrolled their way across the Soviet Union to the outskirts of Moscow in *Blitzkrieg* fashion, the Soviet leadership has been little inclined to countenance a deterrent strategy which tolerates the absorption of any initial strike. Never again will the Soviet leadership endorse a policy which commits the Soviet Union to remaining inert and then lashing out in punitive response. For such a policy contradicts this historical lesson which remains indelibly marked on the minds of the aged Politburo leadership.

In light of the experience gained in the Second World War, it should not be surprising to learn that the Soviet leadership puts a premium on defense in the first instance. Thus Soviet defense and "deterrence" go hand in hand.[51]

50 Here Professor John Erickson observes:
"Deterrence as a concept has never held much appeal for the Soviet military: the terms *ustrashenie* and *sderzhivanie* are rarely used, while *oborona* (defense) increasingly denotes the 'deterrent concept' ... From the outset the Soviet military never accepted the nuclear weapons as an absolute ..."
See his "the Chimera of Mutual Deterrence," *Strategic Review* (Spring, 1978), p.14. If Soviet perceptions can be gauged from public indications, it would seem that the Soviets do not differentiate "deterrence" from "compellance" as sharply as American theorists do. See Henry Trofimenko, *Changing Attitudes toward Deterrence* (Los Angeles: UCLA Center for International and Strategic Affairs, 1980).

51 Some Western military strategists have drawn the wrong conclusion from the tremendous Soviet losses in World War II – approximately 7.5 million military personnel and some 12.5. million civilian dead. As Albert Wohlstetter has written: "Russian casualties in World War II were more than 20 million. Yet Russia recovered extremely well from this catastrophe. There are several quite plausible circumstances in the future when the Russians might be quite confident of being able to limit damage to considerably less than this number ..." See his "The Delicate Balance of Terror," *Foreign Affairs*, Vol. 37, No. 2 (January, 1959). General Thomas S. Power, former Commander of the U.S. Strategic Air Command, puts it more bluntly: "With such grisly tradition and shocking record in the massacre of their own people, the Soviets cannot be expected to let the risk of even millions of Russian lives deter them from starting a nuclear war ..." See his *Design for Survival* (New York: Coward-McCann, 1964), p.111.

As the Soviet leadership generally sees it, the massive Soviet defense buildup – both active and passive – needs little or no advertising. But it, of course, has been the cause of much misgiving and misunderstanding. Paradoxically, the Soviet interest in taking steps to protect itself (including more than just a passing interest in civil defense planning) has fueled American apprehension that the Soviets were determined to develop a first-strike capability. For their part, many Soviet officials saw in the lack of a defense program in the United States more than just a hint that U.S. policy was basically one that emphasized pre-emptive and even first-strike attack, which would deliver a paralyzing blow that would perforce eliminate any retaliation.

The Soviets are, of course, prepared to wage nuclear war. Indeed, the Soviet leadership regards the capability to wage nuclear war as a crucial element of a visible "deterrent." However, "this does *not* indicate any preference for, or inclination towards, regarding nuclear war as a rational instrument of policy." Even more, Soviet deterrent policies "are designed to minimize the incentives for attacking the USSR and, above all, are aimed at preventing the outbreak of hostilities, 'denial' in an absolute sense."[52]

Thus Soviet "deterrence" rests on Soviet capabilities rather than on enemy rationality or goodwill. It relies on retaining the initiative and is skeptical of scenarios that are "managed," especially when the crisis is, or could be, apocalyptic. In this way, the Soviets display a commitment to "war-denial" in their deterrence policy.

The Soviet concept of deterrence by denial serves several theoretical purposes. First, it would prevent the U.S. from actually initiating hostilities. Second, it would reduce the prospect of the United States making military gains at the expense of the Soviet Union and its allies. (This latter objective may be partly responsible for the Soviet Union's determination to play a global role.) Third, it would ensure the survival of the Soviet system. Finally, through the develop-

52 John Erickson, *opus cit.,* p. 245. Ambassador Hillenbrand states here: "I think you sometimes engage in hairsplitting, for example where you try to dinstinguish between the essence of Soviet deterrence and the assumption of enemy rationality. Whether or not the Soviet view of deterrence be called 'deterrence by denial' as dinstinguished from 'deterrence by punishment,' the underlying assumption must still be of rationality or the whole concept of deterrence collapses." Letter, June 4, 1984.

ment of a war-fighting capability it would minimize the incentives for attacking the Soviet Union by guaranteeing a substantial counterstrike.

In summary then, Soviet "deterrence" doctrine may be seen in a positive, active cast. The essence of the policy is not the avoidance of war so much as *preventing it from happening in the first place.* Here the impressive military capability of the U.S.S.R. plays a prominent role. Soviet "deterrence" then is supposed to restrain the imperialists.[53]

The Notion of Mutuality

The notion of "mutuality" or "reciprocity" is very much a part of the American nuclear deterrent doctrine. However, from the Soviet point of view there are some fundamental problems with this concept. To be sure, in one sense there is mutuality of deterrence. That is, Soviet officials – like their American counterparts – recognize that both sides have an overwhelming capability to inflict "unacceptable damage" on each other if nuclear war were initiated. But this realization of political reality should not be construed as the Soviets "accepting the posture of hostage and thus denying any initiative to the Soviet Union ..."[54]

In general, a natural and logical skepticism pervades the Soviet view of MAD. This is partly because the strategy runs counter to the Soviet idea of avoiding having to rely on a potential adversary for Soviet security. But more importantly, Soviet skepticism is due to the fact that they see the notion of mutuality, as it is embodied in "assured destruction" (MAD), as something which is nothing more than a front for what is viewed essentially as an American "counterforce" – and pre-emptive strike – policy.[55]

The reasoning behind Soviet suspicions of the alleged pre-emp-

53 As G.A. Arbatov, a leading Soviet commentator stated in 1974, "the concept of deterrence itself cannot be defended – it is a concept of 'peace built on terror,' which will always be an unstable and a bad peace." See his "The Impasses of the Policy of Force," *Problemy Mira i Sotsializma,* No. 2 (February, 1974).

54 John Erickson, *opus cit.,* p.247.

55 It should be noted here that MAD rests on counter*value* capabilities.

tive nature of the present U.S. counterforce strategy has been stated authoritatively by Major General R. Simonyan, Doctor of Military Science. He observed just a few years ago:[56]

Indeed, a power which sets itself the aim of destroying the 'potential enemy's' [strategic] military facilities must [sic] be the first to deliver a strike, because otherwise its nuclear charges will land on empty missile launch silos and airfields. (emphasis added)

Here the Soviets point to the obvious discrepancy between the *declaratory* policy of the United States, which for a long time was "mutual assured destruction" (MAD), and its *action* policy, which was much different. From the Soviet vantage point, the latter policy was designed to increase its counterforce capabilities. Hence the MX missile program, the Trident submarine program and improvements in Western forward based systems (FBS). Generally, the Soviets see all of these developments as calculated to "outflank" the SALT agreements.

The following statement, penned almost more than ten years ago by two Soviet military writers, provides some insight into how certain military analysts in the U.S.S.R. view nuclear deterrence:[57]

Of course, the concept of 'nuclear deterrence,' which presupposed the existence of enormous nuclear forces capable of 'assured destruction' is not an ideal solution to the problem of peace and the prevention of nuclear conflict.

The authors of the above statement reject such ideas as "acceptable" limited nuclear options, "selective targeting" concepts and the like, which are combined in the U.S. counterforce policy. They maintain that "Preventing nuclear war in any of its forms, large or small, and the limitation of the arms race, are the central problems of Soviet-American relations."[58]

56 R. Simonyan, "In Search of a New Strategy," *Krasnaya zvezda,* March 19, 1979.

57 Lt. General M.A. Mil'shtein and Colonel L.S. Semeyko, "The Problem of the Inadmissibility of a Nuclear Conflict (on New Approaches in the United States)," *SSHA,* No. 11 (November, 1974), p. 4.

58 *Ibid.,* p. 9. See also Colonel D. Proektor, "Two Approaches to Military Policy," *Novoye vremya,* No. 48 (November, 1978). General Goodpaster adds: "I too feel there is evidence to support the Soviet desire to prevent nuclear war. I would add there is also evidence that they want a free hand to pursue adventures in other areas, and to pursue their hostility to Western political-socio-economic systems while the use of nuclear weapons is avoided, or successfully deterred. Somewhere during the past years, the concepts of deterrence advanced by U.S.

Soviet View of Pershing II and Cruise Missile Deployment

A number of discussions in the official Soviet media since these authors wrote have reflected disappointment and concern with the U.S. deterrent position and its increased emphasis on nuclear war fighting. As Secretary General Leonid Brezhnev put it in a speech in May 1977:[59]

I am convinced that not a single statesman, or public figure, or thinking person can avoid his share of responsibility in the struggle against the threat of war, for this means responsibility for the very future of mankind itself. I shall not conceal the fact that our concern over the continuing arms race, including the strategic arms race, has grown in connection with the positions adopted in these matters by the new American administration.

Brezhnev's remarks and other more recent statements by Soviet military and other leaders indicate a growing Soviet concern over increased U.S. counterforce capabilities but also as to *why* this continued increase in capabilities is being sought. As Raymond L. Garthoff, a senior fellow at the Brookings Institution and a noted expert on Soviet military policy writes, "To be sure, some of these expressions of concern doubtless serve other purposes, such as the argument to support requested Soviet military programs. But many have the ring of sincerity about them and many cite incontrovertible evidence to support their arguments on capabilities ..."[60]

In the Soviet perception, the United States has continued, SALT and detente notwithstanding, to seek military superiority. Thus, the NATO two-track deployment decision of December 1979 is viewed by Soviet military analysts as another step in this direction. Of course, these officials also see this move as an attempt to tie NATO even more closely into American strategic nuclear planning, while deflecting or diverting Soviet counteraction towards Europe, – rather than against the United States itself.

writers (although not, however, the programs of actual practitioners) seem to have become unduly narrow and arcane." Letter, June 22, 1984.

59 L.I. Brezhnev, *Radio Moscow,* May 29, 1977.

60 Raymond L. Garthoff, "Mutual Deterrence, Parity and Strategic Arms Limitation in Soviet Policy," in Derek Leebaert (ed.), *Soviet Military Thinking* (London: Allen & Unwin, 1981), p.111.

The Soviet objection to this new capability of the NATO allies to strike targets deep inside the Soviet Union is not merely propaganda. It reflects "a real perception and concern," according to Raymond L. Garthoff.[61] We shall cite but one remark from General of the Army Sergei Akhromeyev, who in September 1984[62] was promoted to Chief of Staff of the Soviet armed forces:[63]

The Soviet Union is not setting for itself the task of striving for military superiority over the United States, but it cannot remain indifferent to the increase in US military potential and cannot permit the existing parity of forces to be upset.

Akhromeyev notes that the Pershing II and theater cruise missiles were being deployed so as to make it possible "to destroy targets over a considerable part of Soviet territory – up to the Volga ... (Thus the) Soviet Union must regard them as weapons of strategic significance." Finally, he says, such "actions automatically call for reflection as to whether they accord with the aims of the negotiations and agreements on limiting strategic offensive arms."[64]

In this context, the newly deployed intermediate-range-nuclear Pershing II is regarded as a pre-emptive, counterforce weapon.[65] The Soviets note that it substantially surpasses the capabilities of the Pershing I and is capable of destroying not only ICBM sites but also centers of command and control. However, what disturbs Soviet officials most is the short flight time of the missile which nulli-

61 Raymond L. Garthoff, "Mutual Deterrence, Parity and Strategic Arms Limitation in Soviet Policy," in Derek Leebaert (ed.), *Soviet Military Thinking* (London: Allen & Unwin, 1981), p. 118.

62 Marshal Akhromeyev, who had succeeded Ogarkov as Chief of the General Staff, was not appointed a First Deputy Defense Minister as was previously the custom. This post was awarded to the Supreme Commander of Land Forces, Marshal Petrov, who had advocated views differing from Ogarkov's on the way the armed forces were to be organized.

63 Sergei F. Akhromeyev, "Dangerous US Aspirations to Nuclear Supremacy, "*Horizont* (East Germany), No. 3, January, 1980, p. 3. This article is based upon a *Novosti* interview which was originally issued on December 24, 1979 in Moscow.

64 *Ibid.* See also G. Dadyants, "Operation Pershing II," *Sotsialisticheskaya industriya,* October 19, 1979; Lt. General N.F. Chervov and V. Zagladin on *Radio Moscow,* Domestic Service, October 20, 1979; and Colonel L. Semeyko, "Where 'Eurostrategy' is Aiming," *Krasnaya Zvezda,* October 28, 1979.

65 From the U.S. point of view the Pershing II is not viewed as a pre-emptive counterforce weapon. As one U.S. official points out: "Only if the Pershing II were in sufficient numbers to destroy all Soviet means of retaliation; it is not and so it would be foolish for NATO to use it pre-emptively."

fies any Soviet resort to launch on warning or even launch under attack.

Thus the Pershing II, together with the ground-launched cruise missiles, heighten the Soviet sense of vulnerability. As the Soviets see things, the deployment of these weapons amounts to an American push for superiority *tout court*. But they also represent the attempt, from the Soviet viewpoint, to implement a "Eurostrategic" strategy of limited nuclear war. Thus, in the European context, a so-called "Eurostrategic" nuclear war might be pursued which would leave the Soviet Union open to attack but which would give sanctuary to the United States.

Given this view of the situation in Europe, the Soviets responded to the Pershing II and cruise missile deployment in a predictable way. They sent the message to Washington that recourse to limited war would produce general war. And they let the West Europeans know that recourse to a limited war would mean the end of Europe.

Conclusions

As we have seen, one does not need to accept at face value official Soviet protestations of innocence regarding their share of responsibility for the arms race and the deterioration of detente, nor their accusations of American culpability, in order to realize that the Soviet perception of nuclear developments differs significantly from our own. To be sure, both Soviet and American approaches in the nuclear era *appear* to be similar. For instance, the military technologies employed by the two sides are similar. Each side generally understands the quantitative and qualitative aspects of the weapons systems of the other side. And both superpowers have been engaged in protracted diplomatic and technical negotiations on strategic arms limitations. Yet the differences between American and Soviet doctrinal views on the role of strategic forces, once largely ignored or dismissed by most Western analysts, are very real. Essentially, they boil down to a fundamental divergence in outlook between U.S. and Soviet elites on the nature of the modern nuclear predicament and the requirements for successfully dealing with it in terms of national security and foreign policy. Within this context, there is a sharp divergence in view over the controversial notion of nuclear deterrence which, from the Soviet vantage point, attempts to compel the U.S.S.R. to follow a foreign policy behavior to the likings of Washington.

In the main, the disparity in doctrine is due to the asymmetrical nature of the two belief systems and different cultural, historical and political influences.[66] American and Soviet views are neither strategically nor politically comparable quantities – except in particular and carefully defined senses. There is no indication that they have identical strategic aims or similar nuclear weapons policies.

Historically, nuclear deterrence was politically attractive to a conservative power like the United States which possessed a vested interest in preserving the post-war *status quo*. The doctrine seemed advantageous to a state with far-flung economic interests and designs and enjoying strategic superiority. Indeed, the policy appeared ideal for dealing with a troublesome and dangerous, but weaker, adversary by making harsh threats of punishment in order to appeal to a bully's sense of survival.[67]

At its heart, Soviet strategy is a strategy of both confrontation and negotiation. Its conceptual underpinning is provided by the concept of the changing correlation of forces, a more subtle variation of the "balance of power" notion. Basically, Soviet strategy rejects the stark choice provided by the American emphasis on deterrence – either stable peace or nuclear incineration.

Soviet officials have adopted a strategy that appears suitable for a quasi-revolutionary power whose particular interests lie in changing the international *status quo*. It seems a proper strategy for a state that emerged on the international scene after the Second World War as a strategic inferior and whose historical tradition favors the brute force of massed armies, guided primarily by continental strategies of defense. Futhermore, it appears appropriate for a country

66 Roman Kolkowicz, Director of the Center for International and Strategic Affairs at the University of California, puts it this way: "We are dealing with two orthodoxies, mutually exclusive by their nature, each claiming a monopoly on scientific truth." Kolkowicz, *opus cit.,* p. 119.

67 "I would note," says General Goodpaster, "that some in the U.S. had hoped that 'deterrence' could deter much more than Soviet nuclear attack, war in Europe, or Soviet tactics of threat and bullying." Letter, June 22, 1984.

having little experience in massive projection of its forces beyond the Eurasian land mass. Soviet strategy appears advantageous, also, to a country with universal ideological and global political interests and aspirations. Moreover, it seems attractive to a state that is not in a hurry, believing that history and time are on its side.

It is clear from this discussion that there is a serious lag in Western, particularly American, appreciation for the Soviet view of nuclear deterrence. Too many U.S. military analysts still evaluate Soviet doctrine using sources which, if not actually outmoded, have become passé. Of particular note here is the stylized recourse to Marshal Sokolovky's *Military Strategy*, which was first published over twenty-four years ago. This book shows Soviet military recognition of the emergence of mutual deterrence (as well as an equivocal and changing view on its public embrace). Indeed in the first edition, which appeared in 1962, there is even a passage which not only attributes the concept to Western strategists and leaders, but also endorses it. However, Soviet military doctrine and its view of deterrence have evolved since the early 1960s.

The authority that Western analysts attribute to Soviet military writings, naturally enough, shapes their ensuing conclusions about Soviet intentions. This is particularly true in the debate in Western circles over the role of war-fighting in Soviet nuclear planning. Already in 1959, Lt. General James Gavin described the classic work of Clausewitz as the Rosetta Stone to understanding Soviet military thinking. This is a metaphor that unfortunately has been used many times since. Gavin, among others, argues that the Soviet conception of both nuclear and conventional force is intertwined with the famous proposition by Clausewitz that war is the continuation of politics by other means. However, the situation is much more complicated than this simplistic portrayal would have us believe.

This preoccupation with outdated source material has contributed in large part to lack of official U.S. recognition that Soviet realism and adherence to military orthodoxy has led to the development of a persistent skepticism towards the "metaphysics" of deterrence. This is particularly true as it finds expression in the present nuclear war-fighting policy of the Reagan Administration, which was largely justified on grounds that the Soviets had moved toward the development of an extended counterforce strategy. Actually, the

Soviets do not generally favor a deterrent posture that views nuclear war as a "rational" instrument of policy – or a process that is "winnable." Why should they? Soviet acknowledgement of limited war scenarios would mean in effect conceding the results of American nuclear advantage, thereby subjecting themselves to nuclear blackmail.

In general, the role of military power is seen from the Soviet point of view as a major instrument in impressing on the "imperialist camp" that military means cannot solve the historical struggle between the two opposing social systems. Moreover, the Soviets want to be able to reduce – if not actually eliminate – the prospect of military gain that could be obtained at the expense of the "socialist camp." While U.S. analysts fret over Soviet military advantages, the undertone in Soviet writings is different. The Soviet Union may no longer be number two. But it is still the United States that shapes the terms of the competition between the superpowers. To put this in the context of deterrence theory, it may be said somewhat simplistically that the Soviet position is one of "deterrence by denial." This contrasts sharply with "deterrence by punishment," which is practiced by the U.S.

To be sure, the Soviet leadership regards the capability to wage nuclear war (*in terms of military preparation*) as a crucial element of its visible "deterrent." But this does not reflect any preference, or inclination, to regard nuclear war as a rational instrument of policy. In short, Soviet "deterrent" policies are designed to minimize the incentives for attacking the U.S.S.R. but, above all, to prevent the outbreak of hostilities. Thus denial becomes a very real function of Soviet "deterrent" strategy. The following statement by the late Major General Nikolai A. Talensky of the U.S.S.R. remains as true today as when he wrote it in the 1960s:[68]

History has taught the Soviet Union to depend mainly on itself in ensuring its security and that of its friends ... After all, when the security of a state is based only on mutual deterrence with the aid of powerful nuclear rockets it is directly dependent on the goodwill and designs of the other side, which is a highly subjective and indefinite factor.

68 N.A. Talensky, "Anti-Missile Systems and Disarmament," in John Erickson (ed.), *The Military-Technical Revolution* (New York: Praeger, 1966), p.227.

There is some reason to believe that in practice the policy of launch on warning would control the policies of both the U.S. and the U.S.S.R., once the warning is believed to be clear and unmistakable."
U.S. Ambassador Martin Hillenbrand

VII. SOVIET COMMAND AND CONTROL

Under the American system of government, the President is the commander-in-chief of the armed forces and possesses the ultimate authority to order the release of nuclear weapons. A fail-safe mechanism ensures that nuclear weapons are not armed until a coded authorization has been received. Wherever the President goes, he is accompanied by a military aide who carries a black briefcase popularly known as the "football," which contains a summary of U.S. nuclear war plans.

In the case of the Soviet Union, analogous arrangement for central control rests with the Defense Council.[1] In the opinion of most Western observers of Soviet military affairs, this is the most crucial party body for military decision-making. However, it is also one of the most secretive party elements.

This chapter examines the basic organizational structure of the Soviet command and control system. Special emphasis is given to the Defense Council, the Ministry of Defense and the General Staff. In this context, Soviet nuclear release procedures are discussed. Finally, allegations that the Soviet Union has adopted a launch-on-warning system are studied.

1 During the Andropov regime the CIA observed an individual in the General Secretary's party who it thought carried the Soviet equivalent to the "football."

Role of the Defense Council

The Politburo of the Central Committee of the Communist Party is the most important political organ in the U.S.S.R. But in nuclear matters, experience seems to show, most important decisions are taken in the Defense Council *(Sovet Oborony).*[2]

This body, which functions today as a kind of subcommittee of the Politburo, has its origins in the Civil War, 1918-1920. At that time, it directed Red Army activities against White Army and foreign troops. Immediately after the Nazi attack on June 22, 1941, this body operated as the State Committee of Defense (GKO). At that time, it was said to comprise the senior party, military-security and state personalities (Stalin, Molotov, Voroshilov, Malenkov and Berya; later Bulganin, Voznesenskiy, Kaganovich and Mikoyan were added). As the GKO, the Defense Council formed the absolute pinnacle of authority for all vital decisions with respect to matters of state, military, economy, security and foreign policy.[3]

For many years following World War II the Soviets were very secretive about the continued existence of the Defense Council. Finally, the public silence was broken in 1973 with a series of articles in the Soviet press on the GKO during World War II. These articles were followed by an acknowledgment in 1976 that the Defense Council continued to exist and that Leonid Brezhnev was its Chairman.[4] One year later an announcement of major importance was made to the effect that Brezhnev was also the "Supreme Commander in Chief" of the Soviet Armed Forces. This was a position about which the Soviets had maintained almost complete silence since the time of Stalin.

As one knowledgeable student of Soviet military affairs writes,

2 It is important to note in this context that since the most influential Politburo members are evidently also members of the Defense Council, and since its deliberations are reportedly chaired by the General Secretary, it is most likely that recommendations worked out in this arena will be approved by the Politburo.

3 Former Defense Minister Andrei Grechko states that *absolute* power was concentrated in its hands. See his *Vooruzhenny Sily Sovetsskogo Gosudarstva,* 2nd ed. (Moscow: Voyenizdat, 1975), p.64.

4 According to a recent Soviet publication, the Defense Council has existed in its contemporary form since at least 1964. See the short biographical sketch on "Brezhnev, Leonid Il'ich," *Voennyi entsiklopedicheskii slovar'* (Moscow: Voenizdat, 1983), p.100.

"These announcements confirmed and reinforced what many analysts suspected: i.e., that the Defense Council served as the primary and final decision point on defense matters, and that the strategic leadership was being consolidated and clarified, under Brezhnev, in a manner very similar to the early Soviet moves of World War II." The major and disturbing difference "now was that these developments were occuring in peacetime, providing yet more signs of a growing militarization of the Soviet system."[5]

The political significance of the Defense Council under Brezhnev and succeeding regimes has rested in a separation of authority. That is, an arrangement was approved which would allow a few members of the Politburo to conduct regular business with the military on behalf of the leadership as a whole, in order to reach decisions on defense-related matters. This arrangement had major political advantages. Perhaps most importantly, it meant that information was segregated within the Politburo – and with it: power.

It is not known for sure what members make up the Defense Council.[6] But the most authoritative and credible descriptions of this body as it existed during the Brezhnev regime agree that it was chaired by the party leader and such *ex officio* members as the Soviet Premier (initially Kosygin), the Soviet President (between 1965 and 1977, Podgorny), the Defense Minister (first Malinovskiy, then Grechko) and the Central Committee secretary in charge of defense production (between 1965 and 1976, Ustinov).[7] It has been pointed out – and it is reasonable to assume – that in addition to these five men, the Chief of the General Staff and the Chairman of the Military-Industrial Commission were participants (although these men were not members of the Politburo). Moreover, in view of the KGB Chairman's military functions, it is also plausible to assume that he was an occasional participant. Finally, there is little reason to doubt

5 John J. Dziak, *Soviet Perception of Military Power: The Interaction of Theory and Practice* (New York: Crane, Russak & Co., 1981), p.44.

6 According to article 121, paragraph 14 of the new Soviet Constitution, the Presidium of the Supreme Soviet has the right to form the Council of Defense. However, in reality, establishment of this Council is very likely determined by the Politburo, acting in the name of the Central Committee. See Harriet Fast Scott *et al., The Soviet Control Structure and Capabilities for Wartime Survival* (New York: Crane, Russak & Co., 1983), p.48.

7 See Henry Goldman, *The Brezhnev Politburo and the Decline of Detente* (Ithaca: Cornell University Press, 1984), p.66.

that a variety of other officials, including the service chiefs, were occasional participants when their interests of responsibilities were involved.[8]

Today, under Mikhail Gorbachev, the Defense Council continues to function as an "inner sanctum" of the Politburo. But some scholars believe that *all* basic policy decisions are now the exclusive domain of the Defense Council.[9] These would pertain to matters such as the size and structure of the armed forces, issues regarding economic costs and priorities, choices with respect to weapons systems and their deployment and the formulation of military doctrinal theses. Also included are such non-military concerns as control over the economy, society and foreign policy. In the view of some Western experts, a "self-perpetuating 'rump' Politburo representing a Soviet-style Party-military-industrial-security complex may very well be running the country."[10] While the idea that the Defense Council may indeed be the governing body through which the present Gorbachev regime is directing the nation may be somewhat farfetched,[11] there is no doubt that this key body wields considerable power.[12]

8 This supposition was confirmed by Kremlinologist Raymond Garthoff at the Brookings Institution who held personal conversations in Moscow with Soviet military leaders. One former general staff officer, Major General M.A. Mil'stein (retired), now working at the Institute for the Study of the USA and Canada, informed the former U.S. Ambassador in September 1983 that the Defense Council at that time not only included CPSU General Secretary Andropov, other selected Politburo members, Marshal Ogarkov, then Chief of the General Staff, but also the five deputy ministers of defense who are commanders in chief of the services. See Edward L. Warner, "Defense Policymaking in the Soviet Union," in Robert J. Art *et al., Reorganizing America's Defense* (New York: Pergamon-Brassey's, 1985), p. 29.

9 See William T. Lee, *Military Decision-Making in the USSR: An Approach to the Problems* (unpublished manuscript, 1977), p. 12.

10 For years emigrés and others have articulated a similar hypothesis concerning the apex of Soviet leadership. Also, such a notion was a recurring theme of the Western spy Oleg Penkovskiy, but until more solid proof emerges such an idea is to be regarded as speculation.

11 Konstantin Chernenko is believed to have assumed the top Defense Council post when he succeeded the late Yuri Andropov as Communist Party leader in February 1984. However, it was not until mid-August 1984 that a Deputy Foreign Minister confirmed that Chernenko was head of the top of the Soviet military policy board in addition to serving as President or head of the Supreme Soviet (Parliament). See *The Minneapolis Star and Tribune,* April 14, 1984.

12 Soviet sources maintain that the Defense Council is responsible for coordinating the acitivities of those state organs that are active in the defense area, for

It is not known whether the contemporary Defense Council has a permanent staff or not. Soviet administrative practice would suggest that it has some sort of organization which would have the task of supporting deliberations and assisting in operationalizing Defense Council decisions into action. According to one scholar, "This function may be performed by an element of the apparatus of the Central Committee, whose General Department provides such administrative support to the Politburo."[13] It is much more likely, however, that such work is performed by the General Staff of the Ministry of Defense.[14]

Supreme High Command

In wartime direct leadership of the Soviet armed forces would be the responsibility of the Supreme High Command (VGK).[15] It is unclear whether the Supreme High Command exists in peacetime. One authoritative Soviet source states that this organ can "sometimes exist in peacetime."[16] In any case, it seems that the Soviet Union is operating today with a peacetime command structure that could very quickly be put on a wartime footing as a full-fledged Supreme High Command.

examining and deciding all fundamental issues relating to the security of the country, for establishing the basic direction of the development of the Soviet armed forces, for approving plans for military development and for creating the basic organization of the defense of the Soviet Union. See Col. P.I. Romanov *et al., Konstitutsiia SSSR i zashchita otchestva* (Moscow: Voenizdat, 1983), p.100.

13 Edward L. Warner, "Defense Policymaking in the Soviet Union," in Robert J. Art *et al., Reorganizing America's Defense* (New York: Pergamon-Brassey's, 1985), p.7.

14 There is a precedent for such an arrangement. General S.M. Shtemenko writes that while serving as Chief of the General Staff in the late 1940s he was secretary of the Higher (Supreme) Military Soviet, the predecessor to the Defense Council. Consult General of the Army S.M. Shtemenko, *General'nyi shtab v gody voiny,* Book 2 (Moscow: Voenizdat, 1973), p.500.

15 See, for instance, Colonel N.P. Skirdo, who states: "Direct leadership of the Armed Forces *both in peacetime and in war* is exercised by the Supreme High Command, the General Staff, and the appropriate military leadership." *The People, the Army, the Commander* (Moscow: Voenizdat, 1970), p.109. This book has been translated and published under the auspices of the U.S. Air Force. The italics are mine.

16 See the article, "Supreme High Command" in *Sovetskaia voennaia entsiklopedia* (Moscow: Voenizdat), Vol. 2, p.113.

The Supreme High Command is headed by the General Secretary of the Party who would act as Supreme Commander-in-Chief. During 1984, former Defense Minister Dmitri Ustinov confirmed the fact Gorbachev's predecessor Konstantin Cherenko held this position even in peacetime.[17]

During wartime the Party leader would also head the General Headquarters (*Stavka*) of the Supreme High Command. The *Stavka* would be in charge of the preparation and conduct of military campaigns and strategic operations. In the words of the Pentagon's *Soviet Military Power*: "It would also resolve issues concerned with the overall wartime situation of the country."

The Ministry of Defense

The Soviet Ministry of Defense (MOD), is, of course, a key element in the nuclear chain of command. While operating under the general guidelines laid down by the senior party leadership, the MOD plays a major contributory role in the formulation and implementation of Soviet nuclear policy.

The most important organizations within the ministry, which have responsibilities for nuclear matters, are the General Staff and the five services of the Soviet armed forces. These are the Strategic Rocket Services, Air Defense Forces, the Air Forces, the Navy and the Ground Forces. The Main Political Administration is also extremely important as well as such central directorates as Civil Defense.[18]

The Ministry of Defense is run by its minister, Marshal Sergei Sokolov with the assistance of three first deputies and ten deputy ministers. Sokolov, 76, is a long-time military man who was a front-line tank commander in World War II. Although Sokolov has been a full member of the Central Committee of the Communist Party since 1968, he is not a full Politburo member, as were his two predeces-

17 U.S. Department of Defense, *Soviet Military Power* (Washington, D.C.: Government Printing Office, 1985), p.19.

18 One of the best accounts of the history and roles of the Main Political Administration is to be found in Timothy Colton, *Commissars, Commanders and Civilian Authority: The Structure of Soviet Military Politics* (Cambridge: Harvard University Press, 1979).

sors Dmitri Ustinov and Marshal Andrei Grechko. Speculation has it that Sokolov, who before his election had served as First Deputy Defense minister for 17 years, was selected as a transitional step reflecting a reluctance on the part of the Kremlin leadership to appoint a younger man to one of the main positions of power in the U.S.S.R.[19] Presumably military professionals were pleased by this appointment which did not threaten the political leadership's supremacy over the armed forces.[20]

The Minister of Defense and his top assistants make up what is called the Collegium of the MOD. According to the *Soviet Military Encyclopedia*, the Collegium is a consultative organ responsible for working out "solutions relating to the development of the Armed Forces, their combat and mobilization readiness, combat and political training, the selection, assignment and indoctrination of military personnel and other important issues," whose decisions are implemented in the form of orders from its chairman, the Minister of Defense.[21]

U.S. intelligence officers believe that Marshal Sokolov convenes the 16-member Collegium at least weekly, if not more often as the situation warrants it. Generally, this high-level defense group serves as a forum for reaching policy decisions on a wide range of issues. In wartime, this body would probably make up the core of the General Headquarters (*Stavka*) of the Supreme High Command.[22]

The Soviet Ministry of Defense is manned, for the most part, by uniformed military personnel. As one student of Soviet military affairs notes, "The senior leadership posts in the ministry are filled almost exclusively by professional military officers who have served

19 In May 1987, General Dmitri T. Yazov was named to replace Marshal Sokolov as Defense Minister. This changeover occurred after a small West German civilian plane penetrated Soviet airspace and flew unimpeded 400 miles to Moscow before landing beside the Kremlin. The new change in leadership was generally seen in the West as putting Gorbachev in a better position to quell any military discontent over his arms control initiatives and over his professed desire to focus national resources on the civilian economy. *The New York Times*, May 31, 1987.

20 See *The Washington Post*, December 23, 1984.

21 See "Collegium of the Ministry of Defense of the U.S.S.R.," *Sovetskaia voennaia entsiklopedia* (Moscow: Voenizdat, 1976), Vol. 4, pp. 235-36.

22 U.S. Defense Department, *Soviet Military Power* (Washington, D.C.: Government Printing Office, 1985), p. 19.

for some thirty to fifty years."[23] In the past, the Minister of Defense was an important exception to this rule, but most recently there has been a return to military leadership over the MOD.

To be sure, there is a substantial number of full-fledged civilians working at the Ministry of Defense. But most of these people serve in nonprofessional, less skilled positions. Importantly, there is no group of civilian defense intellectuals in the central offices of the Ministry of Defense who would address questions of Soviet military doctrine, weapons development or other nuclear matters.

Given the relatively minor role of cilivians in the Ministry of Defense, civilian involvement in Soviet weapons decisions is much lower than it is in the West. "The result," as David B. Rivkin, Jr. points out, "is a nuclear weapons policy that, whatever its substantive merits, is much more unified and consistent than America's."[24]

This is not to suggest that the Ministry of Defense is monolithic. Members of the five military services, for instance, hold very different views on such issues as the assignment of roles and missions among the services and the levels of budgetary support that each should receive. Service parochialism is much in evidence today, but it was perhaps most evident during the early 1960s when the military found itself in a period of doctrinal ferment and confronted strong political pressure to limit defense spending.[25]

General Staff

The General Staff is no doubt the most important staff organ within the Ministry of Defense. It is the central, directing force of the Soviet armed forces. For all practical purposes, it has become – to use the words of two of its creators, Defense Commissar Mikhail Frunze and Marshal Boris Shaposhnikov – "the brain of the army."[26]

23 Edward L. Warner, *opus cit.,* p.14.

24 David B. Rivkin, Jr., "What Does Moscow Think?" *Foreign Policy,* No. 59 (Summer, 1985), p.88.

25 Edward L. Warner, "The Soviet Military", *Problems of Communism,* Vol. 23 (March-April, 1974), p.78.

26 See M.V. Frunze, *Izbranneye proizvedeniia* (Moscow: Voenizdat, 1965), p.155. Also consult Boris Shaposhnikov, *Mozg armii,* which was published in three volumes in 1927-29.

The most important elements of the General Staff are (a) the Main Operations; (b) the Main Intelligence; (c) the Main Organization and Mobilization; (d) the Main Foreign Military Assistance; and (e) the Military Science Directorates. These organizations heavily influence such various undertakings as the drafting of operational plans for theater and intercontinental warfare, the collection and assessment of military intelligence and the refinement of Soviet military organization. They also play the major role in the development of nationwide mobilization plans, the preparation of the annual and long-term economic plants for defense, the management of foreign military assistance arrangements, the formulation of concepts for doctrine, as well as the training during peacetime.

One of the most important directorates under the General Staff is the Military Science Directorate. This directorate is responsible for the development of military strategy. During the decade-long debate (1954-64) in the military over the significance of nuclear weapons in war, it played an active role. It has also published the most important statements concerning strategy. Perhaps most important here is the classified monthly journal, *Military Thought*, which serves as a vehicle for the country's military theorists to present new and sometimes controversial ideas for discussion and peer review.[27]

The General Staff also contains a Treaty and Legal Department. This department plays an important role in international arms control negotiations. Today, the Treaty and Legal Department is headed by Colonel General N. Cherov, who has been a major public relations figure regarding Soviet views on the Intermediate Nuclear Forces negotiations and SDI.[28] Various officers assigned to this department (or its predecessor) have been active participants in Soviet-American arms control talks since the late 1950s.[29]

The General Staff is composed of a cadre of staff officers, a

27 See Robert F. Byrnes (ed.), *After Brezhnev* (Bloomington: Indiana University Press, 1983), p.141.

28 In addition to General Cherov, Marshal Sergei Akhromeyev, the Chief of the General Staff, has served as an important spokesman to the Western press and visiting U.S. congressional delegations on such matters as START and the INF talks as well as Star Wars.

29 For historical background on this involvement, see Edward L. Warner, *The Military in Contemporary Soviet Politics* (New York: Praeger, 1977), pp.224-44.

number of whom have spent decades working in the specialized directorates of the General Staff. In addition, there is a group of the most promising line officers drawn from the different services. Individuals who make up the latter group serve only briefly in the General Staff and from there they are generally posted to key command and staff assignments with the forces in the field, the central directorates of the services in the Soviet capital or other elements of the Ministry of Defense.[30]

The exact relationship between the General Staff and other elements of the Defense Ministry in Moscow is not known in the West. According to one source, Marshal Akhromeyev, the Chief of the General Staff, is the only person who has the right to issue orders in the name of the Minister of Defense.[31] Otherwise, the General Staff has the mandate to ensure "the coordinated actions" of the main staffs of the armed services, the staffs of the Rear Services, Civil Defense, the main and central administrations of the Ministry of Defense and the staffs of the military districts,[32] groups of forces,[33] air defense districts and fleets.[34] Moreover, it appears highly likely that the commanders of the sixteen military districts, the four groups of forces deployed in Eastern Europe and the four fleets, while directly under the Ministry of Defense, function under the general direction of the General Staff.

In a war, the General Staff would serve as operational staff and executive agent for the General Headquarters of the Supreme High Command. Its task would be to work in conjunction with the main

30 Edward L. Warner, "Defense Policymaking in the Soviet Union," in Robert J. Art, (eds.) *Reorganizing America's Defense* (New York: Pergamon-Brassey's, 1985), p.15.

31 Conversation between Michael Sadykiewicz, a former Colonel who completed a two-year course at the Voroshilov Academy of the General staff in 1957, and Edward L. Warner, October 18, 1982.

32 There are sixteen military districts in the Soviet Union. Listed in alphabetical order, these are: the Baltic, Byelorussian, Carpathian, Central Asian, Far Eastern, Kiev, Leningrad, Moscow, North Caucasus, Odessa, Siberian, Transbaikal, Transcaucasia, Turkestan, Ural and Volga military districts.

33 These are four groups of Soviet forces in Eastern Europe. They are the Group of Soviet Forces Germany (GSFG) in East Germany, the Northern Group in Poland, the Central Group in Czechoslovakia and the Southern Group in Hungary.

34 There are four Soviet fleets. These are the Northern, Baltic, Black Sea and Pacific fleets, with headquarters located in Severomorsk, Kaliningrad, Sevastopol and Vladivostok respectively.

staffs of the five services. Its Operations Directorate would draft plans for strategic operations for consideration by the General Headquarters of the Supreme High Command. As soon as these plans were approved, they would be issued to operational commanders as orders of the Supreme High Command.[35]

The Role of the Military in Decision-Making

Most students of Soviet military affairs are unanimous: It is the civilian political leadership that firmly holds the reins of decision-making authority in military as well as other matters in the Soviet Union.[36] Examples from history provide evidence here. For instance, one only has to recall the relative ease with which Khrushchev removed Marshal Zhukov from the Politburo. In a similar vein, the decision to deploy offensive missiles in Cuba and to abolish the independent command of the Ground Forces were reportedly implemented over the vehement objections of the military leadership.[37]

Yet, the above examples do not tell the whole story. It is an observable fact that Soviet professional military men have played an important role at times in decisions relating to contemporary Soviet nuclear policy. For instance, general-grade officers have figured prominently in Soviet delegations during the SALT and MBFR talks and later during the START and space weapons deliberations. There is some reason to believe that Marshal Ogarkov's leading role in the SALT negotiations may have been largely responsible for his promotion to Chief of the General Staff. By the same token, the shooting down of the South Korean airliner in the fall of 1983 was portrayed by Ogarkov and other Soviet representatives as a military decision, made without civilian consultation.

Some Western Soviet military specialists discern a new trend

35 U.S. Defense Department, *Soviet Military Power* (Washington, D.C.: Government Printing Office, 1985), p.19.

36 For a review of this literature consult Stephen M. Meyer, "Soviet Defense Decisionmaking: What Do We Know and What Do We Understand?" *ACIS Working Paper, No. 33* (Los Angeles Center for International and Strategic Affairs, UCLA, 1982).

37 Michael Tatu, *Power in the Kremlin* (New York: Viking Press, 1969), pp.230-244.

evolving in Soviet national security decisionmaking: This is a more fundamental and enduring military influence in this area. In large part, these scholars point to the technological factor as being mainly responsible for this change.[38]

In this view, technology appears to have accomplished what sixty-five years of Soviet party-military relations have attempted to prevent. This is the movement of the professional military into the heart of the defense decisionmaking arena. This trend, it is argued, is particularly evident regarding Soviet military economics where the special treatment accorded the Soviet military economy to the detriment of the civilian economy is well documented.[39] But it is also very clear in the making of the Soviet defense budget.

According to Stephen Meyer, there is important new evidence which points in the direction of increased military influence in the Defense Council. These are the cases for armed intervention in other countries. "Until recently," Meyer concludes, "it was the Politburo members who visited the prospective target country before final decisions were made. Yet, in the most recent cases of Afghanistan and Poland (aborted), senior military officers were sent to assess the situation and report back to the Politburo."[40] (Based on the testimony of a defector from the ranks of the KGB, the Politburo accepted the military view that Afghanistan could be successfully invaded and pacified and rejected KGB advice that such a move was too risky.)

If Meyer's evidence is intriguing, we should recall that it was written before Soviet Defense Minister Dmitri Ustinov died. Ustinov was replaced by Marshal Sergei Sokolov, a career soldier who was not given full Politburo rank. In line with the tradition of keeping the influential military firmly linked with the dominant party, Sokolov had been a member of the Central Committee since 1968.

38 Stephen M. Meyer, "Civilian and Military Influence in Managing the Arms Race in the U.S.S.R.," in Robert J. Art *et al.* (eds.), *Reorganizing America's Defense* (New York: Pergamon-Brassey's, 1985), p.38.

39 See for instance, Arthur Alexander, "Decisionmaking in Soviet Weapons Procurement," *Adelphi Papers Nos. 147-8* (London: International Institute for Strategic Studies, 1978).

40 See Stephen M. Meyer, "Civilian and Military Influence in Managing the Arms Race in the U.S.S.R.," in Robert J. Art *et al.*, (eds.), *Reorganizing America's Defense* (New York: Pergamon-Brassey's, 1985), p.54.

But for almost two years he was deliberately kept out of full-voting membership of the Party's highest decision-making body: the Politburo.

Since coming to power in March, 1985, General Secretary Gorbachev has made it clear that there are limits to military influence. Thus, Party control over the military now seems unchallenged.

Nuclear Release

One of the most secret aspects of Soviet decision-making has to do with nuclear release procedures. While few details are known in the West, the general outlines are understood by senior intelligence officers in the CIA and Defense Intelligence Agency.[41]

First, the decision to authorize military use of nuclear weapons is the exclusive prerogative of the political leadership. "It, first and foremost, and not the military command determines the need to use means of mass destruction, selects the basic objectives and the moments for inflicting strikes with them."[42]

Soviet military writings indicate that nuclear weapons have increased the role of the top leadership in directing wartime operations in a major way. However, it is presently unclear whether Mikhail Gorbachev can actually launch missiles on his own, although Leonid Brezhnev may have used the threat of a surprise attack to arrogate such power to himself when he was Chairman of the Defense Council. The conventional wisdom is that Gorbachev could not act alone in this crucial matter.

It is generally assumed in intelligence circles that once the basic decision has been made in the Defense Council then operational control would be transferred to military commands in the field. This is necessary in order to carry out nuclear strikes efficiently and effectively.

If the order for nuclear release should be given, the General

41 This discussion has benefitted considerably from the analysis in Stephen M. Meyer, "Soviet Theatre Nuclear Forces: Part II: Capabilities and Implications," *Adelphi Paper No. 188* (London: The International Institute for Strategic Studies, 1984), p.32-35.

42 M.P. Skirdo, *Narod armiya, polkovodets* (Moscow: Voenizdat, 1970), p.121.

Staff would take charge of the selection of means of delivery. This might involve the firing of medium-range or intermediate-range ballistic missiles of the Strategic Rocket Forces, the aircraft of Long Range Aviation or the various missiles owned by the Soviet navy. The strike planning for these missiles would most likely be done by a section of the Main Operations Directorate of the General Staff.

In the case of those strategic delivery vehicles deployed on land, they would come under the direct control of Strategic Areas Commands and Ground Force Front and Army Commanders. (In wartime, the Soviet Army would be grouped into Fronts which are formed from the peacetime Military Districts and Groups of Forces. In major theaters, Fronts would be grouped under a Theater Headquarters or TVD.)[43]

In the case of naval operations-tactical cruise missiles and aviation, it is probable that they would be subsumed under the overall command of Fleet Headquarters.

Lastly, the tactical means of delivery on land would be controlled by Ground Force divisional commanders. Analogous naval systems would likely be assigned to battle group commanders.[44]

As presently organized, release authority would flow down the chain of command. Stephen M. Meyer describes the process: "from Supreme High Command (the wartime leadership) to General Staff, from General Staff to theater and strategic sector High Commands (co-ordinating several adjacent Fronts), from High Commands to Front commanders to Army commanders and thence to divisional commanders, and from Fleet Headquarters to battle group commanders."[45]

43 For details see John Erickson *et al., Soviet Military Power and Performance* (Hamden, Ct.: The Shoestring Press), p. 49. The Soviets have divided the world into 13 TVDs, of which five would be along the boundaries of the U.S.S.R.: Northwestern, Western and Southwestern Europe, Central Asia and the Far East (in addition to four intercontinental and four maritime TVDs). Those forces deployed in each military district would be subsumed under the appropriate TVD, as the General Staff decides.

44 One Soviet source comments here: "The transfer of nuclear weapons to the disposal of the strategic, operational and tactical command echelons gives great independence and enables them to choose for themselves the means and methods of military operations within the zones of their responsibility and within the bounds of their authority." I. Zav'yalov, "Evolution in the Correlation of Strategy, Operational Art and Tactics," *Military Thought,* No. II (1971), p. 37.

45 Stephen M. Meyer, *opus cit.,* p. 33.

Meyer notes that in the context of nuclear release, the most vulnerable link in the chain of command is that between the Supreme High Command in the Soviet capital and the High Commands in the field and the Front Commands in the theaters. In contrast, the most secure link is between the Supreme High Command and the General Staff. Herein lies a major problem facing the Soviet political leadership. Release authority may have to be delegated in advance of any decision to launch preemptive nuclear attacks in order best to ensure timely and effective use of forward-based tactical and operation-tactical nuclear systems. "The danger, of course," Meyer points out, "is that once the nuclear weapons are released there is no telling what might happen next."[46]

Soviet military writings suggest that Front Commanders have full authority to employ their nuclear weapons in any way they deem appropriate, once release has been authorized. The same is apparently *not* true for Army and divisional commanders. Whatever the situation, it seems likely that the rigid centralization and hierarchical structure of Soviet military command and control principles (not to mention political control principles) would prevail so that the Soviet political leadership would be able to retain control of nuclear forces until the last possible moment but still have reasonable confidence that a quick response will follow a decision to launch (preemt).

Soviet concerns about the control of nuclear forces have been evident in a number of sources. Most recently, former Soviet Defense Minister Dmitri F. Ustinov stated that Soviet military activities demanded increased attention to:[47]

setting up a still more strict framework in the training of troops and staff, the determination of the composition of arms, the organization of still more rigid control (kontrol) for the assured exclusion of the unsanctioned launch (pusk) of nuclear weapons from tactical to strategic.

Ustinov's choice of words here was important. For one thing, he used *kontrol* rather than *upravlenie* and *pusk* rather than *primenie.* This implied that he was not thinking about problems of battle

46 Stephen M. Meyer, *opus cit.,* p.33.

47 D.F. Ustinov, "Otvesti ugrozu yadernoy voyni," *Pravda,* July 12, 1982.

management. Rather he was concerned with escalation control over the unauthorized *initial* use of Soviet forces.

Emphasis on Preplanning

Western analysts tend to criticize Soviet command and control as being excessively rigid or absolutely centralized. In the United States, for example, rigidity and preplanning are frequently viewed as leading to inflexibility. And this is seen as undesirable.

While it is true that the Soviet Union has had a concept of centralized control for a long time, it has developed procedures and "tools" to make top level control more responsive to battlefield requirements. Especially important here is the apparent Soviet penchant for preplanning. "The Soviet leaders believe in preplanning," Joseph D. Douglass, Jr. writes, "because they anticipate that the command and control apparatus may be temporarily paralyzed in nuclear war."[48] The whole idea behind preplanning is that it would enable lower echelons to know clearly how to proceed even in the absence of command and control.

But the main emphasis in the Soviet command and control system is not just on preplanning. Rather it is on the ability to plan and replan in a minimum amount of time. Time is the crucial factor in the Soviet approach. As former Defense Minister Grechko expressed it in 1975: "The fight to win time is the primary problem of command and control."[49]

Launch on Warning

"There is some reason to believe that in practice the policy of launch on warning would control the policies of both the U.S. and the U.S.S.R., once the warning is believed to be clear and unmistaka-

48 Joseph D. Douglass, Jr., "Soviet Nuclear Strategy in Europe: A Selective Targeting Doctrine?," *Strategic Review,* No. 5 (Fall, 1977), p.24.

49 Marshal A.A. Grechko, *The Armed Forces of the Soviet State* (Moscow, 1975), translated by U.S. Air Force (Washington: Government Printing Office, 1977), p.208.

ble," says U.S. Ambassador Martin Hillenbrand.[50] For its part, the U.S. government has been known to practice "launch on warning," although in simulated circumstances.[51] The same can not be verified for the Soviet Union.

If the Soviets have indeed adopted such a policy,[52] this may mean that the Kremlin plans to launch its nuclear counterstrike as soon as its radars and computers indicate that an enemy attack is on its way. Thus, such a policy represents in a sense the ultimate answer to Soviet anxiety that its missiles and command and control centers are vulnerable.[53]

Automatic quick-launch capabilities may not simply be a by-product of Soviet technology. However, they seem to represent a guiding principle which may have been an integral feature of the Strategic Rocket Forces since their inception. In his memoirs, Khrushchev records that one of the reasons that he disliked the early SS-6 ICBM, which was tested in 1959, was that it could not "be fired at a moment's notice."[54]

The SS-6 was never deployed in large numbers, and a couple of years later the SS-7s and SS-8s were introduced. Khrushchev recounts that the designers of these systems "tackled the problem of perfecting a rocket that could be launched on short notice."[55] Unlike the SS-6, the SS-7 and SS-8 came outfitted with storable liquid fuel that gave them a quick-launch capability.

During his tenure as party leader, Khrushchev made several pro-

50 Letter to this writer, June 1, 1984.

51 Confidential source.

52 General Daniel O. Graham, the former head of the Defense Intelligence Agency, quotes Soviet Marshal Nikolai J. Krylov, former Commander-in-Chief of the Strategic Missile Forces, to this effect in Graham's *Shall America be Defended* (Arlington House, 1979), p 88. See also Lawrence Freedman, *The Evolution of Nuclear Strategy* (New York: St. Martin's Press, 1978), pp. 267-68.

53 According to one U.S. intelligence insider, "Once authority to use nuclear weapons has been obtained by Soviet theater forces, they will be controlled by front and army commands."

54 *Khrushchev Remembers: The Last Testament* (Boston: Little, Brown, 1974), p. 50. According to one Western study, the SS-6's deficiency in this regard was due to "its reliance on nonstorable cryogenic fuels ... [which] makes launching it a long and awkward process during which it is especially vulnerable in conditions of war." See William H. Schauer, *The Politics of Space* (New York: Holmes and Meier, 1976), p. 13.

55 *Ibid.*

nouncements which have been interpreted by some specialists as a Soviet preference for a quick-launch capability. For instance, during the mounting tension over the Berlin question in 1959, Premier Khrushchev warned Averell Harriman:[56]

Your generals talk of maintaining your position in Berlin with force. That is bluff. If you send in tanks, they will burn and make no mistake about it. If you want war, you can have it, but remember, it will be your war. Our rockets will fly automatically.

The term "automatically" was emphasized later as the Soviet leader's colleagues echoed this part of the threat.

Further evidence of Soviet attraction to an automatic firing policy occured during the 1960 U-2 affair. When questioned in 1961 about Soviet control of their nuclear weapons, Deputy Secretary of Defense Roswell Gilpatric stated:[57]

With regard to top-level control over the use of nuclear weapons, the Soviets have not explicitly and formally identified where the responsibility for authorizing use resides, as has the United States. It can be presumed that in the U.S.S.R. this authority is in the hands of Khrushchev alone, or in the Presidium of the Central Committee. At the same time, Soviet statements have indicated that this authority may be delegated to the military under some circumstances. For example, shortly after the U-2 incident, Khrushchev said that Marshal Malinovsky was empowered to respond instantly with missile attacks on any bases from which further U-2s might be sent.

The usual "contemporary" evidence cited as "proof" of a Soviet launch-on-warning policy is the confidential statement by Marshal N.I. Krylov, Commander-in-Chief of the Strategic Missile Forces, who wrote in November 1967:[58]

56 *Life* magazine, July 13, 1959, p.33.

57 Letter from Deputy Secretary of Defense Gilpatric to Senator Hubert Humphrey, August 23, 1961.

58 Marshal N.I. Krylov, "The Nuclear Shield of the Soviet State," *Voyennaya mysl'*, No. 11 (November, 1967), p.20. The Soviet military journal *Voyennaya mysl'* (Military Thought) is the important confidential journal of the Soviet General Staff. Its circulation is restricted to Soviet officers, and it is therefore thought to be comparatively free of concerns over effects on less sophisticated mass military and lay Soviet leaderships – or on non-Soviet audiences. In an unpublished Order (No. 303 of November 6, 1965), then Minister of Defense Marshal Rodion Ya. Malinovsky noted that *Military Thought* is "the main military theoretical organ of the Ministry of Defense of the USSR," and that "it plays an important role in the working out of military-theoretical problems."

Under contemporary circumstances, with the existence of a system for detecting missile launchers, an attempt by an aggressor to inflict a surprise preemptive strike cannot give him a decisive advantage for the achievement of victory in war, and moreover will not save him from great destruction and human losses.

It is worth noting here, however, that Marshal Krylov did not use the Western expression "launch on warning" in the text.

Another passage in the same statement reads:[59]

It must be stressed that under present conditions, when the Soviet Armed Forces are in constant readiness, any aggressor who begins a nuclear war will not remain unpunished, a severe and inevitable retribution awaits him. With the presence in the armament of troops of launchers and missiles which are completely ready for operation, as well as systems for detecting enemy missile launchers and other types of reconnaissance, an aggressor is no longer able suddenly to destroy the missiles before their launch on the territory of the country against which the aggression is committed. They will have time during the flight of the missiles of the aggressor to leave their launchers and inflict a retaliatory strike against the enemy. Even in the most unfavorable circumstances, if a portion of missiles is unable to be launched before the strike of the missiles of the aggressor, as a result of the high degree of protection of the launchers from nuclear explosions, these missiles will be preserved and will carry out the combat missions assigned to them.

Still another document often mentioned in the context of an alleged Soviet "launch-on-warning" policy is the confidential statement by General of the Army S.P. Ivanov, who said in May 1969:[60]

Contemporary means of early detection, moreover, make it possible to discover the initiation of an enemy nuclear attack and to take necessary retaliatory measures in a timely manner.

A number of U.S. military analysts interpret the passage, which is a little less precise, as unmistakably containing the "launch-on-warning" concept.

According to Raymond L. Garthoff, who served on the SALT I negotiating team, the Soviet delegation in the early 1970s, "referred

59 *Ibid.*, p.20.

60 General of the Army S.P. Ivanov, "Soviet Military Doctrine and Strategy," *Voyennaya mysl'*, No. 5 (May, 1969), p.47.

to the existence and continuous improvement of early-warning systems, owing to which ICBM silos might be empty by the time they were hit by an attacker's strike, the ICBMs having been launched by that time." The American delegation reportedly commented later on this statement and "expressed the hope that no government would launch its ICBM force solely on the possibly fallible reading of signals from its early-warning systems." The American side expressed "the view that such a strategic doctrine seemed inconsistent with a proper concern for the problems of accidental or unauthorized launch or provocative third-party attack."

Apparently, the Soviet delegation "was not authorized to enter [into] a discussion of this subject, and had not intended its initial statement to do so," reports Ambassador Garthoff. Accordingly, "it replied with an attempt to disassociate the question from accidental, unauthorized or provocative attacks, and to refer to *American* statements [not made in SALT] about possible launch on warning."

The U.S. team then "provided an official American disavowal of the concept by the Secretary of Defense, with further criticism of the ideas as potentially dangerous for automatic escalation or even for starting a war by accident." But efforts to elicit a statement on Soviet policy with respect to this concept "met with silence." An unofficial comment by a senior military representative was subsequently made that such matters went beyond the proper purview of SALT and should not be discussed with civilians.[61]

Aside from these older, frequently cited sources of a Soviet "launch on warning" policy, there have been a number of authoritative references in recent years as well.[62] In July 1982, for instance, Soviet Defense Minister Dmitri Ustinov (now deceased) hinted at renewed Soviet interest in "launch-on-warning" policies. He said:[63]

With the present-day state of systems of detection, and the combat readiness of the Soviet Union's strategic nuclear means, the USA will not be able to deal a crippling blow to the socialist countries. The ag-

61 See Raymond L. Garthoff, "Mutual Deterrence and Strategic Arms Limitation in Soviet Policy," *International Security,* Vol. III (Summer, 1978), pp.130-131.

62 See for example, Marshal N.V. Ogarkov, "In the Interests of Raising Combat Readiness," *Kommunist vooruzhennykh sil,* No. 14, (July, 1980), p.26.

63 Remarks of Soviet Defense Minister Dmitri Ustinov, "For Averting the Threat of Nuclear War," *Pravda,* July 12, 1982.

gressor will not be able to evade an all-crushing retaliatory strike ... The state of military potential and the military-technological potentials of the sides are such that the imperialist forces will not succeed in ensuring for themselves military superiority either at the stage of preparing a nuclear war or at the moment when they try to start that war.

Some Western military analysts see in the alleged Soviet adoption of launch on warning "a step forward toward stability from preemption."[64] But the majority view is that, if true, the policy remains a potentially destabilizing and dangerous influence. In the view of most U.S. "insiders" and those outside government, the United States should seek ways to discourage the Soviets from any degree of reliance on this policy.

Conclusions

In view of the closed nature of the Soviet political system, outsiders face enormous difficulties in developing a detailed portrayal of the participants and processes involved in policy formation and execution in the Soviet Union. Nowhere is this more true than in the area of command-and-control procedures. The Soviet leadership considers these issues so sensitive that they often hide the very existence of key high-level decisional bodies active in nuclear matters. Moreover, they never discuss openly, in any detail, the nature of contemporary nuclear release procedures which would govern nuclear war.

Having said this, one should not draw the conclusion that it is impossible to identify the individuals and institutions that are of crucial importance in nuclear command and control or to draw general descriptions of the way in which they seemingly interact.

64 See Raymond L. Garthoff, *opus cit.*, p. 132. Garthoff is one of those well known Soviet experts who argue that the Soviets have moved to a launch-on-warning system. As evidence, he points out the lack of adequate air defense coverage of ICBMs. The ICBMs, he says, "would be protected from destruction in the event of an enemy attack not by active antimissile defenses of one or another degree, but by being launched in retaliation before their silos were hit." Raymond L. Garthoff, "BMD and East-West Relations," in Ashton B. Carter *et al.* (eds.), *Ballistic Missile Defense* (Washington, D.C.: The Brookings Institution, 1984), p. 310.

There is a vast body of Soviet books and articles that one can draw upon as well as a number of biographical accounts and personal memoirs of leading military and political figures who were heavily involved in nuclear matters in the past.[65] This chapter draws upon this material to outline and evaluate the basic structure of the Soviet command and control system.[66]

Our findings indicate that the Soviet command-and-control structure is more centralized than its American counterpart. Moreover, the Soviets exercise tighter control over the deployment of their strategic forces, most notably their missile-firing submarines.[67]

The Soviets have gone to great lengths to develop over the years an elaborate peacetime command-and-control network that closely approximates the anticipated wartime structure. At the highest level, the U.S.S.R. has created peacetime national security and military organizations. These organizations are commanded by the secretive Defense Council, which functions as a subcommittee of the Politburo. With little modification, it can operate as the strategic command element in wartime.[68] Or at least this is the theory.

In wartime, this management structure would provide a unified system of command for the armed forces, the Soviet government and the national economy. It would ensure centralized direction, but it would also permit a degree of autonomous operations required by modern warfare.

The present Defense Council, with Gorbachev presiding *ex officio* as Chairman, probably would be expanded during war to in-

65 This study also takes into account some very esoteric evidence such as Harriet Fast Scott's fine analysis of Politburo signatures on the obituaries of defense-related figures between 1960 and 1982. This material suggests that neither Andropov, Chairman of the KGB, nor Gromyko, the Foreign Minister, became members of the Defense Council in 1973 when both were promoted to the Politburo. This original methodoloy indicates that Andropov joined the Defense Council in 1982 after he succeeded Suslov as one of the ranking Secretaries of the Central Committee. See H.F. Scott, "Possible Members of the Council of Defense Derived from Obituaries," unpublished paper (April, 1983).

66 One of the weaknesses of this approach is that it assumes that many of the assumptions about the organizational arrangements and procedural patterns prevailing in some earlier periods are still generally valid today.

67 "Strategic Command and Control," *IISS Strategy Survey 1979* (London: Neil Moore, 1980), p.13.

68 See Marshal V.D. Sokolovsky (ed.), *Soviet Military Strategy,* 3rd ed. (New York: Crane, Russak and Co., 1975). p.361.

clude representatives of the highest party, state and military leadership. Commensurate with the precedent set by World War II, it would function in a way similar to the State Defense Committee in the "Great Patriotic War." Thus, it would provide centralized political direction of the entire war effort.

But even before a war began would the Soviet leadership authorize a launch-on-warning policy? Indeed, do they have one in place at present? There is no clear cut answer here, as the internal debate in the Reagan Administration continues to wage. The best that one can note is that apart from the technical feasibility of such a dangerous policy, it is incompatible with long-standing Soviet command and control practices.[69]

As one noted authority on Soviet military politics has observed, "launch on warning runs diametrically against the grain of Soviet doctrine's emphasis on retaining operational control over the war process at all times." Indeed, "its entire logic rests on the abandonment on any semblance of control in favor of blind reliance on a mindless gamble." As Benjamin Lambeth forcefully concludes, "Launch on warning may be useful as a peacetime deterrent threat, but it could prove suicidal if actually carried out as a wartime strategy."[70]

Here it might be worthwhile to recall that Soviet strategic forces never went on alert, even during the Cuban missile crisis, until the mid-to-late sixties.[71] In short, the Soviets have demonstrated a remarkable command and control conservatism that is not consistent

69 Despite occasional loose statements by U.S. government officials about an American nuclear war-fighting capability, Soviet apprehensions concerning a surprise attack by the United States have probably diminished since the 1950s when "massive retaliation" was U.S. declaratory policy. Not only has the survivability of Soviet strategic forces improved, but the U.S.S.R. is now more confident about receiving adequate strategic warning. As Robert P. Berman and John C. Baker write, "The low alert rates of the Soviet nuclear forces are consistent with the Soviet Union's preference for conserving its military assets by limiting their peacetime operations and holding down the potentially high expense of maintaining a large military force ..." See Robert P. Berman *et al., Soviet Strategic Forces: Requirements and Responses* (Washington, D.C.: The Brookings Institution, 1982), p. 37.

70 Benjamin S. Lambeth, *The State of Western Research on Soviet Military Strategy and Policy* (Santa Monica: RAND, 1984), pp. 40-41.

71 See John J. Holst, *Comparative U.S. and Soviet Deployments, Doctrines and Arms Limitation* (Chicago: University of Chicago, 1970), p. 24.

with placing a premium on being able to launch "on short notice," even after they acquired ICBMs in the 1960s that remedied some of the deficiencies of earlier missiles, like the SS-6.

Soviet military writings have stated that concentration of the leadership of the country and its armed forces in the hands of the highest political agency of government control is necessary for obtaining victory in wartime. But recent authoritative statements by both political and military leaders now discount the goal of "victory" in a nuclear war.

The Soviet leadership has carefully developed (and continues to develop) the details of their system of strategic leadership. Superficially, a system for war fighting and war survival is in place. The nucleus of critical party-state control organs and top military command elements that would be needed in wartime exists in peacetime in the form of high-level political and military organizations. Theoretically, these peacetime structures could shift their activities to wartime operations with a minimum of difficulty.

However, this is only theory. Who knows what would happen in wartime? How vulnerable are these units to nuclear destruction? In the next chapter, we will search for answers to these questions.

Under conditions of a nuclear war, the system for controlling forces and weapons, especially strategic weapons, acquires exceptionally great significance. A disruption of the control over a country and its troops in a theater of military operations can seriously affect the course of events, and in difficult circumstances, can even lead to defeat in a war.

Colonel M. Shirokov in Voennaia Mysl'

VIII. VULNERABILITY OF SOVIET C^3I

"The most likely way that a nuclear war will happen is through a crisis that gets out of control," states one U.S. expert on nuclear war. "The situation that led to World War I is a good example."

Both the United States and the Soviet Union have elaborate systems established to prevent just such an occurence. These are technically known as systems of strategic command, control, communications and intelligence – or C^3I for short. These systems would enable national command authorities (NCA) of both sides to detect a nuclear attack, assess its extent and direct an appropriate retaliatory response.[1]

The Soviets rely upon a system of fixed and mobile command posts with an extensive communications network to enable the leadership to prosecute a war, nuclear or otherwise. However, unlike the U.S. command and control system in which only the very top political and military leadership will hope to be protected, the Soviets are striving to protect leadership throughout the whole country.[2]

1 For a good general analysis of the problems of command and control survivability, see Alan J. Vick, "Post-Attack Strategic Command and Control Survival: Options for the Future," *Orbis,* Vol. 29, No. 1 (Spring, 1985), pp. 95-117.

2 Soviet military writers don't use the phrase C^3I when discussing their own strategic forces. They use the phrases "troop control" (upravleniye voyskami) and "strategic leadership" (strategicheskoye rukovodstvo).

In order to promote party and state control through the protection of high-level party, government and military leaders, the Soviets have put into place an elaborate system of emergency relocation facilities. Many of these are buried, bunkered and designed to withstand considerable blast from nuclear explosions. For the most part, these facilities are outfitted with "hardened" communications equipment, and they are designed to serve as alternate command-and-control posts for the top leadership in wartime.

From a Soviet military and political perspective, the protection of centralized control is essential to ensure continued ability of the U.S.S.R. to fight effectively. Desmond Ball, an Australian specialist on C³I, has highlighted the significance to the Soviets of centralized command and control in the following words:[3]

Observation of Soviet military exercises gives the impression that ships, aircraft, and commands have carefully and specially planned roles, and that operational communications flow directly between headquarters in Moscow and the individual units in the fields. Local commanders seem to have relatively little scope to adapt general orders to field conditions or to use their own initiative if they do not receive central orders. This tendency could be even more pronounced in the strategic forces, since Soviet leaders would be particularly loath to allow lower commanders much room for initiative where nuclear weapons were concerned.

The problem of preserving a survivable command-and-control capability has been nicely summarized in the Soviet literature by Colonel M. Shirokov. As he writes: "Under conditions of a nuclear war, the system for controlling forces and weapons, especially strategic weapons, acquires exceptionally great significance. A disruption of the control over a country and its troops in a theater of military operations can seriously affect the course of events, and in difficult circumstances, can even lead to defeat in a war."[4]

Sensitive to the problem of C³I survivability, the Soviets have constructed a redundant and potentially survivable command-and-control system. However, they are well aware of its deficiencies and

3 Desmond Ball, *Can Nuclear War Be Controlled?* (London: International Institute for Strategic Studies, 1981), p.45.

4 Colonel M. Shirokov, "Military Geography at the Present Stage," *Voennaia Mysl'*, No. 11 (1966), translated in *Foreign Press Digest*, July 27, 1967, p.63.

likely inability to function adequately in a postattack environment. The noted scholar John Steinbrunner makes the case:[5]

Although the Soviets have made extensive investments in measures to protect their command systems and, whether by intention or necessity, have utilized relatively primitive communications equipment significantly less sensitive to nuclear weapons effects, the consequence of their systematic attention to the subject appears to be an awareness of exposure rather than confidence in secure protection.

EMP Effects

For the most part, C^3I systems in the Soviet Union are in large, fixed sites – soft targets with a small number of critical nodal points. Consequently, they are much more vulnerable to the direct and indirect effects of nuclear weapons than the strategic forces they control. In particular, they are vulnerable to the effects of electromagnetic pulse (EMP).[6]

If scientific interest in the effect of electromagnetic pulse was stimulated by American nuclear tests conducted in the early 1960s, this phenomenon and its ramifications for nuclear deterrence were not fully appreciated by strategic thinkers until sometime later. Only recently has EMP begun to receive some of the public attention it deserves. Unfortunately, the publicity given to the prospect of a nuclear winter arising out of a threshold nuclear exchange has tended to obscure this extremely significant aftereffect.

Briefly, EMP represents a short but intense electrical discharge that can do serious damage to most kinds of electronic circuitry, thus posing a threat to unprotected weaponry and computers. Electromagnetic pulse could, for instance, wipe clean all computer memories that are in range of the electromagnetic effects. EMP has an extremely rapid "rise-time" – ten to twenty nanoseconds and lasts only about a microsecond (one millionth of a second). Techni-

5 John Steinbrunner, "Nuclear Decapitation," *Foreign Policy* (Winter, 1981/82), p. 20.

6 There is some debate about the effect of EMP on buried land lines. Planners assume these lines can be protected.

cally, this effect is not generated at a single spot like a lightning bolt but is induced simultaneously throughout an entire electrical grid.[7]

All nuclear explosions generate some EMP. However, only bursts high above the atmosphere give rise to pulses whose effects extend beyond the radius of local devastation. As Janet Raloff points out, a blast fifty miles up would affect an area with a radius of six hundred miles.[8] A burst one hundred miles up would affect an area with a radius of nine hundred miles. *A single nuclear detonation centered over the Soviet Union at an altitude of some two hundred miles would cover much of the country as well as parts of bordering countries with EMP of same intensity and duration.*

Given the vulnerability of electrical transmission lines and electronic hardware to the destructive effects of rapid voltage surges, a series of EMP pulses could have devastating effects on both civilian and military communications systems. In the view of one expert, John Steinbrunner, "several EMP weapons exploded high over the United States could shut down the national power grid for hours or even days and incapacitate large segments of the military command-and-control network."[9] The same could be true of the U.S.S.R.

The chaos-producing effects of electromagnetic pulse have been known for some time by scientists and military communications specialists. But only in the last few years has the American military begun to take major steps to shield or "harden" C^3I systems and other vital electronic equipment that are considered most critical. The Reagan Administration, in particular, with its emphasis on developing a nuclear war fighting capability for "intrawar" deterrence has been concerned that a dedicated strike by the Soviet Union against the American C^3I network would enhance the effectiveness of a Soviet counterforce attack.

Critics are skeptical of recent efforts to pour billions of dollars into schemes that would allegedly protect the American command-and-control system from electromagnetic disruption in a nuclear exchange.[10] They believe the steps now being taken will hardly

7 See Eric J. Lerner, "Electromagnetic Pulse: Potential Crippler," *IEEE Spectrum* (May, 1981), p.42.

8 Janet Raloff, "EMP: A Sleeping Electronic Dragon," *Science News,* May 9, 1981.

9 John Steinbrunner, "Strategic Command and Control Vulnerabilities: Dangers and Remedies," *Orbis,* Vol. 26, No. 4 (Winter, 1983), p.953.

10 The Joint Chiefs of Staff, in their 1983 posture statement, argued that "C^3I sys-

make the C^3I network invulnerable to EMP weapons, and thus are a great waste of money and resources.[11]

The basic problem, of course, is that since the Soviet Union and the United States stopped testing nuclear weapons in the atmosphere, we have not been able substantially to increase our knowledge of EMP. About the most the Pentagon and Soviet Ministry of Defense can do is simulate the effect, and this is not very satisfactory from a military planning perspective. Therefore, many questions remain unanswered about EMP, but so far there has been little public discussion of this important issue.

Do the Soviets Know More about EMP than the U.S.?

Not surprisingly, the Pentagon worries that the Soviets may know more about EMP than it does. One Pentagon argument goes something like this: Soviet high-altitude tests were carried out over central Asia which, though not densely populated, does have some cities. In the view of some Defense Department officials, these tests would have been sufficient to allow Soviet scientists to study the effects of EMP on earth-based electronics systems.[12]

Going back to 1968, Pentagon officials were alarmed to discover that the Soviets were very much aware of EMP effects. Soviet interest here was evidenced by a Soviet Ministry of Defense publication which reported that "powerful nuclear explosions set off at great altitudes" constitute a considerable threat to ICBMs "because the impulses of electromagnetic energy created by such explosions can put out of commission not only the on-board missiles equipment, but also the ground electronic equipment of the launch complexes."

tems must not only support an initial retaliatory response, but also survive and endure through a protracted period of conflict."

11 Former Secretary of State Cyrus Vance, for one, would distinguish between investing money in C^3I for the purpose of making command and control safer and more secure and pouring vast sums of money into C^3I for the purpose of being able to fight and win a nuclear war, which he feels is ridiculous. See his interview with Robert Scheer, *With Enough Shovels: Reagan, Bush and Nuclear War* (New York: Random House, 1982).

12 See Ann M. Cunningham *et al. Future Fire* (New York: Warner Books, 1983), p.199.

Since 1968, Pentagon officials believe that the Soviets have made significant strides in protecting their weapons against EMP. Some of the evidence they use to support their case dates back to 1976, when a Soviet defector flew his MiG-25 to Japan.

Subsequently, the plane was broken down and studied thoroughly. Upon examining the aircraft, officials noted, among other things, that the plane's computer circuitry was technologically up-to-date except for several items. One of these was that it used old-fashioned computer vacuum tubes, which are less sensitive to the effects of EMP. As a result of their analysis, these officials concluded that the Soviets may have known how to "harden" their planes against EMP.

But this is just one plausible explanation. There are others. Perhaps one of the most important of these is provided by John Barron, who wrote an entire book about the MiG pilot and his plane.[13] "The Russians," he writes, "lacked the time and resources to develop all the new technology Western designers and engineers doubtless would have thought necessary for the type of interceptor required. So having no other choice, the Russians elected to make do with what they had. They decided to use, instead of titanium, heavy steel alloy; instead of transistors, vacuum tubes; instead of sophisticated new missiles, those that were available."[14]

Barron points out that the Soviets lagged woefully in certain technological areas. In particular, they lagged in the "technology of transistors, semi-conductors and integrated circuitry, the tininess, lightness, and reliability of which the Americans also considered essential." In sum, there was probably a basic misperception because the Pentagon tended to evaluate the MiG in Western terms and thereby adopted false premises.

If the Soviets have not protected their weapons against EMP (and probably cannot), this is not to say that they are not trying to "harden" their electronic instruments against EMP by means of steel shielding, special grounding, circuit layout, etc. Indeed, they have done a great deal of this, according to U.S. officials with access to classified information on this subject. But it is extremely hard to

13 John Barron, *MIG Pilot: The Final Escape of Lt. Belenko* (New York: Avon Books, 1980).

14 *Ibid.,* p.177-78.

adequately protect a vulnerable system like C^3I, and the difficulties connected with this undertaking should not be underestimated. In any case, there is little evidence that Soviet "hardening" has given them confidence in their ability to maintain secure C^3I facilities in the event of a nuclear war.

ASAT

Some U.S. government experts maintain privately that the Soviet command-and-control system is less vulnerable to some of the effects of EMP than its American counterpart. But this is debatable. It is true, however, that some seventy percent of Pentagon communications are now routed through satellites, a ratio likely to rise in the future.[15] The Soviets also make use of satellites for communications purposes, but not to the extent that the U.S. does. This situation will change in the future, of course, as the U.S.S.R. attempts to close the technological gap.

Given the increasing importance of communications satellites to both sides, the Soviets would like to negotiate a treaty with the United States which would limit the deployment of anti-satellite missiles. Thus, in 1983, they announced a "unilateral moratorium" on launching anti-satellite weapons. This step was coupled with a proposal to negotiate a ban on the testing and deployment of space-based weapons.

The Soviets, of course, were only following their own national self-interest in making this proposal. Among other things, they would like to avoid extending the arms race into space[16] because of the enormous potential cost to them and their technological disadvantage in this area – allegations by the Pentagon to the contrary.

The Air Force, which is heavily committed to its new anti-satellite program, likes to point out that the Soviets possess the world's only "operational" anti-satellite capability. However, what the U.S. military often fails to add is that the U.S. was the first nation to possess an operational ASAT, having begun studies on ASATs before satellites existed. As one authority reports, "In 1963 the Army began

15 *The Defense Monitor,* Vol. 12, No. 7, p.14.

16 "It is too late," says one U.S. arms control official.

testing an ASAT launched by Nike-Zeus missiles which used nuclear warheads. The Air Force began testing its own Thor missile-launched nuclear ASAT in 1964."[17] Even though nuclear explosions in space were banned by the 1963 Limited Test Ban Treaty, the U.S. nuclear ASAT system remained operational until 1975.

Another detail, frequently overlooked in the debate over who is ahead in ASAT technology, is the fact that the Soviet ASAT is primitive and no threat to the most important American satellites which are in high orbit.[18] Moreover, the current American non-nuclear ASAT would be, if fully and successfully tested and deployed, superior to the nuclear Soviet ASAT because it intercepts in a few minutes, rather than hours. Finally, its homing technique is more difficult to foil.[19]

The Reagan Administration, which wants to exploit its technological edge in this important area, has taken the public position in an election year that it is willing to consider negotiations with the Soviets on this matter only if certain preconditions are met.[20] One of the preconditions is that agreement on the troublesome question of verification be resolved first.

Experts are divided over the verification issue. Some believe it is merely a political red herring which the Administration is using to preclude serious talks on a matter of great importance. Others feel the concern is genuine and must be debated on its merits.

17 *The Defense Monitor,* Vol. 12, No. 5 (1983), p.4.

18 According to one U.S. government insider, U.S. reconnaissance, ocean surveillance, electronic intelligence and navigation and meterological satellites operate at altitudes under 600 miles. Of the 50 military, about 26 could be hit by the Soviet ASAT system. Of the 100 Soviet satellites, between 16 and 32 may be within range of the new U.S. ASAT system.

19 Critics have argued that the Soviet ASAT system is a clunker. They point out that many tests have failed. ("This is true of one type of system but not the other," says one U.S. government insider.) Also, the Soviet system is far less flexible than the U.S. system. The Soviet system consists of a ballistic missile that is launched into orbit and then chases down the target satellite. For details, see *The Christian Science Monitor,* September 13, 1985.

20 The Soviets now seem willing to dismantle their existing ASAT capability. On September 28, 1984, Foreign Minister A. Gromyko wrote to the UN Secretary General that "space weapons of *any basing mode* should not be developed, tested or deployed either for antiballistic missile defenses, or as antisatellite systems, or for use against targets on the earth or in the air. *Any such systems already created should be destroyed.*" (Italics mine.) Quoted in Alton Frye, "Strategic Synthesis," *Foreign Policy,* No. 58 (Spring, 1985), p.24.

As the debate over ASAT became publicly more intense in the fall of 1985 the Reagan Administration went through with plans to test its anti-satellite weapons against an object in space. Subsequently, in December 1985, the Congress passed a law banning future tests against objects in space as long as the Soviets continued not to test such a system. Since that time the U.S. Air Force has devised a plan to resume testing an ASAT weapon that they believe does not violate the Congressional ban against testing the weapon on objects in space. (For their part, the Soviets have chosen to observe a Moratorium on ASAT weapon's tests, calling on the U.S. to follow suit.)

Nuclear Decapitation

Both the United States and the Soviet Union are not ruled by civilian leaders who live and work in centrally located, hardened structures at almost all times. Thus, there is the possibility that a carefully planned surprise attack on the White House or the Kremlin could wipe out the entire national command structure.[21] This would throw the C^3I system into chaos – a worst-case scenario that nuclear strategists term "decapitation."

For its part, the United States faces a decapitating threat by Soviet missile-firing submarines positioned on the East coast. Although YANKEE-class submarines have been deployed off the American coast for some time, in February 1984, there was a major change in deployment. As General John Vessey, Jr., Chairman of the Joint Chiefs of Staff stated to Congress at that time, there has been a substantial surge in the number of Soviet SSBNs cruising off the East coast of the U.S. Vessey said that the Soviet activity was part of the long-promised Soviet reaction to the U.S. deployment of Pershing IIs and cruise missiles. The new subs were identified as DELTA-class submarines, which usually operate in the northern Atlantic or the Barents Sea.[22]

21 One U.S. official would argue that the national command structure would remain in place with the devolution of authority that is pre-arranged. But this is optimistic thinking.

22 For details see *The Minneapolis Star and Tribune,* February 15, 1984.

American missile-firing submarines also present a nuclear decapitation threat to the Soviet leadership. Whether or not the Pershing IIs stationed in West Germany do is unclear. Soviet officials say that any attack upon the U.S.S.R. by the Pershings would give them no more than 8-10 minutes warning to respond. U.S. officials maintain, however, that there would be about twelve minutes. At the same time, the Soviets contend the Pershings in West Germany could reach Moscow roughly 1,200 miles away. The Reagan Administration has said publicly that they could not, but its position has been weakened by the lack of credibility in its published figures on the subject in the eyes of many critics.[23]

As Paul Bracken, a political scientist at Yale University and author of an authoritative book on the command and control of nuclear forces, writes: "They (the Pershings) must look to the Soviet military men exactly like the kind of weapon needed to attack their high command before it has time to react." Bracken states that he has no doubt that the Russians are trying to exploit the Pershing deployment "as a propaganda measure." But "that doesn't mean it is not a real military issue as well."

Several Soviet political commentators, including a prominent member of the Central Committee staff, have been quick to point out that the very short flight time of the Pershings would not permit use of the "Hot Line." And some (including most pointedly the former Chief of the General Staff Marshal Nikolai Ogarkov) have suggested what is one of the principal Soviet military concerns over Pershing II. This is that its very short flight time would not even allow "launch on warning" before the missiles struck Soviet ICBM silos or command-and-control centers.[24]

Henry Kissinger, for one, believes that the Soviet argument about the shortened warning time caused by the Pershing IIs is for the "gullible."[25] As he writes in *The Wall Street Journal:* "A Pershing

23 "This is not true," says one U.S. arms control official. "We've published the figure, but people do not believe the figure."

24 See Marshal N.V. Ogarkov, "In the Interests of Raising Combat Readiness," *Kommunist vooruzhennykh sil,* No. 14 (July, 1980), p. 26. Also consult *Pravda,* March 19, 1979. In a frank interview in *Red Star* on May 9, 1984, Ogarkov contradicted himself. At that time, he asserted flatly that a disarming first strike on command-and-control installations or opposing rockets is impossible since a crushing retaliation is unstoppable.

25 William G. Hyland, a former aide to Kissinger, also tends to discount shrill Soviet

takes 8 to 10 minutes to reach the Soviet Union from Western Europe. An ICBM takes 25 to 30 minutes from the U.S.; a submarine-launched missile, depending on its location, requires 15 to 20 minutes. Were the Pershings to be removed, what would the Soviets do with the extra few minutes of warning time?"[26]

In his article, Kissinger explains the real reason for the deployment of the Long-Range Theater Nuclear Forces.[27] He says these weapons which could reach beyond Europe were dispatched to West Germany because they helped prevent the nuclear blackmail of Europe. This they would do by linking their strategic defense with that of the U.S.. "With intermediate-range American weapons in Europe," he argues, "the Soviets could not threaten Europe selectively." Any "nuclear attack and any successful conventional attack would trigger an American counterblow from European installations." Thus, "the Soviets would have to calculate, even in the case of conventional attack, that we would use our missiles before they were overrun." Hence, "the Soviets would have to attack the missiles if they used even conventional weapons in Europe." That in turn "would trigger our strategic forces."

The Soviets, Kissinger maintains, "grasped the significance of the new deployment immediately." They "threatened that any use of these weapons would be answered with an attack on the U.S."[28]

claims of a special threat of a surprise attack because of the short flight time of the Pershing IIs. "A separate attack of 100 Pershings is too foolish to contemplate," he says. "Moreover, the Pershing's range is too limited to attack all Soviet command and control centers. It could not even attack all of the SS-20 sites." See Hyland, "The Struggle for Europe: An American View," in Andrew J. Pierre (ed.), *Nuclear Weapons in Europe,* pp. 33-34.

26 Henry Kissinger, "Arms Control and Europe's Nuclear Shield," *The Wall Street Journal,* January 31, 1984. Herbert Scoville, Jr., a former official with the U.S. Arms Control and Disarmament Agency, attempts to answer that question: "It forces you to go one step further, of trying to guess when there would be an attack and then trying a pre-emptive strike."

27 Kissinger's view here is somewhat different from the opinion he expressed in an interview with the *The Economist,* February 3, 1979.
Question: We have no real answer, do we, at the moment in the European theatre to the SS-20?
Answer: No.
Question: Which is, if you are a European, a little worrying.
Answer: If you assume that every weapon aimed at Europe must be answered by a weapon stationed in Europe. *That is not self evident.* (Italics mine.)

28 *The Wall Street Journal,* January 31, 1984.

Air Defense Program

The Soviet Union relies on several types of military forces to provide protection for its C^3I facilities and strategic offensive forces. However, the most important of these are the forces for air defense. (Soviet Ballistic Missile Defense will be discussed in Chapter 9.)

One of the most basic distinctions between American and Soviet strategic forces is the priority given to defensive forces. For its part, the United States permitted its strategic air defenses to decline after the mid-1960s.[29] At that time, ballistic missiles replaced long-range bombers as the major strategic offensive weapon. By way of comparison, the Soviet Union maintains a large and expensive air defense system despite the fact that nation-wide defenses against ballistic missiles are banned by the ABM Treaty of 1972.[30]

The greater commitment by the Soviets in this area is due, in part, to the fact that strategic bombers/air-launched cruise missiles continue to represent a significant part of the U.S. strategic nuclear delivery system. Bombers and fighter bombers are the primary attack instruments of American regional forces. Furthermore, the character of Soviet deterrence doctrine (i.e., deterrence by denial) requires the use of defensive as well as offensive forces to inhibit attack on the Soviet motherland.

Soviet air defense relies in the main upon interceptor aircraft in conjunction with early-warning networks and surface-to-air missiles (SAMs). Altogether, there are more than 10,000 air defense radars throughout the Soviet Union. As the Pentagon's 1987 edition of *Soviet Strategic Defense Programs* reports, the Air Defense Forces rely upon more than 1,200 interceptor aircraft dedicated to strategic de-

29 In view of the importance attached by the Reagan Administration to its "Star Wars" technology, the U.S. Air Force is lobbying strongly for building up U.S. air defenses in a major way. In addition to a $ 7 billion Air Force plan to modernize radar and interceptor squadrons, Pentagon strategists are seeking ways to meet the so-called "air breathing threat" of Soviet bombers and cruise missiles which would not be stopped by SDI. For details, see *The Washington Post*, August 25, 1984.

30 For one of the better, though now dated, descriptions of Soviet defensive forces, see Robert P. Berman *et al, Soviet Strategic Forces: Requirements and Responses* (Washington, D.C.: The Brookings Institution, 1982), Appendix D.

fense. In additon, 2,800 interceptors assigned to Soviet Air Forces (SAF) could also be employed in strategic defense missions.[31]

The Soviets are deploying the MiG-29 and MiG-31 that, unlike the MiG-23, are capable of attacking low altitude targets effectively. The newest Soviet air defense interceptor is the MiG-31. Code-named the "Foxhound," this interceptor has a "look-down, shoot-down" and multiple-target engagement capability. More than 85 Foxhounds are now (1987) operationally deployed at several locations from the Arkhangelsk area in the north-western U.S.S.R. to the Far East Military District.[32]

Currently, the Soviets have nearly 12,000 SAM launchers which are deployed at more than 1,200 sites. Most of these SAMs are deployed around the Soviet border, particularly in the West. The remainder are used for point defense of cities and military installations.[33] Command centers are also defended. Interestingly, the ICBM fields are given little emphasis by air defense systems. (U.S. strategic bombers are not going to destroy many ICBM silos.)

Historically, the major weakness of the Soviet air defense system has been its inability to defend effectively against a low-altitude bomber threat. And this is exactly the kind of bomber force that the U.S. now deploys. Gordon MacDonald *et al.* summarize the tale:[34]

The currently deployed Soviet system seems to have been designed only for a high altitude bomber attack. Early warning radars cover all the important entry areas for bombers from the United States or Western Europe and can detect high-flying aircraft well beyond Soviet borders. Soviet interceptor aircraft and SAM batteries are numerous enough to inflict heavy attrition on any high-altitude attacking force ... For a low-altitude (500-600 feet) bomber attack the situation is substantially different. Although radar coverage in the northwest

31 Department of Defense, *Soviet Strategic Defense Programs* (Washington, D.C.: Departments of Defense and State, 1985), p.17.

32 *Ibid.*

33 U.S. Defense Intelligence Agency, *Handbook on Soviet Armed Forces* (DIA, 1978), pp.11-14.

34 Gordon MacDonald *et al.*, Soviet Strategic Air Defense," in Richard K. Betts (ed.), *Cruise Missiles: Technology, Strategy, Politics* (Washington, D.C.: The Brookings Institution, 1981), p.67. One U.S. Arms Control official observes: "If this were true, we would not be assigning the B-52 a stand-off role when the B-1 becomes operational."

sector is dense enough to continue to provide some coverage, large gaps appear where radars are not densely distributed. The capability of Soviet strategic SAMs and current aircraft interceptors would be marginal at best against low-flying bombers ... The net effect is that a substantial fraction of the weapons carried in a large, well-planned, low-altitude bomber attack against the Soviet Union would probably be delivered to their targets. Highly defended point sites might inflict significant attrition on such an attacking force, but they would be unlikely to survive a heavy attack.

Although the Soviet capability to intercept low-flying penetrators is marginal, they are in the midst of a major overhaul geared toward fielding an integrated air defense system, according to the 1985 edition of *Soviet Military Power*. "This overhaul includes partial integration of strategic and tactical air defenses; the upgrading of early warning and surveillance capabilities; the deployment of more efficient data transmission systems; and the development and initial deployment of new aircraft, associated air-to-air missiles, surface-to-air missiles, and airborne warning and control (AWACS) aircraft."[35]

The Soviet strategic defense program seems mainly focused on countering U.S. bombers and cruise missiles. These are weapons which are sometimes referred to as "air breathers" since they remain in the atmosphere, unlike ICBMs.

Currently, the U.S.S.R. has a number of relatively primitive air- and sea-launched cruise missile systems. However, it possesses no long-range or strategic cruise missile systems that are operational, although it is moving quickly to catch up with the United States in this vital area.[36]

35 U.S. Department of Defense, *Soviet Military Power* (Washington, D.C.: Government Printing Office, 1985), p. 48.

36 Soviet leaders and the Soviet press have on several occasions in the past reported the testing of long-range cruise missiles, but not until August 26, 1984 were these taken seriously by Western analysts. At that time, the Soviet Defense Ministry announced the conducting of successful tests of these missiles. The brief Soviet statement gave little detail, but said the Soviets had repeatedly suggested the negotiation of a ban on such missiles. For details see *The International Herald Tribune*, August 27, 1984. According to the authoritative International Institute for Strategic Studies in London, the cruise missiles tested by the Soviets have a range of about 1,800 miles. The Institute also reports that the Soviets are testing air- and sea-launched cruise missiles.

While the Soviets have amassed extensive defenses against some kinds of U.S. strategic weapons threatening the Soviet homeland, nevertheless the U.S. Air Force believes that its new B1-B bomber and cruise missiles which hug the terrain and are hard to detect, will be able to penetrate those defenses for many years to come. As a result, Soviet progress in this area is not considered particularly threatening by many U.S. analysts.

Conclusions

Despite the Pentagon's stark portrayal of the Soviet strategic defense threat, a more balanced analysis of the situation would emphasize the vulnerability of air defense to penetration (and consequently Soviet C^3I) by the new technologies being developed by the United States military. The cruise missile is a case in point.

Soviet commentators pretty well recognize the challenge this missile presents to air defense systems. To be sure, the most confident statements have been made by the senior commanders of the Air Defense Forces (PVO), whose responsibility it is to provide air defense.[37] Other Soviet observers are more cautious as the situation warrants, implying a lack of faith in the Soviet Union's air defense system. One military writer, for instance, observes in a piece dealing with recent developments in air-launched cruise missile technology, short-range attack missiles, and advanced strategic air-launched missile technology that "they are all designed to break through strong air defense systems and strike them from various distances ... It is difficult to say at the moment to what extent the hopes of the foreign military specialists are justified, how successful development and testing will be and what final results will be achieved."[38]

A number of Soviet military observers have noted the high

37 See for example Col. Gen. Ye. Yurasov, "Responsible for the Sky of the Motherland," *Izvestia,* April 13, 1980. Also important is Col. Gen. of Aviation I. Podgorny, "Sentries of the Sky," *Trud,* April 8, 1979.

38 Maj. Gen. Artillery V. Zhuravlev, "Air-to-Ground Missiles," *Krasnaya zvezda,* September 30, 1975. Consult here Col. Gen. A. Sozinov, "Sentries of the Sky," *Sovetskaya Rossiya,* April 8, 1979.

penetration capabilities and the high accuracy of cruise missiles.[39] Several military journals have also acknowledged the small radar profile of the missiles, their ability to maneuver evasively and to fly down below radar screening levels, and the low infrared emissions of their propulsion systems. As the Soviet military is obviously aware, these are all factors that seriously complicate detection and interdiction by defenses.

At present, the total additional outlays for upgrading future Soviet strategic defense to counter the challenge of cruise missiles and modern bombers is difficult to project. Generally, Western estimates have ranged from $ 10 billion to $ 50 billion.[40] But given Gorbachev's domestic economic priorities, upgrading means at the very least a substantial and unwanted increase – better, a reallocation – of Soviet defense expenditures.

In summary, although the Soviets are in the midst of a major program to improve their capabilities against aircraft and cruise missiles that fly at low altitude, their air defense system (and consequently their C^3I network) remains extremely vulnerable to the expanding penetration capabilities of U.S. military forces.

C^3I vulnerability has important ramifications for strategic war fighting. Given its serious weaknesses in this area, the Soviet leadership cannot be confident of being able to fight much less win a protracted nuclear war. Such a war could only bring about a severe breakdown of communications and control and lead to a catastrophe for the Soviet Union.

39 See Eng. Col. N. Grishin, "Cruise Missiles: The NATO Variant," *Krasnaya zvezda*, June 18, 1980. [Lt. Col.] L. Nechayuk, "The Pentagon Eurostrategic Creations," *International Affairs* (Moscow), (April, 1980), p. 126.

40 See Robert E. Moffit, "The Cruise Missile and SALT II," *International Security Review*, Vol. 4 (Fall, 1979), p. 227.

When I have trouble sleeping nights, it's because of your (American) offensive missiles, not your defensive missiles.

Alexei Kosygin

IX. BALLISTIC MISSILE DEFENSE

A great deal has been written about the American Strategic Defense Initiative (SDI) – known popularly as "Star Wars." But Soviet ballistic missile defense (BMD) research and capabilities have, by way of contrast, not received much attention. This neglect is unfortunate because Soviet BMD has important political and strategic consequences. It is the purpose of this chapter to redress this imbalance and give the Soviet ballistic missile defense capability some of the attention it deserves.

History of Soviet BMD

Soviet research on BMD was launched prior to U.S. research efforts. Soviet efforts started in the late 1940s and 1950s with Soviet military technologists investigating the possibilities of BMD – then known as ABM.[1] In this regard, Soviet research on BMD paralleled the early development of long-range offensive ballistic missiles.[2]

It is still not completely clear why the Soviet leadership embarked upon a program to develop BMD in the first place. Perhaps, as RAND analyst Thomas Wolfe suggests, the Soviets were motivated by "the belief that a combination of strategic offensive forces

1 Sayre Stevens, "The Soviet BMD Program," in Ashton B. Carter *et al.* (eds.), *Ballistic Missile Defense* (Washington, D.C.: The Brookings Institution, 1984); p. 189.

2 See Khrushchev's interview with Arthur Sulzberger, *The New York Times*, September 8, 1961.

with air and missile defense forces would provide greater military and political flexibility ..."[3]

The first specific claim of Soviet success in this regard was not heard until October 1961, when Marshal Malinovskii reported at the Twenty-Second Party Congress that "the problem of destroying missiles in flight ... has been successfully solved."[4] It was not long thereafter in July 1962 that the U.S.S.R. had developed an anti-missile missile that "can hit a fly in outer space."[5] From that time on, public allusions to Soviet progress in BMD research multiplied rapidly.

Soviet discussions of BMD in the early 1960s continued to affirm the offense-defense interrelationship and to assume BMD would develop. In fact, by 1962-63, the U.S.S.R. was claiming a lead here. However, it was also stressing the fact that BMD was "exceptionally expensive."[6]

The first public display of an alleged BMD missile came on November 7, 1963. Known in the West as GRIFFON, this missile was a two-stage vehicle with an altitude range of 25 to 30 miles and a slant range of approximately 100 miles – according to Western intelligence estimates. Although the Soviets claimed a BMD role for this weapon, this was not at all clear to Western observers.[7]

A more likely candidate for a BMD role was paraded a year later in the Soviet capital in November 1964. Nicknamed the GALOSH, this missile was described by Soviet commentators as capable of intercepting ballistic missiles at long distances from defended targets.[8] Once it was set up around Moscow, Western intelligence estimated that the range of the GALOSH and the capabilities of the radars associated with it enabled the Moscow ABM system to cover an area of many thousands of square miles.

"The display of ABM-associated hardware such as the GRIFFON

3 Thomas W. Wolfe, *Soviet Power and Europe 1945-1970* (Baltimore: The Johns Hopkins University Press, 1970), p.186.

4 *Pravda,* October 25, 1961.

5 *The New York Times,* July 17, 1962. This statement was made by Khrushchev to a group of visiting American newspaper editors.

6 See M.N. Nikolayev, *Snaryad protiv snaryada* (Moscow: Voyenizdat, 1960), pp.145-46.

7 See *The Soviet Military Technological Challenge* (Washington, D.C.: Georgetown University, Center for Strategic Studies, 1967), p.88.

8 *Pravda,* November 8, 1964.

and GALOSH missiles in 1963-64 did not in itself go very far toward answering the prime question whether the Soviet Union had achieved an operationally satisfactory ABM system which it was prepared to deploy on a serious scale," writes Thomas Wolfe.[9] Other Western observers drew similar conclusions. Considerable discussion in the press focused on the possibility that the Soviets had already started deployment of a first generation BMD around Leningrad. But the evidence here was inconclusive.

Not all Soviet commentators were at this time in agreement on the importance of BMD. In March 1965, G. Gerasimov, one of the few Soviet civilian commentators knowledgeable about strategic affairs, published an article in which he polemicized against the view that, through the creation of an anti-ballistic missile defense, it might be possible to achieve "victory" in a nuclear war. This would require "a discovery, bordering on a miracle," he said. "The means of defense lag behind the means of attack. Today there is no absolute defense against a missile salvo. It is possible to intercept and destroy part of the missiles, but to intercept and destroy all of the missiles is technically impossible ..."[10]

In November 1966, U.S. Secretary of Defense Robert McNamara laid doubts to rest about the BMD capability of the Soviet Union. At that time, he disclosed officially that the Soviet Union had embarked on the deployment of anti-ballistic missile (ABM) defenses.[11]

The most important complex was set up to protect Moscow, where the Soviet National Commmand Authority is located. The Moscow system (which may have been deployed at least in part as a possible hedge against the developing Chinese nuclear threat)[12] was very primitive in nature. For one thing, it was vulnerable to decoys and chaff as well as nuclear effects. But most importantly it could defend against only small attacks. (MIRVs were not in existence at this time.)

9 Thomas W. Wolfe, *Soviet Power and Europe 1945-1970* (Baltimore: The Johns Hopkins University Press, 1970), p. 187.

10 G. Gerasimov, "The First-Strike Theory," *International Affairs*, No. 3 (March, 1965), pp. 39-45.

11 See *The New York Times*, November 11, 1966.

12 See President Nixon's press conference of March 14, 1969, in which he stated that Soviet ABM radars are now being directed also against China.

The deployment of a Soviet ABM, no matter how primitive, was the cause of great concern in the United States where alarmists projected the imminent development of a nation-wide system. Subsequently, the Johnson Administration sought to persuade the Soviets to reconsider. In particular, the hope was to gain Soviet agreement to a mutual freeze on ABM deployment in order to head off a new and expensive round of the arms race.

Soviet reaction to President Johnson's plea along these lines in his State of the Union message of January 10, 1967 was both cool and equivocal. However, although the Soviets showed no enthusiasm for a ABM moratorium, they did not shut the door to possible negotiations with the United States.[13]

In fact, discussions between the United States and the Soviet Union on the ABM question had already begun in the form of a probe on December 6, 1966. At that time, U.S. Ambassador Llewellyn Thompson told Soviet Ambassador Anatoly Dobrynin that the United States wished to propose a serious talk on mutually limiting ABM deployment. Dobrynin (and the Soviet government when appraised) responded in a noncommital but open way: What did the U.S. have in mind?[14]

The first Soviet substantive position was communicated in an official exchange of notes in January 1967. It stated that because of the action-reaction interplay of strategic offensive and defensive forces both issues must be included in such discussions and limitations. The U.S. quickly agreed.[15]

At a June 1967 meeting at Glassboro, New Jersey, President Johnson pressed Alexei Kosygin for a firm date for the opening of arms limitation talks. Such a statement would allow Johnson to postpone his decision on the development of a BMD. But the President did not receive a specific answer.

"When I have trouble sleeping nights," Kosygin told Johnson's Defense Secretary McNamara, who had been lecturing him on how

13 See *The New York Times*, June 26, 1967. Kosygin made some inconclusive remarks as early as February, 1967. These are reported in *The New York Times*, February 10, 1967.

14 For details see Raymond L. Garthoff, "SALT I: An Evaluation," *World Politics*, Vol. 31 (October, 1978), pp.1-4.

15 *Ibid.* "That's our position today in Geneva," says one U.S. arms control official, "but the Soviets won't talk."

ABMs would only prompt an offensive-defensive arms race, "it's because of your offensive missiles, not your defensive missiles."[16] The Soviet leader characterized the Soviet ABM as an defensive weapon and therefore unobjectionable. It would not destabilize the arms balance and was therefore not a proper subject for a SALT Treaty.

Soviet footdragging on the ABM issue was the subject of a great deal of speculation at the time. Some observers felt that the American proposal might have touched off an ABM policy debate in the Kremlin.[17] In any case, the lack of positive Soviet response led Secretary McNamara in September 1967 to go ahead with the decision to deploy a relatively light "Chinese oriented" ABM system, which was later dubbed "Sentinel." This decision, it was thought, by some in the Administration, might finally end Soviet reluctance to engage the U.S. in an ABM dialogue.[18]

16 Quoted in Fred Kaplan, *The Wizards of Armageddon* (New York: Simon & Schuster, 1983), p.346.

17 This is the view taken by RAND analyst Thomas W. Wolfe, among others. He argues that "Among signs that internal policy differences in Moscow may have arisen over the question of ABM negotiations was the publication of a *Pravda* article on February 15, 1967, in which Kosygin was made out to be more receptive to the idea of an ABM moratorium than his actual remarks in London a few days before warranted. Two days after the *Pravda* article, written by F. Burlatskii, Western news agencies in Moscow reported that the article had been privately repudiated by Soviet sources, who claimed that the regime's position on ABM negotiations was negative, as would be made clear in a new article." The only problem was that "a corrective article did not appear, suggesting that the isssue was at that point too contentious to handle." On March 31, a "strong statement by a military spokesman of the case for continuing with an ABM deployment program appeared in a *Red Star* article stressing the importance of strategic defense measures along with the value of a powerful offensive posture." Both the article and its timing "again suggested that an internal ABM policy controversy might be going on ..." See Wolfe's prepared statement to the Subcommittee on Military Applications, Joint Committee on Atomic Energy, U.S. Congress and published in *Hearings on the Scope, Magnitude, and Implications of the United States Antiballistic Missile Program,* November 6 and 7, 1967 (Washington, D.C.: Government Printing Office, 1968), pp.63-75.

18 *The New York Times,* September 18, 1967. For a useful "inside" account of the U.S. decision see Morton H. Halperin, "The Decision to Deploy the ABM: Bureaucratic and Domestic Politics in the Johnson Administration," *World Politics,* Vol. 24 (October, 1972), pp.62-95.

ABM Treaty Negotiations

During the late 1960s the two superpowers were finally able to begin serious discussions on ways to limit deployment of Anti-Ballistic Missile systems. In the opinion of the White House, an *absolute* prohibition against each side constructing ABM systems was deemed impossible because both had already begun to construct small ones. Yet the two sides were interested in preventing these systems from expanding across the country. For their part, the Soviets knew that they could overwhelm a limited Safeguard system (the new name for the American ABM), and the Americans knew that they could penetrate the systems around Moscow and Leningrad and destroy these cities. Both sides had a vested interest in a prohibition on further ABM work, since otherwise the two countries would reserve the option of building larger offensive forces certain of overwhelming and/or penetrating possible expanded ABMs of the future.

In retrospect, it seems clear that an absolute ban might have been possible to obtain from the Soviets if the White House had been willing. According to Raymond Garthoff, who participated in the ABM negotiations, "The Soviet Union was even prepared to consider giving up its Moscow defense altogether (although not without appropriate compensation)." But "the possibility of negotiating a 'zero ABM' agreement was prejudiced by an early U.S. proposal, and prompt Soviet acceptance, of a limitation to ABM defense of the National Command Authorities (NCA) in the national capitals."[19]

Why did the Soviets agree so quickly to the American offer when they had been dragging their heels for so long? One can only speculate. But it appears that the technological edge which the U.S. had developed in the field might have been an important factor. As Garthoff concludes: "Soviet acceptance of sharply constrained BMD was certainly facilitated by the fact that the United States had a much superior BMD defense technology and thus capabilites for an important lead in BMD ..."[20]

19 Raymond Garthoff, "BMD and East-West Relations," in Ashton B. Carter *et al.* (eds.), *Ballistic Missile Defense* (Washington, D.C.: The Brookings Institution, 1984), p.286.

20 *Ibid.*

There was also the consideration that by the late 1960s Soviet confidence in its own ABM program may have waned.[21] On the one hand, there were a number of important technical difficulties, rising costs and system inefficiencies. On the other hand, the GALOSH stood to be seriously degraded by the new American technique then under research of equipping land-and-sea based ballistic missiles with MIRVs. This last factor was especially important, as Soviet military writers have noted.[22]

1972 ABM Treaty

In May of 1972, during President Nixon's visit to Moscow, U.S. and Soviet officials signed their treaty on ABMs as well as an interim agreement on offensive missiles. The Senate subsequently approved the two accords.

The 1972 ABM Treaty established the first quantitative arms control limitations in a series of agreed prohibitions on various types of ABM systems. For instance, the testing and deployment of land-mobile, sea-based, air-based and space-based ABM systems were banned. Moreover, MIRVed and other multiple ABM warheads were forbidden, and rapid reload systems were banned. Finally, the deployment of *future* systems substituting for ABM radars, missiles or launchers (e.g. laser interception systems) was effectively prohibited unless agreed upon by both parties. Importantly, the ABM Treaty, which is of indefinite duration, limits each side to anti-missile deployments at strategically insignificant levels. Both the United States and the Soviet Union were restricted to two anti-

21 In late 1968, work on the GALOSH anti-missile system around the Soviet capital apparently came to a standstill about two-thirds of the way toward completion. This suggested to some observers that despite the modest headstart by Moscow in ABM deployment there was some doubt in Soviet leadership circles about the feasibility of obtaining effective missile defense. To be sure, the Soviets continued to pursue a high-level of research interest in the ABM field. See *The New York Times,* February 21, 1969.

22 In a June 1967 article in the confidential Soviet journal *Voyennaya mysl'* by Major General I. Anureyev, Soviet skepticism concerning their ability to surmount these difficulties is evidenced. Three years later, A.A. Sidorenk, author of *The Offensive,* manifested the same pessimism by listing as one of the main qualities of nuclear missiles their "invulnerability in flight."

missile complexes with a maximum of 100 interceptors for each site – not enough to provide meaningful defense for a country's population.[23] One site could be located around the nation's capital and a second in the vicinity of offensive missiles. A subsequent amendment to the treaty limited the number of permissible sites in each country to one with 100 interceptors.[24]

The 1972 ABM Treaty and its 1974 protocol limited the Soviet Union and the United States to one ABM site apiece. The one U.S. ABM site was shut down in 1976 by order of Congress. For their part, the Soviets chose temporarily not to expand their relatively crude ABM system of 64 interceptor missiles (GALOSH) around Moscow.[25]

New ABM Developments

Since the signing of the 1972 ABM Treaty, the Soviet Union has moved to upgrade its ABM capabilities. In the case of a treaty-permitted ABM site around Moscow, half of the sixty-four GALOSH interceptors were removed in 1980.[26] In their place were deployed improved exo-atmospheric GALOSH interceptors and new SH-08 high acceleration endo-atmospheric interceptors. Some Pentagon officials are now projecting that the Soviets will be able to reach the treaty-allowed ceiling of 100 interceptors in the Moscow complex by 1987.[27]

23 The Soviet Union was prepared in 1972 to accept a limit of 75, rather than 100, interceptors for the Moscow deployment. This would, however, have caused complications in the context of balancing equal numbers in view of the American desired deployments for defense of ICBM silos. It was not given serious consideration, according to Raymond Garthoff. See his "BMD and East-West Relations," in Ashton B. Carter *et al.* (eds.), *Ballistic Missile Defense* (Washington, D.C.: The Brookings Institution, 1984), p.314.

24 This protocol was ratified in 1976. See Raymond L. Garthoff, "Negotiating with the Russians: Some Lessons from SALT," *International Security*, Vol. 1, No. 4 (Spring, 1977), pp.3-24.

25 See Nils H. Wessel, "Soviet-American Arms Control Negotiations," *Current History* (May, 1983), p.213.

26 See Rebecca V. Strode, "Space-Based Lasers for Ballistic Missile Defense: Soviet Policy Options," in Keith B. Payne (ed.), *Laser Weapons in Space: Policy and Doctrine* (Boulder, Colo.: Westview, 1983), p.118.

27 U.S. Department of Defense, *Soviet Military Power* (Washington, D.C.: Government Printing Office, 1985), pp.47-48.

U.S. intelligence officers have been observing the upgrading of Soviet ABM facilities with a degree of foreboding. Some more critical observers now maintain that there is mounting evidence that the Soviets may be positioning themselves to "break out" of the ABM Treaty. As these sources see it, the U.S.S.R. is getting ready to deploy systems that are not allowed under the 1972 agreement. Among those systems in dispute is the large phased-array radar at Krasnoyarsk. This radar will be able to track many targets at once, advanced mobile anti-aircraft missiles that could possibly be used against other missiles as well, and ABM launchers that some U.S. intelligence officers say could be quickly reloaded.

At the present time, the evidence of a possible breakout is not conclusive. But developments will bear watching.[28]

SAMs and Their ABM Capability

Perhaps no other ABM issue was, or continues to be, of as much concern to the U.S. as the so-called upgrade issue. This is the fear that the U.S.S.R. might covertly give its widely deployed, anti-aircraft, surface-to-air missile (SAM) forces an ABM capability, thereby putting the United States at a strategic disadvantage.[29]

It was largely because of this worry that American negotiators insisted on a provision in the 1972 ABM treaty which would prohibit either side from giving its non-ABM missiles, launchers or radars ABM capabilities or testing them "in an ABM mode." Importantly, this last phrase was not jointly defined, but the U.S. side inserted into the record a unilateral statement describing events that would in its view constitute testing in an ABM mode. (See Unilateral Statement B in the treaty documents.)

Of the Soviet surface-to-air missiles that are reported to have some ABM capability, there are the SA-5, the SA-10 and the SA-X-12. The SA-5 has been repeatedly improved since the 1960s. But the some 2,000 SA-5 launchers probably still represent little or no ABM capability.

28 See for instance President Reagan's Compliance Report of December, 1985.

29 "The SAMs," observes one U.S. government expert, "would not be effective without Large Phased-Array Radars (LPARs)."

The SA-10 is a separate case. It has been deployed in approximately 800 launchers, and more than half of these have been set up in the vicinity of the Soviet capital. The mobile SA-10 became operational in 1985. In the view of the Pentagon, both the SA-10 and the extensively tested experimental SA-X-12 "may have the potential to intercept some types of U.S. strategic ballistic missiles."[30]

Recently, the SA-X-12 has been the focus of a lot of attention. The Pentagon, for one, believes that it may be an anti-tactical ballistic missile (ATBM). (Although ATBMs are permitted by the ABM Treaty, they may not be used or even tested against strategic missiles.) As the Defense Department publication *Soviet Military Power* writes, the SA-X-12 "may have the capability to engage the Lance and both the Pershing I and Pershing II ballistic missiles."[31] According to one source, the SA-X-12 has been successfully tested against such intermediate-range missiles as the Soviet Scaleboard.[32] There is a great deal of concern over the SA-X-12 in the U.S. intelligence community because its mobility might enable the Kremlin to build thousands of these missiles and hide them in storage until they could be deployed relatively quickly.[33]

One source argues that all three SAMs – the SA-5, the SA-10 and the SA-X-12 – "are more likely to be able to intercept SLBM warheads than ICBM warheads, because the former are generally slower and offer larger radar cross sections." This is especially important, this authority states, "because SLBMs at sea are unlike U.S. ICBMs, and not subject to Soviet counterforce attack."[34]

30 U.S. Department of Defense, *Soviet Military Power* (Washington, D.C.: Government Printing Office, 1985), p.14.

31 U.S. Department of Defense, *Soviet Military Power* (Washington, D.C.: Government Printing Office, 1985), p.48.

32 Hubertus G. Hoffman, "A Missile Defense for Europe?," *Strategic Review* (Summer, 1984), p.53.

33 One insider would describe the numbers battle between CIA, DIA and State as follows: "I was always astonished at the way the Pentagon was trying to manipulate the issue. No matter how far ahead we were/are in technology, they were always crying 'wolf.' using DIA and the service intelligence branches as catspaws. Even after it was determined that the Soviet SH-04 and SH-8s were inferior to the system we abandoned in '76 (as unworkable), the military contintued to push the ABM story, the goal being funding for 'point defense.' (There is a rough parallel in the 'Backfire' bomber issue and the B-1. This is probably why Stansfield Turner (and others) think the Defense Intelligence Agency and company should be abolished.")

34 David S. Yost, "Soviet Ballistic Missile Defense and NATO," *Orbis*, Vol. 29, No. 3 (Summer, 1985), p.284.

System for Detecting and Tracking ICBM Attack

The Soviet system for detecting and tracking a ballistic missile attack consists of a launch-detection satellite network, over-the-horizon radars and a series of large phased-array radars.

According to the Pentagon,[35] the current launch-detection satellite network can provide about a 30-minute warning of any U.S. launch and determine its general origin. Two over-the-horizon radars directed at the ICBM fields in the U.S. also could give 30 minute warning.

Large Phased-Array Radars

The new large phased-array radars (LPARs) being built in the U.S.S.R. are viewed by the CIA as especially important because they could be used to supplement older radars and to form the core of a defense of the national territory. The Reagan Administration has singled out one of these new Soviet LPARs as a violation of the ABM Treaty by virtue of its "siting, orientation and capability."[36] This is the large phased-array radar near the city of Krasnoyarsk in Central-Siberia. This huge facility for ballistic missile early warning and target-tracking was discovered by U.S. officials in 1983. According to the Defense Department, this new radar "closes the final gap" in the Soviet BMD radar coverage network.[37]

When U.S. intelligence first detected the construction site near Krasnoyarsk, they determined that once completed by the late 1980s, this radar would have the appearance and capability of other Soviet LPARs deployed for early warning purposes. The problem was that while other such radars are located at various points along the Soviet periphery, the site of Krasnoyarsk radar is situated on the

35 U.S. Department of Defense, *Soviet Strategic Defense Programs* (Washington, D.C.: Government Printing Office, 1985), p.9.

36 Article VI of the treaty bans the construction of new early warning radars "except ... along the periphery of ... national territory and oriented outwards." See U.S. Arms Control and Disarmament Agency, *Arms Control and Disarmament Agreements* (Washington, D.C.: Government Printing Office, 1982), p.144.

37 U.S. Department of Defense, *Soviet Military Power* (Washington, D.C.: Government Printing Office, 1985), p.46.

interior of the country – nearly 700 kilometers from the Mongolian border. Moreover, its orientation is not toward the People's Republic of China but in a northeasterly direction, towards upper Siberia, the Artic and the Gulf of Alaska. For these reasons, then, the United States claimed that the radar represented a violation of the ABM Treaty which, among other things, spells out the constraints on early-warning radars.

As is well known, the Soviets do not accept this view. As James A. Schear writes: "To the extent that they have offered any explanation, they rely on the provisions of Agreed Statement 'F,' arguing that the radar is permitted because its mission will be to track satellites."[38] Reportedly, "they also point out that its role in space-tracking will become clearer over time – a hint that some have taken as an indication that it will play some role in the next generation of Soviet military space programs."[39]

The role of the new radar site in Soviet BMD is unclear. Some authorities point out that it could aid in determining the size and likely targets of an enemy missile. And this function is critical to ABM defense. However, reports from the U.S. intelligence community suggest that the radar is apparently not designed to function as an ABM battle-management radar.[40] Therefore, if this interpretation is correct, it would not be able to allocate interceptor missiles to incoming warheads. Whatever the true situation, the Soviet Union insists that the radar is being built to perform a mission that the treaty permits, whereas the U.S. is convinced that it will be optimized to perform another, restricted mission. A clear resolution of the dispute remains to be seen.[41]

38 James A. Schear, "Arms Control Treaty Compliance," *International Security*, Vol. 10, No. 2 (Fall, 1985), p.156.

39 See "The Radar at Abalakova – What is it?," F.A.S. *Public Interest Report*, Vol. 37, No. 3 (March, 1984), pp.3-9.

40 See Michael Gordon, "CIA is Skeptical That New Radar is Part of an ABM Defense System," *National Journal* (March 9, 1985), pp.523-24.

41 In October 1985, U.S. and Soviet officials reported an offer by the U.S.S.R. to halt construction on the Krasnoyarsk radar complex if the U.S. dropped its plans to modernize radar systems in Great Britain and Greenland. Some American officials immediately interpreted the Soviet proposal as that the disputed radar facility is a violation of the 1972 treaty. At the same time, the U.S. stated that it was unacceptable to equate the Krasnoyarsk radar with the upgrading of the radars at Fylingdales in Yorkshire and at Thule in Greenland, which officials said were allowable. State Department officials, however, dit not reject the Soviet offer out

Exotic BMD Technologies

Some of the most controversial BMD research is being conducted on what are known as unconventional or "exotic" technologies. These are laser systems, particle beam weapons and millimeter waves or electromagnetics. Unfortunately, little information is publicly available about Soviet programs in these areas.

In the case of millimeter waves, the Kremlin is reportedly developing the very high peak power microwave generators relevant to such application.[42] According to the Defense Intelligence Agency, Soviet particle beam weaponry technological capabilities are approximately equivalent to those of the United States.[43] While it is expected that these approaches will continue to be explored by the Soviets, laser technology appears to hold the greatest ABM promise for space-based systems – however, not now but in the future.

Lasers are a little like flashlights, except that the beam of light is very intensive, highly focused and entirely of one wavelength. As a result, laser devices can produce powerful beams that travel great distances without spreading. But laser systems suffer, among other things, from the fact that they can only operate in good weather, since clouds interfere with the beam. What happens when one tries to blast an intense laser beam through a heavy rainstorm? Steam.

Particle beams can not easily be turned into weapons for similar reasons. In the imagination of military planners, these would be devices that could focus and project atomic particles at the speed of light to intercept and neutralize re-entry vehicles.[44] Scientists have

of hand. "We have neither a positive nor a negative attitude overall to the Soviet proposal," a State Department official said. "There is no decision as of now on how to respond except to probe informally." The *Minneapolis Star and Tribune*, October 29, 1985. "The President's Compliance Report of December, 1985, implicitly resolves this issue," one U.S. arms control official states.

42 See Rebecca V. Strode, "Space-Based Lasers for Ballistic Missile Defense: Soviet Policy Options," in Keith B. Payne (ed.), *Laser Weapons in Space Policy and Doctrine* (Boulder, Colo.: Westview Press, 1983), p.121.

43 The CIA, in a June 26, 1985 statement to a Senate Appropriations subcommittee, predicted that the "Soviets will eventually attempt to build a space-based [particle beam weapon]" but added that the "technical requirements are so severe that we estimate there is a low probability they will test a prototype before the year 2000." Quoted in *The Washington Post*, October 14, 1985. (National Weekly Edition)

44 See Clarence A. Robinson, Jr., "Soviets Push for a Beam Weapon," *Aviation Week and Space Technology*, May 2, 1977, pp.16-61.

been producing high energy particle beams in cyclotrons and other devices for decades. But the laboratory devices require a vacuum, and even large accelerators produce only a weak beam of particles which cannot penetrate the atmosphere. To be used in space, such a weapon would have to have access to large supplies of power for the extraordinarily large amount of energy it would consume.

Soviet BMD research on lasers and particle beams began in the mid-1960s.[45] Already by 1979, the U.S. Defense Department was estimating that Soviet spending on high-energy lasers was five times that of the U.S.[46] Reportedly, the U.S.S.R. is pursuing the technology of ground-based lasers for use against space objects. It is also said to be working on technology for space-based lasers (and particle beams) for use against space objects and aerial targets. According to the 1985 edition of *Soviet Military Power*, "By the late 1980s, the Soviets could have prototypes for ground-based lasers for ballistic missile defense".[47]

John K. Sellers, Chief of the Defense Intelligence Agency's Strategic Defense Branch, recently provided an interesting insight into how estimates on these and other such futuristic systems evolve. "We see small windows into their program – we happen to have one into that area – but we do not get the full scope of what they are working on ... When we say, 'We have evidence that they are working in this area for a space weapon, but no evidence of how many people, how large the effort is,'" Sellers told Congress.

However, as *The Washington Post* noted, when DIA followed up with a program it was much more assertive, insisting that Moscow had a "vigorous program under way for particle beam development and could have a prototype space-based system ready for testing in the later 1990s."[48]

45 Mark E. Miller, *Soviet Strategic Power and Doctrine: The Quest for Superiority* (Bethesda, Md.: Advanced International Studies Institute, 1982), p.244.

46 U.S. Department of Defense, *Soviet Military Power* (Washington, D.C.: Government Printing Office, 1985), p.44.

47 U.S. Department of Defense, *Soviet Military Power* (Washington, D.C.: Government Printing Office, 1985).

48 *The Washington Post*, October 14, 1985. (National Weekly Edition)

Charge and Countercharge

Whether or not the Soviet Union is well ahead of the United States in exotic BMD research, however, is debatable. The Secretary of Defense, Caspar Weinberger, maintains the Soviets are. In a speech before a group of American newspaper editors on April 11, 1985, Weinberger accused the Soviets of possibly preparing to violate existing treaties by deploying a nationwide defense against nuclear missiles. His remarks were part of an effort by the Administration to draw attention to Soviet work on anti-missile defenses and win support for the President's research program for anti-missile weapons. Weinberger maintained that the program was essential as a hedge against such Soviet action.[49]

Weinberger, drawing on the Pentagon's annual assessment of Soviet military power, which had been published the week before, maintained among other things that the Soviet Union was developing moveable radar systems and high-speed missiles to intercept enemy missiles. The assessment stated that the Soviets could develop such a system "within ten years."[50]

Even while they were railing against the American research programs, Weinberger said, the Soviet Union was preparing to use its technological edge to "break out" of the ABM Treaty by establishing an ABM "defense of its national territory ..."[51]

Weinberger's remarks were immediately attacked by opponents of U.S. space-based missile defense and others familiar with the unclassified literature on the subject. For one, John Pike of the Federation of American Scientists stated in rebuttal that the United States was far ahead of the Soviet Union both in missiles that can evade enemy defenses and in radars and computers essential to

49 *The New York Times*, April 12, 1985.

50 In October 1985 the Defense Department released a new booklet which argued that for decades the Soviet Union had devoted more effort and money than the United States to devising ways to defend against nuclear attack. Entitled *Soviet Strategic Defense Programs* (Washington, D.C.: Government Printing Office, 1985), it predicted that the Soviet Union "might" field prototype anti-missile weapons late in this decade, in the 1990s or early in the next century.

51 One U.S. government insider comments here: "The Department of Defense has made similar statements virtually since the ABM Treaty was signed. Arms control treaties are bad for DOD budgets.

build an anti-missile defense system. "There's no doubt that there's an ABM gap, but it's in our favor," Pike argued. He said the Administration's efforts to promote the space-based defense as a hedge against Soviet installation were "laughable."

More authoritative testimony came from within the Pentagon itself from an official knowledgeable about the classified literature on Soviet BMD progress. Robert Cooper, Director of the Defense Advanced Research Projects Agency, said before the Senate Armed Services Committee: "I don't think that the Soviets are far advanced as to where we stand in many, if not most, of these technologies."[52]

Conclusions

As this chapter tries to make clear, the Soviet BMD effort is but part of a much broader attempt by the U.S.S.R. to develop capabilities to pursue major strategic objectives. The Soviet BMD program must thus be seen against this broader background.

Soviet BMD research began shortly after the end of World War II. Evidently, the terrible air raids that the Russian people suffered during the war, particularly in Moscow and Leningrad, demonstrated that the technical means for coping with attack from above was going to be a critical part of war in the future. As one expert on Soviet BMD has observed, "This judgment was coupled with the commitment by the Soviet leadership to protect the homeland from the terrible ravages that it had suffered in World War II, a commitment probably made stronger by perceptions of Soviet unpreparedness at the outset of the war."[53]

Work on the development of an actual BMD program apparently began in the late 1940s or early 1950s. But it was not until the early 1960s that significant ABM systems were actually deployed around Leningrad (later dismantled) and Moscow. Although these two systems were clearly limited and unsophisticated by U.S. standards, they were clear evidence of the Soviet commitment to the development, testing and even deployment of a BMD capability.

52 *The New York Times,* December 22, 1984.

53 Sayre Stevens, "The Soviet BMD Program" in Ashton B. Carter (ed.), *Ballistic Missile Defense* (Washington, D.C.: The Brookings Institution, 1984), p.183.

The question of why the U.S.S.R. chose to deploy the system of first priority around Moscow when its limitations were so obvious still baffles the experts. Some have suggested that the Moscow ABM system had some value in coping with accidental or unauthorized nuclear launch as well as very limited attacks from the U.S. Others have speculated that such a system might have some utility against the British and French deterrent forces which lack MIRV capabilities (although this is now changing). Finally, still other observers have viewed the Moscow complex as an effective system against the small part of the Chinese missile force able to reach the Soviet capital.[54]

The SALT I negotiations, of which the BMD capabilities of the U.S.S.R. played an important part, served to focus one of the great debates relating to Soviet BMD potential. In the main, this controversy concerned the so-called SAM upgrade capabilities of the Soviet Union – whether the U.S.S.R. could somehow enable its widely deployed surface-to-air defenses to serve a useful ABM role. Although some U.S. intelligence analysts have tended to view them in a worst-case context,[55] the general view is that Soviet SAM systems have marginal ABM value at best.

The 1972 ABM Treaty has been widely hailed in the West.[56] But the Soviets, too, accord it much respect.[57] For one thing, it foreclosed an American BMD deployment that could have shored up U.S. superiority in the strategic competition for a while longer. For another, it contributed to Soviet control over the strategic offense-defense interaction. Or so Soviet officials believed. Finally, as a number of other ventures in detente with the United States were abandoned by Moscow, the ABM Treaty took on, in the eyes of the

54 Interestingly, China opposed the 1972 ABM Treaty as part of its opposition to U.S.-Soviet detente and arms control collaboration as a whole.

55 See, for instance, U.S. Department of Defense, *Soviet Military Power* (Washington, D.C.: Government Printing Office, 1985), pp. 46-48.

56 The ABM Treaty is viewed especially favorably by Britain and France. For by limiting Soviet ABM defense to Moscow (and by allowing the Kremlin no more than 100 interceptors) the credibility of the two national deterrents is seen as greatly enhanced. This situation continues to give London and Paris a strong stake in keeping the 1972 ABM Treaty as it is.

57 Military representatives, in particular, have emphasized the importance of the ABM Treaty and its "important contribution to the limitation of strategic arms." See, for example, Semeyko, *Krasnaya zvezda*, April 15, 1983.

Soviet leaders, something of the symbolic significance attributed to it by adherents of detente in the West.

Contrary to some earlier expectations, there is no evidence in the intervening years that Soviet research and development activities in ballistic missile defense (or air defense) have in any significant way been curtailed by the existence of the treaty. In fact, Soviet R&D programs in these areas appear to have flourished. (In the case of air defense, it has led to extensive deployments of new systems.)

Some new ABM equipment began to emerge by the end of the 1970s. These included a new transportable, phased-array radar that appeared to be a product of the air defense technology approach rather than the approach used in the design of the Moscow system. Be that as it may, this time there was little doubt that the radar had a direct ABM function.

Some new ABM interceptors were also tested. These included a long-range missile that represented an improvement over the GALOSH. But more importantly was the testing of a high-acceleration missile which for the first time put the U.S.S.R. in a position to employ atmospheric sorting to discriminate real re-entry vehicles from penetration aids. No doubt, these improvements in the Moscow system will significantly enhance its limited capability. However, given the very large weapons inventories that currently exist in the United States, these defenses cannot seriously hinder an American attack on the Soviet capital.[58]

The same is not true for those exotic systems which are current-

58 Soviet military doctrine recognizes as much. For although the U.S.S.R. has been committed for some time to the development of active defenses, it has concluded that, in general, the offense will overpower the defense. As Marshal V.D. Sokolovsky's classic treatise on Soviet doctrine states, "one must recognize that the present instrumentalities of nuclear attack are undoubtedly superior to the instrumentalities of defense against them." See Marshal V.D. Sokolovsky (Ed.), *Soviet Military Strategy* (Englewood Cliffs, N.J., 1963).
Marshal Sokolovsky's work represented the first major Soviet work on military strategy in thirty-six years. Its editorial bias was unmistakably in favor of the strategic views held by Malinovsky and his followers in the military, and it implicitly criticized some important tenets of Khrushchev. This comprehensive volume is considered a landmark in Soviet military writings, but it is now out of date in many respects. This has not stopped Western writers, however, from quoting it frequently. The quote here can be verified in other more recent authoritative Soviet publications.

ly being researched in the Soviet Union. In the main, little is known about Soviet research on these systems. But claims that Moscow has surpassed the United States in the sort of computer technology and exotic weapons fundamental to a comprehensive shield against enemy nuclear warheads must be approached with skepticism. As U.S. Air Force officers testified before a House Appropriations subcommittee in the spring of 1985; despite years of research on lasers and particle beams, which someday may be used to shoot down incoming warheads, the Soviets "have no identifiable lead in the applications of these technologies to a space-based strategic defense."[59]

As U.S. officials have painfully discovered, in actuality the operational deployment of exotic systems poses numerous problems that are not easily resolved. Even if the Soviets were interested in fielding such a system, it would not be likely in this century. In short, Soviet research interest in this field is evident. But attempts to project "mirror-image" accomplishments in SDI on the Kremlin are unproven.

59 Quoted in *The Washington Post*, October 14, 1985.

"I cannot accept that you don't intend to use it offensively ... you must be contemplating a first strike."
Mikhail Gorbachev

X. SOVIET REACTION TO STAR WARS

The Soviet Union's monopoly on Ballistic Missile Defense came to an abrupt end in March 1983. At that time, President Reagan delivered a major television address to his fellow Americans in which he challenged U.S. scientists to devise a defensive shield capable of eliminating the threat posed by strategic nuclear missiles.[1]

Would it not be better to save lives than to avenge them? Are we not capable of demonstrating our peaceful intentions by applying all our abilities and our ingenuity to achieving a truly lasting stability? I think we are – indeed we must.

After careful consultation with my advisers, including the Joint Chiefs of Staff, I believe there is a way ... It is that we embark on a program to counter the awesome Soviet missile threat with measures that are defensive. Let us turn to the very strengths in technology that spawned our great industrial base ... I know this is a formidable technical task, one that may not be accomplished before the end of the century. Yet, current technology has attained a level of sophistication where it is reasonable for us to begin this effort.

President Reagan, who was counting on his proposal selling well with American voters, called upon the scientific community – "those who gave us nuclear weapons" in the first place – to undertake a long-term missile defense research and development program. This would help us "achieve our ultimate goal of eliminating the threat posed by strategic nuclear missiles." At the time, Reagan did not give out any details about his plan. Only later did Administration officials acknowledge that the project would take decades to reach fruition, with no guarantee of success.

1 The complete text of President Reagan's speech is reproduced in *The New York Times*, March 24, 1983.

The idea for the system, which drew on ideas from the "High Frontier" project, was reportedly planted in the mind of the President by his friend and frequent adviser Edward Teller, the Hungarian-born scientist, often described as the "father of the H-bomb". As *Time* magazine later reported: "Teller's brainstorm became Reagan's dream, and the dream became national policy."[2]

In his original plan, the President envisaged a total shield against nuclear missiles. But Reagan's own senior advisers now regard the immediate purpose of the "Star Wars" program as the defense of American missile silos and military targets, not cities. So far the President refuses to budge on his initial vision. As he said recently, "It's not going to protect missiles. It's going to destroy missiles."

The Critics React

As might be expected, the President's bold, futuristic scheme has encountered a mixed reaction from American politicians and Allied officials who question whether "Buck Rogers" weaponry, however attractive in a visionary sense, offers practical exit from Western strategic doctrine. Some have noted with perhaps a touch of cynicism that Reagan has spent most of his public life opposing arms control agreements and has pressed for bigger and better weapons systems.

Most domestic critics seriously question what they call "Reagan's challenge to America's scientists to achieve a technological miracle that would make the successful race to the moon child's play by comparison." For their part, many members of Congress are deeply concerned about the potentially destabilizing effect of the President's proposal on the arms race. Senator Edward Kennedy (D-Mass.) for one, has termed the plan a "reckless Star Wars scheme." Senator Mark Hatfield (R-Oregon) has declared that Reagan "has, in effect, called for the militarization of the last great hope for international cooperation and peace – outer space."[3]

Allied reaction was also highly critical or, at best, reserved. There are few enthusiastic voices among America's West European

2 *Time*, May 7, 1984.

3 *U.S. News and World Report*, April 4, 1983.

allies. Many commentators in Europe express fears that emphasizing a U.S. missile defense system aimed primarily at Soviet ICBMs would "decouple" Western Europe from the U.S. security umbrella.

Recently, some NATO allies have changed their minds in the wake of a heavy selling campaign by the Reagan Administration. For one, the United Kingdom is now on record as standing behind Washington's research plans. For another, the West German government of Chancellor Helmut Kohl (CDU/CSU/FDP), initially skeptical, has recently decided to follow Britain's decision to close ranks behind Washington's lead.[4] Still other West European allies have allowed their domestic corporations to participate in American research efforts while remaining governmentally aloof.

Initial Soviet Reaction

Soviet response to Reagan's Strategic Defense Initiative (SDI) has been universally negative. From the first TASS account soon after the President's speech, Soviet commentary has stressed that "the deployment of such antimissile defense systems would be a direct violation of the Soviet-American (ABM) Treaty."[5] Military representatives, in particular, have emphasized the importance of the 1972 treaty and "its important contribution to the limitation of strategic arms."[6] Reagan's Star Wars initiative is seen as unsettling the ABM balance.

For his part, General Secretary Yuri Andropov was quick to term the President's plan "irresponsible."[7] It "would open the floodgates," he said, "to a runaway race for all types of strategic arms, both defensive and offensive." Andropov added that in embarking on arms control negotiations the two superpowers had "agreed

4 *The New York Times,* December 12, 1985. On this day Chancellor Kohl's Cabinet agreed to begin negotiations with the U.S. for a role in SDI research. The West German decision came but a month after the Soviets publicly warned West Germany that its participation in President Reagan's Star Wars research project could undermine the 1972 ABM Treaty. For details see *The Washington Post,* November 14, 1985.

5 TASS, Radio Moscow, in FBIS, *Daily Report: Soviet Union,* March 24, 1983, p. AA2.

6 See the interview in *Pravda,* March 27, 1983.

7 Semeyko, *Krasnaya zvezda,* April 15, 1983.

that there is an inseverable interrelationship between strategic offensive and defensive weapons." He stated that it was "not by chance" that the Anti-Ballistic Missile (ABM) Treaty of 1972 was signed simultaneously with the SALT I accord limiting strategic arms. The Soviet leader concluded with the warning that the U.S.S.R. would never allow "the development of ABM systems that could render our ICBMs impotent."

From the perspective of Moscow, one of the greatest dangers inherent in the Reagan proposal has to do with the offensive capability it would give the United States. In the view of Soviet military leaders, the possession by the United States of a system thought to be a foolproof missile defense system might lead U.S. officials to feel they could launch a surprise nuclear attack against the Soviet Union, confident that a retaliatory blow could be stopped or deterred with their own defensive missiles. From the perspective of some American arms control experts outside the Administration, such a situation might sorely tempt the Soviet leadership to launch a preemptive nuclear strike before the U.S. was able to put in place an effective ABM system.

At various times, Ronald Reagan has offered to share U.S. technology with the Soviets so that both sides could work together toward the realization of the U.S. President's dream. But so far the Soviets have been unpersuaded. There are just too many technical problems involved. General Nikolai Chernov of the General Staff, for example, declares that "as a matter of principle, there does not and cannot exist any absolute weapons. 'Absolutely reliable antiballistic missile defense' is just a mirage."[8] Owing to the fact that the superpowers "have reached approximately the same scientific-technical standards and have weapons that are roughly equivalent ... neither side can overtake the other by a great margin. This is also true of BMD." And other Soviet sources repeat "there can be no effective defense means in a nuclear war."[9]

Perhaps the most authoritative early Soviet comment on SDI came from General Secretary Yuri Andropov. On the face of it, he acknowledged that "laymen might find it even attractive as the (American) President speaks about what seems to be defensive meas-

8 Interview in *Pravda,* April 29, 1983.

9 Soltan, FBIS, *Daily Report: Soviet Union,* April 13, 1983, p.AA4.

ures." But "that is true only for those who are not conversant with these matters." Andropov noted that:[10]

in fact the strategic forces of the United States will continue to be developed and upgraded at full tilt and along a quite definite line at that, namely that of acquiring a first-strike nuclear capability. Under these conditions, the intention to acquire the capability of destroying the strategic systems of the other side with the aid of BMD, that is, of rendering the other side incapable of dealing a retaliatory strike, is a bid to disarm the Soviet Union in the face of the American nuclear threat. One must see this clearly in order to appraise correctly the true meaning of this "new concept."

Soviet concern over the development of a deployable ABM system has not decreased since the death of Andropov in February 1983. His immediate successor Konstantin Chernenko stated on a number of occasions the seriousness of a BMD situation which leave the Soviets at a distinct disadvantage. His successor Mikhail Gorbachev has also been much opposed to the idea of a space-based ABM system.

Gorbachev's Interview with Time

The new Soviet leader chose in the September 9, 1985 edition of *Time* magazine to make – among other things – his position on Star Wars absolutely clear to the American people. Five months earlier he told a group of visiting Congressmen that "we don't all live in caves."[11] In a two-hour and twelve-minute conversation with the editors of the U.S. weekly, Gorbachev took the opportunity to stress "the immutable fact that whether we like one another or not, we can either survive or perish together."

"We cannot take in earnest the assertions that the SDI would guarantee invulnerability from nuclear weapons, thus leading to the elimination of nuclear weapons," he said. "In the opinion of our experts (and, to my knowledge, of many of yours), this is sheer fantasy." However, "even on a much more modest scale, in which the Strategic Defense Initiative can be implemented as an antimissile

10 *Pravda*, March 27, 1983.

11 *The Minneapolis Star and Tribune*, May 10, 1985.

defense system of limited capabilities, the SDI is very dangerous. This project will, no doubt, whip up the arms race in all areas, which means that the threat of war will increase. That is why this project is bad for us and for you and for everybody in general."

We approach SDI research from the same point of view, Gorbachev stated. "First of all, we do not consider it to be a research program. In our view, it is the first step stage of the project to develop a new ABM system prohibited under the treaty of 1972. Just think of the scale of it alone – $ 70 billion to be earmarked for the next few years. That is an incredible amount for pure research, as emphasized even by U.S. scientists as well." The point "is that in today's prices those appropriations are more than four times the cost of the Manhattan Project and more than double the cost of the Apollo program that provided for the development of space research for a whole decade – up to the landing of man on the moon. That this is far from being a pure research program is also confirmed by other facts, including tests scheduled for space strike weapons systems."

"That is why the entire SDI Program and its so-called research component are a new and even more dangerous round of the arms race. It is necessary to prevent an arms race in space. We are confident that such an agreement is possible and verifiable. (I have to point out that we trust the Americans no more than they trust us, and that is why we are interested in reliable verification of any agreement as much as they are.)"

Gorbachev went on to say that without such an agreement it would not be possible to reach an agreement on the limitation and reduction of nuclear weapons. "The interrelationship between defensive and offensive arms is sò obvious as to require no proof," he said. "Thus, if the present U.S. position on space weapons is its last word, the Geneva negotiations will lose all sense."

The General Secretary then concluded the written portion of his remarks by declaring: "On behalf of the Soviet leadership and the Soviet people, I would like once again to tell all Americans the most important thing they should know: war will not come from the Soviet Union. We will never start war."

Gorbachev's interview with *Time* laid bare some deep-seated Soviet concerns regarding SDI. But it also showed the new Soviet leader at his best – a party chief who mixes an unprecedented degree of charm and subtlety with the more traditional characteristics of discipline and persistence. Of course, his remarks revealed a one-sided and self-serving view of the world, but they also showed a world leader eager to "talk turkey" with President Reagan at an upcoming summit meeting at which arms control and SDI would be the crucial matters for debate.

Differing Interpretations of the 1972 ABM Treaty

Just a few weeks after Gorbachev's interview with *Time* magazine a controversy broke out in the United States over Star Wars, which was closely followed in Moscow. Basically, this uproar concerned an attempt to reinterpret the 1972 ABM Treaty. It was sparked by a review of the agreement by Philip Kunsberg, a 35-year-old Pentagon staff lawyer whose background included battles against pornographers and the Mafia but no arms control experience.

Kunsberg's study was commissioned by Fred Ikle, the Undersecretary of Defense for Policy, and Richard Perle, Assistant Secretary for International Security Policy in the Pentagon. Both men are strong Star Wars supporters. On their initiative, Kunsberg undertook an investigation of the secret negotiating history of the ABM Treaty. After spending less than a week at his task, he outlined his conclusions in a 19-page report. The bottom line was startling: the treaty allowed for nearly unlimited development and testing of components for President Reagan's Strategic Defense Initiative.

Kunsberg's view, which was subsequently embraced by Defense Secretary Caspar Weinberger,[12] marked a major re-interpretation of the Treaty, which is considered by arms control experts to be one of the most important arms control agreements between the United States and the Soviet Union. It also contradicted the public position of four American presidents, including Ronald Reagan.

Traditionally, in the 13 years since the 1972 ABM Treaty was signed, the United States had taken the position that the agreement bans the testing and development derived from "new physical prin-

12 *The Washington Post*, November 4, 1985.

ciples," such as laser beams. While this ban is not flatly stated in the treaty, it is based on the cumulative evidence of several phrases and statements, some ambiguous.

Nevertheless, trying to fit work on Star Wars within the Treaty restrictions had become increasingly problematical for the Administration as its SDI program moved closer to a phase requiring technical testing of potential components. Therefore, in April, 1985, the Administration had already offered an interpretation of the ABM Treaty that distressed arms control advocates. In a report to Congress, the Pentagon maintained that major SDI tests planned in coming years would involve only restricted "subcomponents" of systems, or would be tested against satellites in space instead of incoming rockets, and thus would not violate ABM stipulations.[13]

As Kunsberg began his review, he was astonished to discover in his study of the treaty the rather large gap between what the treaty said and what was attributed to it. He suggested that the treaty might allow more Star Wars testing than had been previously believed.

Assistant Secretary of Defense Perle "almost fell off the chair" when presented with Kunsberg's report, he later remarked. Suddenly, most of the restrictions posed for future SDI "testing" and "development" by the ABM Treaty seemed of doubtful validity. Moreover, Kunsberg's analysis even questioned whether Star Wars "deployment" would be curbed by the treaty.

Kunsberg's conclusion subsequently set off a hot internal debate in the Administration. For one, Paul Nitze, who helped negotiate the ABM Treaty in 1972 and who was now a senior arms control adviser in the State Department, recalled that the U.S. had tried hard to close the door on all new defensive weapons in 1972 but the Soviets "would not agree to that."[14]

The debate over how to interpret the ABM Treaty pitted Secretary of State George Shultz against Defense Secretary Caspar Weinberger. As the two department secretaries continued to press their arguments, the President's Special Assistant for National Security Affairs Robert C. McFarlane seemed to come down on the side of Weinberger and the civilian leadership of the Defense Department.

13 See *The Washington Post*, October 22, 1985.

14 *The Christian Science Monitor*, October 24, 1985.

On October 6, McFarlane volunteered the view that the "testing" and "development" of ABMs based on "new physical concepts" is "approved and authorized by the treaty" rather than banned.

McFarlane's statement was immediately picked up in Europe where he was seen as speaking for the President on this crucial matter. Reportedly, some of America's closest allies were shocked by the new interpretation with which they did not agree. Generally, they were concerned that differences with the Soviets over this issue might cause a breakdown in the upcoming summit between President Reagan and General Secretary Mikhail Gorbachev.

Washington columnists Rowland Evans and Robert Novak subsequently reported that personal letters from Western European leaders on the subject arrived at the White House soon after McFarlane's "Meet the Press" interview. According to one insider, Chancellor Helmut Kohl of West Germany and British Prime Minister Margaret Thatcher claimed in "hysterical" terms that the new stand taken by McFarlane was intolerable in Europe.[15]

If many outsiders were disturbed by the new line being developed by the Reagan Administration, Gerard Smith was certainly included in this number. Having played an important role in negotiating the 1972 ABM Treaty, he was intimately familiar with not only its public obligations but also its private negotiating history. In general, he denounced the stance being taken by Kunsberg and his allies in the bureaucracy. As he stated in a letter to the *New York Times*,[16] it "is clear that the Reagan Administration has repudiated its former position, and that of all previous administrations, that the anti-ballistic missile treaty bars development and testing of space-based strategic defenses or components of them that use lasers, particle beams and other types of nontraditional technology." This "new interpretation of the treaty has drastic implications for the survival of the treaty and indeed of the whole arms control process."

As the former head of the United States delegation to the stra-

15 See *The Washington Post*, October 21, 1985.

16 *The New York Times*, October 23, 1985. See also Gerard C. Smith, statement before the House Foreign Affairs Subcommittee on Arms Control, International Security and Science on "ABM Treaty and SDI," 99th Congress, 1st session, October 22, 1985, p. 4.

tegic arms limitation talks that negotiated the ABM Treaty, he said, "I would like to record that it was not our intention that any type of technology for space-based ABM systems could be developed or tested under this treaty." According to Smith, the "controlling provision of the treaty (which the Senate ratified by a vote of 88 to 2) is Article 5. Section I reads, 'Each party undertakes not to develop, test or deploy ABM systems or components which are sea-based, air-based, space-based or mobile land-based.'"[17]

Gerard Smith went on to state that the "Article 5 ban seems unambiguous to this writer." However, "if the Administration is concerned about some ambiguity in the negotiating record, it should be recalled that the treaty anticipated this contingency and provided for consultational machinery to clarify any such situation. Would it not at least be prudent, as well as correct international procedure, to undertake such consultation with the other party to the treaty before the Administration implements this new interpretation in carrying out the 'Star Wars' program?"

Many arms control specialists were quick to agree that the legislative record supported the restrictive interpretation taken by Gerard Smith and previous administrations. For one, Alton Frye, an arms control expert on the Council of Foreign Relations, recalled that when the treaty was debated in the Senate Armed Services Committee in 1972, the late Senator Henry M. Jackson berated military witnesses for having accepted limitations on the testing and development of new technologies. Senator Jackson then voted for the accord on the understanding that Article 5 precluded the development and testing of such technologies as lasers, except in fixed, land-based ABM systems. "The Senate was absolutely clear beyond any doubt that this was the interpretation on which it based its rati-

17 Retired Lt. General Royal B. Allison, who was the senior military official on the U.S. ABM negotiating delegation, backs up the view taken by Gerard Smith. According to an interview Allison gave, he said that he was deeply involved in the discussion on this issue because the Joint Chiefs of Staff were determined to leave room for "research and research-testing" in case "exotic" ABMs such as lasers could someday be developed. "Nowhere did I understand that we retained the right to development and full-scale testing of new systems," Allison said. Adding, he stated, "I didn't have any doubt in my mind as to what the Soviets had approved. If there had been any doubt you can be sure we would have announced it." Quoted in *The Washington Post,* November 4, 1985.

fication," asserted Alton Frye. "So I see deep constitutional problems, a usurpation by the executive of the congressional role."[18]

From the beginning of the internal debate, Paul Nitze is reported to have taken the position that was later to prevail. Legalities aside, he argued, the most vital job of the government was to "keep faith" with the interpretation of the treaty previously presented to the Congress, the public and U.S. allies. The Special Adviser to Shultz appears to have been the driving force behind the Secretary of State's proposal, ultimately accepted by the President in a showdown meeting in the White House. This meeting, which took place October 11, resulted in the decision to regard the new interpretation as a matter of law, while retaining the "old" ABM interpretation restricting SDI testing and developing as a matter of administration policy.[19]

The final decision, did not specify how long the President would continue to observe the "old interpretation." Presumably it could be abandoned whenever convenient, since it is only a matter of presidential policy rather than treaty law.

On October 14, 1985, Secretary Shultz was given the job of making the Administration's decision public. He announced on this day that the government would limit its testing and deployment of anti-missile defensive technology to comply with the restrictive interpretation of the 1972 ABM Treaty. Shultz said that the Administration was doing this *even though it believed that interpretation to be wrong.*[20]

The treaty, he said, could "be variously interpreted as to what kinds of development and testing are permitted, particularly with respect to future systems." It is "our view ... that a broader interpretation of our authority is fully justified. This is, however, a moot point. Our SDI research program has been structured and, as the President has reaffirmed, will continue to be conducted in accordance with a restrictive interpretation of the treaty's obligations."

Generally, the "battle over interpretations" was viewed as a "vic-

18 Quoted in *The Christian Science Monitor,* October 24, 1985. For a scholarly discussion of the ambiguities in the ABM Treaty see Alan B. Sheer, "The Language of Arms Control," *Bulletin of the Atomic Scientists* (November, 1985), pp. 23-29.

19 *The Washington Post,* October 22, 1985.

20 *The Minneapolis Star and Tribune,* October 15, 1985.

tory" for the Secretary of State over Defense Department civilians, led by Secretary of Defense Caspar Weinberger, who appeared to want to make the ABM Treaty a "dead letter" (Gerard Smith's words). However, in the view of the supporters of ABM, as long as the "permissive legal interpretation" remained unrepudiated, important treaty restraints, which contribute directly to U.S. security, remained only tenuously in effect.[21]

Marshal Akhromeyev Speaks Out

During the furor in Washington over how the ABM Treaty should be interpreted, the Soviets remained pretty much on the sidelines. Their obvious displeasure, however, was made manifest on October 19, 1985 in an article in *Pravda*. At that time, the Chief of the Soviet General Staff, Marshal Sergei F. Akhromeyev, wrote that recent calls by the Reagan Administration to reinterpret the treaty were "a deliberate deceit."

In the *Pravda* article, Marshal Akhromeyev declared further"The treaty absolutely unambiguously bans the development of ABM systems regardless of whether these systems are based on existing or future technologies." Any other interpretations, he asserted, "contradict reality."

"The present aim of the United States Administration," Akhromeyev stated, is clear: "to prepare a legal base for carrying out all the stages of practical work within the framework of the S D I program, that is, the development, testing and deployment of space-strike weapons."

The Chief of the Soviet General Staff went on to open up the possibility of a major Soviet expansion in space-based defensive weaponry and said that "there will be no American monopoly in outer space." Marshal Akhromeyev threatened that if the Reagan Administration's SDI program is continued, "nothing will remain but for us to adopt countermeasures in the field of both offensive and other armaments, not excluding defensive ones, and including those based in outer space."

21 See, for instance, Michael Krepon, "Dormant Threat to the ABM Treaty," *Bulletin of the Atomic Scientists* (January, 1986), pp.31-33.

Akhromeyev stated that the U.S.S.R. "cannot show naiveté and count only on peaceful assurances by U.S. leaders that serve as a cover for developing strike weapons in space."

The Soviet Marshal's description represented the most detailed public explanation of the Soviet position on space strike weapons since Mikhail Gorbachev's interview in *Time* magazine six weeks earlier. Generally, Western observers in Moscow saw in Akhromeyev's strict definition of the testing allowed by the ABM Treaty a clear signal to Washington of the limits of the Soviet position on SDI research.

Importantly, Akhromeyev stated in response to President Reagan's frequent charge that Moscow was developing its own Star Wars program: "The Soviet Union is not engaged in developing and consequently testing any models of space systems whatsoever. We do not have a program of creating space strike systems or Star Wars plans analogous to the American ones."

An Interview with Soviet Journalists

In late October, hardly two weeks after Secretary of State Shultz's attempt to put a cap on the debate over reinterpreting the ABM Treaty, President Reagan invited a small group of Soviet journalists to interview him in the White House. This freewheeling session, which represented the first Soviet interview of an American President in 24 years, was given with the upcoming U.S.-Soviet summit conference in mind.

Reagan appeared to hold his own during the 42-minute question-and-answer period. But when the interview appeared four days later (on November 4) in *Izvestia*, the official government newspaper of the Soviet Union, a number of controversial responses were deleted, along with other passages where the President disputed official Soviet policy explanations.[22] Perhaps more impor-

22 Deputy *Izvestia* editor Nicholai Efimov told Western journalists in Moscow that his paper ran the interview exactly as TASS' Washington office transmitted it. Efimov said the four-day delay in publishing the interview was a result of technical productions and distribution schedules not disputes in editing. *Izvestia* played down the interview by putting it on page 4 without illustration.

tantly, the President's offer to share Star Wars research was also deleted. This was in keeping with official Soviet depictions of his stance on the issue as hard-line and intractable.

No doubt, the President startled his guests when he stated in the interview that the deployment of his proposed space-based missile defense system would come about only *after* an agreement to eliminate offensive nuclear missiles. By making this statement Reagan seemed to be adding a major new twist to the U.S. plan for SDI. Previously, the President had indicated that he hoped to make nuclear weapons obsolete with the missile defense. By saying that "the terms for getting it" would be "the elimination of the offensive weapons," the President appeared to be expanding on his earlier pledge to share the technology.

When questioned about the President's new proposal to make the elimination of offensive weapons a condition for deployment of defensive weapons, a White House spokesman tried to play down the idea. He said that the President was referring to a "transition period" for negotiations before deployment of the missile defense sytem. He said that Reagan was discussing a goal "to do away with all offensive weapons and end up with everybody sharing a star shield or nuclear shield."[23]

Nevertheless, in his interview, the President said matter of factly: "We would not deploy ... until we sit down with the other nations of the world, and those that have nuclear arsenals, and see if we cannot come to an agreement on which there will be deployment only if there is elimination of the nuclear weapons." Reagan said he would make this point to Gorbachev. "We won't put this weapons, or this system in place, this defensive system, until we do away with our nuclear missiles, our offensive missiles," he stated. "But we will make it available to other countries, including the Soviet Union, to do the same thing."[24]

23 See *The Washington Post*, November 5, 1985.

24 Later in an interview with news agency correspondents, President Reagan said that he had been misunderstood when he remarked that his space-based missile defense system would not be deployed until all nuclear missiles are eliminated. Reagan said he would still seek elimination of nuclear weapons in talks with the allies and Soviets about sharing the strategic defense system. He added that if the Soviets refused to go along, "we would go ahead and deploy it." See *The Washington Post*, November 7, 1985.

"And if the Soviet Union and the United States both say we will eliminate our offensive weapons, we will put in this defensive thing in case some place in the world a madman some day tries to create these weapons again," he said.

Reagan compared strategic defense to the decision to outlaw poison gas after World War I. We "all kept our gas masks," the President said. "Well this weapon, if such can be developed, would be today's gas mask."

In response to a question, Reagan acknowledged criticism that his SDI, coupled with offensive missiles, could put one state in a position where they might be more likely to dare a first strike. However, the President said this would not be the case if the technology is shared. And "I can assure you we are not going to try and monopolize this ... for a first-strike capability."

Twice in the interview Reagan proposed to share Star Wars research with the Soviet Union. But neither offer appeared in *Izvestia*. The President's assurances that the U.S. would not deploy a space-strike weapon in violation of the 1972 ABM Treaty was also omitted by the Soviet publication.

In his interview, Reagan defended research on SDI vigorously. But in an extensive critique, *Izvestia* rebutted the President's defense of U.S. arms control policy point by point. The rebuttal, which like the interview covered a page of the nationally distributed newspaper, dismissed the interview as "nothing new," "propaganda" and a distortion of facts. "Nevertheless, the TASS commentary said, "the awareness of the need for extensive Soviet-U.S. dialogue is a positive development."

A Leak to the Press

The Reagan interview with *Izvestia* was published in the Soviet Union just as Secretary of State George P. Shultz arrived in Moscow to begin working out final arrangements for the President's November 19-20, 1985 meeting in Geneva with Soviet leader Mikhail Gorbachev. The White House had sought the interview to put Reagan's views before the Soviet people before the summit. (Requests for a presummit appearance by the President on Soviet TV had been ignored.)

Shultz's talks in the Soviet capital were for the most part frustrating and inconclusive. Differences were so great between the two sides that not even the usual communiqué for the summit could be agreed upon. And once again SDI was a major sticking point. The Soviets were still attempting to block the program from going beyond the research stage, and the American side was equally firm in maintaining its options.

When the two principals finally sat down for extended face-to-face talks, things were not much better at first. The atmosphere had been overshadowed, in part, by the controversy surrounding publication of a private letter to President Reagan by Defense Secretary Weinberger. In the letter, which was leaked to the press just before the meeting to maximize its impact, Weinberger strongly advised the President not to give the Soviets any assurances "that you will continue to be bound" by current SDI research limits because that "would diminish significantly the prospects that we will succeed in bringing our search for a strategic defense to fruition." Weinberger also urged Reagan to avoid a Geneva agreement pledging U.S. adherence to the unratified SALT II Treaty because it "would limit severely your options for responding to Soviet [treaty] violations." (The treaty was due to expire at the end of the following month.)

Weinberger's tough advice was carried in a three-page cover letter to the Defense Department's study of alleged Soviet violations of SALT that was delivered to the White House. A copy of the letter was secretly obtained by *The Washington Post* and subsequently published, touching off a furor.

Reportedly, the President was outraged with the leak of Weinberger's letter, interpreting it as a flagrant attempt by the Pentagon to influence his hand in the upcoming negotiations with Gorbachev. However, if severely perturbed, the President ended up following Weinberger's advice to the letter on the issue of SDI and SALT.

U.S.-Soviet Summit Conference

By most accounts, the discussions between the two leaders were cordial if heated at times. As expected, both sides made a special point of addressing the Strategic Defense Initiative in the talks. For his part, the President tried to sell missile defense to the Soviets ("there is a new technology here which may give us a different way of doing things better"); and for his part, Gorbachev accused Reagan of spreading the arms race into space ("Don't you believe us when we say we won't wage a first strike?")

The President pulled no punches in his campaign to persuade the Soviet leader. At one place in the discussions, he tried to make the point that the underlying premises on which nuclear deterrence was founded had been undermined. "Wouldn't it be better to adopt a system that does not involve threats at all," he is reported to have told Gorbachev.[25]

But the Soviet leader was not impressed with Reagan's intensive lobbying efforts. "I can't deal in visions," Gorbachev said.

The following short dialogue, as excerpted from *Newsweek*,[26] is typical of the kind of exchanges the two leaders must have had over SDI.

Reagan reached into his pocket and brought out a document that was written in Russian. It contained a U.S. proposal for reducing strategic nuclear weapons by 50 percent – but without eliminating Star Wars. Gorbachev just shrugged off the piece of paper. "We just disagree," he stated.

Later in the discussions Gorbachev spelled out some of his concern. "I understand exactly what you are saying," he told the President, "and I disagree with it." The General Secretary argued that Reagan's plan was "a feeling based on emotion and not on a realistic reckoning with the facts." He maintained that SDI would never work and that it made no sense for Reagan to spend billions on the system unless he had another motive. "I cannot accept that you don't intend to use it offensively," declared Gorbachev. He insisted that "you must be contemplating a first strike."

25 For a report on what the President intended to say to Gorbachev see *The New York Times*, September 27, 1985.

26 The dialogue is taken from *Newsweek*, December 2, 1985.

"I've explained to you that when [after World War II] we had a monopoly on offense, we didn't use it," the President replied. "Why don't you trust me?"

"Would you believe me if I said that the Soviet Union will never attack the United States," asked Gorbachev. "As a leader, I can't take it on faith alone. We won't be run out of the game. We should negotiate now. A year or 18 months from now, it will be more difficult. You're trying to catch a firebird ..."

Shortly Thereafter, the Talk Adjourned

Despite the lack of progress on SDI, the summit was generally viewed by Western analysts as a moderate success. President Reagan told his Cabinet after the talks that his face-to-face meeting with Gorbachev had "cleared the air." He said the two men had agreed to "keep in touch, keep in contact," even before they were scheduled to meet again the following year.[27]

If the American side seemed fairly happy with the results of the superpower discussions, the Soviets continued to emphasize Star Wars as the major stumbling block to normalizing relations. Generally, as the Soviets saw things, the Reagan Administration was determined to regain military superiority over the U.S.S.R. And the space-based ABM initiative was seen as the main instrument for doing so.[28]

Possible Soviet Countermeasures to SDI

At their summit President Reagan and Soviet Party leader Gorbachev discussed the Star Wars issue at length. But neither could convince the other of his point of view. Reagan said that the U.S. reserved the right to continue research on space-based missile defense, whereas Gorbachev said he wanted a ban on any research, testing or deployment of space strike weapons.

27 *The New York Times*, November 23, 1985.

28 This opinion was expressed by Genrikh Trofimenko of the Soviet Institute of the U.S.A. and Canada, in *The New York Times*, October 10, 1985.

Gorbachev, reportedly, did not spell out what the Soviets would do against SDI. This was in keeping with past remarks for public consumption which only vaguely hinted at possible Soviet countermeasures. Previously, Gorbachev himself and other officials had stated on various occasions that they would merely take "adequate" measures against the antiballistic missile defense system envisioned by the U.S. President.

What specific countermeasures might the Soviets take against the new technologies of SDI? For one thing, the Kremlin could decide to match the United States and build a defensive shield of its own. As Soviet officials stated on October 22, 1985, Moscow was prepared to devote whatever resources were necessary to develop a space-based missile defense if the U.S. did not abandon its own efforts.[29] While denying American assertions that the U.S.S.R. is already conducting an extensive effort in this area, the officials said the Soviet Union could afford to divert resources to the new weapons systems without compromising plans to spur economic growth.

If a Soviet counter SDI program is one option, it is not the most likely one, according to many outside experts. Eric Stubbs, a Harvard University economist and specialist on Soviet military affairs, tells why.[30] For one thing, Soviet efforts in this area are hobbled by a lack of key technology and management expertise. Stubbs' recent study, which challenges assertions by Pentagon officials, says that Soviet scientists are perhaps a decade behind the U.S. in computers, advanced sensors, integrated circuits, optics, signal processing and software. These are all critical components to the development of an effective defense against ballistic missiles.

More importantly, Stubbs argues, the apparent absence of any central coordination of its space defense research may frustrate Soviet efforts to manage the huge amount of resources and personnel required to rival the American program. According to Stubbs, Soviet military research is fragmented. Several military bureaucracies are

29 The Soviet officials were Marshal Sergei F. Akhromeyev, who has been a leading spokesman on Soviet military policy, as well as Chief of the General Staff; Georgi M. Korniyenko, a First Deputy Foreign Minister; and Leonid M. Zamyatin, the Soviet leadership's spokesman..They appeared at a news conference in Moscow. See *The New York Times*, October 23, 1985.

30 Stubb's study was published in January 1986 by the Council on Economic Priorities.

secretly working on similar projects with little communications among them. "Resources are often allocated to those pet projects of the most influential officials" rather than on the basis of strategic priority, Stubbs maintains.

To be sure, Stubbs' study acknowledges that the Soviets have made "some provocative and impressive strides in bringing the exotic technologies closer to some semblance of prototype systems." But he insists that without the advanced sensors and computers to detect and track enemy missiles, sort out decoys, direct weapons firings and provide damage assessments, these exotic weapons technologies cannot be tied into a workable system.

Stubbs further maintains that by concentrating on the rapid and premature development of a few "conspicuous, technologically prestigious" prototypes, rather than investigating a broad range of technologies, the Soviet Union runs the risk of suddenly discovering it has been pursuing unworkable solutions.

In view of the many serious problems connected with the development of a space-based ABM system, the Soviets are much more likely to turn to ways which would frustrate the defensive system being researched by the United States. For one thing, the technologies required for countermeasures are in a much more advanced state than those required for Star Wars itself.[31] Indeed, much of the necessary technology already exists. Here a number of promising options are available to the Kremlin.

In the case of lasers, ICBM and SLBM boosters might be hardened in order to improve their survivability under laser attack. Some other defensive measures could also be implemented to defend Soviet missiles from the effects of lasers. For example, Richard Garwin has suggested that boosters might be protected from laser illumination by "hiding" behind aluminum foil screens perhaps 100 meters square. Missiles could also be equipped with electronic countermeasures for use against the command and control system of the laser. Also, the surface of a missile could be made highly reflective so that little light is absorbed. The Soviets might experiment with these and other options.[32]

31 See Stephen Shenfield, "Soviets may not imitate Star Wars," *Bulletin of the Atomic Scientists* (June-July, 1985), p.38.

32 For a good discussion of Soviet policy options see Rebecca V. Strode, "Space-

Rather than try to protect missiles against the effects of lasers, the Soviets might well try to overwhelm the BMD system with a large number of targets. Theoretically, the Soviet Union could saturate the target acquisitions and aiming capacities of the opposing laser satellites by greatly proliferating the number of boosters. "Fractionalization" or increasing the number of MIRVs carried by Soviet missiles is easier for the U.S.S.R. because its large missiles have greater payloads. Recently, the Joint Chiefs of Staff told Congress that Soviet SS-18 ICBMs could be fitted with 30 warheads each instead of the 10 now permitted by an unratified SALT II Treaty.[33]

Most Soviet military experts also expect the Soviets to step up the development – already in progress – of cruise missiles and submarines with which to launch them. As now organized, the Pentagon's Strategic Defense Initiative Office directing Star Wars research has no programs to deal with cruise missiles or aircraft.

Another Soviet countermeasure often discussed by strategic analysts involves firing ballistic missiles from offshore submarines on what are called "depressed" or low-angle trajectories. By using such low-angle trajectories, boosters and warheads would spend much less time in space outside the atmosphere. Moreover, the elapsed time from launching to target would be significantly less. These factors would go far toward complicating nuclear defense.

"Precursor attacks" are still another possible Soviet countermeasure. And, in the view of a number of experts, they are one of the most likely. Such attacks would be timed to take place shortly before salvos of missiles were launched at key targets in the United States. Conceivably, they could take a variety of forms. But in basic terms, they would involve detonating nuclear weapons in space to blind, cripple or destroy the defensive armada. Also, they could attack the relatively delicate ground stations in the U.S. that would be relaying battle data to and from the defensive weapons. A combination of several countermeasures would probably be the most effective way of neutralizing a space-based defense, say the experts.

A more passive measure would be for the Soviets to deploy

Based Lasers for Ballistic Missile Defense: Soviet Policy Options," in Keith B. Payne (ed.), *Laser Weapons in Space: Policy and Doctrine* (Boulder, Colo.: Westview Press, 1983), pp. 123-24.

33 See *The New York Times*, March 6, 1985.

space mines. These would be satellites parked in orbit near U.S. warning sensors or space-based defensive devices. The explosive charges in the mines could be detonated by radio before, or during, the attack.

For a long time no one in the West knew for sure which of these countermeasures the Soviets might seek to deploy. But recently the Soviets gave some indication of those ploys it is favoring. In December 1985, barely three weeks after the summit, the Kremlin outlined specific possible countermeasures to render U.S. space-based systems into what one Soviet military specialist called "useless junk."[34]

In an article dated December 16, 1985, retired Army Colonel Vasily Morozov, a military writer for the press agency Novosti, stated that the Soviets would deploy space mines and other objects in orbit to destroy or interfere with U.S. systems. Morozov also said that the Soviets could launch dummy missiles to distract American anti-missile satellites and use special coatings on Soviet missiles that would deflect laser beams.

Morozov maintained that the Soviets already had the technology for these countermeasures. It was estimated that these measures would cost only one percent or two percent of any Star Wars scheme. (The Reagan Administration plans to sink $26 billion in research for a space-based system over five years.)

The Soviet commentator went on to declare that "There is another effective way of replying to an American space-based antiballistic missile system: increasing the number and improving the ... accuracy and yields of Soviet offensive arms. In this case, it is not Soviet missiles that would become useless junk, as American SDI champions expect, but the allegedly invulnerable antimissile shield."

In a separate lengthy commentary, Major General Yuri Lebedev, identified by Novosti as a spokesman for the general staff of the Soviet armed forces and as a participant in past disarmament talks, said: "Such a defense cannot, for one, counter cruise missiles and strategic bombers. Each system, ABM included, has its saturation limit, an ability to counter a definite number of missiles but no

34 See the English-language commentary in *The New York Times*, December 17, 1985.

more. Radio jamming and some other factors may lower its effectiveness."

The thrust of the two articles was to call into question the feasibility of SDI and to link Star Wars to the U.S.-Soviet disarmament talks in Geneva. Interestingly, nothing was said about Soviet Star Wars type research.

A Change of Plans

In the three years and more since the President shocked the world with his exotic space-based ABM plan, officials in the Administration have had a chance to take a long, hard look at how such an idea might be operationalized. Although official enthusiasm is still great, there has been a less well known change of plans on the instrumentalities that are to be used in putting together a feasible system.

In the beginning the Pentagon's Strategic Defense Initiative Organization (SDIO), the formal name of the office conducting Star Wars research, spent a great deal of time researching the possibilities of such directed energy weapons as lasers and particle beams. But two years later this office concluded that the dream of exotic space-based battle stations firing powerful laser beams to knock out Soviet missiles and warheads was beyond America's technological research for the foreseeable future.[35] Instead, the Pentagon now intends to rely on kinetic energy weapons like "smart rocks" (projectiles that home in on the heat produced by warheads) and "railguns" (devices that use electromagnets to accelerate a projectile along a rail to thousands of miles an hour).

The implications of this new strategy are that two separate generations of a space-based missile defense system would be necessary. According to SDIO officials, the "first generation" of the space-based defense system would basically represent an extension of the technology used in a successful experiment, June 1984. At that time, the Army fired a ground-based, maneuverable, non-nuclear missile at an incoming dummy warhead and succeeded in hitting it more than 100 miles into space.

35 See *The Washington Post,* May 27, 1985.

A "second generation" defense system would have to await significantly more research on the kinds of futuristic systems that gave Reagan's strategic defense plan its Star Wars nickname. This, of course, assumes that the efforts eventually prove workable. However, the growing conviction among top Pentagon officials connected with SDI research is that the use of directed energy weapons will remain beyond U.S. technological reach for many years.

Thus, Star Wars research continues. But its research focus now is entirely different.

Sharing Star Wars with the Soviets?

President Reagan's pledge to share a space-based ABM system with the Soviet Union has baffled many officials in industry and the Pentagon. The Soviets, too, have indicated they are suspicious of the President's offer.

President Reagan first mentioned the possibility of sharing the space-based ABM technology in 1983 when the research on this system began. When asked in October of that year by the BBC whether he would be willing to provide the SDI system "off the shelf" to the Soviets, he responded: "Why not?" But he quickly added that "there would have to be reductions of offensive missiles."[36]

Presumably, the President feels that sharing the fruits of research into SDI is necessary to prevent the Soviets from trying to overwhelm the system with a huge buildup in nuclear arms. Nevertheless, even many of the Strategic Defense Initiative's strongest supporters are skeptical. They contend that any plan to put the nation's most critical technology into Soviet hands is doomed to failure.

The critics maintain that there are some important drawbacks to any sharing of BMD technology with the Russians. For one thing, these people point out the technologies underlying these programs such as advanced computers, software and lasers, are exactly the same the Defense Department is presently fighting to keep out of the hands of the Soviets.

"It seems to run counter to everything else that [we] are doing,"

36 Quoted in *The New York Times*, November 30, 1985.

says William Rector, Vice President of Space Systems at General Dynamics Corporation. "It just doesn't make sense."[37]

Importantly, the President has not gone into detail publicly exactly how the U.S. might share its Star Wars technology. For instance, would the Soviets be handed it all, or would the system be administered for both states by a third party?

Recently, some Pentagon officials have suggested that it might be possible to give the Soviets access to an American-developed system without permitting them to delve into its inner workings. Others have said that perhaps U.S. and Soviet engineers could jointly deploy a space-based defense system, each contributing different technologies. The latter view, however, only represents a minority school of thought.

The main problem with Reagan's sharing idea, in the view of the experts, is the double-edged nature of the technology. While the main goal of the system is defensive, certain components of the SDI clearly have potential to be turned into devastating offensive weapons. The most obvious are ground-based and space-based lasers, which could be used in a pre-emptive nuclear attack. But there are also the so-called "supercomputers" which would act as SDI's central nervous system.

According to U.S. scientists sympathetic to SDI research, the supercomputer, or S-1 as it is officially known, may be the key to establishing a defense against enemy missiles. As Presidential scientific adviser Edward Teller told Congress in April 1983, "By using these upcoming supercomputers we can make decisions in proper time so that we can orchestrate our defenses, and we can make sure that we do the best possible job in shielding ourselves from any strategic attack."[38]

But this is only theory – at least for the short term. As James Fletcher, Chairman of the Reagan Administration's Defense Technologies Study Team that helped define the President's Strategic Defense Initiative, reports: the crucial ABM battle management technologies are not presently within reach of the United States.[39]

37 *The New York Times,* November 30, 1985.

38 Quoted in *The New York Times,* November 4, 1985.

39 James C. Fletcher, "The Technologies for Ballistic Missile Defense," *Issues in Science and Technology* (Fall, 1984), pp. 24-25.

The computers must be very fast, performing on the order of one billion operations a second ... The computers must be able to operate in a nuclear environment and must be hardened against radiation and shock. These critical technologies may well require research programs of 10 to 20 years before they are ready for deployment in a ballistic missile defense system ...

If defense experts see a great deal of promise in these powerful supercomputers, they are fearful that they could be easily reprogrammed to help solve an array of complicated technical issues in the U.S.S.R. These include problems in aerospace and nuclear weapons design. Because of the importance of supercomputer technology, the Pentagon has gone to extraordinary lengths in recent years to insure that Soviet scientists are denied access to it.

However the President chooses to implement his sharing idea, the Soviets are showing no interest so far. They continue to remain supremely skeptical of the whole scheme, which they put in the context of the United States striving for a first strike capability against the Soviet Union.

When asked by a reporter if he would give the Soviets a veto power over the Strategic Defense Initiative, the President responded: "hell, no." He added that if the Soviets refused to go along, the United States would go ahead and deploy it.[40]

Conclusions

Few would probably deny the appeal of President Reagan's stated long-term goal of "rendering nuclear weapons impotent and obsolete." This goal, which is attractive to large segments of the U.S. population and its allies is made even more attractive politically by recent progress with sophisticated techniques that can shoot down missiles without using nuclear explosives. Moreover, there can be little doubt that the idea of developing an Anti-Ballistic Missile system continues to have a large constituency in the American arms industry, which sees billions of dollars in contracts over the next two decades. There is nothing surprising about this.

40 *The Washington Post*, November 7, 1985.

However, there are many pitfalls to the building of "space-strike weapons," as the Soviets call them. For one thing, they are enormously costly. For another, there is no guarantee that they would work in the end. Finally, they are very threatening to the Soviets, who generally see them in the context of an attempt by the U.S. to regain military superiority over them. As Gorbachev later told reporters about his talk with President Reagan: "I said to the President, bear in mind that we are not simpletons. If the President was committed to that idea, then my task as Soviet leader was to disabuse him of it."

For Gorbachev, his summit with President Reagan was a pivot point of history. The Soviet leader has rapidly consolidated his power and is now fixing a long-term course. His first priority is to modernize the Soviet economy, and the summit helped him to set the crucial balance between civilian and military spending.

As one Soviet diplomat explained things to an American journalist, "The key decisions on our investment allocations must be made in the next three months." For Gorbachev, "it is important to check whether it is possible not make an accommodation with the Reagan Administration, and if not, then we have to tighten our belts and try to do both economic reform and a new military buildup at the same time."[41]

For the Soviet leader, the issue is whether Reagan has changed enough to strike an acceptable bargain to check the arms race. For the last five years, the Kremlin has been bitterly offended by the President's hostile rhetoric and adamantly distrustful of doing business with him. Now the General Secretary has advanced the following gambit: "Will Reagan agree to severely restrict work on a space-based defense in exchange for a well-hedged 50 percent cutback in offensive arsenals?"

After giving the matter a great deal of thought, the Soviets appear now to have chosen *not* to compete with the United States in the development of a space-based missile defense system – even though the Pentagon continues to maintain that Moscow has invested heavily in research here. Although the evidence is not conclusive, the U.S.S.R. seems determined to defeat the possible adop-

41 See Hedrick Smith, "Geneva: A Test of Two Wills," *The New York Times Magazine,* November 17, 1985.

tion of such an American system by implementing a wide-ranging program of defensive and offensive countermeasures. As a result, a new arms race may be in the making.[42]

Stephen M. Meyer of the Massachusetts Institute of Technology and a Pentagon consultant on Soviet military policy sums up the situation: "It's not going to be a race between our 'Star Wars' and their 'Star Wars,' but a race against our system and their efforts to overwhelm or neutralize it."[43]

The Soviets have already made their position clear publicly, although one must be careful here to dinstinguish the *operational* policy from the declaratory policy. The Soviets have indicated that they will meet a decision by the United States to deploy SDI by a decision to significantly increase the numbers and striking power of their offensive missile forces. At the same time, they will develop a wide array of countermeasures and possibly create a nationwide, more traditional, land-based antiballistic missile system of the type prohibited by the 1972 ABM Treaty.

As Mikhail Gorbachev told President Reagan at the summit conference in Geneva, the Soviet Union would develop countermeasures if work on Star Wars continues and the system is deployed. The Soviet leader said that Soviet countermeasures "will be effective, though less expensive, and quicker to produce."

In an interview in the fall of 1985, Marshal Sergei Akhromeyev, Chief of the Soviet General Staff, was more specific about the testing of Star Wars related projects: "If this process goes on we will have nothing to do but take up retaliatory measures in the field of both offensive and defensive weapons."

42 President Reagan envisions a world where strategic defenses would make nuclear weapons unusable. However, work by the U.S. Air Force on missile "penetration aids" indicates that the more likely scenario is a continuing race between offensive and defensive weapons technology.
To be sure, to the Pentagon, the missile work is a way for the U.S. to hedge its bets. Here the following scenario is outlined: If the Soviets achieve a breakthrough in defense technology before the U.S. and quickly establish a nationwide antimissile system, better missiles would keep the United States from falling into a dangerous strategic disadvantage.
A great deal of Air Force thinking about new ways to "sneak" warheads through defenses is being done under the auspices of the Advanced Strategic Missile Systems (ASMS) at Norton Air Base in California. The ASMS program is among the most secret of the Administration's programs. See *The Christian Science Monitor,* December 10, 1985.

43 Quoted in *The New York Times,* March 6, 1985.

The President's way out of this spiraling arms race is to share Star Wars technology with Moscow. He first broached this idea in 1983 when the research project started. Since that time, he has often repeated his hope of giving the Soviets the results of the $26-billion U.S. research effort. But there has been considerable grumbling about this idea. For instance, the Congressional Office of Technology Assessment noted in a recent report that if plans or actual hardware are shared, "potential adversaries" could figure out a way to circumvent the system. Moreover, if that technology is shared the OTA said, "the American advantage which had enabled us to develop that technology first would necessarily be compromised."[44]

For their part, the Soviets have thus far shown no interest in the President's sharing scheme. The best evidence that is available – Soviet strategic writings and official policy statements crosschecked with actual Soviet military decisions – reveals the Soviets to be agnostics when it comes to strategic defense. As the Soviets generally see things, Star Wars is being researched in order to give the United States a first-strike capability. Gorbachev said as much in his private talks with the President.

The Administration is counting on a mutually agreed reduction in offensive nuclear weapons in order to ensure a "highly effective" missile defense system. However, Gorbachev, in a speech before the Supreme Soviet, the country's nominal parliament, said flatly that there could be no cuts in nuclear arsenals until the SDI program was abandoned. "We hope," he said, in what amounted to a report card on the Geneva summit, "that what was said at Geneva about SDI was not the last word of the American side."

If the Soviets seem *publicly* determined to block the testing, development and deployment of space-strike weapons, they are slightly more flexible in private.[45] For instance, the Kremlin has indi-

44 Quoted in *The Washington Post*, November 5, 1985.

45 One U.S. official would disagree here. "It boggles the mind that the Russians are still playing from two sheets of music," being conciliatory in public and less so in private." He cites the interview given in August by Gorbachev to *Time* magazine. There the Soviet leader said the Soviet Union was not trying to ban research, but only the design of weapons in the SDI program. However, in the Geneva talks, this source says, the Russians continue to call for a ban on "scientific research, testing and deployment." According to this official, "this means that there has not been one iota of change in their language on research at Geneva."

cated to U.S. negotiators at Geneva that it is prepared to allow U.S. research testing in space of sensors and other devices that could be associated either with SDI's futuristic weapons. But the Kremlin will not permit tests of space-based weapons or "models, pilot samples, separate assemblies and components," as Marshal Sergei Akhromeyev put it, of missile-killing lasers, particle beams or hypervelocity guns that could also be part of the Strategic Defense Initiative.

Soviet reservations notwithstanding, the U.S. is determined to proceed with Star Wars research and development. This is being done to see if the President's dream of a space-based missile defense is practical. According to one source, the tests in space planned by the Pentagon over the next five years will not use models of SDI weapons. Rather they will utilize components to determine if weapons can be built eventually along with the associated warning and guidance sensors critical to missile defense.[46]

Thus far, the American negotiating team in Geneva has not decided on what proposals, if any, should be offered to the Soviets on how to accommodate the U.S. viewpoint on space-based weapons. While they continue to mull over the problem, American negotiators have described to the Soviets how SDI research and testing over the next few years would stay within the limits of the ABM Treaty. According to one insider, they have also indicated that it will be three to five years before SDI research suggests what modifications would be necessary in the treaty to permit SDI to continue.[47]

Paul Nitze, Special Adviser to Secretary of State Shultz on arms control matters, offers the following explanation to clear up the dispute over research. According to Nitze, the Russians feel that even basic research, if directed toward the creation of what they call space strike weapons, should be barred. Such weapons, in the Soviet definition, would be those in space designed for the purpose of counterring objects in space or on earth, or those on earth designed to counter objects in space. The Soviet approach, Nitze states, would bar research into U.S. space weapons, but Russians contend that their program on lasers and other advanced techniques is not directed toward the creation of space weapons. See *The New York Times,* November 12, 1985.

46 *The Washington Post,* November 11, 1985. (National Weekly Edition)

47 The Reagan Administration clearly believes that its SDI research program will not violate the provisions of the 1972 ABM Treaty. However, Lt. General James A. Abrahamson, Director of the Pentagon's Strategic Defense Initiative Organization, told a Senate Armed Services subcommittee on October 30, 1985: "There clearly will come a time [in the 1990s] when we enter the development phases and ... require much more direct testing [of components of a defensive system]

To be sure, the Soviets are still heavily committed to the 1972 ABM Treaty. However, they now appear to recognize that both sides will conduct tests in space of devices with certain ABM capabilities. Moscow's present concern is to develop a strategy which would isolate American testing of space weapons.

The Soviet position in this regard has undergone important change. At one time, the U.S.S.R. wanted to ban all research connected with SDI. Now it appears to have backed away from that extreme position. The most detailed presentation on the Soviet approach here came directly from Marshal Akhromeyev in an interview with *Pravda*. This interview was considered so important by the Soviets that they translated it and reprinted it in the *Washington Post* in a full-scale ad in the October 25, 1985 edition.

The Soviet chief of staff maintained that the Soviet position "does not deny the right and possibility of conducting basic research in outer space." But he quickly added that Moscow views as "impermissible" the development and testing of models.

Akhromeyev also pointed out that a test of impermissible "space-strike weapons" could be verified by national technical means. This is a phrase used by arms controllers to mean electronic intelligence systems, including spy satellites maintained by each state.

In a slight, but highly significant, change of wording, the Soviet spokesman stated that everything being done for the "subsequent design and production of space-strike systems – not just space-strike weapons themselves – should be banned." By using the verb form "should," Akhromeyev implied that those steps are not prohibited by the treaty.

In summary, the Soviet Union wants to ban SDI. But it also recognizes that research programs including tests are permissible up to a certain point without modification of the 1972 ABM Treaty. It remains to be seen whether the two sides can now agree on where that threshold lies.

that we will have to have a modified [ABM] treaty in some way in order to proceed ..." Quoted in *The Washington Post*, November 18, 1985.

... a traditional emphasis on 'bigness' as a symbol of 'goodness' or greater effectiveness has seemingly maintained a persistent influence over Soviet approaches to weaponry.

Dennis Ross

XI. SOVIET NUCLEAR WEAPONS POLICIES

The Soviets have gone to extreme lengths to ensure that their forces will not be able to launch a nuclear weapon without the proper authority. What are these procedures? Who handles nuclear warheads? How are they fired? These are some of the questions dealt with in this chapter. However, because of the extreme sensitivity of these issues, the answers to these questions must be very incomplete.

ICBM Deployment

The Soviet ICBM force is deployed in 26 complexes. And contrary to common assumption that these complexes lie in a broad band astride the Trans-Siberian Railway, they are in fact distributed quite widely throughout the U.S.S.R. About half of them are situated west of the Ural Mountains.[1]

According to U.S. intelligence sources, some Soviet ICBMs came to be deployed along the Trans-Siberian rail link because it was the only means of transportation for the large, land-based missiles. "There was simply no other way of getting them there in a dispersed fashion," says one U.S. official.

1 For details, see Desmond Ball, "Research Note: Soviet ICBM Deployment," *Survival* (July-August, 1980), pp. 167-68.

The distribution of Soviet ICBMs over a wide area poses a number of problems for U.S. targeting experts. For one thing, the Soviet ICBM fields cut through the largest concentration of the ethnic Russian population. For another,[2]

Unlike the United States, which has deployed her ICBMs generally in the center of the country, the Soviet ICBMs extend across virtually the entire USSR. A Soviet attack limited to the United States ICBM sites would fall completely east of 115 W longitude and west of the Mississippi River, and would be less difficult for United States early-warning and attack assessment systems to differentiate from an attack involving the major United States population and industrial centers and the national capital. A United States retaliatory strike against the Soviet ICBM fields, on the other hand, must cover nearly the entire geographic expanse of the Soviet Union, including the more heavily populated and industrialized area west of the Urals. Processing data on some 1,000 to 2,000 warheads and other objects such as penetration aids and booster fragments targeted over this vast region might pose insuperable problems for the Soviet attack assessment system. This is especially the case vis-à-vis the three of four ICBM fields in the Moscow area.

The locations of the Soviet ICBM complexes have significant implications for U.S. targeting strategy. For one thing, about two-thirds of the complexes are situated deep within the U.S.S.R. This enhances American concern with respect to both the range and defense penetration capabilities of its strategic forces.[3] Moreover, the depth and intensity of Soviet air defense forces poses special problems for bombers and air-delivered weapons. These include the short-range attack missiles (SRAMs) and air-launched cruise missiles (ALCMs) that might be considered for use against some ICBM sites or their command-and-control posts and support systems.

2 Desmond Ball, "Research Note: Soviet ICBM Deployment," *Survival* (July-August, 1980), p.169. One U.S. official inserts here: "But the U.S. would know which Soviet ICBM fields have missiles remaining, and if the Soviets fired all their ICBMs near their populated areas, U.S. retaliatory forces would not be aimed at empty Soviet silos."

3 This is an especially important point says one U.S. official in the Arms Control and Disarmament Agency. The SS-18, for instance, is located farthest from U.S. retaliatory forces.

Nuclear Targeting Strategy

One of the most closely held secrets in the U.S.S.R. is Soviet nuclear targeting policy. Little information on this subject is available in the classified literature, and still less is written on this secretive matter in "open" studies. In both cases, the bulk of these writings must necessarily be highly speculative. In view of the lack of hard data, the following discussion on Soviet nuclear targeting will be very sketchy.

The first point to note here is that Soviet nuclear targeting policy follows directly from doctrinal strategy. Here the emphasis is, as already observed, on the preemptive nuclear strike in the last resort. Soviet discussions of nuclear war invariably stress the importance of initial nuclear strikes and of seizing the initiative in those strikes.

The second point to note is that the general principles of Soviet nuclear targeting strategy must be applied to specific geographic areas of strategic military operations. As William T. Lee, a former CIA specialist in Soviet military affairs, writes: "The targets located in each geographic area differ, and Soviet politico-military objectives are not identical in all potential areas of conflict. Each area must be analyzed for differences in the targets, and the most vulnerable points of each target, in order to maximize the military effectiveness of an attack with the least collateral damage commensurate with Soviet politico-military objectives in that area."[4]

The third point to understand is that the Strategic Rocket Forces (SRF) consisted entirely of medium-range ballistic missiles (MRBM) units when it was formed in 1959. (A possible exception is the handful of SS-6 ICBMs which may have been under SRF control.) Until around 1968 or 1969, the SRF had more intermediate-range/medium-range ballistic missiles than ICBMs. Thus, the early history of Soviet strategic missile targeting focused in the main on the European and Asian theaters of military operations (TVDs).

A fourth point to bear in mind here concerns the difference between the Soviet Union and the United States over the term "strategic." To American war planners, the concept strategic nuclear operations is limited to intercontinental exchanges. However, as far

4 William T. Lee, "Soviet Targeting Strategy and SALT," *Air Force Magazine* (September, 1978), p.121.

as the Soviets are concerned, strategic operations begin at their borders. This difference in view is not a minor one; it has far-reaching consequences for the size and characteristics of Soviet strategic nuclear forces.

Finally, one must take into account the general factors affecting the conduct of strategic nuclear operations in the theaters of military operations. These include (a) the political objectives of Soviet political leaders; (b) the nature and objectives of planned Soviet military operations in each theater; and (c) the most vulnerable components of the targets to be attacked. These factors have been explicitly stated or have been inferred from the unclassified Soviet military and political literature for more than two decades.

Given the orientation of present Soviet nuclear strategy, in the event of a nuclear war, Soviet strategic forces would most likely be used massively rather than sequentially.[5] They would target a wide range of nuclear and conventional military targets, command-and-control facilities, centers of political and administrative leadership, economic and industrial facilities, power supplies, and other targets more selectively. Urban areas would not be excluded, especially those that were near military, political or industrial targets.

The extent of Soviet strategic nuclear targeting is evident from the following quotations:

The Strategic Rocket Forces, which form the basis of the combat might of our Armed Forces, are intended for the destruction of the enemy's means of nuclear attack, his large troop formations and military bases, the destruction of the aggressor's industry, the disorgani-

5 The Soviet Union, of course, exercises some selectivity in the choice of targets to be attacked in the event of a nuclear war. For instance, Soviet Colonel Shirokov writes that "the quantity of objectives, especially military-economic, located on the territory of warring states ... is very great. Therefore, the belligerents will strive to select from the objectives those which have the greatest influence on the outcome of the armed struggle." (Cited by Leon Goure *et al.*, "The Soviet Strategic View," *Strategic Review* [Winter, 1980], p.81.) Less there be misunderstanding, it should be noted that the notion of selective responses or selective options in a kind of escalation ladder is foreign to Soviet nuclear strategy. In the Soviet context, the word selective should not be equated with the term "limited" or "few." It does not imply a demonstration use, a limited battlefield option, or even tit-for-tat exchanges. Selective, in the Soviet sense, still includes the notion of larg-scale nuclear strikes. Consult Joseph D. Douglass, Jr., "Soviet Nuclear Strategy in Europe: A Selective Targeting Doctrine?," *Strategic Review* (Fall, 1977), p.19.

zation of [his] state and military command and control, and of the operations of his rear and transportation.[6]

Very important strategic missions of the armed forces can be the destruction of the largest industrial and administrative-political centers, power systems, and stocks of strategic raw materials; disorganization of the system of state and military control; destruction of the main transport centers; and destruction of the main groupings of troops, especially of the means of nuclear attack.[7]

Despite the fact that a wide range of targets would be subject to massive and simultaneous attacks, there are some specific priorities regarding the destruction of particular elements of the U.S. and allied target sets. Since World War II, for example, the Soviets have consistently argued that defeat of an enemy's armed forces is the first and primary objective of military operations in a nuclear war. In order to defeat a nuclear-armed adversary, it is first necessary to destroy his nuclear weapons and the means of delivering them. As Soviet Major General Dzhelaukhov indicated in 1966, "Strategic rockets are regarded as the most important strategic objectives."[8]

Some of the most important targets listed in the primary category are strategic bomber bases, forward-based missiles (FBM), submarine bases and support facilities as well as nuclear stockpiles and strategic command-and-control centers.[9]

In the view of one well known student of American and Soviet nuclear strategy, Desmond Ball, the second target category consists "of theater nuclear weapons and associated systems." These include tactical and carrier aviation, cruise missiles, tactical missiles, airfields, and tactical command-and-control systems."[10]

The third category "consists of other military targets, such as large ground troop formations, tank concentrations, reserve forces,

6 Marshal A.A. Grechko, cited by Leon Goure *et al.*, *The Role of Nuclear Forces in Current Soviet Strategy* (Miami: Center for Advanced International Studies, University of Miami, 1974), p.107.

7 V. Zenskov, cited by Joseph D. Douglass, Jr. *et al.*, *Soviet Strategy for Nuclear War* (Stanford: Hoover Institution Press, 1979), p.36.

8 Cited in Joseph D. Douglass, Jr. *et al.*, *opus cit.*, p.75.

9 Consult Joseph D. Douglass, Jr., *Soviet Military Strategy in Europe* (Elmsford, N.Y.: Pergamon Press, 1980), p.74.

10 Desmond Ball, "Soviet Strategic Planning and the Control of Nuclear War," in Roman Kolkowitz *et al.* (eds.), *The Soviet Calculus of Nuclear War* (Massachusetts: Lexington Books, 1986), p.53.

storehouses of arms and munitions, equipment and fuel, naval bases, interceptor airfields, anti-aircraft artillery and missiles, and associated command-and-control systems and facilities."[11]

The fourth category "consists of political-administrative targets, such as government centers and areas where the political leadership is concentrated."[12]

Finally, the fifth category "consists of a wide range of economic-industrial facilities, including power stations (perhaps the most important nonmilitary targets in Soviet war planning), stocks of strategic raw materials, oil refineries and storage sites, metallurgical plants, chemical industries, and transport operations (such as 'rail centers, and marshalling yards, bridges, tunnels, train ferries and trains on land, and ports and vessels on the water')."[13]

No mention is made in this scheme of targeting urban areas per se, and this is perhaps its greatest shortcoming. But it is important to recall that there is a surplus of nuclear warheads. That is, there are more warheads than suitable targets, so a considerable amount of over-targeting is inevitable and cities would be directly affected here. So far as is known, the Soviets have never had a "no cities" targeting doctrine.

Low Alert Status of ICBMs

Generally, American ICBMs maintain a 98 percent alert rate. (This is apart from a dwindling number of aged Titan II missiles which are liquid-fueled.) It is believed that the alert rate of Soviet ICBMs is much lower.

Some sources in the U.S. intelligence community say that Soviet peak-readiness alert may be as low as 25 percent. The exact figure is difficult to pin down, but, according to one report, it is almost no higher than 70 percent. (The remaining 30 percent are in the overhaul stage at any one time, unavailable for action.)

The relatively low alert rate for Soviet ICBMs has important ram-

11 Desmond Ball, *opus cit.,* p.53.

12 *Ibid.*

13 *Ibid.* See also Colonel Shirokov, cited in Leon Goure *et al.,* The Soviet Strategic View," *Strategic Review* (Winter, 1980), pp.81-83.

ifications for those who debate the pros and cons of alleged Soviet "first strike" plans. As Andrew Cockburn writes: "If we assume that the alert figure is 70 percent, that cuts Tolubko's (former SRF commander) operational force from 1,398 ICBMs to about 980. Taking the reliability rate as 50 percent, which is a very conservative figure, the number of Soviet ICBMs that could be expected to perform to specifications comes out at about 490. This would be quite enough to obliterate the fabric of American society, but it leaves very little margin for error in any kind of counterforce operations."[14]

Until recently, the U.S.S.R. was known to keep only a small portion of its land-based missiles on full alert. The inability of the Soviet Union to maintain, without great expense, a large number of missiles on combat alert arose in part from the fact that the gyroscope in its guidance systems – necessary to induce stability in the ICBM – rotated on metal ball bearings. Thus, the guidance system needed some time to warm up before a missile could be launched. Moreover, during any sustained period of holding a missile ready for immediate launching, the entire guidance system would fail because the ball bearings, which were mass produced to less than perfect tolerances, would fail under such continued stress.[15]

An additional limitation to keeping Soviet ICBMs on full alert concerns their liquid fuel. Liquid fueled ICBMs simply cannot be maintained at the same continuous state of alert. However, in a crisis (which the Soviets say would precede any hostilities), they could be raised to full readiness rather rapidly.

The experience of the U.S. Air Force with its remaining liquid-fueled missiles – the Titans – gives a clear picture of the kind of dangers liquid-fuel rockets pose. "It is dangerous, it is dangerous," Sergeant Jeff Kennedy of the U.S. Air Force informed the CBS program 60 Minutes in 1981. "It's dangerous to the people that work on it. It's dangerous to the people that are in the surrounding area around the missile, for the simple reason that once the tank's punctured, that's it. There's nothing we can do to prevent it, to stop it ... There's so many places for a Titan missile to leak, it's just unbelievable. It's

14 Andrew Cockburn, *The Threat: Inside the Soviet Military Machine* (New York: Vintage Books, 1984), p.313.

15 See Robert P. Berman *et al.*, *Soviet Strategic Forces: Requirements and Responses* (Washington, D.C.: The Brookings Institution, 1982), pp.88-89.

not uncommon to have three or four Titan missiles leaking at once." The danger stems from the fact that vapor given off by leaking fuels is highly poisonous and has a tendency to explode.

In September 1980, an airman working on a Titan at a base in Damascus, Arkansas dropped a 9-pound wrench, which fell some 66 feet down the silo and punctured the "skin" of the missile. From that time on the fuel began to leak. Nine hours later the missile exploded. The force of the explosion blew the 750-ton concrete lid a distance of 1,000 feet and Sergeant Kennedy, who just emerged from the silo, 150 feet.[16]

The volatility of Soviet liquid-fueled rockets has been demonstrated more than once. But of partiuclar importance was an incident in 1960. In October of that year, an advanced Soviet missile engine exploded during a test launch, killing the first head of the Soviet Strategic Rocket Forces, Marshal Mitrofan Nedelin and over 300 other observers. This tragedy was described by the Western spy who served in the General Staff, Colonel Oleg Penkovskiy.[17] It is not clear whether this accident was associated with an atomic-powered rocket, which the Soviets were thought to be developing, or with a more conventional SS-6 ICBM.

Today the only Soviet ICBMs to use solid fuel as opposed to liquid fuel for their propulsion systems are the obsolescent SS-13s and the newly deployed mobile SS-25s. Solid fueled missiles have the big advantage of being able to be fired at the turn of the key. The Soviets rely upon storable liquid fuels for the majority of their strategic rocket propulsion systems. These missiles can be launched on relatively short notice, somewhere on the order of four to eight minutes.[18]

16 For details see Andrew Cockburn, *The Threat: Inside the Soviet Military Machine* (New York: Random House, 1983).

17 See *The Penkovskiy Papers* (New York: Doubleday, 1965). This book was published by the CIA through Doubleday and much of the material was compiled from CIA records.

18 Robbin F. Laird *et al., The Soviet Union and Strategic Arms* (Boulder, Colo.: Westview Press, 1984), p.34.

Test Firing

In contrast to the U.S. Air Force, which never test-fires even a single missile out of an operational silo,[19] the Soviets do. (This practice is sometimes construed by U.S. officials as yet another indication that the Soviets are both ready and able to fight a nuclear war with the goal of emerging victorious.) For instance, on June 19, 1982, the U.S. government publicized the fact that the Soviets had carried out a series of tests of nuclear missiles the day before.

Although some American publications like *Aviation Week* chose to highlight these tests as a demonstration that a nuclear war-fighting capability had been sucessfully tested, what the Soviets had actually done was this: They had launched two aging SS-11 ICBMs from their operational silos in the western and central U.S.S.R. across Siberia to the desolate Kamchatka peninsula. About the same time, they also fired an intermediate-range SS-20 missile at Kamchatka, an SS-N-8 missile from a submarine in the White Sea and two antiballistic missiles as well as an anti-satellite missile. The Soviet launches were particularly impressive in view of the fact that the U.S. had not fired more than one ICBM at a time since 1971.

If U.S. authorities tended to view the Soviet test as somewhat menacing, author Andrew Cockburn takes a different view. "The test was not unique," the controversial writer says, "since the Soviet Union has carried out similar exercises at least once before in the last five years. The two SS-11s were not the kind of missiles that would be used in a first strike. That role is reserved, according to the Pentagon scenarists, for the larger and MIRVed SS-18. SS-11s were used because these missiles are being phased out, and "it is somewhat hazardous to manhandle a Soviet missile, especially an old one, from its silo." The Soviets thus displayed "an admirable sense

19 The U.S. Air Force has not fired an ICBM out of a silo that would be used in wartime since the 1960s. At that time there were four such attempts. The results were inauspicious: three missiles failed to show any signs of life whatsoever, and the fourth exploded early in flight. Since then, the Air Force undertakes operational testing by removing a designated missile from its silo and transporting it to a special test launch site at Vandenburg Air Force Base in southern California. There it is given a careful going over by experts and then fired into the South Pacific.

of economy in using the junking process to exercise a crew in firing a missile off into the wastes of Kamchatka."[20]

Reports from governmental "insiders" indicate that Soviet ICBM test shots from operational silos are not generally good. In fact, the failure rate is said to be extremely high. According to one such source, it would be "inconceivable" for the Soviets to risk a pre-emptive strike in view of their reliability problem.[21]

Soviet Reloading Capabilities

Soviet reload capabilities for their land-based ICBMs is a hotly debated topic within Western intelligence circles. But before this issue can be understood, it is first necessary to distinguish between so-called "hot" and "cold" launched missiles.

An example of a hot launched missile is the SS-19. The engine ignition of this Soviet missile takes place while it is in the silo. Thus, the silo becomes severely damaged upon launch.

By way of contrast, there is the SS-18 missile, which uses a cold-launched technique. Main engine ignition of this missile does not take place in the silo; it occurs after the ICBM has exited the silo. Thus, cold-launching minimizes damage to the hardened silo.

Cold launching was developed originally for firing missiles from submarines. It involves the use of a low pressure gas to force the missile out of its silo into the atmosphere where its first-stage propellants ignite. In the eyes of strategic theorists, the cold-launch technique is consistent with the development of a capability to reload and refire during a protracted nuclear conflict. But this is just theory.

20 Andrew Cockburn, *The Threat: Inside the Soviet Military Machine* (New York: Vintage Books, 1984), p. 312. Former CIA Director William Colby calls this book "A major contribution." But other Soviet specialists find it suspect. As James T. Reitz writes in "Underrating Soviet Might" in *Problems of Communism* (November-December, 1983), p. 86: "For reasons best known to himself, [Cockburn] does his level best to indicate that the threat is far less ominous than popularly assumed by a series of Western governments (including the US) and by a host of well-known and reputable Western military scholars and writers."

21 "Their accuracy stinks, reliability is so bad you can't believe it," one such intelligence analyst told a reporter in 1983. See Jonathan Marshall, "Missiles That Fissile," *Inquiry* magazine (March, 1983).

In actuality, there is considerable misconception about the true purpose and nature of Soviet cold-launched missiles. Generally, these missiles are kept encased in a close-fitting metal tube inside the silo. This tube serves the purpose of providing additional hardening for the missile against explosions in the vicinity as well as making it easier to transport and assemble the weapon. When the missile is "popped" out of the tube and silo, however, the silo still suffers a great deal of damage. Thus, any silo that has cold-launched a missile needs considerable repair before it can be used again.

According to one source, the quickest that the Soviets have ever been observed to reload an ICBM silo after a test launch is three months.[22] In the late 1970s, an intensive investigation by the CIA failed to produce any evidence that the Soviets were planning to reload and refire their ICBM silos during hostilities. However, this situation may now be changing.

A former Defense Intelligence Agency official maintains that when the CIA "failed to produce any evidence there was a rigorous on-going argument in the U.S. analytic community." It is important to note, he says, the period during which the CIA found no evidence. This was "when the pressures were for ratification of the SALT II treaty and when preoccupation and mirror-imaging argued that such a procedure was obviously unrealistic." Moreover, "the argument at the time was badly confused by the focus on the SALT II definitions of *rapid* reload (which SALT II forbade for ICBM launchers)." These definitions had "little theoretical relevance to many possible scenarios where a refire capability, in somewhat more time than the few hours defined for this in the treaty understandings, could have real utility."

Finally, this confidential source suggests that CIA, in the intervening years, may well have changed its mind about Soviet capabilities here. He points out that "U.S. government publications (Secretary of Defense Reports, the DOD series on *Soviet Military Power*, etc.) which have *subsequently* even more firmly attributed a reload capability to the Soviets, are not produced in a vacuum. They are

22 Andrew Cockburn, *The Threat: Inside the Soviet Military Machine* (New York: Vintage Books, 1984), p. 312. Reload time for the solid-fueled SS-20, which is an intermediate-range ballistic missile, is of the order of one hour, according to U.S. government officials.

coordinated throughout the official intelligence community and any differences are reflected by at least caveats and qualifiers. This stongly suggests that the CIA judgments have changed," he says, "and so has the three months figure cited: simple technical analysis would show a much more meaningful theoretical capability."

Strobe Talbott, the author of several inside accounts of arms control negotiations, takes a different view. "A spare artillery shell can be loaded in an instant," he says. But "reload ICBMs would have to be taken out of storage facilities, put on railroad cars, transported hundreds of miles to transshipment points, loaded onto trucks and hauled, along with a great deal of cumbersome equipment, to silos for launching." Moreover, the "Soviets would have to carry out this time-consuming and complicated procedure while a nuclear war was in progress."[23] Since U.S. intelligence knows the location of Soviet storage sites and rail lines that could be used to transport extra missiles to launching areas, Talbott feels that these could be targeted in the Single Integrated Operational Plan (SIOP).

The best judgment in U.S. intelligence is that the Soviets probably cannot refurbish and reload silo launchers in a period less than several days. However, it is worth noting that the Soviets in an exercise in the autumn of 1980 practiced the reloading of twenty-five to forty SS-18 silos during a period of two to five days. This evidence would seem to suggest that the Soviet military has not entirely succumbed to the political leadership in its rejection of the notion of the feasibility of a protracted nuclear war.

Theoretically, reloads represent an additional threat to both sides, but this threat is very marginal compared to the capabilities for initial use. The missile forces of the adversary are a primary target for both sides' "time-urgent" forces. Regardless of which side actually goes first, few functional silos are likely to survive the initial nuclear exchange. And even if some do survive relatively unscathed, their marginal utility will have declined sharply. As one authority notes, "without a survivable communication linkage between the surviving force and the central leadership, effective targeting tied to political and military objectives would be virtually impossible."[24]

23 Strobe Talbott, *Deadly Gambits* (New York: Alfred A. Knopf, 1984), p.288.

24 Robin F. Laird and Dale R. Herspring, *The Soviet Union and Strategic Arms* (Boulder, Colo.: Westview Press, 1984), p.33.

Nuclear Warheads

Reliable figures on the total number of Soviet nuclear warheads are hard to come by. For a long time it was thought that the United States possessed a greater stockpile of warheads, while the Soviet Union was assumed to have a larger number of means of delivery, primarily in missiles. Recently, however, there have been indications that the U.S.S.R. might have moved ahead of the U.S. in numbers of nuclear warheads.[25]

According to the new Defense Department "force loading" estimates, the Soviet Union has about 34,000 nuclear warheads for its bombers, long-range and medium-range missiles, artillery and cruise missiles.[26] The United States, by comparison, is said to have 26,000.

The new estimates, prepared in 1984 by the Pentagon, show that the U.S.S.R. overtook the United States in nuclear warheads more than eight years ago. A spokesman for the Defense Department claimed that the new estimates are based on intelligence assumptions which are more "sophisticated" than those for earlier weapons.

According to critics, the new figures were more the product of politics in the Reagan Administration than anything else. For instance, the White House has used the new estimates in confidential briefings to Congress to argue that the Soviet Union is leading the arms race and thus the U.S. must expand and modernize its nuclear weapons program.

In an article published in the June 1984 issue of *Arms Control Today,* William M. Arkin, a specialist in nuclear arms at the Institute for Policy Studies in Washington, D.C., and Jeffrey I. Sands, a researcher at the National Resources Defense Council, reach a different conclusion on the number of Soviet warheads. They estimate that the Soviet stockpile of warheads ranges from 21,400 to 41,250

25 According to the well-respected International Institute for Strategic Studies in London, the Soviet Union has increased the number of its long-range nuclear warheads by 37 percent in the past three years. In the view of the IISS, the Soviets now have a substantial edge over the United States in the number of ground- and submarine-launched missile warheads and in their overall destructive capacity. See *The Christian Science Monitor,* November 1, 1985.

26 See *The New York Times,* June 18, 1984.

– about half of them built since 1979. The maximum number, they explain, reflects an assumption that all Soviet missiles able to carry multiple independently targeted warheads are indeed armed to the limit. Moreover, they assume all silos able to be reloaded have warheads available for reloading and that artillery pieces and missiles able to fire both nuclear and conventional warheads have a full supply of nuclear warheads. The minimum figure assumes that the Soviet Union has assembled only enough warheads to load its weapons with the minimum number of warheads they are capable of firing.[27]

Arkin and Sands, who are collaborating on a Soviet data book on nuclear weapons, assert that the Pentagon deliberately has inflated its figures and called that a "warhead gap."

In truth, the U.S. intelligence community does not really know the exact size of the Soviet nuclear stockpile. "With regard to the warheads themselves, Richard Wagner, Assistant to the Secretary of Defense (Atomic Energy), testified before a House Subcommittee on March 14, 1984, "we know almost nothing about what capabilities the Soviet have."[28] Other sources confirm this statement.

KGB Control of Warheads

It may surprise some, but nuclear stockpiles in the Soviet Union are not in the custody of the regular forces but of the KGB. Soviet silos contain four men generally. Two are regular servicemen who launch the rocket, and two are KGB personnel who carry out the separate function of arming the missile's nuclear warhead. (In earlier years, these safety precautions included keeping the warheads physically separated and under KGB control away from the actual rockets that would carry them.)

According to one authoritative source, "Soviet nuclear storage sites are separate from the delivery systems and heavily guarded by KGB troops." The warheads "are moved to the delivery systems in

27 William M. Arkin *et al.*, "The Soviet Nuclear Stockpile," *Arms Control Today* (June, 1984).

28 Quoted in *ibid.*, p.3.

closed vans as part of small, heavily guarded convoys, often with light aircraft overhead to maintain communications." Alternatively, "warheads may be delivered by helicopters with a close escort of gunships and a top cover of fighters."[29]

Stockpiling Nuclear Weapons Outside the U.S.S.R.

Despite the fact that the U.S. has nuclear stockpiles littered at its various bases around the world, the Soviet Union has been careful about keeping its nuclear weapons within its own territory. (The shipment of MRBMs and IRBMs to Cuba in 1962 was a major exception to this policy.) Thus, the short-range missiles, artillery pieces and bombers stationed in East Europe that would fire or deliver nuclear warheads and bombs were without their ammunition.[30] Since the warheads were stored inside the Soviet Union, they could only be mated up with the delivery systems in times of extreme emergency or for regular exercise. But now all this is changing.

Beginning in late 1981, it became clear that the Soviet Union was deploying nuclear weapons in East Europe for the first time. This deployment began with the stationing of Fencer aircraft in Poland and East Germany (with nuclear bombs) and the replacement of old Soviet short-range missiles with SS-21s, SS-22s and SS-23s. In East Europe, the Soviets have nuclear weapons concentrated at a small number of closely guarded, central storage sites and airbases.

Now it appears that Czechoslovakia, East Germany, Hungary and Poland have Soviet nuclear warheads under Soviet control. (Unlike the U.S. and its NATO allies, the U.S.S.R. does not share warheads with the Warsaw Pact.) According to one authority, there are probably about thirty nuclear storage sites in Eastern Europe.[31]

29 David C. Isby, *Weapons and Tactics of the Soviet Army* (New York: Jares, 1981), p. 210.

30 During the 1950s and 1960s nuclear weapons and delivery systems were often maintained at separate locations. And states of readiness were relatively low. Take for example the situation during the Cuban Missile Crisis. Soviet ICBM silos evidently stood empty through the crisis with their warheads in storage bunkers as far as some fifty miles away.

31 William M. Arkin *et al.*, *Nuclear Battlefields: Global Links in the Arms Race* (Cambridge: Ballinger Publishing Co., 1985), p. 38.

Emphasis on Large Rockets

A question that may be asked here is "Why do the Soviets continue to rely in large part on huge rockets?" The Soviet SS-18, for instance, is twice the size of the American MX. For a long time their nuclear weapons were fairly efficient and with improvements in accuracy they did not require such large rockets and warheads.

Among students of Soviet missiles, there are a number of competing hypotheses as to why the Soviets have continued to build large ICBMs (though this trend appears to be tapering off with the new emphasis on mobile ICBMs).[32] One theory holds that the Soviets wanted to loft very high-yield warheads as a way of compensating for their lack of accuracy on hardened targets (e.g. ICBM silos). Another hypothesis focuses on the usefulness of the heavy missiles in implementing a preemptive strike if war broke out. "Giant Soviet ICBMs with highly destructive multiple warheads are the most effective means of delivering the biggest blow first."[33]

A third theory holds that large warheads on large rockets were intended simply for "city busting." This strategy would maximize Soviet residual megatonnage that could be sent in retaliation if the United States ever launched a preemptive strike on the Soviet Union. A fourth idea was that the SS-18s would play to Russian cultural affinity, connoting a solid or good nuclear deterrent. A fifth argument was that large warheads and rockets were intended to provide a propaganda advantage; they would enable the Soviets to claim possession of the ultimate "terror" weapon. Still another theory was that the large payload of Soviet rockets could be intended to maximize the process of MIRVing. Up to thirty warheads could be placed on the SS-18 alone, according to U.S. arms control officials. (SALT restricts the maximum number to ten.) Finally, there is the simple point that to the Soviets bigness is better.

This last point is especially important given that a unique Soviet strategic style grows out of a peculiarly Russian-Soviet psychology. As Dennis Ross, a noted student of Soviet nuclear strategy, writes:

32 This discussion has benefitted considerably from John Prados, *The Soviet Estimate* (New York: The Dial Press, 1982), pp. 204-05.

33 Gerard Smith, *Doubletalk: The Story of the First Strategic Arms Limitations Talks* (New York: Doubleday, 1980), pp. 94-95.

"For example, a tradional emphasis on 'bigness' as a symbol of 'goodness' or greater effectiveness has seemingly maintained a persistent influence over Soviet approaches to weaponry."[34] Thus, the Soviet approach, even with regard to the most advanced ICBM, remains the same as it historically has been toward artillery-like weapons: "The bigger the better."

Stockpile Reliability

U.S. experts generally agree that American nuclear warheads are superior to Soviet warheads in several important aspects. One of these is the ratio of nuclear yield to the weight of the warhead. However, Soviet warheads which, like their American counterparts, are coming down in overall weight are still generally much larger and more powerful.[35] In the past, they needed to be because they were not as accurate as U.S. warheads.

Over the years, the American testing program has been more extensive than the Soviet one. Overall, it has conducted about 760 nuclear tests whereas the U.S.S.R. has conducted about 560.

The Soviets have proposed a moratorium on all nuclear testing. But the Reagan Administration has refused to go along or agree to a total test ban treaty. The White House maintains that because U.S. warheads are more sophisticated than Soviet ones they require more testing.

This position is challenged by Richard L. Garwin of the Thomas J. Watson Research Center, who says that stockpile reliability can be determined in other ways. He acknowledged that a ban on tests would stand in the way of some safety improvements, such as the use of intensive high-explosive mixtures that are used to detonate nuclear weapons. But he said, "Our weapons are adequately safe."[36]

34 Dennis Ross, "Rethinking Soviet Strategic Policy: Inputs and Implications," in John Batlis *et al., Soviet Strategy* (London: Croom Helm, 1981), pp.125-26.

35 The year 1965 saw the start of an effort by the Soviet nuclear weapons laboratories to develop smaller-yield warheads for their tactical nuclear forces, something the Soviet military had desired since 1960. See Stephen M. Meyer, "Soviet Theatre Nuclear Forces: Part II: Capabilities and Implications," *Adelphi Paper No. 188* (London: The International Institute for Strategic Studies, 1984), p.19.

36 *The New York Times,* October 4, 1985.

Paul Warnke, chief negotiator in the Carter Administration, goes much farther than Garwin. He dismisses as nonsense the argument by Kenneth Adelman, the former U.S. arms control director, that nuclear weapons must be tested for safety and reliability. "There's no basis for that," Warnke says. "We do very little in the way of proof-testing." The usual procedure, he said, is to inspect weapons stockpiles for rust and corrosion and to test the trigger mechanism. All that can be done without a nuclear explosion, Warnke says.[37]

On-Site Inspection?

Only recently have U.S. officials begun to make much publicly of the link between stockpile reliability and nuclear testing. Generally, past administrations were not unsympathetic to the notion of obtaining a *comprehensive* test ban, a step which they linked to "on-site" inspection.

For various reasons, the question of on-site inspections has been a bone of contention in American-Soviet negotiations over arms control,[38] although less so with the development of sophisticated national technical means of verification such as satellite photography.[39] Some U.S. disarmament officials maintain that nuclear arms agreements can best be verified by monitoring on the ground. And the United States has stated its willingness in the past to open its facilities to such examination.

For a long time, the Soviets refused even to consider on-site inspection a serious negotiating issue. As Premier Khrushchev once exclaimed to a Western visitor: "You can't let a cat into the kitchen and expect it just to drink the milk."

In this folksy way, the Soviet leader was attempting in the early 1960s to express Soviet concern about how the controversial issue

37 Quoted in *The Minneapolis Star and Tribune,* April 1, 1986.

38 U.S. capabilities in this area are highly controversial. According to one U.S. Pentagon official, "U.S. capability in this area is much less than portrayed by the news media."

39 One Reagan Administration official would disagree here: He asserts that "the verification situation has changed since this Administration seeks qualitative constraints, not quantative, and National Technical Means are not sufficient for such agreements."

of arms control verification might be used by the United States. In particular, Khrushchev was worried about the intelligence ramifications of caving in to American compliance with a proposed treaty allowing for on-site inspection of nuclear weapons facilities. Except for a Soviet proposal in 1963, in the context of negotiations on a nuclear test ban treaty,[40] the Soviets continued to reject any foreign inspection of its nuclear installations.

With the development of sophisticated satellite capabilities by both superpowers in the 1960s, the question of on-site inspection became less important for awhile. Both American and Soviet leaders felt confident that with the new monitoring technology they could independently verify arms control agreements of that period.

In the mid-1970s, however, both sides began to evidence growing concern that with the proliferation of new weapons technologies, such as the small yet lethal cruise missiles which were being developed first by the U.S. then by the Soviets, on-site inspection should be given another serious look. This was especially true of the Soviet position, which traditionally was most sensitive on this issue.

In 1976, after protracted negotiations, a treaty governing peaceful nuclear explosions was signed by President Ford and General Secretary Brezhnev. This accord, which was never ratified by the U.S. Senate, provided for on-site inspections.

Subsequently, U.S., Soviet and British negotiators also agreed on the concept of on-site inspections during negotiations on a comprehensive test ban. But these were broken off in the context of the Soviet invasion of Afghanistan in 1979.

Beginning in June 1982, Leonid Brezhnev attempted to move both sides again in the direction of on-site inspection. At that time, he offered to open "a part of the civilian nuclear facilities in the

40 In an interview with Norman Cousins in April 1963, Khrushchev asserted that he had with difficulty persuaded his colleagues in the Politburo to go along with three on-site inspections for a comprehensive test ban treaty, only to be made "to look foolish" when the United States declined to accept a limit of three inspections. See "Notes on a 1963 Visit with Khrushchev," *Saturday Review*, November 7, 1964, pp.16-21, 58-60. According to a book by Glenn T. Seaborg, Chairman of the Atomic Energy Commission during the Kennedy Administration, both Kennedy and Khrushchev had a deep commitment to a total ban on nuclear testing. See his *Kennedy, Khrushchev and the Test Ban* (Berkeley: University of California Press, 1981).

U.S.S.R. to inspection by the International Atomic Energy Agency in Vienna." (Soviet weapons facilities were exempted in the Brezhnev proposal.)[41]

The United States refused to take up Brezhnev's offer at the time, and it was not until three years later that the Soviets moved to reopen the question once again. In August of that year, the U.S.S.R. permitted the first international inspection of its nuclear power reactors. Three months later, in November, Mikhail Gorbachev said after his meeting with President Reagan that if a ban on the development of space-based weapons were negotiated, the Soviet Union would open its laboratories to outside inspection to verify Soviet compliance. Then, in December 1985, the Soviets offered to permit the United States some on-site inspection of nuclear test ranges in return for American participation in a test moratorium.[42]

In a *Pravda* article, dated December, 1985, Moscow said that the Soviet Union would accept an international verification system that would involve special monitoring stations placed in third countries. It added: "The Soviet Union is prepared to go even further. It stands for coming to terms with the United States ... also on certain measures of on-site verification to remove the possible doubts about compliance with such a moratorium."

The Soviet proposal, which was first made in a private letter on December 5, from Mikhail Gorbachev to President Reagan, was rejected out of hand by Washington, even if U.S. officials were encouraged by its tone and by Gorbachev's willingness to consider on-site inspection. In the main, the Administration wanted to maintain the option of continuing to test new weapons, particularly possible "subcomponents" of the Strategic Defense Initiative. However, there were some other considerations. These were spelled out by a spokesman for the Administration who insisted that weapons testing was needed to insure the reliability of weapons. He noted that the Soviet proposal for a moratorium came shortly after the Soviets finished a round of testing, while the United States was now in a phase of updating its nuclear arsenal. Almost as an afterthought, the spokesman said the Russians could not be trusted to adhere to the ban.

41 *Pravda,* June 16, 1982.

42 *Pravda,* December 19, 1985.

But the Administration could not afford to abandon the public relations forum to the Soviet Union, so the President responded with a counter-proposal: He wrote Gorbachev proposing that Soviet and American experts meet to discuss ways to improve the verification of agreements on underground nuclear tests. The President even repeated an invitation, which was rejected by Gorbachev, to attend a U.S. underground nuclear test in Nevada.[43]

Later in December, before a year-end reception of foreign diplomats in Moscow, Gorbachev again voiced Soviet willingness to move toward on-site inspection. "The Soviet Union is prepared," he said, "to take most resolute steps down to on-site inspection as regards control over the ending of nuclear testing." He added: "Our country has a stake in reliable and rigorous control no less than any other country. Under the present international conditions, given the deficit of mutual trust, verification measures are simply indispensable."[44]

Pressing his case further, the Soviet leader declared: "Let us act so that 1986 should go down in history as the year when people mustered up enough common sense to rise above narrow motives and stop disfiguring their own planet."

Conclusions

Soviet nuclear weapons policies are tightly held secrets. But even so what little is known about these policies reinforces the view of a very rigid Soviet command-and-control system. The Soviets have gone to great pains to ensure complete control over nuclear delivery systems and warheads.

There is a great deal of debate over the link betwen stockpile reliability and nuclear testing. Some defense officials claim that the United States must continue nuclear testing to maintain confidence in the continued operability of weapons already deployed. Some test ban opponents add the argument that testing is needed to confirm new designs including those for exotic new systems being con-

43 *The Washington Post*, December 24, 1985.
44 Quoted in *The New York Times*, December 28, 1985.

sidered for possible use in future strategic defense systems. In actual fact, most U.S. – and probably most Soviet – tests have been conducted for design purposes, not for reliability. Nuclear weapons technology is quite mature and innovation tends to occur in modest increments.[45]

The Soviets apparently recognize this: still the increasing Soviet trend toward greater openess on the question of on-site inspection is remarkable indeed. Their most recent proposal, which ties a bilateral moratorium on nuclear testing to an offer to open up Soviet nuclear sites for some kind of inspection, is obviously aimed at stopping Reagan's SDI program (which necessitates testing). But given the Soviet penchant for secretness in this area it is most welcome.

The Administration takes a different tack. It generally views the Soviet proposal in the context of a public relations challenge. Firmly committed to pursuing Star Wars, it tends to view the Soviet offer as a major threat. Consequently, it emphasizes the need to keep testing until there are deep cuts in offensive nuclear stockpiles and as long as these weapons are required to deter attack.

This position is unfortunate for a test ban is in the interests of both countries. A simultaneous test ban, by itself, could go far in slowing the onrushing pace of the nuclear arms race. Moreover, it could prove to be an important first step in achieving other important measures to slow, halt and reserve this costly and fatal arms competition.[46]

45 In early April 1986, Reagan Administration officials let it be known that the CIA had changed its procedures for estimating the yields of large Soviet nuclear tests because it had decided its previous estimates were too high. THe CIA decision, which was approved January 21, immediately raised questions about past Administration assertions that the U.S.S.R. probably had violated the Threshold Test Ban Treaty of 1974. (This accord limits the size of warheads being tested underground to no more than 150 kilotons.) Experts familiar with the change said it would lower yield estimates of Soviet tests by approximately 20 percent. For details see *The New York Times,* April 2, 1986.

46 On April 11, 1986, the Soviet Union announced that it was ending its eight-months moratorium on nuclear testing because of continued U.S. tests. Soviet officials accused the United States of putting military interest ahead of mankind's desire to end "nuclear madness." For its part, the U.S. said that the United States would continue nuclear testing because national security required it. For details, see *The New York Times,* April 12, 1986.

> Can you picture what would be left after a few hydrogen bombs fell on Moscow? Forget about 'a few' – imagine just one. Or Washington? Or New York? Or Bonn? It staggers the mind. All the mathematical calculations made during the war games, all our computers are worthless in trying to comprehend the magnitude of the destruction we would face.
>
> *Nikita Khrushchev*
> *Khrushchev Remembers*

XII. SOVIET CIVIL DEFENSE EFFORTS

The Reagan Administration's civil defense effort is based primarily on the fear that the Soviets have an evacuation program that would somehow embolden them. But the Central Intelligence Agency disputes this assertion. In general, CIA officials say privately that they do not believe that the Soviets have put their civil defense program in motion with the idea that they could credibly plan to survive a nuclear war and use this as part of a nuclear war strategy. But if this were the case, these sources note, "we could neutralize such an effort."

One high-level CIA official notes in passing that, although the Soviet civil defense program has many ardent admirers in the United States, in truth it is a lowly branch of the service. Telling indication of the overall status of Soviet civil defense is the appointment of the recently disgraced Ivan D. Yershov to be chief of staff of the civil defense troops. His perquisites are quite modest: they include one apartment in Moscow and one dacha of reportedly modest proportions on which he has to pay rent.

CIA officials point out in private conversations that the Soviet civil defense program has been in existence for a long time. (Its specific adaptation to the requirements of the nuclear era dates back to 1961, when responsibility was transferred from the Ministry of Interior to the Ministry of Defense. At that time, Marshal Chuykov, a Deputy Minister of Defense and Commander-in-Chief of the Ground Forces, was appointed to head the effort.)

But in all this time the Soviets have never conducted an evacuation drill in a major city or entirely emptied even a small town.[1] Moreover, these intelligence officials, who closely monitor the situation in the Soviet Union, say that they have found little evidence of serious efforts at mass indoctrination of the population on civil defense. (In fact many local citizens seem to take an ironic pleasure from the observation that the acronym for "civil defense" in Russian forms the word "coffin.") There is also little evidence that would suggest a comprehensive program for hardening economic installations.[2] Thus, overall, the measures the Soviets have taken to protect their economy would not prevent massive damage from an attack designed to destroy Soviet facilities.

It is important to note here that Soviet attitudes toward civil defense have undergone considerable change over the years. In the 1960s passive measures were accorded an important place along with a system of active defense as an integral part of the U.S.S.R.'s military posture in the nuclear age. As a prominent Soviet military leader asserted early in 1964, "not a single defense measure can be decided under modern conditions without considering civil defense needs."[3]

Over the past decade the Soviets have invested some $ 2 billion a year in civil defense. But some officials in the CIA would take issue with the assertion that this can be taken as evidence that the Soviets are preparing not only to survive, but to prevail in a nuclear war. First, these intelligence sources say that $ 2 billion is not really what the Soviets spend; it is an *estimate* of what they would spend if they paid their workers on the same wage scale that American workers are paid. Second, they point to a CIA study done in 1978 which discounted the notion that the Soviets believe that their civil defense

1 The U.S. Defense Intelligence Agency disputes this. It claims that on one occasion the Soviets did practice the evacuation of the work force of one industry from one city.

2 According to one U.S. government insider, "there is little evidence in the unclassified literature, but there is in the classified materials."

3 Marshal V.I. Chuikov, "The Defense of the Population is the Main Task of Civil Defense," *Military Knowledge*, No. 1 (January, 1964), p.3.

system gives them a strategic edge. In part this study read as follows: The Soviets "cannot have confidence ... in the degree of protection their civil defenses would afford them, given the many uncertainties attendant to a nuclear exchange. We do not believe that the Soviet's present civil defense would embolden them deliberately to expose the U.S.S.R. to a higher risk of nuclear attack."[4]

A study by the U.S. Office of Technology Assessment several years ago concluded that just three Minuteman II intercontinental ballistic missiles and seven Poseidon missiles with multiple warheads could wipe out 73 percent of the Soviet industrial refining capacity.[5] In this connection, one "insider" notes that about 75 percent of the basic industrial capacity of the U.S.S.R. (primary metals, chemicals, petroleum construction, synthetic rubber, agricultural and railroad equipment and power generators) is concentrated in approximately 400 plants.

Evacuation Plans

On paper, Soviet evacuation plans appear impressive at first glance. "There are nine warning signals," writes Fred Kaplan, "each indicating different stages of a crisis and alerting the citizenry to par-

4 Some Westerners maintain that we do not know what the Soviets consider to be "unacceptable damage." Thus, it is argued, we can never be certain about exactly what is enough to deter. By Soviet statements which contend that nuclear war would cause unprecedented damage, or that the results are unimaginable or other statements about the dire consequences of such a war have been presented in detail in this paper. They are also a good indication that the U.S. can still inflict what the Soviets consider unacceptable damage upon the U.S.S.R. Other Westerners argue that the Soviet view of what would be unacceptable damage is different from the American view. The argument goes like this: Since the Soviets killed so many of their own people in the purges and held up under such devastation in World War II, the level of damage which they could consider to be unacceptable will be much higher than the level the U.S. would consider to be unacceptable. Acutally, the opposite conclusion is just as – if not more – likely. Because the Soviets have suffered so much, and are so aware of the consequences of great destruction on their country, their threshold of what is considered to be unacceptable may really be lower than the U.S. estimates. See Robert L. Arnett, "Soviet Attitudes Towards Nuclear War: Do They Really Think They Can Win?," *Journal of Strategic Studies*, Vol. 2 (September, 1979), pp. 190-91.

5 U.S. Office of Technology Assessment, *The Effects of the Nuclear War* (Washington, D.C.: Government Printing Office, 1979), p. 76.

ticular forms of action. At the final alarm, ordering urban evacuation, the people are to take prespecified motorcars, trains or buses to prespecified shelters in rural areas." The rest of the population "is to find shelter in the city or to start walking (in orderly columns of 500 to 1,000). They are then to build 'expedient shelters,' for which printed instructions exist."[6] According to Soviet sources, this entire procedure is to take approximately 72 hours.

But this is only theory. According to CIA analysts familiar with the Soviet civil defense program, the problems the Russians face in safeguarding the bulk of their civilian population in a nuclear war are immense if not insurmountable. For instance, Soviet cities are far more concentrated than many cities of the American South and West that developed after the introduction of the automobile and the freeway. The evacuation of these large urban population centers and "evenly" distributing city dwellers in less populated areas would pose immense logistical problems under the most favorable of circumstances.

In a deteriorating international situation leading to the contemplated use of nuclear weapons, the circumstances would certainly be less than favorable. And the U.S.S.R.'s creaky public transportation system is hardly the world's best.

As CIA officials explain, Soviet plans envisage the urban population moving out of the danger areas in trains, in motor vehicles or on foot. Yet there are only about two million cars, two million trucks and approximately 200,000 buses for the entire Soviet Union. Furthermore, there are few roads in that vast and underdeveloped (when compared with the U.S.) country. No more than a third of these have hard surfaces. For the most part, railroads are the preferred method of long-distance travel in the U.S.S.R. However, most of the lines are single-track and most of the trains are loaded with freight at any given time. It is unlikely that the trains would be in the right place at the right time in sufficient quantities to pick up the millions of people in danger and transport them to distant, presumably less dangerous areas.

6 Fred Kaplan, "The Soviet Civil Defense Myth," *The Bulletin of Atomic Scientists,* Vol. 34, Nos 3 & 4 (March/April, 1978), p.16. Kaplan was a fellow at the M.I.T. Center for International Studies Arms Control Project at the time of this writing. He is also the author of *Dubious Specter: A Second Look at the Soviet Threat* (1977).

Take the case of the Soviet national capital. Present plans for evacuating Moscow call for most residents simply to walk out of the city, since there is inadequate transportation to move approximately eight million people in an expeditious way by train, bus or automobile. According to the CIA, this evacuation would take three to seven days, and the Agency would discover almost immediately that it was happening. (Since this state of affairs would imply that Soviet authorities believed that nuclear war was imminent, it is probable that the Administration would respond by ordering the rapid evacuation of American cities.) Soviet city dwellers would be directed to designated areas in the countryside for regrouping; yet some method of feeding and sheltering all these people would have to be found. This task would be difficult under any conditions, but particularly so should evacuation occur in winter. Not surprisingly, therefore, many CIA officials have serious doubt that this system would be implemented effectively amid the breakdown of social order, disruption of services and so forth that would be expected to accompany a nuclear war.[7]

According to a U.S. Defense Department report, the Soviet civil defense system would be able to protect only 6-12 percent of the total work force at key industrial installations. This report also pointed out that one key aspect of the Soviet effort to protect industry – its geographical dispersal – has not been implemented to any important degree: [8]

New plants have often been built next to major existing plants. Existing plants and complexes have been expanded. No effort has been made to increase the distance between buildings or to locate additions in such a way as to minimize fire and other hazards in the event of a nuclear attack. Previously open spaces at fuel storage sites have been filled with new storage tanks and processing units. In sum, the value of overall production capacity has been increased proportionately more in existing sites than in new areas.

The Soviet program providing for the protection of workers in hardened shelters is also generally viewed with skepticism by the

7 For background see Director of Central Intelligence, *Soviet Civil Defense,* N178-10003, July 1978.

8 U.S. Defense Department, *Annual Report, 1981* (Washington, D.C.: Government Printing Office, 1980), p.78.

CIA. These people point out that the shelters are normally located at the sites of major factories, most of which are targeted by U.S. nuclear warheads.

Russians in such shelters would most probably have a difficult time surviving the multiple effects of nuclear weapons use on or about their shelters. These might well include blast, burial of their shelters under tons of rubble, fire storms and conflagrations that would literally suck the air out of their shelters, denying them oxygen and causing temperatures to rise to unbearable levels.[9]

All of these considerations led Stansfield Turner, when he was CIA Director, to testify to Congress that he was not aware of any civil defense plan in the U.S.S.R. that could conceivably protect the Russian population effectively against nuclear attack. More importantly, he said, he knew of no such plan which would give the leaders of the Soviet Union the delusion that effective protection of their population and industry was possible against nuclear attack.

Frequently, proponents of civil defense in this country cite official Soviet publications as evidence that the Soviet leadership attaches great importance to civil defense measures as a means of ensuring the ability of the U.S.S.R. to survive a nuclear attack and for the attainment of victory. These include handbooks, leaflets, propaganda posters, which have led critics to comment slyly that the "most visible product of the Soviet civil defense bureaucracy is paper."[10] Actually, there is more to it than that, say the critics. Just as those publications distributed by civil defense planners in the U.S. give cause for optimism that one could possibly fight and survive a nuclear attack, so do many Soviet C.D. publications paint a generally positive picture. However, as one student of Soviet civil defense

9 For a detailed analysis of Soviet civil defense capabilities see Leon Goure, *War Survival in Soviet Strategy: Soviet Civil Defense* (Coral Gables, Fla.: Center for Advanced International Studies, University of Miami, 1976).

10 See for instance, Andrew Cockburn, *The Threat: Inside the Soviet Military Machine* (New York: Random House, 1983), p. 230. He writes: "The millions of Soviet school-children who attend Pionieer camps (roughly equivalent to boy-scout camps) each as the standard time for putting on a cotton and gauze mask (2 1/2 minutes), unpacking a 10-foot by 12-foot "trench shelter" (3 minutes for a team of three,) and decontaminating irradiated clothing with a soap and oil solvent (7 minutes). It also advises youthful readers that a nuclear blast wave takes 2 seconds to travel the first six-tenths of a mile, while those farther away will have "a few seconds" or more to seek shelter.

has noted, even Soviet publications admit that "civil defense by itself cannot solve the problem of effectively protecting large segments of the population and the essential sectors of the economy from destruction ..."[11]

Already 16 years ago Zh. Dyusheyev wrote in a brochure on the nature of a future nuclear war: "The devastation and losses in civilian population which occurred in past wars cannot be compared to the great losses in the civilian population or the tremendous amount of destruction that will occur if a nuclear missile war is unleashed."[12] Since that time a number of strong statements have been made in this regard. One such statement was made by V.M. Berezhkov, editior of SSCA, the journal of the USA Institute. He argued in 1977 that the nuclear arsenals of the U.S. and the U.S.S.R. are so powerful that nuclear war would not serve as a practical instrument of policy, and that neither side could expect to survive such a conflict in any meaningful sense of the word.[13]

To be sure, Soviet military writers tend to disagree about the utility of civil defense. But many civilian writers do not believe that their country could avoid unprecedented destruction in a nuclear war.

According to Jack Geiger, Professor of Community Medicine at the School of Biomedical Education, City College of New York, Russian physicians recently spent two and a half hours of prime time on the Soviet national television network presenting to the Soviet people some of the major consequences of nuclear war. He says that Dr. Ye I. Chazov and his colleagues pointed out "the futility of any defensive measures." This information, he says, "has also appeared recently in Soviet newspapers and magazines."[14]

11 Leon Goure *et al., The Role of Nuclear Forces in Current Soviet Strategy* (Coral Gables, Fla.: Center for Advanced International Studies, University of Miami, 1974), p.119.

12 Zh. Dyusheyev, *Samopomoshch i Vzaimopomoshch Pri Primenii Oruzhiya Massovogo Porazheniya i Pri Neschastnykh Sluchayak* (1972), cited in JPRS 59294, *Translation on USSR Military Affairs,* No. 925, p.22.

13 V.M. Berezhkov, "Basic Principles of Soviet-US Relations," *SSHA: Ekonomika, Politika i Ideologiya,* No. 4 (1977), p.8. Care should be taken with this source, since it is written with a foreign audience in mind.

14 See Patrick O'Herrernan, *opus cit.,* p.265.

Late 1980s

As we move into the last half of the 1980s, we no longer find opposition in the U.S.S.R. to the official no-victory nuclear war stance expressed so openly. Indeed, the new Chief of Staff, Marshal Akhromeyev, has publicly affirmed the official position. Importantly, writings by military men which identify nuclear war with the destruction of civilization have recently become more common. Take for example the statement by Lieutenant General Volkogonov:[15] *He who fires his missiles first will perish second, but perish just the same... One can turn the adversary into ashes, but cannot thereby emerge victorious. There will be no witnesses to pass judgment ... Nuclear might is a means not only of annihilation but also of self-annihilation ... The threat of war is ... a threat to the whole of civilization. More than that if we suppose that our civilization is alone and unique in the universe, and nobody has yet proven otherwise.*

If the military position may thus be moving closer to the political stance, there are, of course, quite a few indications that the possibility of victory is still defended in at least some quarters in the military. So one must be cautious about drawing any hard and fast conclusions here about actual Soviet perceptions.

Perhaps the most important conclusion that one can draw about Soviet civil defense measures is the following: Through the civil defense programs, the Soviet military is able to foster and maintain in the populace a war-preparedness attitude. At the same time, it encourages a certain kind of discipline and paramilitary habits. In recent years the programs have received more serious attention from the Party and the military and have consequently been expanded and intensified.

Views of the Aftereffects of Nuclear Weapons

The official Soviet position toward the bomb and its pervasive aftereffects has undergone significant change, as a number of scholars readily have observed. In the immediate postwar period Soviet

15 *Znamya*, 2 (1984), p.175.

military doctrine, which was determined in the main by Stalin, emphasized the "constantly operating factors" such as manpower, morale and the stability of the home front. In this context, the atomic bomb – while it was condemned as a weapon of mass destruction – was not the ultimate weapon. In keeping with this doctrine *Pravda*, as late as January 1950, was asserting that only 8,400 people were affected at Hiroshima. No public mention was made of the first American explosion of a thermonuclear device at Eniwetok in November 1952. And it was not until 1954 that the first picture of the atomic mushroom cloud was published in the Soviet Union.[16]

Beginning shortly after Stalin died in 1953, a number of efforts (largely by the military) were made to cut the restrictive bonds of "Stalinist military science" and somewhat belatedly adapt to the world of nuclear weapons. Between 1953 and 1957 a debate took place in the pages of Soviet publications which, for all its textual obscurity, indicated to some Kremlinologists that a new school of Soviet strategic thinking had arisen to challenge the conventional wisdom.[17] One of the most articulate spokesmen of this "new school" was the late Major General Nikolai Talensky, editor of the influential military journal *Military Thought*. He argued that the advent of nuclear weapons, particularly the hydrogen bomb which had just appeared on the Soviet scene, had fundamentally altered the nature of warfare. The sheer destructiveness of these weapons was such that one could no longer talk of a socialist strategy automatically overcoming the strategy of the capitalist countries. In the oblique way in which Soviet debates on issues of great import are invariably conducted, General Talensky was saying in effect that perhaps, after all, war had ceased to represent a viable instrument of state policy.[18]

16 According to Raymond Garthoff, a long-time student of Soviet military affairs and former U.S. Ambassador to Bulgaria, "not a single article on atomic energy or atomic weapons is known to have appeared in the period from 1947 through 1953 in the Soviet military daily and periodical press, open or restricted in circulation." See his *Soviet Strategy in the Nuclear Age* (New York: Praeger, 1958), p. 67.

17 Herbert Dinerstein has sought to explain the doctrinal discussions of the 1950s as a reflection of internal infighting over the adequacy of Soviet strategic expenditures and the influence of this issue on the struggle for power within the Politburo. See his *War and the Soviet Union: Nuclear Weapons and the Revolution in Soviet Military and Political Thinking* (New York: Praeger, 1959), p. 91

18 Talensky's "heresy" brought an immediate and vehement response from serving

But more important than Talensky's controversial utterances were the speeches delivered by leading Soviet politicians in the winter of 1953-54. These seemed to support the thesis advanced by President Eisenhower in his address before the United Nations of December 1953 – namely, that nuclear war could spell the demise of civilization. In his address delivered on March 12, 1954, Stalin's immediate successor, Georgi Malenkov, echoed the sentiments earlier expressed by Eisenhower. Malenkov said that a new world war would unleash a holocaust which, "with the present means of warfare, means the destruction of world civilization."[19]

The attack on the traditional thinking of the Soviet military establishment triggered a furious reaction. The military leaders of the Red Army were not about to let the Soviet armed forces be relegated to the status of a militia whose principal task was averting war rather than winning it. In the view of several historians of the period, Malenkov's unorthodox views on war may well have contributed to his downfall.[20] In any case, his dimissal in February 1955 as party leader was accompanied by a barrage of press denunciations of the idea that war had suddenly become unfeasible.

There are some indications that the chief rival of Malenkov – Khrushchev – capitalized on the discontent within the military establishment to form with it an alliance with whose help he eventually rose to power. The successful military counter-attack appears to have been led by the World War II hero Marshall Georgi Zhukov,

Soviet officers, who rushed into the military press to criticize him by name – a move that rarely happens to Soviet general officers. They did not, however, take issue with Talensky's views so much as they did to his having stated them in public. Such loose talk, his opponents made clear, was tactless in the extreme because it dangerously undermined the case for a strong and prosperous military establishment in the U.S.S.R. For instance, General K. Bochkarev, Deputy Commandant of the Soviet General Staff Academy, argued that if ideas like those expressed by Talensky took hold, "the armed forces of the socialist states ... will not be able to set for themselves the goal of defeating imperialism and the global nuclear war which it unleashes and the mission of attaining victory in it, and our military science should not even work out a strategy for the conduct of war since the latter has lost its meaning and its significance ... *In this case, the very call to raise the combat readiness of our armed forces and improve their capability to defeat any aggressor is senseless.*" (Italics mine.) See Andrew Cockburn, *opus cit.*, p.214.

19 *Pravda*, March 13, 1954.

20 See for instance, Leon Goure *et al.*, *The Role of Nuclear Forces in Current Soviet Strategy* (Coral Gables: University of Miami, 1974), p.XV.

whom Khrushchev made his Minister of Defense and brought into the Presidium (as the Politburo was then called).

The guidelines of Soviet nuclear policy during this period of Khrushchev's tenure were formulated during 1955-57 under the leadership of Zhukov himself. Their collaboration resulted in the rejection of the notion that there existed an "absolute weapon."

During the late 1950s, the Soviet position on nuclear policy changed once again. This was in large part due to Khrushchev's solemn conviction that nuclear war had become politically useless,[21] since there would be no victors and the damage would be so devastating that organized society would cease to exist.[22]

In the aftermath of the Cuban Missile crisis of October 1962, Khrushchev painted this grim picture:[23]

According to the calculations of scientists the very first blow [in a thermonuclear war] would destroy between 700 and 800 million people. All large cities, not only in the United States and the Soviet Union, the two leading nuclear powers, but also in France, Britain, Germany, Italy, China, Japan, and many other countries would be razed to the ground and destroyed. The consequences of atomic-hydrogen bomb war would persist during the lives of many generations and would result in disease, death, and would cripple the human race.

"The atomic bomb," stated the Soviet Party Central Committee in an open letter of July 14, 1963 to the Communist Party of China, "does not adhere to the class principle; it destroys everybody within range of its devastating force."[24]

21 It is important to note here that Khrushchev arrived at this position gradually. In 1954, he maintained that in the event of a nuclear war the "imperialists will choke on it and it will end up in a catastrophe for the imperialist world." (*Pravda,* June 13, 1954.) In 1955, he still subscribed to the view that "we cannot be intimidated by fables that in the event of a new world war civilization will perish." (*Pravda,* March 27, 1955.) In 1956, Khrushchev began to hedge, stating that "war is not fatalistically inevitable." (TASS, February 14, 1956) By 1958, Khrushchev had reversed himself, now maintaining that "a future war ... would cause immeasurable harm to all mankind." (Radio Budapest, April 3, 1958.)

22 See Roman Kolkowicz, "Strategic Parity and Beyond: Soviet Perspectives," *World Politics* (April, 1971), p. 437. In 1959 Khrushchev remarked that he did "not trust appraisals of generals on questions of strategic importance." Quoted in Lawrence Freedman, *The Evolution of Nuclear Strategy* (New York: St. Martin's Press, 1983), p. 262.

23 *Pravda,* January 17, 1963.

24 *Pravda,* July 14, 1963.

In this context, a study undertaken in the mid-1960s by Thomas W. Wolfe, a senior staff member of the Rand Corporation and a faculty member of George Washington University, is worth citing. In analyzing the Sino-Soviet dispute of that era, he wrote: "The Soviet Union ... has charged that the Chinese fail to appreciate the destructive consequences of a nuclear war and have in effect courted it by being willing to provoke the United States. Peking in turn has retorted that the Soviet leaders ... are so afraid of nuclear war that they have allowed this fact to paralyze their policy."[25]

Following Khrushchev's removal as First Secretary in 1964, the "collective leadership" of party leader Leonid Brezhnev, Prime Minister Aleksei Kosygin and President Nikolai Podgorny made a number of important changes in Soviet nuclear strategy. However, they did retain the central assumption of Khrushchev's policy that a nuclear war would be a catastrophe for both the East and West.[26]

If the political leadership in the Soviet Union seems to have been the first to recognize the devastating effects of nuclear warfare, there were signs in the 1960s that a number of military men were now willing to acknowledge this reality. For instance, in 1968, Major General L. Bochkarev stated in a confidential Soviet military journal that "it is inadmissible" to ignore the conclusions of scientists on the catastrophic effects of the use of "even a part" of the vast existing nuclear stockpiles.[27]

25 See Wolfe's *The Soviet Union and the Sino-Soviet Dispute* (Calif.: The Rand Corporation, 1965), pp. 16-22. In a famous interview with Edgar Snow in 1965, Mao Tse-tung described how he went to the trouble of reading reports of an investigation of the effects of hydrogen bomb tests conducted over the Bikini Islands in the South Pacific in the early 1950s. Mao became almost lyrical in describing how research workers in 1959 found "mice scampering about and fish swimming in the streams ... foliage ... flourishing, and birds ... twittering in the trees" and vegatation so thick they had to "cut paths through the undergrowth." Although things might have been problematical for a year or two, Mao claimed, "nature had gone on." However, Mao was incorrect. Nature had not quite gone on as he said. Subsequent studies revealed significant radiation effects among some of the people of the islands and lingering dangers from radiation still affecting the habitat. See Robert J. Lifton and Richard Falk, *Indefensible Weapons: The Political and Psychological Case Against Nuclearism* (New York: Basic Books, 1982), p. 75.

26 *Ibid.*

27 See L. Bochkarev, "The Question of the Sociological Aspect of the Struggle Against the Forces of Aggression and War," *Voyennaya mysl'*, No. 9 (September, 1968), pp. 8-9

Just as U.S. officials were observing the evolution of Soviet policy on this important issue, Soviet authorities were following trends in the United States. Writing in 1971, G.A. Arbatov, Director of the USA Institute in the Soviet Union, noted: "Americans today do not doubt the fact that [thermonuclear war] would be suicidal for the American people. The conclusion that a world thermonuclear war has become a 'useless' instrument of policy is now shared by *most* representatives of the ruling circles as well."[28]

Since the early 1980s, Soviet officials and political leaders have been unanimous in addressing the issue of the devastating effects of nuclear war. The official Soviet policy in this regard did not change during the fifteen-month tenure of Yuri Andropov. And when Andropov died in early 1984, Konstantin Chernenko moved quickly to affirm this policy. Subsequently, Mikhail Gorbachev reiterated this policy at his summit meeting with President Reagan in November 1985: "... a nuclear war cannot be won and must never be fought."[29]

Nuclear Winter

Recently, a new element has been introduced into the Soviet-American debate over the long term effects of nuclear war. This is the finding by Carl Sagan, Paul Ehrlich and his fellow American scientists that nuclear war could constitute a global catastrophe. While this has long been suspected by people both inside and outside the U.S. government, it is interesting to note that the Soviets claim they had reached a similar conclusion through experiments in their own laboratories.

According to Sagan, there exists a rough "threshold" at which severe meteorological consequences are triggered.[30] In the case of nuclear warheads exploding in *surface* bursts against counterforce targets (e.g., missile silos), this threshold is about 2,000 warheads.

28 See G.A. Arbatov, "A Step in the Interests of Peace," *SSHA*, No. 11 (November, 1971).

29 See *The New York Times*, November 22, 1985.

30 It should be noted that the concept of a "nuclear *threshold*" is disputed even by some of those scientific supporters of Sagan's "nuclear winter" idea.

Given the large number of warheads in the arsenals of the two superpowers (about 50,000 with an aggregate yield near 15,000 megatons), the number of nuclear warheads that could destroy the world is small indeed. As in all calculations of this complexity, Sagan and Ehrlich acknowledge, there are uncertainties. Some factors tend, for instance, to work towards more severe or more prolonged effects; others tend to ameliorate the effects. As Sagan writes, "it is the soot produced by urban fires that is the most sensitive trigger of the climatic catastrophe."

As Sagan and Ehrlich report, the cumulative effects of a nuclear strike of between 500 and 2,000 warheads could trigger a "nuclear winter" and shatter the interconnecting web of systems that sustain life on the planet. Smoke and soot would obscure sunlight, causing temperatures to plunge below freezing levels even in the summer. Food crops and other ecological systems would be wiped out. And radiation would be several times more intense than previously. Finally, when this pall lifted, ultra-violet rays from the sun would reach intolerable levels.[31] In the words of Paul Ehrlich: "The population size of *Homo Sapiens* conceivably could be reduced to prehistoric levels or below, and extinction of the human species itself cannot be excluded."

At a special scientific conference held in Washington, D.C. October 31 through November 1, 1983, Soviet scientists were asked to comment via satellite on the studies done by Sagan and Ehrlich. The Soviet delegation was led by Evgeny P. Velikhov, Vice President of the Soviet Academy of Sciences, and they devoted considerable time to discussing new research findings in the Soviet Union similar to those in America.

The Soviet scientists reported that their research work indicated that a nuclear war could possibly create a global "toxic smog," unchecked biological epidemics and substantial depletion of the earth's oxygen supply. For one, Sergei P. Kapitza of the Physicotechnical Institute in Moscow said he agreed with his U.S. counterparts that recent findings mean that the use of nuclear weapons is "suicidal."[32]

31 See also C.H. Kruger *et al., Causes and Effects of Stratospheric Ozone Reduction: An Update* (Washington, D.C.: National Academy of Sciences, 1982).

32 See *The New York Times*, December 9, 1983.

Conclusions

The findings of Sagan and Ehrlich have a number of clear policy implications for the Soviet Union and the United States alike. For one thing, it means that a Soviet nuclear strike would be suicide – *even if there was no retaliatory strike by the United States.* As Carl Sagan and Paul Ehrlich have convincingly shown, and this is recognized by the U.S.S.R., an attack by the Soviets, using only a small fraction of its existing nuclear warheads, could literally mean the death of the planet and the extinction of the human race. (The present French *force de frappe,* said to target Soviet cities exclusively, may itself be adequate to trigger a global nuclear winter.)[33]

But Sagan and Ehrlich's findings have important ramifications for Soviet civil defense efforts. Put bluntly, they mean that no state can count on surviving a nuclear war. Thus, any civil defense program is questionable. To be sure, this knowledge of nuclear winter has not stopped the Soviets from continuing to make provisions in this disputed area. But the evidence would suggest that the Soviet political leadership no longer shares the enthusiasm of the military for this program. It seems also to recognize the impracticality of implementing civil defense plans on a large scale, even though a large number of persons continue to be involved bureaucratically.

Of course, the Soviets have plans to "protect" their top leadership. But they cannot protect the vast majority of their people in the event of nuclear war. In the words of William Hyland, a long-time student of Soviet affairs and a former aide to Henry Kissinger: "It is a mistake to confuse a program to protect leaders and key industrial personnel with effective civil defense for the population."[34]

Khrushchev, in his memoirs,[35] paints a vivid picture of the con-

33 See Carl Sagan's letter in "Comment and Correspondence," *Foreign Affairs,* Vol. 62, No. 4 (Spring, 1984), p.1001.

34 See *The New York Times,* June 10, 1982.

35 See Nikita Khrushchev, *Khrushchev Remembers: The Last Testament* (New York: Bantam Books, 1976), pp.619, 561. Khrushchev's memoirs are used widely, if carefully, by scholars of Soviet affairs. The following is not atypical: "Khrushchev's account must ... be approached with great care and discretion. It is highly biased, full of inaccuracies and faulty recollections, and extremely contentious. Yet it coincides remarkably well with the accounts of Djilas and Svetlana ..." See Juri Valenti *et al., Soviet Decisionmaking for National Security* (London: George Allen & Unwin, 1984), p.32.

ditions which must go through the minds of the present Soviet leadership when plans are discussed by the military to survive a nuclear war. Leaders, Khrushchev says, "must be careful not to look at the world through the eyeglasses of the military." They "should keep in mind exactly what sort of destruction we're capable of today." Leaders should be aware of the losses their own countries "will suffer" even if, "God willing," they are able to destroy their enemies.

"There are those," Khrushchev observes, "who don't seem to be able to get it through their heads that in the next war, the victor will be barely distinguished from the vanquished." Thus, "a war between the Soviet Union and the United States would almost certainly end in mutual defeat."

"Can you picture what would be left after a few hydrogen bombs fell on Moscow," Khrushchev asks. "Forget about 'a few' – imagine just one. Or Washington? Or New York? Or Bonn? It staggers the mind. All the mathematical calculations made during the war games, all our computers are worthless in trying to comprehend the magnitude of the destruction we would face."

Continuing in this fashion, Khrushchev suggests that it is "infinitely better to prevent a war than to try to survive one. I know all about bomb shelters and command posts and emergency communications and so on. But listen here: in a single flash, a bunker can be turned into a burial vault for a country's leaders and military commanders."

If an evil empire does exist, let it exist. I'm sure remaking the Soviet Union is not a goal of the United States.

Mikhail Gorbachev in a Moscow meeting with House Speaker Thomas P. O'Neil, April, 1985.

XIII. FROM NUCLEAR WAR FIGHTING TO ARMS CONTROL?

For many years the majority of American observers assumed that the central dilemmas of the nuclear age – the awesome destructiveness of nuclear weapons and the absence of meaningful defenses against them – would lead Soviet and American strategic thinkers to similar views on the proper role of nuclear weapons in the foreign policy of their country. Somewhat arrogantly, Americans have ignored the injunction offered well over fifteen years ago by Raymond L. Garthoff, who said that "in order to establish the strategic thought and doctrine of an alien military culture, it is first necessary to escape the confines of one's own implicit and unconscious strategic concept."[1] Americans, who were dominated by an ethnocentric bias that projected Western strategic premises and practices onto Soviet military planning, tended to assume that whatever is logical or preferable for U.S. military theoreticians must also be acceptable to Soviet political-military leaders.[2] If this situation was clearly not the case, Americans often took it for granted that Soviet strategic thinking was "lagging" behind American thinking. Thus,

1 Raymond L. Garthoff, *Soviet Strategy in the Nuclear Age* (New York: Praeger, 1962), p.XI.

2 A classic example is the influential work by Bernard Brodie, one of the pioneers of U.S. nuclear doctrine. His book, *Strategy in the Missile Age*, which originally was published in 1959 and then reprinted in 1965, makes only a few offhand allusions to Soviet nuclear strategy. And then either he notes with approval that it is "developing along lines familiar in the United States" (p.171) or else, when the Soviets prefer to follow their own track, he dismisses it as a "ridiculous and reckless fantasy." (p.215).

they saw it as their appointed task in arms control negotiations to educate their Soviet counterparts on the facts of life in the nuclear age.[3]

But the Soviets needed no tutoring from the United States about nuclear matters. Soviet strategic philosophy remains fundamentally unlike that of the United States. It is an undeniable reality that Soviet nuclear strategy is shaped primarily by peculiar Soviet influences – what Jack L. Snyder in his provocative RAND study terms a unique "strategic culture."[4] Of particular importance here is Marxist-Leninist political theory, Russian and Soviet historical experience, traditional Russian military doctrine and the geographical position of the U.S.S.R. in the Eurasian landmass surrounded by potentially hostile countries.

All of these factors suggest that Soviet nuclear strategy is different from American strategy, which Soviet strategic thinkers tend to regard as second-rate. In their view, U.S. strategic doctrine seems obsessed with a single weapon, which it "absolutizes" at the expense of almost everything else that military experience teaches soldiers to take into account.

Given what we now know about Soviet nuclear strategy, one would think that American strategic thinkers would be beyond the point where three familiar schools of thought on Soviet doctrine used to argue past each other somewhat in this vein: one saying "Whatever they say, they think as we do"; the second insisting, "Whatever they say, it does not matter"; and the third insisting, "They think what they say, and therefore, they are out for superiority over us." However, this is not the case, as recent experience shows.[5]

3 Explaining this particular expression of our cultural self-centeredness is a fascinating field for speculation. Fritz W. Ermarth, a former analyst of Soviet and American strategic policies at the Central Intelligence Agency, observes: "I think it goes beyond the American habit of value projection. It may result from the fact that post-war developments in U.S. strategy were an institutional and intellectual offspring of the nature sciences that spawned modern weapons. Scientific truth is transnational, not culturally determined. But, unfortunately, strategy is more like *politics* than like science." See his "Contrasts in American and Soviet Strategic Thought," *International Security,* Vol. 3 No. 2 (Fall, 1978), p. 140.

4 Jack L. Snyder, *The Soviet Strategic Culture: Implications for Limited Nuclear Operations* (Santa Monica: RAND Corporation, 1977), p.V. It is important to note that the Soviet "strategic culture" is not a monolith.

5 Where the lack of direct access to strategic doctrine complicates our under-

The late arrival of the Soviet Union on the nuclear scene seems naturally to have influenced early Soviet attitudes towards nuclear weaponry. For one thing it meant, in the first decade after 1945, dealing with a situation of utter vulnerability (regarding its air defenses) to the uncertain designs of an increasingly suspicious and hostile opponent. For another, it created an important incentive to neutralize the intimidating features of nuclear weaponry by challenging their acceptability on all possible grounds.

For a practical matter, the best that Stalin could hope for during a period when the U.S.S.R. lacked atomic weapons and an adequate delivery capability was to prevent war by holding Western Europe hostage to Soviet conventional superiority.[6] Since the American desire to provoke a nuclear war, or even to alter the *status quo* at this time, was small, the ability to threaten Europe was a realistic strategy.

But the development of the capability to threaten the United States with destruction was preferable to reliance on American self-restraint or solicitude for the survival of Western Europe. So Stalin decided soon after the Second World War to promote the development of ballistic missiles that could reach the United States. When intercontinental ballistic missiles became organic Soviet weapons in the early 1960s, what Khrushchev had been saying since December 1956 became true: no state would be safe from devastating damage in a nuclear war.

In the 1950s Khrushchev anticipated this development and behaved as if it were already true in his public statements. Taking advantage of all the opportunities offered by a closed society for manipulating information, he tried desperately after the first successful Soviet testing of an ICBM and the placing of the first space satellite in orbit in 1957 to translate the *perception* of a new nuclear balance into significant Soviet political gains. Consequently, Premier Khrush-

standing of Soviet nuclear strategy, an overwhelming abundance of data or interpretation of the data serves to confuse Soviet understanding of the American side. This is a point the Soviets make with some justification when berated with the evils of Soviet society.

6 One U.S. defense expert would assert here: "You are begging the issue of whether or not the Soviets had any offensive plans against Western Europe, or whether Western hostility towards the U.S.S.R. was legitimate."

chev embarked on a vigorous diplomatic campaign carried out by means of nuclear blackmail.

Almost instinctively, Khrushchev appreciated the far-reaching political ramifications for the Soviet Union of acquiring long-range nuclear "rockets" – as he liked to call them. Realizing that strategic nuclear weapons symbolized the opening of a new era in East-West competition on a global scale, he created the Strategic Rocket Forces as a separate entity. And he encouraged the development and production of its associated military hardware. The first three generations of Russian intercontinental ballistic missiles and ballistic missile-launching submarines were developed during his tenure. (This new-look Soviet defense policy, which also called for significant cuts in conventional forces, has been termed by one scholar "more rubble for the ruble.")[7]

From the vantage of the West, particularly the United States, it looked like the Soviet leader was "obsessed with nuclear weapons as the only feasible means of conducting modern warfare."[8] However, in actuality, as Richard Smoke writes, Khrushchev was bluffing.[9] To be sure, Khrushchev's nuclear "saber rattling" did intimidate the West, e.g. during the 1956 Suez Canal crisis. And various negotiations were undertaken by U.S., British and French officials to mollify the Soviet leader. But by late 1961, satellite photography, which had replaced the U-2 as a prime source of American intelligence about Soviet missile capabilities, left no doubt that the Soviet intercontinental capacity was only marginal. Realizing that the West was now very well informed of Soviet nuclear inferiority, Khrushchev resorted to the desperate gamble of placing nuclear weapons in Cuba in 1962. However, this move ended in failure, and two years later Khrushchev was removed from power.

Since Khrushchev's removal over twenty years ago, succeeding Soviet leaders have indicated publicly their unwillingness to *use* nuclear weapons for political gain. This changed state of affairs has

7 Raymond L. Garthoff, "Khrushchev and the Military," in Alexander Dallin and Alan F. Westin (eds.), *Politics in the Soviet Union* (New York: Harcourt, Brace and World, 1966), p.255.

8 William G. Hyland, *opus cit.*, p.49.

9 Richard Smoke, *National Security and the Nuclear Dilemma: An Introduction to the American Experience* (Massachusetts: Addison-Wesley Publishing Co., 1984), p.99.

not meant, however, that the Kremlin sees no political utility to be derived from the *possession* of these weapons of mass destruction. To the contrary. The attainment of parity, for instance, has compelled the United States to take Soviet positions on international issues more fully into account. As former Soviet Foreign Minister Andrei Gromyko has observed:[10]

The Soviet Union is a great power situated on two continents, Europe and Asia, but the range of our country's international interests is not determined by its geographic position alone ... The Soviet people do not plead with anybody to be allowed to have their say in the solution of any question concerning the maintenance of international peace, concerning the freedom and independence of the peoples and our country's extensive interests. This is our right, due to the Soviet Union's position as a great power. During any acute situation, however far away it appears from our country, the Soviet Union's reaction is to be expected in all capitals of the world.

For more than two decades a wide rhetorical gap on the question of the consequences of nuclear war existed between Soviet military and political leaders. During this period one could find in the writings of Soviet military officers and civilian strategists ample statements leading U.S. officials to believe that the Soviet leadership thought it was possible to fight and win a nuclear war. At the same time one could also find statements to the contrary, such as those which hailed the 1973 Soviet-American Agreement on "Prevention of Nuclear War" as reduction of the danger of nuclear war. The situation is radically different today. Almost all Soviet writers and political leaders addressing this important question now solemnly declare in effect that there will be no victors in a nuclear war.

As a result of this change in policy, there is today a large body of political statements that come perilously close to Malenkov's "heresy" of 1954 – that nuclear war would mean the end of civilization. In June, 1981, Brezhnev said that "... the future of all mankind would be at stake in a nuclear war."[11] Specifically denying the notion of

10 Quoted by Herbert Block, "Value and Burden of Soviet Defense," in Joint Economic Committee, eds., *Soviet Economic Prospects for the Seventies* (Washington, D.C.: U.S. Government Printing Office, 1973), p.201.

11 *Pravda*, June 23, 1981.

winning a nuclear war, the late General Secretary proclaimed: "It is dangerous madness to try to defeat each other in the arms race and to count on victory in nuclear war." Brezhnev also asserted that "anyone who starts a nuclear war in the hope of winning it has thereby decided to commit suicide."[12] All Brezhnev's successors have affirmed this rhetoric, which of course is intended in part for popular consumption, especially in Europe. (Recently, Gorbachev stated in a *Time* interview: "I would like once again to tell all Americans the most important thing they should know: war will not come from the Soviet Union. We will never start war.")

If Soviet military writings today and the remarks by Soviet leaders all suggest that the Kremlin will not use nuclear weapons militarily for political gain, the Soviet leadership still fears that the United States, untempered by the horrors of war on its own territory, might be tempted to attack or that war might arise out of third-party conflict. Consequently, Soviet leaders must be prepared to make the best of things if war does erupt. Their military strategy is designed accordingly.

But one is advised to put this "war fighting" doctrine into the proper perspective, particularly its emphasis on "survival" and "victory." As Fritz W. Ermarth observes: "the system decided it *had* to believe in survival and victory of some form." Not so to believe "would mean that the most basic processes of history, on which Soviet ideology and political legitimacy are founded, would be derailed by the technological works of man and the caprice of an historically doomed opponent." Moreover, as the defenders of doctrinal rectitude in the U.S.S.R. have continued to point out, "failure to believe in the 'manageability' of nuclear disaster would lead to pacificism, defeatism, and lassitude in the Soviet military effort."[13]

For the Soviet Union, the decisive influence in the formulation of its military strategy were the lessons of World War II with which, for understandable reasons, Soviet military leaders are virtually obsessed. Some twenty million Soviet citizens died in what the Russians like to call "the Great Patriotic War." This figure contrasts sharply with American losses in World War II of approximately

12 *Pravda*, October 21, 1981.

13 Fritz W. Ermarth, *opus cit.*, p.144.

325,000 and the absence of warfare and occupation at home. Soviet spokesmen are fond of pointing out that the United States did not have to suffer the horrors of war as they did. The Soviet regime came very close to being crushed by the Nazi armies in the Second World War. This experience underpins the fundamental belief of the Soviet leadership that the U.S.S.R. must be able to defend itself under any circumstances and cannot rely on the peaceful professions of an adversary who advocates mutual deterrence.[14]

Does this major shift in policy suggest that the Kremlin is no longer prepared for nuclear war? Certainly not. The Soviets are busy modernizing their strategic theater and tactical nuclear forces.

In short, the official Soviet position is that although war with the West is no longer "fatalistically inevitable," and indeed that the present correlation of forces has significantly reduced the danger of an attack on the Soviet Union, the possibility of the occurrence of war cannot be completely discounted, either for the present or the future.

Recent Efforts at Arms Control

During the last few years the Soviets have shown an increasing interest in arms control negotiations with the United States. But here the major stumbling block to progress has been the SDI program and President Reagan's determination not to give it up. In the main, Gorbachev endeavoured to reach agreement with the U.S. in this crucial area because it would allow him to concentrate national resources on a troubled civilian economy.

The year 1986 began on a upbeat note. For one thing, the United States started the year by extending its political commitment to the SALT II Treaty. This accord would have expired on December 31, 1985, if SALT II had been ratified.

In mid-January, 1986, General Secretary Mikhail Gorbachev proclaimed a comprehensive disarmament proposal. This bold plan called, among other things, for the elimination of all nuclear weapons by the end of the century. Obviously, Gorbachev's sweeping

14 See Nathan Leites, *Soviet Style in War* (New York: Crane, Russak & Co., 1982).

proposal was designed, in part, to capture the propaganda initiative. But to U.S. arms control experts the details of the proposal suggested a new flexibility in the Soviet negotiating position on nuclear weapons. Important here was the concession to accept a zero level for INF missiles without seeking compensation for British and French nuclear forces which were in the process of undergoing extensive modernization.[15]

If the Soviet proposal offered some promising concessions, a major setback occured four months later, on May 27. For it was at this time that President Reagan formally repudiated the American commitment to SALT II. He indicated that the United States would exceed the limits of this agreement later in the year. This meant, among other things, that the Soviet Union would be free to deploy its new mobile ICBM's without feeling an obligation to remove other missiles as was true in the past. At the same time, the USSR could increase the number of MIRVed warheads on each of its heavy SS-18s. The President's decision was based in part, at least, on alleged violations of the agreement by the Soviet Union.

The President's SALT II decision cast a pall over Soviet-American relations for the next few months. Then, in early October, the political scene suddenly changed to one of anticipation and hope. The announcement was made that in less than two weeks Reagan and Gorbachev would meet at Reykjavik.

The Iceland Summit

Initial accounts of the Iceland summit of October 11-12 went a long way to deflate the optimism that had sprung up around the superpower conference. Among other things, they made clear that the gathering had been a bitter disappointment for both statesmen. For one thing, the two men had been unable to set a future date for a full-scale summit conference in the U.S. But much more significantly, President Reagan had passed up an arms accord of sweeping historical proportions in order to protect his pet project, Star Wars.

15 U.S. Arms Control Association, *Annual Report 1986* (Washington, D.C., 1987) p.1.

For his part, Gorbachev reaped some political rewards from the postsummit publicity. Even though he came back from Reykjavik pretty much empty-handed, he had put President Reagan and his Strategic Defense Initiative on the spot. And his public self assurance and his candid report to the Soviet people made him look like a winner.[16]

For a moment, the two men shared the breathtaking vision of a nuclear-free world. That is, both had agreed, if only for a moment, to eliminate all nuclear weapons. But this commitment did not survive the summit; in fact, it was denied by Administration spokesmen. Had it survived, the commitment would have left the United States and its allies in a position of inferiority *vis-à-vis* the larger conventional forces of the Soviet camp.

The package deal fell apart, of course, when President Reagan rejected Gorbachev's restrictions of SDI. Now, however, there were signs of greater Soviet flexibility. Importantly, there were reports that the Soviets were finally willing to make significant compromises on Star Wars. These included possibly allowing some work on SDI space weapons outside the laboratory, although not in space. "We have something up our sleeve," promised one Soviet official.[17]

Until the talk focused on Star Wars, the two leaders had made remarkable progress in their conversations. On INF, for instance, Gorbachev agreed that U.S. and Soviet medium-range nuclear missiles should be withdrawn from Europe. At first, Reagan seemed reluctant, but then the Soviet leader brought him around. He pointed out that the American President had been the first to suggest a

16 From the point of view of the Soviet Union, "The agreements almost reached in Reykjavik were undermined at the very last minute by American intransigence on SDI." Or so says Georgi Fedyashin, Deputy Director of Novosti, the Soviet press agency, and one of the principal architects of the Kremlin's image in the West. "The Soviet delegation made very serious concessions to reach agreement in Reykjavik," Fedyashin said. But he added, the U.S. was "unfortunately" not prepared to do the same.
In a TV address to the Soviet people, Gorbachev claimed: "Our conscience is clear. One cannot reproach us for anything. We did all we could do." *The Christian Science Monitor,* October 16, 1986.

17 American officials reported in this connection that Soviet diplomats in Washington have been hinting that a new interpretation of the word "laboratory" might be possible. "They say that a laboratory does not necessarily have to be within walls," states one sources. "The way they are talking, a laboratory could mean practically anywhere except out in space." See *Newsweek,* October 27, 1986.

"zero option." As Gorbachev later described it, he put Reagan on the spot: "How can you abandon your own child, your zero option?"[18]

The Soviet leader agreed to cut his Asian-based SS-20 missiles from 513 warheads to only 100. These cuts were to be matched by an equal number of warheads to be based in the U.S. Gorbachev also agreed to freeze shorter range nuclear missiles in Europe and to negotiate reductions. Surprisingly, the Soviet leader consented on strategic weapons to a stunning fifty percent cut to 1,600 delivery vehicles and 6,000 warheads. "They've given us one heck of a proposal," Reagan told his senior staff the first day.

On SDI, some of Reagan's advisers thought they might be able to fudge the problem. The Soviet Foreign Minister, for one, seemed to agree that for ten years, work on SDI should be restricted "in accordance with the current understanding" of the 1972 ABM Treaty.[19] In that both Moscow and Washington sharply disagreed on the interpretation of the treaty, the U.S. side took Shevardnadze's consent as a sign that Gorbachev was willing to finesse the problem for the time being.

By Sunday afternoon, October 12, the two leaders were hammering out details personally. According to one insider, the final American proposal offered to eliminate all ballistic missiles after ten years. For his part, Gorbachev countered with an offer to eliminate all *strategic* nuclear weapons after a decade. (This would allow the U.S.S.R. to dominate Europe with shorter-range nuclear missiles.) For their part, Reagan and his advisers insisted on the elimination of "all offensive ballistic missiles." Then, Gorbachev startled the group by making his boldest suggestion to date.

White House Chief of Staff Donald Regan reconstructs it as follows: The Soviet leader asked: "Why not make this everything?"

18 *Newsweek*, October 27, 1986.

19 According to a bipartisan panel headed by leading specialists, President Reagan's notion of a "star wars" dome to protect the United States from nuclear warheads could not even go into development in the next ten years. "It is very unlikely that any sort of wide area BMD we could put into full-scale engineering development before that point ... would be worth having," stated a report of the Aspen Strategic Group. Co-chairmen of the group were William J. Perry, Assistant Secretary of Defense for Research and Development in the Carter Administration, and Brent Scowcroft, Special Assistant for National Security Affairs in the Ford Administration. See *The New York Times*, October 22, 1986.

President Reagan responded: "You mean *everything* – artillery shells and the like?" The Soviet leader affirmed: "Yes." Reagan replied: "O.K. I'll agree to that, everything."

This amazing deal was never committed to formal agreement. And soon the American side was backing away from it. As one side later remarked: "No, you can't have a nuclear-free world because people know how to build these weapons."[20]

In the end, it was vigorous disagreement over SDI that scuttled the summit. The Soviet leader insisted that work on "space-strike" weapons had to stay in the laboratory for ten years. But Reagan and his advisers saw this as a Soviet plan calculated to sabotage SDI. As Reagan later said on T.V., "he was killing SDI, and unless I agreed, all the work toward eliminating nuclear weapons would go down the drain – cancelled."

As the summit ended, Max Kampelman, the chief U.S. negotiator at the Geneva arms talks, was led to exclaim: "in every way except the end" it was "a fantastic thing ... It was the most appealing package ever negotiated by the two countries."[21]

Later aides reconstructed the final dialogue. As the two men exited the Hofdi House, Gorbachev declared to Reagan, "I think we can still deal. There is still time." But the President replied: "I don't think you really wanted a deal." As they approached his limousine, the President said: "I don't know when we'll meet again."

20 In the hours immediately following the conclusion of the summit, U.S. government spokesmen indicated that all-out elimination of nuclear weapons was the position of the administration. Days later they were asserting that while Reagan discussed the elimination of all nuclear arms, he never proposed more than destruction of all ballistic or long-range guided missiles, in two five-year phases. The distinction is strategically important because the American position as now stated would leave both sides with substantial arsenals of cruise missiles, nuclear bombs and tactical nuclear weapons fired from conventional artillery pieces. Disputing White House accounts of the summit, Soviet officials claimed that President Reagan had agreed to eliminate all strategic nuclear weapons in ten years. Deputy Foreign Minister Alexander Bessmertnykh told a press conference that the Kremlin considered White House assertions to the contrary deliberate distortions. Bessmertnykh quoted what he asserted were Reagan's own words to back up his statements. In a television address several days earlier, Gorbachev stated: "The President did, albeit without special enthusiasm, consent to the elimination of all – I emphasize, all – not only certain individual strategic offensive arms, to be destroyed precisely over ten years, in two stages." See *The Minneapolis Star and Tribune*, October 26, 1986.

21 *The Minneapolis Star and Tribune*, October 13, 1986.

Then Gorbachev replied: "I don't know what else I could have done." Reagan: "You could have said yes."[22]

The Summit Aftermath

First impressions of arms control prospects in the aftermath of the summit were predictably pessimistic. But then several events occured which helped to brighten the picture considerably.

First the negative side of the ledger. A little over a month after Reagan and Gorbachev confronted each other face to face, the United States exceeded a critical limit of SALT with the deployment of the 131st strategic bomber equipped with cruise missiles. This move effectively destroyed the only existing constraint on strategic offensive arms by eliminating the possibility that the U.S. might remain in *de facto* compliance with SALT II.

As the year ended, Washington announced that it was giving serious consideration to reorienting its SDI program to "early" deployment of a technically less ambitious system. It also indicated that it would soon begin testing of a program that would violate the traditional interpretation of the ABM Treaty.[23]

For their part, the Soviets announced that they would resume underground nuclear testing if the U.S. continued testing in 1987 (which it did). The White House reacted to this important Soviet decision by ignoring it. This, in effect, signaled the end of the thrice renewed, 19-month Soviet moratorium.

Despite these grim developments in 1986, the picture began to change for the better in early 1987. And again the Soviets beat Reagan to the punch.

On February 28, 1987, Mikhail Gorbachev said he was ready to sign "without delay", an agreement to remove medium-range nuclear missiles from Europe in five years. Importantly, the Soviet leader no longer tied concessions on INF to SDI restraint.[24]

22 Following the summit, Gorbachev accused the U.S. of deliberately misrepresenting the results of his meeting with President Reagan. At the same time, he affirmed that his proposals to Reagan in Reykjavik still stood, but only as an indivisible package. *The New York Times,* October 22, 1986.

23 U.S. Arms Control Association, *Annual Report 1986* (Washington, D.C., 1987), p.2.

24 See *Newsweek,* March 16, 1987.

The American response was immediately forthcoming. A "breakthrough" has been achieved, said Reagan, who told an audience of newspaper editors: "This is a great moment of hope for all mankind."[25]

With this boost, INF talks took on a new seriousness of purpose. To be sure, major differences remained to be settled. But if a deal could be closed, it would be a landmark in the history of arms control: the first treaty to dismantle existing missiles instead of merely imposing limits on future deployments.

The Soviet goal was to have an agreement ready for signature during the summer of 1987. This major event would clear the way for a third summit between Reagan and Gorbachev.

A Change in Leadership

While intense bargaining was underway, an unexpected event occurred in late May 1987 which was to have repercussions for the arms control talks. On May 30, Soviet Defense Minister Sergei L. Sokolov was relieved of his duties, and the Soviet military was sharply rebuked by Gorbachev after a small West German civilian plane penetrated Soviet airspace and flew unimpeded 400 miles to Moscow before landing beside the Kremlin. The 75-year-old World War II veteran Sokolov was replaced by General Dmitri T. Yazov, Deputy Minister of Defense for Personnel.[26]

The new change of leadership was generally seen in the West as a consolidation of power by Mikhail Gorbachev. Importantly, it was expected to put him in a better position to quell any military discontent over his arms control initiatives and over his professed desire to focus national resources on the civilian economy. "This really brings the generational change into the military at last," a Western military attaché exclaimed.[27]

25 *Ibid.*
26 See *The New York Times*, May 31, 1987.
27 *Ibid.*

INF Agreement

Serious INF negotiations took place all during the spring and summer of 1987. And it was not until September that an accord in principle could be reached. Final agreement, however, was held up over a condition set by the Soviet side. This was that Gorbachev would only come to the United States for a summit if assured that he and President Reagan would be able to transact some major business.[28]

With the signing of the INF "agreement in principle to conclude a treaty," there was a great deal of euphoria in Washington. But this was premature as the INF treaty may yet have some difficulty winning the necessary two-thirds Senate majority. Nevertheless, there is some reason to think that the INF deal may set the tone for additional U.S.-Soviet agreements.

This process has already begun. In a ceremony in the White House Rose Garden, Secretary of State Shultz and Foreign Minister Shevardnadze signed a minor but symbolically important accord setting up two "nuclear risk-reduction centers." Two days later, they announced the beginning of "full scale" negotiations looking forward to eventual ban on nuclear tests.

Western Reaction

Since 1981, when President Reagan first proposed what became known as the "zero-zero" option (meaning the dismantling of all intermediate range missiles in Central Europe), an INF treaty has become the touchstone of whether the United States and the Soviet Union can summon the political will to start a reversal of the arms race. There has been a long series of negotiations on the issue, interrupted by a Soviet walkout that began in 1983 and lasted for 16 months. Towards the end of the talks, one of the last sticking points was what to do with the 72 Pershing 1A shorter-range missiles owned by the Federal Republic of Germany and outfitted with U.S. warheads. In the end, this problem was solved by a decision by

28 *Time*, September 28, 1987.

Chancellor Helmut Kohl to have the missiles destroyed once the U.S. and Soviet weapons were dismantled.

In general, the INF agreement received a mixed welcome in Western Europe. The grass roots reaction was, for the most part, very favorable. This was particularly true in West Germany where the controversial Pershing II missiles were deployed. For their part, the British and French governments, two independent nuclear powers, appeared somewhat nervous that the elimination of some superpower weaponry might raise public demands for the abolition of their own nuclear weapons. But both pledged to strengthen their arsenals. On the other hand, the Belgian, Dutch and Italian governments, reluctant hosts to U.S. cruise missiles, were pretty much relieved that they would soon lose the politically volatile weapons.

If there was general popular relief over the INF agreement in Europe, there was also some official concern. As NATO Secretary General Lord Carrington warned, the alliance "should not let any euphoria it engenders push us toward some mythical nonnuclear nirvana."[29] Perhaps, the issue most often raised in this context concerned Western fears of Soviet predominance in conventional weapons. Many West European commentators argued that the Soviet position would be enhanced by the elimination of medium-range missiles. In effect, Moscow would be left with greater leverage over Western Europe.

Star Wars Moves Forward

Just as Washington and Moscow were concluding a successful series of negotiations on INF, the Reagan Administration was pressing forward with an ambitious program that the Soviets regard as a major obstacle to peace. This is the controversial Strategic Defense Initiative (SDI). And the Pentagon was now preparing to advance to the Milestone I stage, an official term indicating that the system is ready to pass from "exploration" to "demonstration." In other words, Star Wars was now deemed fit to move from the drawing board to the production stage.

29 *Newsweek*, September 28, 1987.

The Soviet response was to clarify its position on SDI. Moscow now argued that both sides should adhere for an additional ten years to the 1972 ABM treaty, which restricts defensive weapons. The Kremlin then offered the White House an option: It could either negotiate a long list of objects that cannot be put into space or it can agree that both sides will "strictly abide by the ABM treaty as it was signed and ratified in 1972."

If the Soviet offer on SDI was designed, in part, to help move bilateral talks along on strategic weapons, it did not take into consideration the fact that Reagan remained as committed to Star Wars as ever. This was his dream, and he was irrevocably determined to hand on the program, recently accelerated, to his successor.

Conclusions

The INF agreement is viewed as a dangerous *quid pro quo* by Henry Kissinger. Writing in the October 12, 1987 edition of *Newsweek*, he claims that it is responsible for touching off a "grave crisis of confidence" among America's NATO allies. This NATO "crisis" can be summed up as follows:

First, Kissinger sees as a consequence to INF the development of an apparent change in military doctrine pursued by the last five administrations. This new situation would place the burden of nuclear defense on weapons based in the United States or at sea.

Second, the former Secretary of State sees in INF the "decoupling" of American and European defenses. In his view, this would enable the Soviet Union to threaten Western Europe while sparing the United States.

Third, Kissinger believes that with the removal of INF forces Soviet conventional superiority will become more important.

The upshot of all this, Kissinger argues, is that Europe probably "will seek new directions in the years ahead." While some countries will be tempted to maneuver between East and West and in the process extend the Reagan Administration's denuclearization rhetoric to battlefield weapons, others will seek to build up their own nuclear forces. In either case, "the old pattern of American tutelage will end."

If Kissinger's concerns here seem exaggerated, some of his views are shared by West European leaders. As the INF accord took shape, they had little choice but to come out for disarmament. (Even the usually hawkish French proclaimed their support for the zero-zero option.) But there were many doubts in private. In the main, few were convinced that their governments would come up with the money to build up NATO's conventional forces once part of the nuclear umbrella was withdrawn.

But the INF treaty will not split the NATO alliance. Nor will it come close to leaving Western Europe defenseless. Afterall, NATO unity is in the last analysis more an article of faith than firepower.

In the meantime, the years ahead promise to be uncertain. But they also pose a challenging period for the supporters of arms control and improved Soviet-American relations. Both the Soviet and American political leadership have decided that the INF accord is in their vested interests. Of course, it represents a small step forward, but if it commits the Reagan Administration to the arms control process and re-establishes bipartisanship in this crucial area, it can serve a valuable function beyond its original scope.

Going beyond INF, both the U.S.S.R. and the U.S. have endorsed the goal of significant reductions in strategic arms. Moreover, the new Soviet leadership has demonstrated unprecedented negotiating flexibility. (The Soviets may be hoping that progress on arms control will prompt Congress to cut funds for the development of SDI.) At the same time, Washington seems to be moving toward a less rigid ideological approach to the overall Soviet-American relationship.

We ought to pay attention to Gorbachev and what he is trying to do. He sounds like he means business.
Helmut Kohl, Chancellor of West Germany

XIV. ABOUT-FACE ON ARMS: INF AND BEYOND

"It is just amazing how much detail we got in this INF Treaty," one U.S. official exclaims. "Here the Soviets have handed over reams and reams of sensitive data, and in the early 1970s they wouldn't even tell us how many missiles they had."[1]

The INF (Intermediate-Range Nuclear Forces) agreement, which was signed by Mikhail Gorbachev and Ronald Reagan on December 8, 1987, is truly an unprecedented treaty. "We have completed very important work," said Eduard A. Shevardnadze, the Soviet Foreign Minister. "I think that what we have done is in the interest of all nations of this planet." Secretary of State George Shultz also hailed the treaty. President Reagan said in this context that he and Gorbachev had established "an entirely different relationship."[2] For his part, the Soviet leader declared that he and Reagan now "trust each other more."

What made it all possible? Surely, General Secretary Gorbachev and President Reagan deserve a lot of the credit. For his part, Gorbachev announced on February 28, 1987 that the Soviets were now willing to take up the American offer to sign a separate agreement on medium-range nuclear weapons in Europe.[3] Previously, the So-

1 Ralph Earle II, chief U.S. negotiator of the SALT II Treaty from 1978 to 1980, tells the following similar story: "... in 1978, the chief Soviet negotiator, Vladimir Semenov, orally advised me of the exact number of heavy bombers possessed by his nation, commenting that he had just 'violated' 400 years of Russian history .." *The Washington Post,* December 5, 1987.

2 *The Minneapolis Star and Tribune,* December 12, 1987.

3 See Heinrich Bechtoldt, "Gorbachev: Initiatives or Reactions?" *Außenpolitik* (English Edition), Vol. 38, No. 4 (1987), p.325.

viet leader had argued that there should be a complete arms-control package, including cuts in long-range missiles and limits on SDI – or no deal at all. On this note the Soviet-American summit at Reykjavik had broken up.[4]

Why the sudden change of heart? There is no clear-cut answer, although the simplest explanation may be the best. This is that having failed at Iceland in 1986, Gorbachev decided to settle for a deal that he could get in 1987 with a strong President and a Congress predisposed to ratify it. If this meant foregoing twisting the President's arm too much for concessions on SDI, so be it. And in the end (after some more posturing), the Soviets did indeed decide to put aside temporarily their differences with the United States over "Star Wars."

Later, some Soviet officials tried to rationalize their new approach. This was said to have something to do with the recent decision by Congress to cut back sharply on funding for the Administration's SDI research program. (This decision led the Administration to postpone the planned expansion of its testing program for a space-based missile defense system.)[5] "Why argue about possible future quarrels?" asked Gennadi Gerasimov, the Soviet Foreign Ministry spokesman.[6]

If it appeared on the face of things that the Soviets were now surrendering their basic position on SDI, this was not the case. They

4 When President Reagan's "zero option" (i.e. the elimination of all intermediate-range nuclear weapons in Europe) was first proposed in 1981, Moscow dismissed it out of hand. A years later, the head of the Soviet delegation to the INF talks, Yuli Kvitsinsky, described it as "a formula for unilateral disarmament by our side and frankly, an insult to our intelligence." See Strobe and Talbott, *Deadly Gambits: The Reagan Administration and the Stalemate in Nuclear Arms Control* (London: Pan, 1985), pp. 114-15.

5 In late November 1987, the Reagan Administration, facing a research budget substantially smaller than it had envisioned, said it was planning sharp cutbacks and delays of up to two years in key experiments and development projects. As a result of this development, the government will now not be able to decide by 1992, the current target date, whether to begin manufacturing equipment that could actually be deployed in the first phase of a missile defense system in space. For details see, *The New York Times*, November 22, 1987. On December 13, 1987, Secretary of State Shultz said that the Reagan Administration would no longer insist that Congress accept the Administration's broad interpretation of the ABM Treaty. Rather, the Administration will now seek Congressional approval of funds for "Star Wars" tests on a case-by-case basis. *The New York Times*, December 14, 1987.

6 Quoted in *The New York Times*, December 6, 1987.

had just shifted tactics to buy some more time. General Secretary Gorbachev now said that if reductions on long-range arms were to be carried out, the ABM Treaty as signed would have to be *strictly* observed. Since President Reagan was committed to a *broad* interpretation of the agreement that would allow unlimited testing of some new types of antimissile systems (SDI related), this issue continued to fester through the December summit, when it was ambiguously – but not finally – resolved.[7]

According to American sources, Gorbachev agreed at the three-day summit – which was positive but achieved less than was expected[8] – that the ABM Treaty permits research and development and "if necessary, tests." But this may have just been an "understanding," since there was no detailed written agreement on this matter.[9] A senior Administration spokesman stated later that Reagan had made clear to Gorbachev that he and his successors would feel free to test in space but not to deploy any SDI system for seven to ten years, the exact time to be negotiated.

Reagan's Change of Heart

But the INF Treaty was not only the result of a change in Soviet policy. It also came about to some degree because of a change in heart of Ronald Reagan (although he publicly denies it). Paul M. Weyrich of the conservative Free Congress Foundation describes in detail how this change in heart affected the President. At a private White House meeting in September 1987, Reagan startled a group of right-wing leaders with his positive evaluation of Gorbachev. As Weyrich recalls, Reagan went on to say that "Gorbachev is a different kind of Soviet leader, the first to say that his goal is not con-

7 Some U.S. officials were claiming after the summit that the matter had been resolved, but it is likely that the Soviets will raise SDI again before a strategic arms treaty is completed. According to a joint statement at the summit, it was agreed that SDI testing would be permitted "as required." See *St. Paul Pioneer Press Dispatch*, December 11, 1987.

8 Reagan said there was "dramatic progress" on arms control. Gorbachev claimed there was only "some headway" towards an agreement, but he pledged to "work hard" to have it ready for signing in Moscow in the spring of 1988.

9 *The Minneapolis Star and Tribune*, December 11, 1987.

quering the West ... Reagan's view was that internal conditions in the Soviet Union were forcing Gorbachev to deal differently with the West."[10]

The conservatives pressed their case that the Soviets remained the "evil empire" that Reagan had once labeled them. And they cited examples of Soviet misconduct in Afghanistan and elsewhere to back up their case. But the President did not acknowledge these points.

Later, at the summit meeting in Washington, Reagan exuded warmth towards his Soviet counterpart. "My first name is Ron," he told Gorbachev. "Mine is Mikhail," responded the Soviet leader. Subsequently, Reagan and Gorbachev quickly established eye contact and what appeared to be good rapport. "I have often felt," the President said in his welcoming remarks, "that our people should have been better friends long ago."

"We can only hope that this history-making agreement will not be an end in itself", President Reagan stated "but the beginning of a working relationship that will enable us to tackle the other issues, urgent issues, before us: strategic offensive nuclear weapons, the balance of conventional forces in Europe, the destructive and tragic regional conflict that beset so many parts of our globe, and respect for the human and natural rights that God has granted to all men."[11]

Echoing some of these statements, Gorbachev said: "for everyone, and above all for our two great powers, the treaty whose text is on this table offers a big chance, at last, to get onto the road leading away from the threat of catastrophe ... It is our duty to take full advantage of that chance and move together toward a nuclear free world, which holds children, the promise of a fulfilling and happy life, without fear and withouth a senseless waste of resources on weapons of destruction."[12]

If the President was not beguiled by his Soviet guest at the summit, he was clearly impressed. "There was a certain chemistry between us," he said later.[13]

10 Quoted in *The Washington Post* (National Weekly Edition), December 14, 1987.
11 Quoted in *The New York Times*, December 9, 1987.
12 *Ibid.*
13 Quoted in *The Minneapolis Star and Tribune*, December 12, 1987.

INF Main Provisions[14]

The 19-page treaty, which is the product of more than seven years of hard bargaining, outlines the step-by-step procedures for eliminating all American and Soviet intermediate-range and shorter-range nuclear missiles. These are missiles with a range of 315 to 3,125 miles.

The agreement is accompanied by a 16-page, single-space manual of how each side's missiles are to be destroyed. There is also a 21-page, single-spaced annex on procedures for monitoring the treaty by carrying out surprise visits at some missile installations. The protocol also explains how the parties will weigh, measure and open missile canisters outside missile production plants to make sure that no illegal missiles are being produced there.

In a highly unusual procedure, the United States decided not to publish a detailed memorandum of understanding which is an integral part of the treaty. This secret document says where the missiles and their launchers are located and how many are at each site. It also provides valuable technical data about them.

In making the decision not to publish the sensitive memorandum, the White House apparently yielded to the wishes of the Defense Department, which claimed that data in the document could be of potential use to terrorists. "We don't want to offer terrorists a target," said a senior Administration official.[15] (Despite U.S. reservations, the Soviets are going ahead with publication of this sensitive annex. So now is the United States.)

Provisions

Those American nuclear missiles that are affected by the treaty are the 442 deployed Cruise and Pershing II missiles in West Germany, the United Kingdom, Italy and Belgium. They will be destroyed over a period of three years. Those Soviet missiles included in the accord are the 553 SS-20 and SS-4 missiles. Another 130

14 Excerpts of the INF Treaty are printed in *The Washington Post*, December 9, 1987. See Appendix A of this book, p.313-68.

15 *The New York Times*, December 9, 1987.

shorter-range Soviet SS-12 and SS-23 missiles, including about fifty in East Germany and Czechoslovakia, will also be dismantled over 18 months. In short, this treaty pertains to about 1,487 Soviet warheads and about 442 U.S. delivery vehicles – or approximately six percent of their combined nuclear arsenals.

Monitoring

Under the treaty, U.S. inspectors will monitor the Soviets' dismantling and then remain to guard against violations for ten years. For their part, the Soviets have the corresponding inspection right in Western Europe and the United States. An inspection system has been established which provides for 20 checks a year during the three years the missiles are to be destroyed. The monitoring will continue over ten additional years, with 15 checks annually in the first five years and ten annually in the last five years.[16]

Plant Inspection

One of the last obstacles to be cleared by the treaty negotiators concerned the right of the U.S. to inspect a Soviet plant where SS-25 mobile ICBMs are assembled. (SS-25s are not covered under the pact, since they are long-range missiles, but their first stage is similar in configuration to the banned SS-20s.) American monitors will be able to make sure the SS-25s are not modified to replace the SS-20s. In exchange, the Soviets will be able to send inspectors to one U.S. missile plant at Magna Utah where Pershing II's were produced and where the MX and Trident are now being produced.

16 Conservative critics of the treaty will probably focus on the fact that it fails to permit U.S. inspections at sites not listed in the lengthy appendix. But these persons should know that the American side initially advocated U.S. inspection rights anywhere in the U.S.S.R. However, as the Soviets moved closer to acceptance of the proposal, the American negotiators backed away in fear that the Soviets would abuse a similar right to inspect anywhere in the United States. In the words of State Department adviser Paul H. Nitze, it would be "detrimental to U.S. security interests to give Soviet inspectors such unlimited access." See *The Washington Post*, December 7, 1987.

Verification

Under the verification provisions of the accord, the Soviet Union and the United States will establish the Special Verification Commission to resolve questions relating to compliance with the treaty. They also agree to such measures as may be necessary to improve the viability and effectiveness of the treaty.

Treaty Duration

The treaty is of unlimited duration. But each party has the right to withdraw if it decides that extraordinary events related to the treaty have jeopardized its overriding interests.

A "Potemkin Village" Surprise

One of the real surprises that arose out of the extended negotiations leading to the INF agreement was the discovery by U.S. officials that the Soviets had "Potemkin village" nuclear missiles. The Soviets told U.S. officials that about 200 of their medium-range missiles, earlier described as operational weapons, were really just "training missiles" – many of them filled with concrete. The account of the "training missiles" was offered by the Soviets to explain a discrepancy between their initial count of 1,950 warheads and the 1,487 total contained in the new INF accord.[17]

But the "training missiles" revelation was not the only surprise to come from the Soviet side during the INF negotiations. Equally, compelling was the discovery of large numbers of non-deployed, or stored, Soviet missiles. This figure was "on the high side" of U.S. intelligence estimates according to one American insider.[18]

17 But the U.S. side also hat its surprises. For one, it appears that the U.S. had deployed dozens more medium-range missiles in Europe than previously had been acknowledged. This revelation came out in the secret annex to the INF Treaty.

18 For details see *The Minneapolis Star and Tribune*, December 11, 1987.

American Reaction to the Treaty

The feeling that President Reagan is betraying his principles by signing the INF Treaty is running high among American conservatives, provoking unusual personal criticism (e.g. "The President is selling us out!"). The most intense criticism of Reagan's behavior is coming from unelected conservative activists such as Paul M. Weyrich of the Free Congress Foundation. Weyrich, who has formed an alliance of conservatives under the banner of the Anti-Appeasement Alliance to campaign publicly against Senate ratification of the INF Treaty, terms Reagan "a weakened president, weakened in spirit as well as clout, and not in a position to make judgments about Gorbachev at this time."[19]

To be sure, this view is not shared by the majority of Americans, who support the President on this issue. A new survey taken by the Democratic firm Marttila and Kiley affirms this attitude. 74 percent of Republicans and 69 percent of Democrats are favorable to the treaty.[20] The poll also found that the voters generally regard the military build-up that has marked the Reagan years as a public mandate.

An Evaluation of the Treaty

Denunciations by those on the far right notwithstanding, the terms of the INF agreement are generally favorable to the West. For example, the U.S.S.R. will be eliminating nearly a thousand more nuclear delivery vehicles than the U.S. And the "mind boggling" verification measures are the most detailed ever to be gained from the usually secretive Russians. (In a striking turnaround, Marshal Sergei F. Akhromeyev, the Soviet Chief of the General Staff, boasted: "We raised questions concerning inspections more often than our partners did!") These provisions break new ground and will both facilitate Senate ratification and set a precedent for future arms control agreements.

Critics of the INF Treaty generally focus on the claim that the

19 *The Washington Post* (National Weekly Edition), December 14, 1987.
20 *Ibid.*

deal will leave Western Europe vulnerable to the superior Warsaw Pact forces. As General Bernard Rogers, former NATO Commander, wrote recently, "denuclearization will make Western Europe safe again for conventional war or, more likely, neutralization."[21]

However, the critics exaggerate their case. For one thing, the reductions in nuclear weapons are relatively minor. (To be sure, more far-reaching changes are in the making.) For another, the critics of INF exaggerate Soviet ambitions – particularly under Gorbachev. But finally, they give undue weight to the disparity in conventional arms in Central Europe. The imbalance is, in reality, not as great as often depicted. (For example, former published NATO descriptions of the balance of forces fail to include substantial French forces, which were counted in the 1970's – even though France was not militarily integrated in NATO.[22] At the same time, Spanish forces are not generally included in Western estimates of the conventional balance, although Spain has been a NATO member since 1982. If these Western forces are added to the balance, the discrepancy is not strategically important.)[23]

Even granting Soviet superiority in conventional forces, what would the Soviets have to gain by an invasion of Western Europe? For one thing, the human and economic consequences of a war with NATO – even if successful – and even if it did not draw nuclear retaliation, would be excessive. Moreover, when taking into account the problems the Soviets are experiencing in Afghanistan, what could they hope to achieve in confronting a better-equipped and equally defiant Western alliance? Finally, given the problems of keeping in line the U.S.S.R.'s socialist allies in Eastern Europe, why would they want to take on the much more awesome task of trying to control millions of West Europeans? No, the INF Treaty, to use the words of Norman Podhoretz, is not giving the Soviets "a bloodless victory."

21 Quoted in *The Minneapolis Star and Tribune,* November 23, 1987.

22 According to the International Institute for Strategic Studies in London, a conservative organization, NATO has 796,000 ground forces facing 995,000 Warsaw pact troops along the East-West border.

23 New official studies in both the United States and Western Europe have noted that NATO and Warsaw Pact forces are on a much more equal footing than the official statistics would seem to show. See *The Washington Post,* December 5, 1987. One critic would argue here that the Spanish forces are not in the same category as the French.

It is important to note here that limits on French and British nuclear armaments are not included in the treaty – although the Soviet Union for a long time sougth to include them. These two states are currently credited by the International Institute for Strategic Studies with 368 submarine – launched ballistic missile warheads – up from 128 in 1979. For its part, the French share of submarine-launched warheads continues to increase through the MIRVing of its missile force. France also possesses 18 single-warhead intermediate-range ballistic missiles. For its part, Great Britain, which is increasing its warheads total, plans to install MIRVs on U.S. built Trident D-5 missiles.

Then, there is the modernization that is going on in NATO. The 400-plus Poseidon submarine-launched warheads assigned to NATO through its commander will be gradually replaced in the coming years by more accurate Trident D-5 missiles. Both types of missiles will be capable of destroying military installations in the Soviet Union, which were previously targeted by the Pershing IIs and ground-launched cruise missiles. So, while some important military capabilities are being phased out, others are being quietly added.[24]

The crucial point in all this, of course, remains the fact that after the INF Treaty the U.S.S.R. will have considerably fewer theater nuclear weapons targeted on Western Europe than it had in 1979. The Soviet Union will have begun not only the elimination of all its SS-20s, but will complete the elimination of the 600 or so SS-4s and SS-5s which have been deployed since the late 1950's as well.

What about the so-called shorter-range intermediate nuclear forces or SRINF? The United States has no missiles of this range deployed in Europe. But the Soviets have a number of SS-12s and SS-23s deployed in East Germany and Czechoslovakia. During the negotiations, the Soviets offered to eliminate their SRINF missiles deployed in Eastern Europe and in the European part of the U.S.S.R. In exchange, the U.S. was expected to forego the deployment of any SRINF and give up its warheads for the Pershing Ia in West Germany. In the end, a deal was struck with the last minute help of the Kohl government, and a ban on SRINF was agreed upon.

24 Jonathan Dean, "The INF Agreement: Pluses and Minuses for Western Security," *Arms Control Today*, Vol. 17, No. 6 (July-August, 1987), p. 4.

But nothing was agreed upon regarding the tactical missile question, i.e., missiles with a range of 300 miles or less. According to the Pentagon, the Soviet Union is credited with about 500 SS-1c SCUD launchers and a further 500 FROG and SS-21 missiles – all of which are deployed against European NATO.[25] The Warsaw Pact is also credited with about 3,500 nuclear-capable artillery pieces. For its part, NATO has roughly the same number of nuclear-capable artillery pieces, but only about 200 nuclear missiles to match the larger Soviet figure. Although the Soviets now have an advantage in total numbers of tactical nuclear missiles, their tactical missiles are not as accurate as those possessed by NATO.

Despite apparent Soviet advantage in this area, Gorbachev has offered to begin negotiations on their elimination. The General Secretary first proposed such talks in January 1986 as part of his program to eliminate all nuclear weapons by the year 2,000. Subsequently, this proposal was picked up by the Warsaw Pact in June 1986. It has been repeated several times since.

But the West is divided on how to respond to this initiative. The Federal Republic of Germany, for one, considers itself to be the main target of such weapons in a possible conflict, and understandably it wishes to negotiate reductions in this area. The governments of other NATO allies are not so enthusiastic. Apprehensive over the "denuclearization" of Europe in the face of Soviet superiority in conventional forces, they tend to prefer to wait for prior agreement on the reduction of conventional forces and elimination of chemical weapons.

A New Soviet Military Doctrine?

The INF accord represents in large part the culmination of a number of important proposed changes in Soviet and Warsaw Pact military doctrines. Taken together, these changes – which are to be seen in the context of Gorbachev's call: "We require a radical break with traditions of political thinking" – promise to have a profound impact on European security and the overall East-West relationship.

25 U.S. Department of Defense, *Soviet Military Power* (Washington, D.C.: U.S. Government Printing Office, 1987).

Some of the more important signals of this radical rethinking have taken the form of very recent – but little noticed in the West – public statements that have been made by both Soviet and Warsaw Pact officials.[26]

First, there is the Warsaw Pact address of June 11, 1986. This public statement contained the following key passage: "In the interests of security in Europe and the whole world, the military concepts and doctrines of the military alliances must be based on *defensive* principles." (At this time, the Warsaw Pact, in what became known as the "Budapest Appeal," called for the reduction of troops, complete with arms and combat technology, by 100,000 to 150,000 men by about 1990.)[27]

Second, there is the speech in Moscow by Mikhail Gorbachev on February 16, 1987. This declared: "It is important, in our view, while scaling down military confrontation, to carry through such measures as would make it possible to lessen, or better still, altogether exclude the possibility of a surprise attack. The most dangerous offensive arms must be removed from the zone of contact. Quite naturally, military doctrines must be of purely defensive nature."

Third, on April 25, 1987, Soviet Ambassador Yuri Deryabin revealed in an interview that the U.S.S.R. had "begun to analyze the ideas about non-offensive defense, having been inspired by the work on this subject that has been going on in Denmark and the Federal Republic of Germany." More specifically, he suggested that the most dangerous offensive weapons be withdrawn from a zone in Central Europe. When told that this approach seemed to contradict decades of traditional Soviet military planning in which offensive capabilities have been stressed, he declared: "Yes, but it is time to break with tradition, also in the military field. A withdrawal of offensive systems would already change the traditional military patterns."

If non-offensive defense seems like an attractive idea to the

26 This writer is indebted to Professor Neild for compiling most of these statements. Unless otherwise indicated all quoted passages are taken from his important article "Beyond INF: A New Approach to Nonnuclear Forces," *World Policy Journal*, Vol. 4, No. 4 (Fall, 1987), pp.605-620.

27 See Karl Heinz Kamp, "Perspectives of Conventional Arms Control in Europe," *Außenpolitik* (English Edition), Vol. 38, No. 4 (1987), p.332.

Kremlin political leadership, there are some problems with it from the Soviet military point of view. For one thing, it is highly controversial. As Edward L. Warner, senior defense analyst of the RAND Corporation and a noted expert on the Red Army, states: "Nothing could be more in conflict with reality" than the idea that Soviet ground forces are mainly defensive in their character. "In the last decade the Soviets have developed the doctrine, organization and capability to fight an offensive war ... a *Blitzkrieg* especially in Europe."[28]

Other experts have noted that there seems to be a sharp difference of opinion about "non-offensive defense" between Soviet diplomats and the few military officials with quasi-political jobs at the Central Committee, on the one hand, and the purely career military officers on the other. "The career military people don't buy it," observed one American official. But only time will tell.

A fourth major Soviet military statement with policy ramifications was made on May 4, 1987 by Anatoly Dobrynin, former long-term Russian Ambassador to the United States and now a close foreign policy adviser to Mikhail Gorbachev. He expounded on a new controversial national security concept – that of "reasonable sufficiency". As explained by Dobrynin, this means "the level necessary for defense purposes only."[29] In his speech, the Secretary of the Central Committee in charge of the International Department pointed to various concepts of "non-offensive defense" being propounded by "a number of opposition socialdemocratic parties of Western Europe." This development, Dobrynin said, represents "a search in a rational direction which offers scope for comparing views and exchanging opinions."

Fifth, there is the statement issued by the Warsaw Pact on May 29, 1987. This emphasized the necessity to avoid war in a nuclear age. Among other things, this declaration called for a number of measures which are proposed to achieve "a balance of military

28 Quoted in *The Washington Post*, November 30, 1987.

29 Defense Minister Dmitri Yazov, writing in *Pravda* on July 27, 1987, also defined "reasonable sufficiency" in vague terms. He said that currently it means "precisely the magnitude of armed forces necessary to defend oneself against an attack from the outside ... (Some U.S. officials have interpreted this "meaningless" definition as reflecting the Soviet military's lack of enthusiasm for the new concept.) For the future, Yazov wrote, the Warsaw Pact proposes to employ the sufficiency principle to reduce East-West force levels "on a mutually agreed basis."

force at an even lower level." These measures include a call for the prohibition of chemical weapons,[30] the reduction of force levels and the creation of zones free of various types of forces and weapons, which would lead to the eventual and simultaneous dissolution of NATO and the Warsaw Pact. Importantly, for the first time mention was made that *no more* forces were needed than were necessary to defend and preserve the peace.[31]

At the end of the public statement came the following startling proposal:

The Warsaw Treaty members propose to the North Atlantic Alliance member states to hold consultations with the aim of comparing the military doctrine of both alliances, analyzing their character and jointly studying the directions of their further evolution with a view to removing the mutual suspiciousness and mistrust that have accumulated for years, attaining a better understanding of each other's intentions and ensuring that the military concepts and doctrines of the military blocs and their members be based on defense principles.

The existing imbalances and asymmetries in separate types of armaments and services of armed forces and the search for ways of removing them on the basis of reductions by the side that is ahead on the understanding that such reductions will lead to the establishment of ever lower levels, could also be a subject of consultations.

The socialist member states of the Treaty propose to hold such consultations at an authoritative expert level with the participation of military specialists of countries of both sides. They are prepared to hold such consultations already in 1987. The consultations could be held in Warsaw or Brussels, or in each of those cities alternately.

The last major statement on the new military rethinking (before this book goes to press) concerns the interview in November, 1987, with Lev Mendelevich, the Director of Policy Planning in the Soviet

30 For several years the Soviet Union and the United States have conducted talks on banning chemical weapons. But these negotiations have largely been stymied by Moscow's refusal to accept extensive on-site verification measures. Early in 1987, however, the Soviets embraced this principle, so the prospects are good for the completion of a new chemical weapons' treaty in the next year or so. The big problem remains how to persuade all the nations with chemical weapons to join in the new treaty. (Recently, the U.S. side seems to be backing out of this proposed agreement, arguing that verification is impossible.)

31 See Heinrich Bechtoldt, "Gorbachev: Initiatives or Reactions?" *Außenpolitik* (English Edition), Vol. 38, No. 4 (1987), pp. 328-29.

Foreign Ministry.[32] Mendelevich reportedly has been deeply involved in the evolution of the new national security concept of "reasonable sufficiency." So far, most Soviet statements in public about this disputed concept have been very general and have been made by semi-official experts and publications rather than by Soviet officials. But now for possibly the first time, an important Soviet official was being more specific – at least to Western observers.

When interviewed, Mendelevich drew a distinction between the application of "reasonable sufficiency" in the nuclear field and in the field of conventional forces. In the nuclear arena, the concept was said to call ultimately for the complete elimination of nuclear weapons. But in the meantime, it describes a condition of "strategic stability." This condition was defined by Mendelevich as "when each side retains the compatibility for a retaliatory (nuclear) strike, but neither side (has the weapons) for a "disarming first strike."[33]

As things now stand, no official Soviet calculation has been made public on the level of nuclear force required for this condition. But U.S. experts say it would be well below the proposed cuts of up to fifty percent in U.S. and Soviet strategic nuclear forces under negotiation by both sides.

Mendelevich informed *The Washington Post* that "reasonable sufficiency" in conventional forces relies on the axiomatic concept of "balance" at lower levels and on less threatening deployments. These include the removal of tanks and other offensive weapons from front-line areas. "It is impossible to put these things into practice unilaterally," Mendelevich pointed out. "It may only be done through a process of agreement."

Prospects for the Future

If all these public statements can be taken as impressive evidence pointing in the direction of a new trend in Soviet military and political thinking,[34] a very large question nevertheless remains. This

32 See *The Washington Post*, November 30, 1987.

33 It is important to note here that this new thinking on reasonable sufficiency does *not* mean that the Soviets are now moving in the direction of MAD.

34 For a more detailed statement, see Mikhail Gorbachev, *Perestroika* (New York: Harper and Row, 1987).

is how to interpret these unprecendented signals. It would seem on the face of things that the Soviets have been engaged – and still are – in a vigorous and far-reaching interrial debate on how best to secure the future national-security of the Soviet Union and its socialist allies. The result of this rethinking has led the Soviet leadership, which now stresses the "interdependence" of nations and the importance of multilateral diplomacy and institutions like the United Nations,[35] to come belatedly to the recognition that security is "increasingly a political function that can be accomplished only by political means."[36] As Anatoly Dobrynin wrote in an article in the June 1987 issue of the party monthly, *Kommunist*, "the time has come for new political thinking." And this "new political thinking" calls for a global approach to diplomacy that encompasses "all the elements of world politics – military, political, economic and humanitarian." In other words, the time has come for the U.S.S.R. to "establish relations between countries on a more solid basis than that of arms."

Is this just rhetoric? No, there is much more to it than that. To be sure, the Soviet Union has not been "under Gorbachev" long enough for even the keenest observers to be sure how much change – military and political – the new leadership intends. Nor can one say with confidence at this early date how far it will succeed. However, enough change has already occurred – and is in the making – to discuss, albeit with a wariness of concluding too much too soon, some future prospects and policies of Gorbachev.

First, it is important to put his controversial proposed strategic changes into the proper context. Here U.S. Ambassador Harlan Cleveland offers the following incomplete list of other breathtaking changes the Soviets have recently proposed. Gorbachev who, more

35 In sharp contrast to previous practice, the Soviet Union is now pressing the General Assembly of the U.N. to help draw up "a new comprehensive system of international security" that would give the United Nations an enhanced role in preserving peace. The United States and most of its allies oppose such a Soviet initiative, terming it essentially a propaganda move that is intended to present Moscow as the principal exponent of enlightened internationalism. See *The New York Times,* November 4, 1987. Mikhail Gorbachev, in a *Pravda* article of September 17, 1987 announced a new Soviet interest in bolstering the role of the United Nations. The Soviets subsequently declared that they would pay their back dues in full for U.N. activities, including peacekeeping efforts that Moscow had previously opposed.

36 See *Le Monde* (Paris) August 7, 1987.

than any other Soviet leader before him, has been outspoken about the shortcomings of the domestic systems, has "come out for a comprehensive test ban, for a world agreement on nuclear piracy and terrorism, for using the U.N. Security Council to keep peace in turbulent regions, for a U.N. World Space Organization, for U.N. specialized agencies to become 'regulators of international processes,' for mutual monitoring, military observers and U.N. peacekeeping, for a multilateral conflict-resolving hot line, and for a doctrine of military sufficiency." Moreover, if the removal of nuclear weapons leaves a "conventional disparity" in armed forces, Gorbachev says that the U.S.S.R. ought to remove that disparity, too. Just like that.[37]

If the Soviets are really serious about reducing East-West tensions, then the development of a new military doctrine and force posture, which is less threatening to NATO,[38] would be an important development. To be sure, Moscow is determined to match its new policy with demands for simultaneous changes in Western strategy. And there is no denying that the Soviet Union believes that the elimination of nuclear weapons in Europe is to its operational advantage and will also reduce the likelihood that conflict will escalate to nuclear strikes on the U.S.S.R.[39] But they also, no doubt, are concerned that NATO might be tempted to take advantage of the new military situation. In any case, it does seem that the Soviet leadership has now decided to enter into a long-term dialogue with the West that could lead to the encouragement and acceptance of some of these ideas both at home and abroad.

37 Quoted in *The Minneapolis Star and Tribune*, November 8, 1987.

38 For more on this point see Michael MccGwire, "Why the Soviets are Serious about Arms Control," *The Brookings Review* (Spring, 1987), p.18.

39 At his news conference before departing for home on December 10, 1987 Gorbachev renewed a proposal calling for the creation of a demilitarized, de-nuclearized zone in Europe that would widen the space between NATO and Warsaw Pact forces. "We should sit down at the negotiating table," the Soviet leader said, lamenting the long impasse over reducing conventional weapons in Europe. "We should lay our cards on the table, and that will surely show who is in earnest and who is perhaps trying to be too sly, because we all know what each side has. We know about the quantities, the locations, everything." Gorbachev went on to explain that he was referring to the establishment of "a corridor of limited armaments" – a region stripped of tanks, mobile heavy artillery and rockets, attack helicopters, tactical aircraft and nuclear artillery, rockets, mortars and bombs. See *St. Paul Pioneer Press Dispatch*, December 13, 1987.

So far, the West has remained largely skeptical of the new Soviet strategy,[40] which now apparently emphasizes mutual security (is international relations no longer to be viewed as a zero-sum game?) and maintaining only enough conventional might necessary to defend the Soviet Union and its allies. However, some NATO countries are urging that this rhetoric be put to the test on the negotiating table to see how far Gorbachev is prepared to go. Having expressed interest in the Warsaw Pact proposal for consultations on doctrine, NATO is now considering a detailed response. Given the modest success of the Gorbachev-Reagan summit in Washington,[41] there is good reason to be optimistic about the outcome.[42] Consequently, a new era in East-West relations may well be in the making.[43]

40 See for instance, David B. Rivkin, Jr., "The Soviet Approach to Nuclear Arms Control: Continuity and Change," *Survival*, Vol. 29, No. 6 (Nov.-Dec., 1987), p. 494. Skeptical U.S. officials do not hesitate to point out in this context that Gorbachev is not the first Soviet leader to make farreaching disarmament proposals. Nikita Khrushchev, for instance, put forward various plans for "general and complete disarmament" during the 1950s. However, as Matthew Evangelista points out: "The scope and intensity of Gorbachev's disarmament diplomacy do ... mark a sharp break with the practice of his predecessors." See his article "The New Soviet Approach to Security," *World Policy Journal*, Vol. 3, No. 4 (Fall, 1986), p. 563.

41 Both Reagan and Gorbachev claimed, among other things, to have narrowed their differences in the talks on strategic arms at the summit. They agreed, for example, on a new sub-limit of a 4,900 for land and sea-based ballistic missiles as part of a 6,000 limit for all kinds of strategic nuclear delivery systems. The effect of this agreement means that the Soviets will be forced to cut back on their land-based ICBMs, which the U.S. finds most threatening in exchange for large cuts in U.S. SLBMs.
The two sides also agreed to put a limit of 1.540 warheads on so-called "heavy" missiles, such as the SS-18. This figure – a fifty percent reduction – was suggested by the Soviets several weeks earlier. It represented a major Soviet concession in an area that has deeply concerned the U.S. policymakers. For details, see *St. Paul Pioneer Press Dispatch*, December 11, 1987. On START, the Soviets made verification easier by agreeing to ban the encryption of telemetry from missile test flights.

42 According to British Prime Minister Margaret Thatcher, "Relations are good (with the Russians). I think they are better than they have ever been before." Quoted in *The Washington Post*, December 8, 1987.

43 It is worth noting in this context that East Germany's leader Erich Honecker has reportedly ordered GDR guards at the Berlin Wall and along the West German border to stop shooting civilians trying to flee to the West. According to the testimony of several former frontier guards, who have escaped across the heavily fortified border in recent times, their superiors told them to use their firearms only in self-defense, or if a soldier or policeman tried to flee. *The Washington Post*, December 9, 1987.

APPENDIX A:
THE INTERMEDIATE-RANGE NUCLEAR FORCES TREATY BETWEEN THE U.S.A. AND U.S.S.R.
- INF-TREATY -

Treaty between the United States of America and the Union of Soviet Socialist Republics on the Elimination of Their Intermediate-Range and Shorter-Range Missiles

of December 8, 1987

The United States of America and the Union of Soviet Socialist Republics, hereinafter referred to as the Parties,

Conscious that nuclear war would have devastating consequences for all mankind,

Guided by the objective of strengthening strategic stability,

Convinced that the measures set forth in this Treaty will help to reduce the risk of outbreak of war and strengthen international peace and security, and

Mindful of their obligations under Article VI of the Treaty on the Non-Proliferation of Nuclear Weapons,

Have agreed as follows:

Article I

In accordance with the provisions of this Treaty which includes the Memorandum of Understanding and Protocols which form an integral part thereof, each Party shall eliminate its intermediate-range and shorter-range missiles, not have such systems thereafter, and carry out the other obligations set forth in this Treaty.

Article II

For the purposes of this Treaty:

1. The term "ballistic missile" means a missile that has a ballistic trajectory over most of its flight path. The term "ground-launched ballistic missile (GLBM)" means a ground-launched ballistic missile that is a weapon-delivery vehicle.

2. The term "cruise missile" means an unmanned, self-propelled vehicle that sustains flight through the use of aerodynamic lift over most of its flight path. The term "ground-launched cruise missile (GLCM)" means a ground-launched cruise missile that is a weapon-delivery vehicle.

3. The term "GLBM launcher" means a fixed launcher or a mobile land-based transporter-erector-launcher mechanism for launching a GLBM.

4. The term "GLCM launcher" means a fixed launcher or a mobile land-based transporter-erector-launcher mechanism for launching a GLCM.

5. The term "intermediate-range missile" means a GLBM or a GLCM having a range capability in excess of 1000 kilometers but not in excess of 5500 kilometers.

6. The term "shorter-range missile" means a GLBM or a GLCM having a range capability equal to or in excess of 500 kilometers but not in excess of 1000 kilometers.

7. The term "deployment area" means a designated area within which intermediate-range missiles and launchers of such missiles may operate and within which one or more missile operating bases are located.

8. The term "missile operating base" means:

(a) in the case of intermediate-range missiles, a complex of facilities, located within a deployment area, at which intermediate-range missiles and launchers of such missiles normally operate, in which support structures associated with such missiles and launchers are also located and in which support equipment associated with such missiles and launchers is normally located; and

(b) in the case of shorter-range missiles, a complex of facilities, located any place, at which shorter-range missiles and launchers of such missiles normally operate and in which support equipment associated with such missiles and launchers is normally located.

9. The term "missile support facility," as regards intermediate-range or shorter-range missiles and launchers of such missiles,

means a missile production facility or a launcher production facility, a missile repair facility or a launcher repair facility, a training facility, a missile storage facility or a launcher storage facility, a test range, or an elimination facility as those terms are defined in the Memorandum of Understanding.

10. The term "transit" means movement, notified in accordance with paragraph 5(f) of Article IX of this Treaty, of an intermediate-range missile or a launcher of such a missile between missile support facilities, between such a facility and a deployment area or between deployment areas, or of a shorter-range missile or a launcher of such a missile from a missile support facility or a missile operating base to an elimination facility.

11. The term "deployed missile" means an intermediate-range missile located within a deployment area or a shorter-range missile located at a missile operating base.

12. The term "non-deployed missile" means an intermediate-range missile located outside a deployment area or a shorter-range missile located outside a missile operating base.

13. The term "deployed launcher" means a launcher of an intermediate-range missile located within a deployment area or a launcher of a shorter-range missile located at a missile operating base.

14. The term "non-deployed launcher" means a launcher of an intermediate-range missile located outside a deployment area or a launcher of a shorter-range missile located outside a missile operating base.

15. The term "basing country" means a country other than the United States of America or the Union of Soviet Socialist Republics on whose territory intermediate-range or shorter-range missiles of the Parties, launchers of such missiles or support structures associated with such missiles and launchers were located at any time after November 1, 1987. Missiles or launchers in transit are not considered to be "located."

Article III

1. For the purposes of this Treaty, existing types of intermediate-range missiles are:

(a) for the United States of America, missiles of the types designated by the United States of America as the Pershing II and the BGM-109G, which are known to the Union of Soviet Socialist Republics by the same designations; and

(b) for the Union of Soviet Socialist Republics, missiles of the types designated by the Union of Soviet Socialist Republics as the RSD-10, the R-12 and the R-14, which are known to the United States of America as the SS-20, the SS-4 and the SS-5, respectively.

2. For the purposes of this Treaty, existing types of shorter-range missiles are:

(a) for the United States of America, missiles of the type designated by the United States of America as the Pershing IA, which is known to the Union of Soviet Socialist Republics by the same designation; and

(b) for the Union of Soviet Socialist Republics, missiles of the types designated by the Union of Soviet Socialist Republics as the OTR-22 and the OTR-23, which are known to the United States of America as the SS-12 and the SS-23, respectively.

Article IV

1. Each Party shall eliminate all its intermediate-range missiles and launchers of such missiles, and all support structures and support equipment of the categories listed in the Memorandum of Understanding associated with such missiles and launchers, so that no later than three years after entry into force of this Treaty and thereafter no such missiles, launchers, support structures or support equipment shall be possessed by either Party.

2. To implement paragraph I of this Article, upon entry into force of this Treaty, both Parties shall begin and continue throughout the duration of each phase, the reduction of all types of their deployed and non-deployed intermediate-range missiles and deployed and non-deployed launchers of such missiles and support structures and support equipment associated with such missiles and launchers in accordance with the provisions of this Treaty. These reductions shall be implemented in two phases so that:

(a) by the end of the first phase, that is, no later than 29 months after entry into force of this Treaty:

(i) the number of deployed launchers of intermediate-range missiles for each Party shall not exceed the number of launchers that are capable of carrying or containing at one time missiles considered by the Parties to carry 171 warheads;

(ii) the number of deployed intermediate-range missiles for each Party shall not exceed the number of such missiles considered by the Parties to carry 180 warheads;

(iii) the aggregate number of deployed and non-deployed launchers of intermediate-range missiles for each Party shall not exceed the number of launchers that are capable of carrying or containing at one time missiles considered by the Parties to carry 200 warheads;

(iv) the aggregate number of deployed and non-deployed intermediate-range missiles for each Party shall not exceed the number of such missiles considered by the Parties to carry 200 warheads; and

(v) the ratio of the aggregate number of deployed and non-deployed intermediate-range GLBMs of existing types for each Party to the aggregate number of deployed and non-deployed intermediate-range missiles of existing types possessed by that Party shall not exceed the ratio of such intermediate-range GLBMs to such intermediate-range missiles for that Party as of November 1, 1987, as set forth in the Memorandum of Understanding; and

(b) by the end of the second phase, that is, no later than three years after entry into force of this Treaty, all intermediate-range missiles of each Party, launchers of such missiles and all support structures and support equipment of the categories listed in the Memorandum of Understanding associated with such missiles and launchers, shall be eliminated.

Article V

1. Each Party shall eliminate all its shorter-range missiles and launchers of such missiles, and all support equipment of the categories listed in the Memorandum of Understanding associated with such missiles and launchers, so that no later than 18 months after entry into force of this Treaty and thereafter no such missiles, launchers or support equipment shall be possessed by either Party.

2. No later than 90 days after entry into force of this Treaty, each Party shall complete the removal of all its deployed shorter-range missiles and deployed and non-deployed launchers of such missiles to elimination facilities and shall retain them at those locations until they are eliminated in accordance with the procedures

set forth in the Protocol on Elimination. No later than 12 months after entry into force of this Treaty, each Party shall complete the removal of all its non-deployed shorter-range missiles to elimination facilities and shall retain them at those locations until they are eliminated in accordance with the procedures set forth in the Protocol on Elimination.

3. Shorter-range missiles and launchers of such missiles shall not be located at the same elimination facility. Such facilities shall be separated by no less than 1000 kilometers.

Article VI

1. Upon entry into force of this Treaty and thereafter, neither Party shall:

(a) produce or flight-test any intermediate-range missiles or produce any stages of such missiles or any launchers of such missiles; or

(b) produce, flight-test or launch any shorter-range missiles or produce any stages of such missiles or any launchers of such missiles.

2. Notwithstanding paragraph I of this Article, each Party shall have the right to produce a type of GLBM not limited by this Treaty which uses a stage which is outwardly similar to, but not interchangeable with, a stage of an existing type of intermediate-range GLBM having more than one stage, providing that that Party does not produce any other stage which is outwardly similar to, but not interchangeable with, any other stage of an existing type of intermediate-range GLBM.

Article VII

For the purposes of this Treaty:

1. If a ballistic missile or a cruise missile has been flight-tested or deployed for weapon delivery, all missiles of that type shall be considered to be weapon-delivery vehicles.

2. If a GLBM or GLCM is an intermediate-range missile, all GLBMs or GLCMs of that type shall be considered to be intermediate-range missiles. If a GLBM or GLCM is a shorter-range missile, all GLBMs or GLCMs of that type shall be considered to be shorter-range missiles.

3. If a GLBM is of a type developed and tested solely to intercept and counter objects not located on the surface of the earth, it shall not be considered to be a missile to which the limitations of this Treaty apply.

4. The range capability of a GLBM not listed in Article III of this Treaty shall be considered to be the maximum range to which it has been tested. The range capability of a GLCM not listed in Article III of this Treaty shall be considered to be the maximum distance which can be covered by the missile in its standard design mode flying until fuel exhaustion, determined by projecting its flight path onto the earth's sphere from the point of launch to the point of impact. GLBMs or GLCMs that have a range capability equal to or in excess of 500 kilometers but not in excess of 1000 kilometers shall be considered to be shorter-range missiles. GLBMs or GLCMs that have a range capability in excess of 1000 kilometers but not in excess of 5500 kilometers shall be considered to be intermediate-range missiles.

5. The maximum number of warheads an existing type of intermediate-range missile or shorter-range missile carries shall be considered to be the number listed for missiles of that type in the Memorandum of Understanding.

6. Each GLBM or GLCM shall be considered to carry the maximum number of warheads listed for a GLBM or GLCM of that type in the Memorandum of Understanding.

7. If a launcher has been tested for launching a GLBM or a GLCM, all launchers of that type shall be considered to have been tested for launching GLBMs or GLCMs.

8. If a launcher has contained or launched a particular type of GLBM or GLCM, all launchers of that type shall be considered to be launchers of that type of GLBM or GLCM.

9. The number of missiles each launcher of an existing type of intermediate-range missile or shorter-range missile shall be considered to be capable of carrying or containing at one time is the number listed for launchers of missiles of that type in the Memorandum of Understanding.

10. Except in the case of elimination in accordance with the procedures set forth in the Protocol on Elimination, the following shall apply:

(a) for GLBMs which are stored or moved in separate stages,

the longest stage of an intermediate-range or shorter-range GLBM shall be counted as a complete missile;

(b) for GLBMs which are not stored or moved in separate stages, a canister of the type used in the launch of an intermediate-range GLBM, unless a Party proves to the satisfaction of the other Party that it does not contain such a missile, or an assembled intermediate-range or shorter-range GLBM, shall be counted as a complete missile; and

(c) for GLCMs, the airframe of an intermediate-range or shorter-range GLCM shall be counted as a complete missile.

11. A ballistic missile which is not a missile to be used in a ground-based mode shall not be considered to be a GLBM if it is test-launched at a test site from a fixed land-based launcher which is used solely for test purposes and which is distinguishable from GLBM launchers. A cruise missile which is not a missile to be used in a ground-based mode shall not be considered to be a GLCM if it is test-launched at a test site from a fixed land-based launcher which is used solely for test purposes and which is distinguishable from GLCM launchers.

12. Each Party shall have the right to produce and use for booster systems, which might otherwise be considered to be intermediate-range or shorter-range missiles, only existing types of booster stages for such booster systems. Launches of such booster systems shall not be considered to be flight-testing of intermediate-range or shorter-range missiles provided that:

(a) stages used in such booster systems are different from stages used in those missiles listed as existing types of intermediate-range or shorter-range missiles in Article III of this Treaty;

(b) such booster systems are used only for research and development purposes to test objects other than the booster systems themselves;

(c) the aggregate number of launchers for such booster systems shall not exceed 35 for each Party at any one time; and

(d) the launchers for such booster systems are fixed, emplaced above ground and located only at research and development launch sites which are specified in the Memorandum of Understanding.

Research and development launch sites shall not be subject to inspection pursuant to Article XI of this Treaty.

Article VIII

1. All intermediate-range missiles and launchers of such missiles shall be located in deployment areas, at missile support facilities or shall be in transit. Intermediate-range missiles or launchers of such missiles shall not be located elsewhere.

2. Stages of intermediate-range missiles shall be located in deployment areas, at missile support facilities or moving between deployment areas, between missile support facilities or between missile support facilities and deployment areas.

3. Until their removal to elimination facilities as required by paragraph 2 of Article V of this Treaty, all shorter-range missiles and launchers of such missiles shall be located at missile operating bases, at missile support facilities or shall be in transit. Shorter-range missiles or launchers of such missiles shall not be located elsewhere.

4. Transit of a missile or launcher subject to the provisions of this Treaty shall be completed within 25 days.

5. All deployment areas, missile operating bases and missile support facilities are specified in the Memorandum of Understanding or in subsequent updates of data pursuant to paragraphs 3, 5(a) or 5(b) of Article IX of this Treaty. Neither Party shall increase the number of, or change the location or boundaries of, deployment areas, missile operating bases or missile support facilities, except for elimination facilities, from those set forth in the Memorandum of Understanding. A missile support facility shall not be considered to be part of a deployment area even though it may be located within the geographic boundaries of a deployment area.

6. Beginning 30 days after entry into force of this Treaty, neither Party shall locate intermediate-range or shorter-range missiles, including stages of such missiles, or launchers of such missiles at missile production facilities, launcher production facilities or test ranges listed in the Memorandum of Understanding.

7. Neither Party shall locate any intermediate-range or shorter-range missiles at training facilities.

8. A non-deployed intermediate-range or shorter-range missile shall not be carried on or contained within a launcher of such a type of missile, except as required for maintenance conducted at repair facilities or for elimination by means of launching conducted at elimination facilities.

9. Training missiles and training launchers for intermediate-range or shorter-range missiles shall be subject to the same locational restrictions as are set forth for intermediate-range and shorter-range missiles and launchers of such missiles in paragraphs 1 and 3 of this Article.

Article IX

1. The Memorandum of Understanding contains categories of data relevant to obligations undertaken with regard to this Treaty and lists all intermediate-range and shorter-range missiles, launchers of such missiles, and support structures and support equipment associated with such missiles and launchers, possessed by the Parties as of November 1, 1987. Updates of that data and notifications required by this Article shall be provided according to the categories of data contained in the Memorandum of Understanding.

2. The Parties shall update that data and provide the notifications required by this Treaty through the Nuclear Risk Reduction Centers, established pursuant to the Agreement Between the United States of America and the Union of Soviet Socialist Republics on the Establishment of Nuclear Risk Reduction Centers of September 15, 1987.*

3. No later than 30 days after entry into force of this Treaty, each Party shall provide the other Party with updated data, as of the date of entry into force of this Treaty, for all categories of data contained in the Memorandum of Understanding.

4. No later than 30 days after the end of each six-month interval following the entry into force of this Treaty, each Party shall provide updated data for all categories of data contained in the Memorandum of Understanding by informing the other Party of all changes, completed and in process, in that data, which have occurred during the six-month interval since the preceding data exchange, and the net effect of those changes.

5. Upon entry into force of this Treaty and thereafter, each Party shall provide the following notifications to the other Party:

(a) notification, no less than 30 days in advance, of the scheduled date of the elimination of a specific deployment area, missile operating base or missile support facility;

* Text of the Agreement and the Protocols on the Establishment of Nuclear Risk Reduction Centers see: at the end of this treaty, p. 369-75.

(b) notification, no less than 30 days in advance, of changes in the number or location of elimination facilities, including the location and scheduled date of each change;

(c) notification, except with respect to launches of intermediate-range missiles for the purpose of their elimination, no less than 30 days in advance, of the scheduled date of the initiation of the elimination of intermediate-range and shorter-range missiles, and stages of such missiles, and launchers of such missiles and support structures and support equipment associated with such missiles and launchers, including:

(i) the number and type of items of missile systems to be eliminated;

(ii) the elimination site;

(iii) for intermediate-range missiles, the location from which such missiles, launchers of such missiles and support equipment associated with such missiles and launchers are moved to the elimination facility; and

(iv) except in the case of support structures, the point of entry to be used by an inspection team conducting an inspection pursuant to paragraph 7 of Article XI of this Treaty and the estimated time of departure of an inspection team from the point of entry to the elimination facility;

(d) notification, no less than ten days in advance, of the scheduled date of the launch, or the scheduled date of the initiation of a series of launches, of intermediate-range missiles for the purpose of their elimination, including:

(i) the type of missiles to be eliminated;

(ii) the location of the launch, or, if elimination is by a series of launches, the location of such launches and the number of launches in the series;

(iii) the point of entry to be used by an inspection team conducting an inspection pursuant to paragraph 7 of Article XI of this Treaty; and

(iv) the estimated time of departure of an inspection team from the point of entry to the elimination facility;

(e) notification, no later than 48 hours after they occur, of changes in the number of intermediate-range and shorter-range missiles, launchers of such missiles and support structures and support equipment associated with such missiles and launchers resulting from elimination as described in the Protocol on Elimination, including:

(i) the number and type of items of a missile system which were eliminated; and
(ii) the date and location of such elimination; and

(f) notification of transit of intermediate-range or shorter-range missiles or launchers of such missiles, or the movement of training missiles or training launchers for such intermediate-range and shorter-range missiles, no later than 48 hours after it has been completed, including:
(i) the number of missiles or launchers;
(ii) the points, dates and times of departure and arrival;
(iii) the mode of transport; and
(iv) the location and time at that location at least once every four days during the period of transit.

6. Upon entry into force of this Treaty and thereafter, each Party shall notify the other Party, no less than ten days in advance, of the scheduled date and location of the launch of a research and development booster system as described in paragraph 12 of Article VII of this Treaty.

Article X

1. Each Party shall eliminate its intermediate-range and shorter-range missiles and launchers of such missiles and support structures and support equipment associated with such missiles and launchers in accordance with the procedures set forth in the Protocol on Elimination.

2. Verification by on-site inspection of the elimination of items of missile systems specified in the Protocol on Elimination shall be carried out in accordance with Article XI of this Treaty, the Protocol on Elimination and the Protocol on Inspection.

3. When a Party removes its intermediate-range missiles, launchers of such missiles and support equipment associated with such missiles and launchers from deployment areas to elimination facilities for the purpose of their elimination, it shall do so in complete deployed organizational units. For the United States of America, these units shall be Pershing II batteries and BGM-109G flights. For the Union of Soviet Socialist Republics, these units shall be SS-20 regiments composed of two or three battalions.

4. Elimination of intermediate-range and shorter-range missiles and launchers of such missiles and support equipment associated

with such missiles and launchers shall be carried out at the facilities that are specified in the Memorandum of Understanding or notified in accordance with paragraph 5(b) of Article IX of this Treaty, unless eliminated in accordance with Sections IV or V of the Protocol on Elimination. Support structures, associated with the missiles and launchers subject to this Treaty, that are subject to elimination shall be eliminated in situ.

5. Each Party shall have the right, during the first six months after entry into force of this Treaty, to eliminate by means of launching no more than 100 of its intermediate-range missiles.

6. Intermediate-range and shorter-range missiles which have been tested prior to entry into force of this Treaty, but never deployed, and which are not existing types of intermediate-range or shorter-range missiles listed in Article III of this Treaty, and launchers of such missiles, shall be eliminated within six months after entry into force of this Treaty in accordance with the procedures set forth in the Protocol on Elimination. Such missiles are:

(a) for the United States of America, missiles of the type designated by the United States of America as the Pershing IB, which is known to the Union of Soviet Socialist Republics by the same designation; and

(b) for the Union of Soviet Socialist Republics, missiles of the type designated by the Union of Soviet Socialist Republics as the RK-55, which is known to the United States of America as the SSC-X-4.

7. Intermediate-range and shorter-range missiles and launchers of such missiles and support structures and support equipment associated with such missiles and launchers shall be considered to be eliminated after completion of the procedures set forth in the Protocol on Elimination and upon the notification provided for in paragraph 5(e) of Article IX of this Treaty.

8. Each Party shall eliminate its deployment areas, missile operating bases and missile support facilities. A Party shall notify the other Party pursuant to paragraph 5(a) of Article IX of this Treaty once the conditions set forth below are fulfilled:

(a) all intermediate-range and shorter-range missiles, launchers of such missiles and support equipment associated with such missiles and launchers located there have been removed.

(b) all support structures associated with such missiles and launchers located there have been eliminated; and

(c) all activity related to production, flight-testing, training, repair, storage or deployment of such missiles and launchers has ceased there.

Such deployment areas, missile operating bases and missile support facilities shall be considered to be eliminated either when they have been inspected pursuant to paragraph 4 of Article XI of this Treaty or when 60 days have elapsed since the date of the scheduled elimination which was notified pursuant to paragraph 5(a) of Article IX of this Treaty. A deployment area, missile operating base or missile support facility listed in the Memorandum of Understanding that met the above conditions prior to entry into force of this Treaty, and is not included in the initial data exchange pursuant to paragraph 3 of Article IX of this Treaty, shall be considered to be eliminated.

9. If a Party intends to convert a missile operating base listed in the Memorandum of Understanding for use as a base associated with GLBM or GLCM systems not subject to this Treaty, then that Party shall notify the other Party, no less than 30 days in advance of the scheduled date of the initiation of the conversion, of the scheduled date and the purpose for which the base will be converted.

Article XI

1. For the purpose of ensuring verification of compliance with the provisions of this Treaty, each Party shall have the right to conduct on-site inspections. The Parties shall implement on-site inspections in accordance with this Article, the Protocol on Inspection and the Protocol on Elimination.

2. Each Party shall have the right to conduct inspections provided for by this Article both within the territory of the other Party and within the territories of basing countries.

3. Beginning 30 days after entry into force of this Treaty, each Party shall have the right to conduct inspections at all missile operating bases and missile support facilities specified in the Memorandum of Understanding other than missile production facilities, and at all elimination facilities included in the initial data update required by paragraph 3 of Article IX of this Treaty. These inspections shall be completed no later than 90 days after entry into force of this Treaty. The purpose of these inspections shall be to

verify the number of missiles, launchers, support structures and support equipment and other data, as of the date of entry into force of this Treaty, provided pursuant to paragraph 3 of Article IX of this Treaty.

4. Each Party shall have the right to conduct inspections to verify the elimination, notified pursuant to paragraph 5(a) of Article IX of this Treaty, of missile operating bases and missile support facilities other than missile production facilities, which are thus no longer subject to inspections pursuant to paragraph 5(a) of this Article. Such an inspection shall be carried out within 60 days after the scheduled date of the elimination of that facility. If a Party conducts an inspection at a particular facility pursuant to paragraph 3 of this Article after the scheduled date of the elimination of that facility, then no additional inspection of that facility pursuant to this paragraph shall be permitted.

5. Each Party shall have the right to conduct inspections pursuant to this paragraph for 13 years after entry into force of this Treaty. Each Party shall have the right to conduct 20 such inspections per calendar year during the first three years after entry into force of this Treaty, 15 such inspections per calendar year during the subsequent five years, and ten such inspections per calendar year during the last five years. Neither Party shall use more than half of its total number of these inspections per calendar year within the territory of any one basing country. Each Party shall have the right to conduct:

(a) inspections, beginning 90 days after entry into force of this Treaty, of missile operating bases and missile support facilities other than elimination facilities and missile production facilities, to ascertain, according to the categories of data specified in the Memorandum of Understanding, the numbers of missiles, launchers, support structures and support equipment located at each missile operating base or missile support facility at the time of the inspection; and

(b) inspections of former missile operating bases and former missile support facilities eliminated pursuant to paragraph 8 of Article X of this Treaty other than former missile production facilities.

6. Beginning 30 days after entry into force of this Treaty, each Party shall have the right, for 13 years after entry into force of this Treaty, to inspect by means of continuous monitoring:

(a) the portals of any facility of the other Party at which the final assembly of a GLBM using stages, any of which is outwardly similar to a stage of a solid-propellant GLBM listed in Article III of this Treaty, is accomplished; or

(b) if a Party has no such facility, the portals of an agreed former missile production facility at which existing types of intermediate-range or shorter-range GLBMs were produced.

The Party whose facility is to be inspected pursuant to this paragraph shall ensure that the other Party is able to establish a permanent continuous monitoring system at that facility within six months after entry into force of this Treaty or within six months of initiation of the process of final assembly described in subparagraph (a). If, after the end of the second year after entry into force of this Treaty, neither Party conducts the process of final assembly described in subparagraph (a) for a period of 12 consecutive months, then neither Party shall have the right to inspect by means of continuous monitoring any missile production facility of the other Party unless the process of final assembly as described in subparagraph (a) is initiated again. Upon entry into force of this Treaty, the facilities to be inspected by continuous monitoring shall be: in accordance with subparagraph (b), for the United States of America, Hercules Plant Number 1, at Magna, Utah; in accordance with subparagraph (a), for the Union of Soviet Socialist Republics, the Votkinsk Machine Building Plant, Udmurt Autonomous Soviet Socialist Republic, Russian Soviet Federative Socialist Republic.

7. Each Party shall conduct inspections of the process of elimination, including elimination of intermediate-range missiles by means of launching, of intermediate-range and shorter-range missiles and launchers of such missiles and support equipment associated with such missiles and launchers carried out at elimination facilities in accordance with Article X of this Treaty and the Protocol on Elimination. Inspectors conducting inspections provided for in this paragraph shall determine that the processes specified for the elimination of the missiles, launchers and support equipment have been completed.

8. Each Party shall have the right to conduct inspections to confirm the completion of the process of elimination of intermediate-range and shorter-range missiles and launchers of such missiles and support equipment associated with such missiles and

launchers eliminated pursuant to Section V of the Protocol on Elimination, and of training missiles, training missile stages, training launch canisters and training launchers eliminated pursuant to Sections II, IV and V of the Protocol on Elimination.

Article XII

1. For the purpose of ensuring verification of compliance with the provisions of this Treaty, each Party shall use national technical means of verification at its disposal in a manner consistent with generally recognized principles of international law.

2. Neither Party shall:

(a) interfere with national technical means of verification of the other Party operating in accordance with paragraph 1 of this Article; or

(b) use concealment measures which impede verification of compliance with the provisions of this Treaty by national technical means of verification carried out in accordance with paragraph 1 of this Article. This obligation does not apply to cover or concealment practices, within a deployment area, associated with normal training, maintenance and operations, including the use of environmental shelters to protect missiles and launchers.

3. To enhance observation by national technical means of verification, each Party shall have the right until a treaty between the Parties reducing and limiting strategic offensive arms enters into force, but in any event for no more than three years after entry into force of this Treaty, to request the implementation of cooperative measures at deployment bases for road-mobile GLBMs with a range capability in excess of 5,500 kilometers, which are not former missile operating bases eliminated pursuant to paragraph 8 of Article X of this Treaty. The Party making such a request shall inform the other Party of the deployment base at which cooperative measures shall be implemented. The Party whose base is to be observed shall carry out the following cooperative measures:

(a) no later than six hours after such a request, the Party shall have opened the roofs of all fixed structures for launchers located at the bases removed completely all missiles on launchers from such fixed structures for launchers and displayed such missiles on launchers in the open without using concealment measures; and

(b) the Party shall leave the roofs open and the missiles on launchers in place until twelve hours have elapsed from the time of the receipt of a request for such an observation.

Each Party shall have the right to make six such requests per calendar year. Only one deployment base shall be subject to these cooperative measures at any one time.

Article XIII

1. To promote the objectives and implementation of the provisions of this Treaty, the Parties hereby establish the Special Verification Commission. The Parties agree that, if either Party so requests, they shall meet within the framework of the Special Verification Commission to:

(a) resolve questions relating to compliance with the obligations assumed; and

(b) agree upon such measures as may be necessary to improve the viability and effectiveness of this Treaty.

2. The Parties shall use the Nuclear Risk Reduction Centers, which provide for continuous communication between the Parties, to:

(a) exchange data and provide notifications as required by paragraphs 3, 4, 5 and 6 of Article IX of this Treaty and the Protocol on Elimination;

(b) provide and receive the information required by paragraph 9 of Article X of this Treaty;

(c) provide and receive notifications of inspections as required by Article XI of this Treaty and the Protocol on Inspection; and

(d) provide and receive requests for cooperative measures as provided for in paragraph 3 of Article XII of this Treaty.

Article XIV

The Parties shall comply with this Treaty and shall not assume any international obligations or undertakings which would conflict with its provisions.

Article XV

1. This Treaty shall be of unlimited duration.
2. Each Party shall, in exercising its national sovereignty, have

the right to withdraw from this Treaty if it decides that extraordinary events related to the subject matter of this Treaty have jeopardized its supreme interests. It shall give notice of its decision to withdraw to the other Party six months prior to withdrawal from this Treaty. Such notice shall include a statement of the extraordinary events the notifying Party regards as having jeopardized its supreme interests.

Article XVI

Each Party may propose amendments to this Treaty. Agreed amendments shall enter into force in accordance with the procedures set forth in Article XVII governing the entry into force of this Treaty.

Article XVII

1. This Treaty, including the Memorandum of Understanding and Protocols, which form an integral part thereof, shall be subject to ratification in accordance with the constitutional procedures of each Party. This Treaty shall enter into force on the date of the exchange of instruments of ratification.
2. This Treaty shall be registered pursuant to Article 102 of the Charter of the United Nations.

DONE at Washington on December 8, 1987, in two copies, each in the English and Russian languages, both texts being equally authentic.

Protocol on Procedures Governing the Elimination of the Missile Systems Subject to the Treaty Between the United States of America and the Union of Soviet Socialist Republics on the Elimination of Their Intermediate-Range and Shorter-Range Missiles

of December 8, 1987

Pursuant to and in implementation of the Treaty Between the United States of America and the Union of Soviet Socialist Republics on the Elimination of Their Intermediate-Range and Shorter-Range Missiles of December 8, 1987, hereinafter referred to as the Treaty, the Parties hereby agree upon procedures governing the elimination of the missile systems subject to the Treaty.

I. Items of Missile Systems Subject to Elimination

The specific items for each type of missile system to be eliminated are:

1. For the United States of America:

Pershing II: missile, launcher and launch pad shelter;
BGM-109G: missile, launch canister and launcher;
Pershing IA: missile and launcher; and
Pershing IB: missile.

2. For the Union of Soviet Socialist Republics:

SS-20: missile, launch canister, launcher, missile transporter vehicle and fixed structure for a launcher;
SS-4: missile, missile transporter vehicle, missile erector, launch stand and propellant tanks;
SS-5: missile;
SSC-X-4: missile, launch canister and launcher;
SS-12: missile, launcher and missile transporter vehicle; and
SS-23: missile, launcher and missile transporter vehicle.

3. For both Parties, all training missiles, training missile stages, training launch canisters and training launchers shall be subject to elimination.

4. For both Parties, all stages of intermediate-range and shorter-range GLBMs shall be subject to elimination.

5. For both Parties, all front sections of deployed intermediate-range and shorter-range missiles shall be subject to elimination.

II. Procedures for Elimination at Elimination Facilities

1. In order to ensure the reliable determination of the type and number of missiles, missile stages, front sections, launch canisters, launchers, missile transporter vehicles, missile erectors and launch stands, as well as training missiles, training missile stages, training launch canisters and training launchers, indicated in Section I of this Protocol, being eliminated at elimination facilities, and to preclude the possibility of restoration of such items for purposes inconsistent with the provisions of the Treaty, the Parties shall fulfill the requirements below.

2. The conduct of the elimination procedures for the items of missile systems listed in paragraph 1 of this Section, except for training missiles, training missile stages, training launch canisters and training launchers, shall be subject to on-site inspection in accordance with Article XI of the Treaty and the Protocol on Inspection. The Parties shall have the right to conduct on-site inspections to confirm the completion of the elimination procedures set forth in paragraph 11 of this Section for training missiles, training missile stages, training launch canisters and training launchers. The Party possessing such a training missile, training missile stage, training launch canister or training launcher shall inform the other Party of the name and coordinates of the elimination facility at which the on-site inspection may be conducted as well as the date on which it may be conducted. Such information shall be provided no less than 30 days in advance of that date.

3. Prior to a missile's arrival at the elimination facility, its nuclear warhead device and guidance elements may be removed.

4. Each Party shall select the particular technological means necessary to implement the procedures required in paragraphs 10 and 11 of this Section and to allow for on-site inspection of the conduct of the elimination procedures required in paragraph 10 of this Section in accordance with Article XI of the Treaty, this Protocol and the Protocol on Inspection.

5. The initiation of the elimination of the items of missile systems subject to this Section shall be considered to be the commencement of the procedures set forth in paragraph 10 or 11 of this Section.

6. Immediately prior to the initiation of the elimination procedures set forth in paragraph 10 of this Section, an inspector from the Party receiving the pertinent notification required by paragraph 5(c) of Article IX of the Treaty shall confirm and record the type and number of items of missile systems, listed in paragraph 1 of this Section, which are to be eliminated. If the inspecting Party deems it necessary, this shall include a visual inspection of the contents of launch canisters.

7. A missile stage being eliminated by burning in accordance with the procedures set forth in paragraph 10 of this Section shall not be instrumented for data collection. Prior to the initiation of the elimination procedures set forth in paragraph 10 of this Section, an inspector from the inspecting Party shall confirm that such missile stages are not instrumented for data collection. Those missile stages shall be subject to continuous observation by such an inspector from the time of that inspection until the burning is completed.

8. The completion of the elimination procedures set forth in this Section, except those for training missiles, training missile stages, training launch canisters and training launchers, along with the type and number of items of missile systems for which those procedures have been completed, shall be confirmed in writing by the representative of the Party carrying out the elimination and by the inspection team leader of the other Party. The elimination of a training missile, training missile stage, training launch canister or training launcher shall be considered to have been completed upon completion of the procedures set forth in paragraph 11 of this Section and notification as required by paragraph 5(e) of Article IX of the Treaty following the date specified pursuant to paragraph 2 of this Section.

9. The Parties agree that all United States and Soviet intermediate-range and shorter-range missiles and their associated reentry vehicles shall be eliminated within an agreed overall period of elimination. It is further agreed that all such missiles shall, in fact, be eliminated 15 days prior to the end of the overall period of elimination. During the last 15 days, a Party shall withdraw to its

national territory reentry vehicles which, by unilateral decision, have been released from existing programs of cooperation and eliminate them during the same timeframe in accordance with the procedures set forth in this Section.

10. The specific procedures for the elimination of the items of missile systems listed in paragraph 1 of this Section shall be as follows, unless the Parties agree upon different procedures to achieve the same result as the procedures identified in this paragraph:

For the Pershing II:

Missile:

(a) missile stages shall be eliminated by explosive demolition or burning;

(b) solid fuel, rocket nozzles and motor cases not destroyed in this process shall be burned, crushed, flattened or destroyed by explosion; and

(c) front section, minus nuclear warhead device and guidance elements, shall be crushed or flattened.

Launcher:

(a) erector-launcher mechanism shall be removed from launcher chassis;

(b) all components of erector-launcher mechanism shall be cut at locations that are not assembly joints into two pieces of approximately equal size;

(c) missile launch support equipment, including external instrumentation compartments, shall be removed from launcher chassis; and

(d) launcher chassis shall be cut at a location that is not an assembly joint into two pieces of approximately equal size.

For the BGM-109G:

Missile:

(a) missile airframe shall be cut longitudinally into two pieces;

(b) wings and tail section shall be severed from missile airframe at locations that are not assembly joints; and

(c) front section, minus nuclear warhead device and guidance elements, shall be crushed or flattened.

Launch Canister:

Launch canister shall be crushed, flattened, cut into two pieces of approximately equal size or destroyed by explosion.

Launcher:

(a) erector-launcher mechanism shall be removed from launcher chassis;

(b) all components of erector-launcher mechanism shall be cut at locations that are not assembly joints into two pieces of approximately equal size;

(c) missile launch support equipment, including external instrumentation compartments, shall be removed from launcher chassis; and

(d) launcher chassis shall be cut at a location that is not an assembly joint into two pieces of approximately equal size.

For the Pershing IA:

Missile:

(a) missile stages shall be eliminated by explosive demolition or burning;

(b) solid fuel, rocket nozzles and motor cases not destroyed in this process shall be burned, crushed, flattened or destroyed by explosion; and

(c) front section, minus nuclear warhead device and guidance elements, shall be crushed or flattened.

Launcher:

(a) erector-launcher mechanism shall be removed from launcher chassis;

(b) all components of erector-launcher mechanism shall be cut at locations that are not assembly joints into two pieces of approximately equal size;

(c) missile launch support equipment, including external instrumentation compartments, shall be removed from launcher chassis; and

(d) launcher chassis shall be cut at a location that is not an assembly joint into two pieces of approximately equal size.

For the Pershing IB:

Missile:

(a) missile stage shall be eliminated by explosive demolition or burning:

(b) solid fuel, rocket nozzle and motor case not destroyed in this process shall be burned, crushed, flattened or destroyed by explosion; and

(c) front section, minus nuclear warhead device and guidance elements, shall be crushed or flattened.

For the SS-20:

Missile:

(a) missile shall be eliminated by explosive demolition of the missile in its launch canister or by burning missile stages;

(b) solid fuel, rocket nozzles and motor cases not destroyed in this process shall be burned, crushed, flattened or destroyed by explosion; and

(c) front section, including reentry vehicles, minus nuclear warhead devices, and instrumentation compartment, minus guidance elements, shall be crushed or flattened.

Launch Canister:

Launch canister shall be destroyed by explosive demolition together with a missile, or shall be destroyed separately by explosion, cut into two pieces of approximately equal size, crushed or flattened.

Launcher:

(a) erector-launcher mechanism shall be removed from launcher chassis;

(b) all components of erector-launcher mechanism shall be cut at locations that are not assembly joints into two pieces of approximately equal size;

(c) missile launch support equipment, including external instrumentation compartments, shall be removed from launcher chassis;

(d) mountings of erector-launcher mechanism and launcher leveling supports shall be cut off launcher chassis;

(e) launcher leveling supports shall be cut at locations that are not assembly joints into two pieces of approximately equal size; and

(f) a portion of the launcher chassis, at least 0.78 meters in length, shall be cut off aft of the rear axle.

Missile Transporter Vehicle:

(a) all mechanisms associated with missile loading and mounting shall be removed from transporter vehicle chassis;

(b) all mountings of such mechanisms shall be cut off transporter vehicle chassis;

(c) all components of the mechanisms associated with missile loading and mounting shall be cut at locations that are not assembly joints into two pieces of approximately equal size;

(d) external instrumentation compartments shall be removed from transporter vehicle chassis;

(e) transporter vehicle leveling supports shall be cut off transporter vehicle chassis and cut at locations that are not assembly joints into two pieces of approximately equal size; and

(f) a portion of the transporter vehicle chassis, at least 0.78 meters in length, shall be cut off aft of the rear axle.

For the SS-4:

Missile:

(a) nozzles of propulsion system shall be cut off at locations that are not assembly joints;

(b) all propellant tanks shall be cut into two pieces of approximately equal size;

(c) instrumentation compartment, minus guidance elements, shall be cut into two pieces of approximately equal size; and

(d) front section, minus nuclear warhead device, shall be crushed or flattened.

Launch Stand:

Launch stand components shall be cut at locations that are not assembly joints into two pieces of approximately equal size.

Missile Erector:

(a) jib, missile erector leveling supports and missile erector mechanism shall be cut off missile erector at locations that are not assembly joints; and

(b) jib and missile erector leveling supports shall be cut into two pieces of approximately equal size.

Missile Transporter Vehicle:

Mounting components for a missile and for a missile erector mechanism as well as supports for erecting a missile onto a launcher shall be cut off transporter vehicle at locations that are not assembly joints.

For the SS-5:

Missile:

(a) nozzles of propulsion system shall be cut off at locations that are not assembly joints;

(b) all propellant tanks shall be cut into two pieces of approximately equal size; and

(c) instrumentation compartment, minus guidance elements, shall be cut into two pieces of approximately equal size.

For the SSC-X-4:

Missile:

(a) missile airframe shall be cut longitudinally into two pieces;

(b) wings and tail section shall be severed from missile airframe at locations that are not assembly joints; and

(c) front section, minus nuclear warhead device and guidance elements, shall be crushed or flattened.

Launch Canister:

Launch canister shall be crushed, flattened, cut into two pieces of approximately equal size or destroyed by explosion.

Launcher:

(a) erector-launcher mechanism shall be removed from launcher chassis;

(b) all components of erector-launcher mechanism shall be cut at locations that are not assembly joints into two pieces of approximately equal size;

(c) missile launch support equipment, including external instrumentation compartments, shall be removed from launcher chassis;

(d) mountings of erector-launcher mechanism and launcher leveling supports shall be cut off launcher chassis;

(e) launcher leveling supports shall be cut at locations that are not assembly joints into two pieces of approximately equal size; and

(f) the launcher chassis shall be severed at a location determined by measuring no more than 0.70 meters rearward from the rear axle.

For the SS-12:

Missile:

(a) missile shall be eliminated by explosive demolition or by burning missile stages;

(b) solid fuel, rocket nozzles and motor cases not destroyed in this process shall be burned, crushed, flattened or destroyed by explosion; and

(c) front section, minus nuclear warhead device, and instrumentation compartment, minus guidance elements, shall be crushed, flattened or destroyed by explosive demolition together with a missile.

Launcher:

(a) erector-launcher mechanism shall be removed from launcher chassis;

(b) all components of erector-launcher mechanism shall be cut at locations that are not assembly joints into two pieces of approximately equal size;

(c) missile launch support equipment, including external instrumentation compartments, shall be removed from launcher chassis;

(d) mountings of erector-launcher mechanism and launcher leveling supports shall be cut off launcher chassis;

(e) launcher leveling supports shall be cut at locations that are not assembly joints into two pieces of approximately equal size; and

(f) a portion of the launcher chassis, at least 1.10 meters in length, shall be cut off aft of the rear axle.

Missile Transporter Vehicle:

(a) all mechanisms associated with missile loading and mounting shall be removed from transporter vehicle chassis;

(b) all mountings of such mechanisms shall be cut off transporter vehicle chassis;

(c) all components of the mechanisms associated with missile loading and mounting shall be cut at locations that are not assembly joints into two pieces of approximately equal size;

(d) external instrumentation compartments shall be removed from transporter vehicle chassis;

(e) transporter vehicle leveling supports shall be cut off transporter vehicle chassis and cut at locations that are not assembly joints into two pieces of approximately equal size; and

(f) a portion of the transporter vehicle chassis, at least 1.10 meters in length, shall be cut off aft of the rear axle.

For the SS-23:

Missile:

(a) missile shall be eliminated by explosive demolition or by burning the missile stage;

(b) solid fuel, rocket nozzle and motor case not destroyed in this process shall be burned, crushed, flattened or destroyed by explosion; and

(c) front section, minus nuclear warhead device, and instrumentation compartment, minus guidance elements, shall be crushed, flattened, or destroyed by explosive demolition together with a missile.

Launcher:

(a) erector-launcher mechanism shall be removed from launcher body;

(b) all components of erector-launcher mechanism shall be cut at locations that are not assembly joints into two pieces of approximately equal size;

(c) missile launch support equipment shall be removed from launcher body;

(d) mountings of erector-launcher mechanism and launcher leveling supports shall be cut off launcher body;

(e) launcher leveling supports shall be cut at locations that are not assembly joints into two pieces of approximately equal size;

(f) each environmental cover of the launcher body shall be removed and cut into two pieces of approximately equal size; and

(g) a portion of the launcher body, at least 0.85 meters in length, shall be cut off aft of the rear axle.

Missile Transporter Vehicle:

(a) all mechanisms associated with missile loading and mounting shall be removed from transporter vehicle body;

(b) all mountings of such mechanisms shall be cut off transporter vehicle body;

(c) all components of mechanisms associated with missile loading and mounting shall be cut at locations that are not assembly joints into two pieces of approximately equal size;

(d) control equipment of the mechanism associated with missile loading shall be removed from transporter vehicle body;

(e) transporter vehicle leveling supports shall be cut off transporter vehicle body and cut at locations that are not assembly joints into two pieces of approximately equal size; and

(f) a portion of the transporter vehicle body, at least 0.85 meters in length, shall be cut off aft of the rear axle.

11. The specific procedures for the elimination of the training missiles, training missile stages, training launch canisters and training launchers indicated in paragraph 1 of this Section shall be as follows:

Training Missile and Training Missile Stage:

– Training missile and training missile stage shall be crushed, flattened, cut into two pieces of approximately equal size or destroyed by explosion.

Training Launch Canister:

– Training launch canister shall be crushed, flattened, cut into two pieces of approximately equal size or destroyed by explosion.

Training Launcher:

– Training launcher chassis shall be cut at the same location designated in paragraph 10 of this Section for launcher of the same type of missile.

III. Elimination of Missiles by Means of Launching

1. Elimination of missiles by means of launching pursuant to paragraph 5 of Article X of the Treaty shall be subject to on-site inspection in accordance with paragraph 7 of Article XI of the Treaty and the Protocol on Inspection. Immediately prior to each launch conducted for the purpose of elimination, an inspector from the inspecting Party shall confirm by visual observation the type of missile to be launched.

2. All missiles being eliminated by means of launching shall be launched from designated elimination facilities to existing impact areas for such missiles. No such missile shall be used as a target vehicle for a ballistic missile interceptor.

3. Missiles being eliminated by means of launching shall be launched one at a time, and no less than six hours shall elapse between such launches.

4. Such launches shall involve ignition of all missile stages. Neither Party shall transmit or recover data from missiles being eliminated by means of launching except for unencrypted data used for range safety purposes.

5. The completion of the elimination procedures set forth in this Section, and the type and number of missiles for which those procedures have been completed, shall be confirmed in writing by the representative of the Party carrying out the elimination and by the inspection team leader of the other Party.

6. A missile shall be considered to be eliminated by means of launching after completion of the procedures set forth in this Section and upon notification required by paragraph 5(e) of Article IX of the Treaty.

IV. Procedures for Elimination In Situ

1. Support Structures

(a) Support structures listed in Section I of this Protocol shall be eliminated in situ.

(b) The initiation of the elimination of support structures shall be considered to be the commencement of the elimination procedures required in paragraph 1(d) of this Section.

(c) The elimination of support structures shall be subject to verification by on-site inspection in accordance with paragraph 4 of Article XI of the Treaty.

(d) The specific elimination procedures for support structures shall be as follows:

(i) the superstructure of the fixed structure or shelter shall be dismantled or demolished, and removed from its base or foundation;

(ii) the base or foundation of the fixed structure or shelter shall be destroyed by excavation or explosion;

(iii) the destroyed base or foundation of a fixed structure or shelter shall remain visible to national technical means of verification for six months or until completion of an on-site inspection conducted in accordance with Article XI of the Treaty; and

(iv) upon completion of the above requirements, the elimination procedures shall be considered to have been completed.

2. Propellant Tanks for SS-4 Missiles

Fixed and transportable propellant tanks for SS-4 missiles shall be removed from launch sites.

3. Training Missiles, Training Missile Stages, Training Launch Canisters and Training Launchers

(a) Training missiles, training missile stages, training launch canisters and training launchers not eliminated at elimination facilities shall be eliminated in situ.

(b) Training missiles, training missile stages, training launch canisters and training launchers being eliminated in situ shall be eliminated in accordance with the specific procedures set forth in paragraph 11 of Section II of this Protocol.

(c) Each Party shall have the right to conduct an on-site inspection to confirm the completion of the elimination procedures for training missiles, training missile stages, training launch canisters and training launchers.

(d) The Party possessing such a training missile, training missile stage, training launch canister or training launcher shall inform the other Party of the place-name and coordinates of the location at which the on-site inspection provided for in paragraph 3(c) of this Section may be conducted as well as the date on which it may be conducted. Such information shall be provided no less than 30 days in advance of that date.

(e) Elimination of a training missile, training missile stage, training launch canister or training launcher shall be considered to have been completed upon the completion of the procedures required by this paragraph and upon notification as required by paragraph 5(e) of Article IX of the Treaty following the date specified pursuant to paragraph 3(d) of this Section.

V. Other Types of Elimination

1. Loss or Accidental Destruction

(a) If an item listed in Section I of this Protocol is lost or destroyed as a result of an accident, the possessing Party shall notify the other Party within 48 hours, as required in paragraph 5(e) of Article IX of the Treaty, that the item has been eliminated.

(b) Such notification shall include the type of the eliminated item, its approximate or assumed location and the circumstances related to the loss or accidental destruction.

(c) In such a case, the other Party shall have the right to conduct an inspection of the specific point at which the accident occurred to provide confidence that the item has been eliminated.

2. Static Display

(a) The Parties shall have the right to eliminate missiles, launch canisters and launchers, as well as training missiles, training launch canisters and training launchers, listed in Section I of this Protocol by placing them on static display. Each Party shall be limited to a total of 15 missiles, 15 launch canisters and 15 launchers on such static display.

(b) Prior to being placed on static display, a missile, launch canister or launcher shall be rendered unusable for purposes inconsistent with the Treaty. Missile propellant shall be removed and erector-launcher mechanisms shall be rendered inoperative.

(c) The Party possessing a missile, launch canister or launcher, as well as a training missile, training launch canister or training launcher that is to be eliminated by placing it on static display shall provide the other Party with the place-name and coordinates of the location at which such a missile, launch canister or launcher is to be on static display, as well as the location at which the on-site inspection provided for in paragraph 2(d) of this Section, may take place.

(d) Each Party shall have the right to conduct an on-site inspection of such a missile, launch canister or launcher within 60 days of receipt of the notification required in paragraph 2(c) of this Section.

(e) Elimination of a missile, launch canister or launcher, as well as a training missile, training launch canister or training launcher, by placing it on static display shall be considered to have been completed upon completion of the procedures required by this paragraph and notification as required by paragraph 5(e) of Article IX of the Treaty.

This Protocol is an integral part of the Treaty. It shall enter into force on the date of the entry into force of the Treaty and shall remain in force so long as the Treaty remains in force. As provided for in paragraph 1(b) of Article XIII of the Treaty, the Parties may agree upon such measures as may be necessary to improve the viability and effectiveness of this Protocol. Such measures shall not be deemed amendments to the Treaty.

DONE at Washington on December 8, 1987, in two copies, each in the English and Russian languages, both texts being equally authentic.

Protocol Regarding Inspections Relating to the Treaty Between the United States of America and the Union of Soviet Socialist Republics on the Elimination of Their Intermediate-Range and Shorter-Range Missiles

of December 8, 1987

Pursuant to and in implementation of the Treaty Between the United States of America and the Union of Soviet Socialist Republics on the Elimination of Their Intermediate-Range and Shorter-Range Missiles of December 8, 1987, hereinafter referred to as the Treaty, the Parties hereby agree upon procedures governing the conduct of inspections provided for in Article XI of the Treaty.

I. Definitions

For the purposes of this Protocol, the Treaty, the Memorandum of Understanding and the Protocol on Elimination:

1. The term "inspected Party" means the Party to the Treaty whose sites are subject to inspection as provided for by Article XI of the Treaty.
2. The term "inspecting Party" means the Party to the Treaty carrying out an inspection.
3. The term "inspector" means an individual designated by one of the Parties to carry out inspections and included on that Party's list of inspectors in accordance with the provisions of Section III of this Protocol.
4. The term "inspection team" means the group of inspectors assigned by the inspecting Party to conduct a particular inspection.
5. The term "inspection site" means an area, location or facility at which an inspection is carried out.
6. The term "period of inspection" means the period of time from arrival of the inspection team at the inspection site until its departure from the inspection site, exclusive of time spent on any pre-and post-inspection procedures.

7. The term "point of entry" means: Washington, D.C., or San Francisco, California, the United States of America; Brussels (National Airport), The Kingdom of Belgium; Frankfurt (Rhein Main Airbase), The Federal Republic of Germany; Rome (Ciampino), The Republic of Italy; Schiphol, The Kingdom of the Netherlands; RAF Greenham Common, The United Kingdom of Great Britain and Northern Ireland; Moscow, or Irkutsk, the Union of Soviet Socialist Republics; Schkeuditz Airport, the German Democratic Republic; and International Airport Ruzyne, the Czechoslovak Socialist'Republic.

8. The term "in-country period" means the period from the arrival of the inspection team at the point of entry until its departure from the country through the point of entry.

9. The term "in-country escort" means individuals specified by the inspected Party to accompany and assist inspectors and aircrew members as necessary throughout the in-country period.

10. The term "aircrew member" means an individual who performs duties related to the operation of an airplane and who is included on a Party's list of aircrew members in accordance with the provisions of Section III of this Protocol.

II. General Obligations

1. For the purpose of ensuring verification of compliance with the provisions of the Treaty, each Party shall facilitate inspection by the other Party pursuant to this Protocol.

2. Each Party takes note of the assurances received from the other Party regarding understandings reached between the other Party and the basing countries to the effect that the basing countries have agreed to the conduct of inspections, in accordance with the provisions of this Protocol, on their territories.

III. Pre-Inspection Requirements

1. Inspections to ensure verification of compliance by the Parties with the obligations assumed under the Treaty shall be carried out by inspectors designated in accordance with paragraphs 3 and 4 of this Section.

2. No later than one day after entry into force of the Treaty, each Party shall provide to the other Party: a list of its proposed aircrew members; a list of its proposed inspectors who will carry out inspections pursuant to paragraphs 3, 4, 5, 7 and 8 of Article XI of the Treaty; and a list of its proposed inspectors who will carry out inspection activities pursuant to paragraph 6 of Article XI of the Treaty. None of these lists shall contain at any time more than 200 individuals.

3. Each Party shall review the lists of inspectors and aircrew members proposed by the other Party. With respect to an individual included on the list of proposed inspectors who will carry out inspection activities pursuant to paragraph 6 of Article XI of the Treaty, if such an individual is unacceptable to the Party reviewing the list, that Party shall, within 20 days, so inform the Party providing the list, and the individual shall be deemed not accepted and shall be deleted from the list. With respect to an individual on the list of proposed aircrew members or the list of proposed inspectors who will carry out inspections pursuant to paragraphs 3, 4, 5, 7 and 8 of Article XI of the Treaty, each Party, within 20 days after the receipt of such lists, shall inform the other Party of its agreement to the designation of each inspector and aircrew member proposed. Inspectors shall be citizens of the inspecting Party.

4. Each Party shall have the right to amend its lists of inspectors and aircrew members. New inspectors and aircrew members shall be designated in the same manner as set forth in paragraph 3 of this Section with respect to the initial lists.

5. Within 30 days of receipt of the initial lists of inspectors and aircrew members, or of subsequent changes thereto, the Party receiving such information shall provide, or shall ensure the provision of, such visas and other documents to each individual to whom it has agreed as may be required to ensure that each inspector or aircrew member may enter and remain in the territory of the Party or basing country in which an inspection site is located throughout the in-country period for the purpose of carrying out inspection activities in accordance with the provisions of this Protocol. Such visas and documents shall be valid for a period of at least 24 months.

6. To exercise their functions effectively, inspectors and aircrew members shall be accorded, throughout the in-country period,

privileges and immunities in the country of the inspection site as set forth in the Annex to this Protocol.

7. Without prejudice to their privileges and immunities, inspectors and aircrew members shall be obliged to respect the laws and regulations of the State on whose territory an inspection is carried out and shall be obliged not to interfere in the internal affairs of that State. In the event the inspected Party determines that an inspector or aircrew member of the other Party has violated the conditions governing inspection activities set forth in this Protocol, or has ever committed a criminal offense on the territory of the inspected Party or a basing country, or has ever been sentenced for committing a criminal offense or expelled by the inspected Party or a basing country, the inspected Party making such a determination shall so notify the inspecting Party, which shall immediately strike the individual from the lists of inspectors or the list of aircrew members. If, at that time, the individual is on the territory of the inspected Party or a basing country, the inspecting Party shall immediately remove that individual from the country.

8. Within 30 days after entry into force of the Treaty, each Party shall inform the other Party of the standing diplomatic clearance number for airplanes of the Party transporting inspectors and equipment necessary for inspection into and out of the territory of the Party or basing country in which an inspection site is located. Aircraft routings to and from the designated point of entry shall be along established international airways that are agreed upon by the Parties as the basis for such diplomatic clearance.

IV. Notifications

1. Notification of an intention to conduct an inspection shall be made through the Nuclear Risk Reduction Centers. The receipt of this notification shall be acknowledged through the Nuclear Risk Reduction Centers by the inspected Party within one hour of its receipt.

(a) For inspections conducted pursuant to paragraphs 3, 4 or 5 of Article XI of the Treaty, such notifications shall be made no less than 16 hours in advance of the estimated time of arrival of the inspection team at the point of entry and shall include:

(i) the point of entry;
(ii) the date and estimated time of arrival at the point of entry;
(iii) the date and time when the specification of the inspection site will be provided; and
(iv) the names of inspectors and aircrew members.

(b) For inspections conducted pursuant to paragraphs 7 or 8 of Article XI of the Treaty, such notifications shall be made no less than 72 hours in advance of the estimated time of arrival of the inspection team at the point of entry and shall include:

(i) the point of entry;
(ii) the date and estimated time of arrival at the point of entry;
(iii) the site to be inspected and the type of inspection; and
(iv) the names of inspectors and aircrew members.

2. The date and time of the specification of the inspected site as notified pursuant to paragraph 1(a) of this Section shall fall within the following time intervals:

(a) for inspections conducted pursuant to paragraphs 4 or 5 of Article XI of the Treaty, neither less than four hours nor more than 24 hours after the estimated date and time of arrival at the point of entry; and

(b) for inspections conducted pursuant to paragraph 3 of Article XI of the Treaty, neither less than four hours nor more than 48 hours after the estimated date and time of arrival at the point of entry.

3. The inspecting Party shall provide the inspected Party with a flight plan, through the Nuclear Risk Reduction Centers, for its flight from the last airfield prior to entering the airspace of the country in which the inspection site is located to the point of entry, no less than six hours before the scheduled departure time from that airfield. Such a plan shall be filed in accordance with the procedures of the International Civil Aviation Organization applicable to civil aircraft. The inspecting Party shall include in the remarks section of each flight plan the standing diplomatic clearance number and the notation: "Inspection aircraft. Priority clearance processing required."

4. No less than three hours prior to the scheduled departure of the inspection team from the last airfield prior to entering the airspace of the country in which the inspection is to take place, the inspected Party shall ensure that the flight plan filed in accordance with paragraph 3 of this Section is approved so that the in-

spection team may arrive at the point of entry by the estimated arrival time.

5. Either Party may change the point or points of entry to the territories of the countries within which its deployment areas, missile operating bases or missile support facilities are located, by giving notice of such change to the other Party. A change in a point of entry shall become effective five months after receipt of such notification by the other Party.

V. Activities Beginning Upon Arrival at the Point of Entry

1. The in-country escort and a diplomatic aircrew escort accredited to the Government of either the inspected Party or the basing country in which the inspection site is located shall meet the inspection team and aircrew members at the point of entry as soon as the airplane of the inspecting Party lands. The number of aircrew members for each airplane shall not exceed ten. The in-country escort shall expedite the entry of the inspection team and aircrew, their baggage, and equipment and supplies necessary for inspection, into the country in which the inspection site is located. A diplomatic aircrew escort shall have the right to accompany and assist aircrew members throughout the in-country period. In the case of an inspection taking place on the territory of a basing country, the in-country escort may include representatives of that basing country.

2. An inspector shall be considered to have assumed his duties upon arrival at the point of entry on the territory of the inspected Party or a basing country, and shall be considered to have ceased performing those duties when he has left the territory of the inspected Party or basing country.

3. Each Party shall ensure that equipment and supplies are exempt from all customs duties.

4. Equipment and supplies which the inspecting Party brings into the country in which an inspection site is located shall be subject to examination at the point of entry each time they are brought into that country. This examination shall be completed prior to the departure of the inspection team from the point of entry to conduct an inspection. Such equipment and supplies shall be examined by the in-country escort in the presence of the in-

spection team members to ascertain to the satisfaction of each Party that the equipment and supplies cannot perform functions unconnected with the inspection requirements of the Treaty. If it is established upon examination that the equipment or supplies are unconnected with these inspection requirements, then they shall not be cleared for use and shall be impounded at the point of entry until the departure of the inspection team from the country where the inspection is conducted. Storage of the inspecting Party's equipment and supplies at each point of entry shall be within tamper-proof containers within a secure facility. Access to each secure facility shall be controlled by a "dual key" system requiring the presence of both Parties to gain access to the equipment and supplies.

5. Throughout the in-country period, the inspected Party shall provide, or arrange for the provision of, meals, lodging, work space, transportation and, as necessary, medical care for the inspection team and aircrew of the inspecting Party. All the costs in connection with the stay of inspectors carrying out inspection activities pursuant to paragraph 6 of Article XI of the Treaty, on the territory of the inspected Party, including meals, services, lodging, work space, transportation and medical care shall be borne by the inspecting Party.

6. The inspected Party shall provide parking, security protection, servicing and fuel for the airplane of the inspecting Party at the point of entry. The inspecting Party shall bear the cost of such fuel and servicing.

7. For inspections conducted on the territory of the Parties, the inspection team shall enter at the point of entry on the territory of the inspected Party that is closest to the inspection site. In the case of inspections carried out in accordance with paragraphs 3, 4 or 5 of Article XI of the Treaty, the inspection team leader shall, at or before the time notified pursuant to paragraph 1(a) (iii) of Section IV of this Protocol, inform the inspected Party at the point of entry through the in-country escort of the type of inspection and the inspection site, by place-name and geographic coordinates.

VI. General Rules for Conducting Inspections

1. Inspectors shall discharge their functions in accordance with this Protocol.

2. Inspectors shall not disclose information received during inspections except with the express permission of the inspecting Party. They shall remain bound by this obligation after their assignment as inspectors has ended.

3. In discharging their functions, inspectors shall not interfere directly with on-going activities at the inspection site and shall avoid unnecessarily hampering or delaying the operation of a facility or taking actions affecting its safe operation.

4. Inspections shall be conducted in accordance with the objectives set forth in Article XI of the Treaty as applicable for the type of inspection specified by the inspecting Party under paragraph 1(b) of Section IV or paragraph 7 of Section V of this Protocol.

5. The in-country escort shall have the right to accompany and assist inspectors and aircrew members as considered necessary by the inspected Party throughout the in-country period. Except as otherwise provided in this Protocol, the movement and travel of inspectors and aircrew members shall be at the discretion of the in-country escort.

6. Inspectors carrying out inspection activities pursuant to paragraph 6 of Article XI of the Treaty shall be allowed to travel within 50 kilometers from the inspection site with the permission of the in-country escort, and as considered necessary by the inspected Party, shall be accompanied by the in-country escort. Such travel shall be taken solely as a leisure activity.

7. Inspectors shall have the right throughout the period of inspection to be in communication with the embassy of the inspecting Party located within the territory of the country where the inspection is taking place using the telephone communications provided by the inspected Party.

8. At the inspection site, representatives of the inspected facility shall be included among the in-country escort.

9. The inspection team may bring onto the inspection site such documents as needed to conduct the inspection, as well as linear measurement devices; cameras; portable weighing devices; radiation detection devices; and other equipment, as agreed by the

Parties. The characteristics and method of use of the equipment listed above, shall also be agreed upon within 30 days after entry into force of the Treaty. During inspections conducted pursuant to paragraphs 3, 4, 5(a), 7 or 8 of Article XI of the Treaty, the inspection team may use any of the equipment listed above, except for cameras, which shall be for use only by the inspected Party at the request of the inspecting Party. During inspections conducted pursuant to paragraph 5(b) of Article XI of the Treaty, all measurements shall be made by the inspected Party at the request of the inspecting Party. At the request of inspectors, the in-country escort shall take photographs of the inspected facilities using the inspecting Party's camera systems which are capable of producing duplicate, instant development photographic prints. Each Party shall receive one copy of every photograph.

10. For inspections conducted pursuant to paragraphs 3, 4, 5, 7 or 8 of Article XI of the Treaty, inspectors shall permit the in-country escort to observe the equipment used during the inspection by the inspection team.

11. Measurements recorded during inspections shall be certified by the signature of a member of the inspection team and a member of the in-country escort when they are taken. Such certified data shall be included in the inspection report.

12. Inspectors shall have the right to request clarifications in connection with ambiguities that arise during an inspection. Such requests shall be made promptly through the in-country escort. The in-country escort shall provide the inspection team, during the inspection, with such clarifications as may be necessary to remove the ambiguity. In the event questions relating to an object or building located within the inspection site are not resolved, the inspected Party shall photograph the object or building as requested by the inspecting Party for the purpose of clarifying its nature and function. If the ambiguity cannot be removed during the inspection, then the question, relevant clarifications and a copy of any photographs taken shall be included in the inspection report.

13. In carrying out their activities, inspectors shall observe safety regulations established at the inspection site, including those for the protection of controlled environments within a facility and for personal safety. Individual protective clothing and equipment shall be provided by the inspected Party, as necessary.

14. For inspections pursuant to paragraphs 3, 4, 5, 7 or 8 of Article XI of the Treaty, pre-inspection procedures, including briefings and safety-related activities, shall begin upon arrival of the inspection team at the inspection site and shall be completed within one hour. The inspection team shall begin the inspection immediately upon completion of the pre-inspection procedures. The period of inspection shall not exceed 24 hours, except for inspections pursuant to paragraphs 6, 7 or 8 of Article XI of the Treaty. The period of inspection may be extended, by agreement with the in-country escort, by no more than eight hours. Post-inspection procedures, which include completing the inspection report in accordance with the provisions of Section XI of this Protocol, shall begin immediately upon completion of the inspection and shall be completed at the inspection site within four hours.

15. An inspection team conducting an inspection pursuant to Article XI of the Treaty shall include no more than ten inspectors, except for an inspection team conducting an inspection pursuant to paragraphs 7 or 8 of that Article, which shall include no more than 20 inspectors and an inspection team conducting inspection activities pursuant to paragraph 6 of that Article, which shall include no more than 30 inspectors. At least two inspectors on each team must speak the language of the inspected Party. An inspection team shall operate under the direction of the team leader and deputy team leader. Upon arrival at the inspection site, the inspection team may divide itself into subgroups consisting of no fewer than two inspectors each. There shall be no more than one inspection team at an inspection site at any one time.

16. Except in the case of inspections conducted pursuant to paragraphs 3, 4, 7 or 8 of Article XI of the Treaty, upon completion of the post-inspection procedures, the inspection team shall return promptly to the point of entry from which it commenced inspection activities and shall then leave, within 24 hours, the territory of the country in which the inspection site is located, using its own airplane. In the case of inspections conducted pursuant to paragraphs 3, 4, 7 or 8 of Article XI of the Treaty, if the inspection team intends to conduct another inspection it shall either:

(a) notify the inspected Party of its intent upon return to the point of entry; or

(b) notify the inspected Party of the type of inspection and the inspection site upon completion of the post-inspection procedures. In this case it shall be the responsibility of the inspected Party to ensure that the inspection team reaches the next inspection site without unjustified delay. The inspected Party shall determine the means of transportation and route involved in such travel.

With respect to subparagraph (a), the procedures set forth in paragraph 7 of Section V of this Protocol and paragraphs 1 and 2 of Section VII of this Protocol shall apply.

VII. Inspections Conducted Pursuant to Paragraphs 3, 4 or 5 of Article XI of the Treaty

1. Within one hour after the time for the specification of the inspection site notified pursuant to paragraph 1(a) of Section IV of this Protocol, the inspected Party shall implement pre-inspection movement restrictions at the inspection site, which shall remain in effect until the inspection team arrives at the inspection site. During the period that pre-inspection movement restrictions are in effect, missiles, stages of such missiles, launchers or support equipment subject to the Treaty shall not be removed from the inspection site.

2. The inspected Party shall transport the inspection team from the point of entry to the inspection site so that the inspection team arrives at the inspection site no later than nine hours after the time for the specification of the inspection site notified pursuant to paragraph 1(a) of Section IV of this Protocol.

3. In the event that an inspection is conducted in a basing country, the aircrew of the inspected Party may include representatives of the basing country.

4. Neither Party shall conduct more than one inspection pursuant to paragraph 5(a) of Article XI of the Treaty at any one time, more than one inspection pursuant to paragraph 5(b) of Article XI of the Treaty at any one time, or more than 10 inspections pursuant to paragraph 3 of Article XI of the Treaty at any one time.

5. The boundaries of the inspection site at the facility to be inspected shall be the boundaries of that facility set forth in the Memorandum of Understanding.

6. Except in the case of an inspection conducted pursuant to paragraphs 4 or 5(b) of Article XI of the Treaty, upon arrival of the inspection team at the inspection site, the in-country escort shall inform the inspection team leader of the number of missiles, stages of missiles, launchers, support structures and support equipment at the site that are subject to the Treaty and provide the inspection team leader with a diagram of the inspection site indicating the location of these missiles, stages of missiles, launchers, support structures and support equipment at the inspection site.

7. Subject to the procedures of paragraphs 8 through 14 of this Section, inspectors shall have the right to inspect the entire inspection site, including the interior of structures, containers or vehicles, or including covered objects, whose dimensions are equal to or greater than the dimensions specified in Section VI of the Memorandum of Understanding for the missiles, stages of such missiles, launchers or support equipment of the inspected Party.

8. A missile, a stage of such a missile or a launcher subject to the Treaty shall be subject to inspection only by external visual observation, including measuring, as necessary, the dimensions of such a missile, stage of such a missile or launcher. A container that the inspected Party declares to contain a missile or stage of a missile subject to the Treaty, and which is not sufficiently large to be capable of containing more than one missile or stage of such a missile of the inspected Party subject to the Treaty, shall be subject to inspection only by external visual observation, including measuring, as necessary, the dimensions of such a container to confirm that it cannot contain more than one missile or stage of such a missile of the inspected Party subject to the Treaty. Except as provided for in paragraph 14 of this Section, a container that is sufficiently large to contain a missile or stage of such a missile of the inspected Party subject to the Treaty that the inspected Party declares not to contain a missile or stage of such a missile subject to the Treaty shall be subject to inspection only by means of weighing or visual observation of the interior of the container, as necessary, to confirm that it does not, in fact, contain a missile or stage of such a missile of the inspected Party subject to the Treaty. If such a container is a launch canister associated with a type of missile not subject to the Treaty, and declared by the inspected Party to contain such a missile, it shall be subject to external inspection only, including use of radiation detection de-

vices, visual observation and linear measurement, as necessary, of the dimensions of such a canister.

9. A structure or container that is not sufficiently large to contain a missile, stage of such a missle or launcher of the inspected Party subject to the Treaty shall be subject to inspection only by external visual observation including measuring, as necessary, the dimensions of such a structure or container to confirm that it is not sufficiently large to be capable of containing a missile, stage of such a missile or launcher of the inspected Party subject to the Treaty.

10. Within a structure, a space which is sufficiently large to contain a missile, stage of such a missile or launcher of the inspected Party subject to the Treaty, but which is demonstrated to the satisfaction of the inspection team not to be accessible by the smallest missile, stage of such a missile or launcher of the inspected Party subject to the Treaty shall not be subject to further inspection. If the inspected Party demonstrates to the satisfaction of the inspection team by means of a visual inspection of the interior of an enclosed space from its entrance that the enclosed space does not contain any missile, stage of such a missile or launcher of the inspected Party subject to the Treaty, such an enclosed space shall not be subject to further satisfaction of the inspection team by means of a visual inspection of the interior of an enclosed space from its entrance that the enclosed space does not contain any missile, stage of such a missile or launcher of the inspected Party subject to the Treaty, such an enclosed space shall not be subject to further inspection.

11. The inspection team shall be permitted to patrol the perimeter of the inspection site and station inspectors at the exits of the site for the duration of the inspection.

12. The inspection team shall be permitted to inspect any vehicle capable of carrying missiles, stages of such missiles, launchers or support equipment of the inspected Party subject to the Treaty at any time during the course of an inspection and no such vehicle shall leave the inspection site during the course of the inspection until inspected at site exits by the inspection team.

13. Prior to inspection of a building within the inspection site, the inspection team may station subgroups at the exits of the building that are large enough to permit passage of any missile, stage of such missile, launcher or support equipment of the in-

spected Party subject to the Treaty. During the time that the building is being inspected, no vehicle or subject capable of containing any missile, stage of such a missile, launcher or support equipment of the inspected Party subject to the Treaty shall be permitted to leave the building until inspected.

14. During an inspection conducted pursuant to paragraph 5(b) of Article XI of the Treaty, it shall be the responsibility of the inspected Party to demonstrate that a shrouded or environmentally protected object which is equal to or larger than the smallest missile, stage of a missile or launcher of the inspected Party subject to the Treaty is not, in fact, a missile, stage of such a missile or launcher of the inspected Party subject to the Treaty. This may be accomplished by partial removal of the shroud or environmental protection cover, measuring, or weighing the covered object or by other methods. If the inspected Party satisfies the inspection team by its demonstration that the object is not a missile, stage of such a missile or launcher of the inspected Party subject to the Treaty, then there shall be no further inspection of that object. If the container is a launch canister associated with a type of missile not subject to the Treaty, and declared by the inspected Party to contain such a missile, then it shall be subject to external inspection only, including use of radiation detection devices, visual observation and linear measurement, as necessary, of the dimensions of such a canister.

VIII. Inspections Conducted Pursuant to Paragraphs 7 or 8 of Article XI of the Treaty

1. Inspections of the process of elimination of items of missile systems specified in the Protocol on Elimination carried out pursuant to paragraph 7 of Article XI of the Treaty shall be conducted in accordance with the procedures set forth in this paragraph and the Protocol on Elimination.

(a) Upon arrival at the elimination facility, inspectors shall be provided with a schedule of elimination activities.

(b) Inspectors shall check the data which are specified in the notification provided by the inspected Party regarding the number and type of items of missile systems to be eliminated against the number and type of such items which are at the elimination facility prior to the initiation of the elimination procedures.

(c) Subject to paragraphs 3 and 11 of Section VI of this Protocol, inspectors shall observe the execution of the specific procedures for the elimination of the items of missile systems as provided for in the Protocol on Elimination. If any deviations from the agreed elimination procedures are found, the inspectors shall have the right to call the attention of the in-country escort to the need for strict compliance with the above-mentioned procedures. The completion of such procedures shall be confirmed in accordance with the procedures specified in the Protocol on Elimination.

(d) During the elimination of missiles by means of launching, the inspectors shall have the right to ascertain by visual observation that a missile prepared for launch is a missile of the type subject to elimination. The inspectors shall also be allowed to observe such a missile from a safe location specified by the inspected Party until the completion of its launch. During the inspection of a series of launches for the elimination of missiles by means of launching, the inspected Party shall determine the means of transport and route for the transportation of inspectors between inspection sites.

2. Inspections of the elimination of items of missile systems specified in the Protocol on Elimination carried out pursuant to paragraph 8 of Article XI of the Treaty shall be conducted in accordance with the procedures set forth in Sections II, IV or V of the Protocol on Elimination or as otherwise agreed by the Parties.

IX. Inspection Activities Conducted Pursuant to Paragraph 6 of Article XI of the Treaty

1. The inspected Party shall maintain an agreed perimeter around the periphery of the inspection site and shall designate a portal with not more than one rail line and one road which shall be within 50 meters of each other. All vehicles which can contain an intermediate-range GLBM or longest stage of such a GLBM of the inspected Party shall exit only through this portal.

2. For the purposes of this Section, the provisions of paragraph 10 of Article VII of the Treaty shall be applied to intermediate-range GLBMs of the inspected Party and the longest stage of such GLBMs.

3. There shall not be more than two other exits from the inspection site. Such exits shall be monitored by appropriate sensors. The perimeter of and exits from the inspection site may be monitored as provided for by paragraph 11 of Section VII of this Protocol.

4. The inspecting Party shall have the right to establish continuous monitoring systems at the portal specified in paragraph 1 of this Section and appropriate sensors at the exits specified in paragraph 3 of this Section and carry out necessary engineering surveys, construction, repair and replacement of monitoring systems.

5. The inspected Party shall, at the request of and at the expense of the inspecting Party, provide the following:

(a) all necessary utilities for the construction and operation of the monitoring systems, including electrical power, water, fuel, heating and sewage;

(b) basic construction materials including concrete and lumber;

(c) the site preparation necessary to accommodate the installation of continuously operating systems for monitoring the portal specified in paragraph 1 of this Section, appropriate sensors for other exits specified in paragraph 3 of this Section and the center for collecting data obtained during inspections. Such preparation may include ground excavation, laying of concrete foundations, trenching between equipment locations and utility connections;

(d) transportation for necessary installation tools, materials and equipment from the point of entry to the inspection site; and

(e) a minimum of two telephone lines and, as necessary, high frequency radio equipment capable of allowing direct communication with the embassy of the inspecting Party in the country in which the site is located.

6. Outside the perimeter of the inspection site, the inspecting Party shall have the right to:

(a) build no more than three buildings with a total floor space of not more than 150 square meters for a data center and inspection team headquarters, and one additional building with floor space not to exceed 500 square meters for the storage of supplies and equipment;

(b) install systems to monitor the exits to include weight sensors, vehicle sensors, surveillance systems and vehicle dimensional measuring equipment;

(c) install at the portal specified in paragraph 1 of this Section equipment for measuring the length and diameter of missile stages contained inside of launch canisters or shipping containers;

(d) install at the portal specified in paragraph 1 of this Section non-damaging image producing equipment for imaging the contents of launch canisters or shipping containers declared to contain missiles or missile stages as provided for in paragraph 11 of this Section;

(e) install a primary and back-up power source; and

(f) use, as necessary, data authentication devices.

7. During the installation or operation of the monitoring systems, the inspecting Party shall not deny the inspected Party access to any existing structures or security systems. The inspecting Party shall not take any actions with respect to such structures without consent of the inspected Party. If the Parties agree that such structures are to be rebuilt or demolished, either partially or completely, the inspecting Party shall provide the necessary compensation.

8. The inspected Party shall not interfere with the installed equipment or restrict the access of the inspection team to such equipment.

9. The inspecting Party shall have the right to use its own two-way systems of radio communication between inspectors patrolling the perimeter and the data collection center. Such systems shall conform to power and frequency restrictions established on the territory of the inspected Party.

10. Aircraft shall not be permitted to land within the perimeter of the monitored site except for emergencies at the site and with prior notification to the inspection team.

11. Any shipment exiting through the portal specified in paragraph 1 of this Section which is large enough and heavy enough to contain an intermediate-range GLBM or longest stage of such a GLBM of the inspected Party shall be declared by the inspected Party to the inspection team before the shipment arrives at the portal. The declaration shall state whether such a shipment contains a missile or missile stage as large or larger than and as heavy or heavier than an intermediate-range GLBM or longest stage of such a GLBM of the inspected Party.

12. The inspection team shall have the right to weigh and measure the dimensions of any vehicle, including railcars, exiting

the site to ascertain whether it is large enough and heavy enough to contain an intermediate-range GLBM or longest stage of such a GLBM of the inspected Party. These measurements shall be performed so as to minimize the delay of vehicles exiting the site. Vehicles that are either not large enough or not heavy enough to contain an intermediate-range GLBM or longest stage of such a GLBM of the inspected Party shall not be subject to further inspection.

13. Vehicles exiting through the portal specified in paragraph 1 of this Section that are large enough and heavy enough to contain an intermediate-range GLBM or longest stage of such a GLBM of the inspected Party but that are declared not to contain a missile or missile stage as large or larger than and as heavy or heavier than an intermediate-range GLBM or longest stage of such a GLBM of the inspected Party shall be subject to the following procedures.

(a) The inspecting Party shall have the right to inspect the interior of all such vehicles.

(b) If the inspecting Party can determine by visual observation or dimensional measurement that, inside a particular vehicle, there are no containers or shrouded objects large enough to be or to contain an intermediate-range GLBM or longest stage of such a GLBM of the inspected Party, then that vehicle shall not be subject to further inspection.

(c) If inside a vehicle there are one or more containers or shrouded objects large enough to be or to contain an intermediate-range GLBM or longest stage of such a GLBM of the inspected Party, it shall be the responsibility of the inspected Party to demonstrate that such containers or shrouded objects are not and do not contain intermediate-range GLBMs or the longest stages of such GLBMs of the inspected Party.

14. Vehicles exiting through the portal specified in paragraph 1 of this Section that are declared to contain a missile or missile stage as large or larger than and as heavy or heavier than an intermediate-range GLBM or longest stage of such a GLBM of the inspected Party shall be subject to the following procedures.

(a) The inspecting Party shall preserve the integrity of the inspected missile or stage of a missile.

(b) Measuring equipment shall be placed only outside of the launch canister or shipping container; all measurements shall be made by the inspecting Party using the equipment provided for in paragraph 6 of this Section. Such measurements shall be observed and certified by the in-country escort.

(c) The inspecting Party shall have the right to weigh and measure the dimensions of any launch canister or of any shipping container declared to contain such a missile or missile stage and to image the contents of any launch canister or of any shipping container declared to contain such a missile or missile stage; it shall have the right to view such missiles or missile stages contained in launch canisters or shipping containers eight times per calendar year. The in-country escort shall be present during all phases of such viewing. During such interior viewing:

(i) the front end of the launch canister or the cover of the shipping container shall be opened;

(ii) the missile or missile stage shall not be removed from its launch canister or shipping container; and

(iii) the length and diameter of the stages of the missile shall be measured in accordance with the methods agreed by the Parties so as to ascertain that the missile or missile stage is not an intermediate-range GLBM of the inspected Party, or the longest stage of such a GLBM, and that the missile has no more than one stage which is outwardly similar to a stage of an existing type of intermediate-range GLBM.

(d) The inspecting Party shall also have the right to inspect any other containers or shrouded objects inside the vehicle containing such a missile or missile stage in accordance with the procedures in paragraph 13 of this Section.

X. Cancellation of Inspection

An inspection shall be cancelled if, due to circumstances brought about by force majeure, it cannot be carried out. In the case of a delay that prevents an inspection team performing an inspection pursuant to paragraphs 3, 4 or 5 of Article XI of the Treaty, from arriving at the inspection site during the time specified in paragraph 2 of Section VII of this Protocol, the inspecting Party may either cancel or carry out the inspection. If an inspection is cancelled due to circumstances brought about by force majeure or delay, then the number of inspections to which the inspecting Party is entitled shall not be reduced.

XI. Inspection Report

1. For inspections conducted pursuant to paragraphs 3, 4, 5, 7 or 8 of Article XI of the Treaty, during post-inspection procedures, and no later than two hours after the inspection has been completed, the inspection team leader shall provide the in-country escort with a written inspection report in both the English and Russian languages. The report shall be factual. It shall include the type of inspection carried out, the inspection site, the number of missiles, stages of missiles, launchers and items of support equipment subject to the Treaty observed during the period of inspection and any measurements recorded pursuant to paragraph 10 of Section VI of this Protocol. Photographs taken during the inspection in accordance with agreed procedures, as well as the inspection site diagram provided for by paragraph 6 of Section VII of this Protocol, shall be attached to this report.

2. For inspection activities conducted pursuant to paragraph 6 of Article XI of the Treaty, within 3 days after the end of each month, the inspection team leader shall provide the in-country escort with a written inspection report both in the English and Russian languages. The report shall be factual. It shall include the number of vehicles declared to contain a missile or stage of a missile as large or larger than and as heavy or heavier than an intermediate-range GLBM or longest stage of such a GLBM of the inspected Party that left the inspection site through the portal specified in paragraph 1 of Section IX of this Protocol during that month. The report shall also include any measurements of launch canisters or shipping containers contained in these vehicles recorded pursuant to paragraph 11 of Section VI of this Protocol. In the event the inspecting Party, under the provisions of paragraph 14(c) of Section IX of this Protocol, has viewed the interior of a launch canister or shipping container declared to contain a missile or stage of a missile as large or larger than and as heavy or heavier than an intermediate-range GLBM or longest stage of such a GLBM of the inspected Party, the report shall also include the measurements of the length and diameter of missile stages obtained during the inspection and recorded pursuant to paragraph 11 of Section VI of this Protocol. Photographs taken during the inspection in accordance with agreed procedures shall be attached to this report.

3. The inspected Party shall have the right to include written comments in the report.

4. The Parties shall, when possible, resolve ambiguities regarding factual information contained in the inspection report. Relevant clarifications shall be recorded in the report. The report shall be signed by the inspection team leader and by one of the members of the in-country escort. Each Party shall retain one copy of the report.

This Protocol is an integral part of the Treaty. It shall enter into force on the date of entry into force of the Treaty and shall remain in force as long as the Treaty remains in force. As provided for in paragraph 1(b) of Article XIII of the Treaty, the Parties may agree upon such measures as may be necessary to improve the viability and effectiveness of this Protocol. Such measures shall not be deemed amendments to the Treaty.

DONE at Washington on December 8, 1987, in two copies, each in the English and Russian languages, both texts being equally authentic.

FOR THE UNITED STATES OF AMERICA:

President of the United States of America

FOR THE UNION OF SOVIET SOCIALIST REPUBLICS:

General Secretary of the Central Committee of the CPSU

Annex

Provisions on Privileges and Immunities of Inspectors and Aircrew Members

In order to exercise their functions effectively, for the purpose of implementing the Treaty and not for their personal benefit, the inspectors and aircrew members referred to in Section III of this Protocol shall be accorded the privileges and immunities contained in this Annex. Privileges and immunities shall be accorded for the entire in-country period in the country in which an inspection site is located, and thereafter with respect to acts previously performed in the exercise of official functions as an inspector or aircrew member.

1. Inspectors and aircrew members shall be accorded the inviolability enjoyed by diplomatic agents pursuant to Article 29 of the Vienna Convention on Diplomatic Relations of April 18, 1961.

2. The living quarters and office premises occupied by an inspector carrying out inspection activities pursuant to paragraph 6 of Article XI of the Treaty shall be accorded the inviolability and protection accorded the premises of diplomatic agents pursuant to Article 30 of the Vienna Convention on Diplomatic Relations.

3. The papers and correspondence of inspectors and aircrew members shall enjoy the inviolability accorded to the papers and correspondence of diplomatic agents pursuant to Article 30 of the Vienna Convention on Diplomatic Relations. In addition, the aircraft of the inspection team shall be inviolable.

4. Inspectors and aircrew members shall be accorded the immunities accorded diplomatic agents pursuant to paragraphs 1, 2 and 3 of Article 31 of the Vienna Convention on Diplomatic Relations. The immunity from jurisdiction of an inspector or an aircrew member may be waived by the inspecting Party in those cases when it is of the opinion that immunity would impede the course of justice and that it can be waived without prejudice to the implementation of the provisions of the Treaty. Waiver must always be express.

5. Inspectors carrying out inspection activities pursuant to paragraph 6 of Article XI of the Treaty shall be accorded the exemption from dues and taxes accorded to diplomatic agents pursuant to Article 34 of the Vienna Convention on Diplomatic Relations.

6. Inspectors and aircrew members of a Party shall be permitted to bring into the territory of the other Party or a basing country in which an inspection site is located, without payment of any customs duties or related charges, articles for their personal use, with the exception of articles the import or export of which is prohibited by law or controlled by quarantine regulations.

7. An inspector or aircrew member shall not engage in any professional or commercial activity for personal profit on the territory of the inspected Party or that of the basing countries.

8. If the inspected Party considers that there has been an abuse of privileges and immunities specified in this Annex, consultations shall be held between the Parties to determine whether such an abuse has occurred and, if so determined, to prevent a repetition of such an abuse.

Agreement between the United States of America and the Union of Soviet Socialist Republics on the Establishment of Nuclear Risk Reduction Centers

of September 15, 1987

The United States of America and the Union of Soviet Socialist Republics, hereinafter referred to as the Parties,

Affirming their desire to reduce and ultimately eliminate the risk of outbreak of nuclear war, in particular, as a result of misinterpretation, miscalculation, or accident,

Believing that a nuclear war cannot be won and must never be fought,

Believing that agreement on measures for reducing the risk of outbreak of nuclear war serves the interests of strengthening international peace and security,

Reaffirming their obligations under the Agreement on Measures to Reduce the Risk of Outbreak of Nuclear War between the United States of America and the Union of Soviet Socialist Republics of September 30, 1971, and the Agreement between the Government of the United States of America and the Government of the Union of Soviet Socialist Republics on the Prevention of Incidents on and over the High Seas of May 25, 1972,

Have agreed as follows:

Article 1

Each Party shall establish, in its capital, a national Nuclear Risk Reduction Center that shall operate on behalf of and under the control of its respective Government.

Article 2

The Parties shall use the Nuclear Risk Reduction Centers to transmit notifications identified in Protocol I which constitutes an integral part of this Agreement.

In the future, the list of notifications transmitted through the Centers may be altered by agreement between the Parties, as relevant new agreements are reached.

Article 3

The Parties shall establish a special facsimile communications link between their national Nuclear Risk Reduction Centers in accordance with Protocol II which constitutes an integral part of this Agreement.

Article 4

The Parties shall staff their national Nuclear Risk Reduction Centers as they deem appropriate, so as to ensure their normal functioning.

Article 5

The Parties shall hold regular meetings between representatives of the Nuclear Risk Reduction Centers at least once each year to consider matters related to the functioning of such Centers.

Article 6

This agreement shall not affect the obligations of either Party under other agreements.

Article 7

This agreement shall enter into force on the date of its signature.

The duration of this Agreement shall not be limited.

This Agreement may be terminated by either Party upon 12 months written notice to the other Party.

Done at Washington on September 15, 1987, in two copies, each in the English and Russian languages, both texts being equally authentic.

George P. Shultz
For the United States of America

Eduard A. Shevardnadze
For the Union of Soviet Socialist Republics

PROTOCOL I

Pursuant to the provisions and in implementation of the Agreement between the United States of America and the Union of Soviet Socialist Republics on the Establishment of Nuclear Risk Reduction Centers, the Parties have agreed as follows:

Article 1

The Parties shall transmit the following types of notifications through the Nuclear Risk Reduction Centers:

(a) notifications of ballistic missile launches under Article 4 of the Agreement on Measures to Reduce the Risk of Outbreak of Nuclear War between the United States of America and the Union of Soviet Socialist Republics of September 30, 1971;

(b) notifications of ballistic missile launches under paragraph 1 of Article VI of the Agreement between the Government of the United States of America and the Government of the Union of Soviet Socialist Republics on the Prevention of Incidents on and over the High Seas of May 25, 1972.

Article 2

The scope and format of the information to be transmitted through the Nuclear Risk Reduction Centers shall be agreed upon.

Article 3

Each Party also may, at its own discretion as a display of good will and with a view to building confidence, transmit through the Nuclear Risk Reduction Centers communications other than those provided for under Article 1 of this Protocol.

Article 4

Unless the Parties agree otherwise, all communications transmitted through and communications procedures of the Nuclear Risk Reduction Centers' communication link will be confidential.

Article 5

This Protocol shall enter into force on the date of its signature and shall remain in force as long as the Agreement between the United States of America and Union of Soviet Socialist Republics on the Establishment of Nuclear Risk Reduction Centers of September 15, 1987, remains in force.

PROTOCOL II

Pursuant to the provisions and in implementation of the Agreement between the United States of America and the Union of Soviet Socialist Republics on the Establishment of Nuclear Risk Reduction Centers, the Parties have agreed as follows:

Article 1

To establish and maintain for the purpose of providing direct facsimile communications between their national Nuclear Risk Reduction Centers, established in accordance with Article 1 of this Agreement, hereinafter referred to as the National Centers, an Intelsat satellite circuit and a Statsionar satellite circuit, each with a secure orderwire communication capability for operational monitoring. In this regard:

(a) There shall be terminals equipped for communication between the National Centers;

(b) Each Party shall provide communication circuits capable of simultaneously transmitting and receiving 4800 bits per second;

(c) Communication shall begin with test operation of the Intelsat satellite circuit, as soon as purchase, delivery and installation of the necessary equipment by the Parties are completed. Thereafter, taking into account the results of test operations, the Parties shall agree on the transition to a fully operational status;

(d) To the extent practicable, test operation of the Statsionar satellite circuit shall begin simultaneously with test operation of the Intelsat satellite circuit. Taking into account the results of test operations, the Parties shall agree on the transition to a fully operational status.

Article 2

To employ agreed-upon information security devices to assure secure transmission of facsimile messages. In this regard:

(a) The information security devices shall consist of microprocessors that will combine the digital message output with buffered random data read from standard 5 1/4 inch floppy disks;

(b) Each Party shall provide, through its embassy, necessary keying material to the other.

Article 3

To establish and maintain at each operating end of the two circuits, facsimile terminals of the same make and model. In this regard:

(a) Each Party shall be responsible for the purchase, installation, operation and maintenance of its own terminals, the related information security devices, and local transmission circuit appropriate to the implementation of this protocol;

(b) A group 3 facsimile unit which meets CCITT recommendations T.4 and T.30 and operates at 4800 bits per second shall be used;

(c) Direct facsimile messages from the USSR National Center to the U.S. National Center shall be transmitted and received in the Russian language, and from the U.S. National Center to the USSR National Center in the English language;

(d) Transmission and operation procedures shall be in conformity with procedures employed on the direct communication link and adapted as necessary for the purpose of communications between the National Centers.

Article 4

To establish and maintain a secure orderwire communication capability necessary to coordinate facsimile operation. In this regard:

(a) The orderwire terminals used with the information security devices described in paragraph (a) of Article 2 shall incorporate standard USSR cyrillic and United States latin keyboards and cathode ray tube displays to permit the exchange of messages between operators. The specific layout of the cyrillic keyboard shall be as specified by the Soviet side;

(b) To coordinate the work of operators, the orderwire shall be configured so as to permit, prior to the transmission and reception of messages, the exchange of all information pertinent to the coordination of such messages;

(c) Orderwire messages concerning transmissions shall be encoded using the same information security devices specified in paragraph (a) of Article 2;

(d) The orderwire shall use the same modem and communication link as used for facsimile messages transmission;

(e) A printer shall be included to provide a record copy of all information exchanged on the orderwire.

Article 5

To use the same type of equipment and the same maintenance procedures as currently in use for the direct communication link for the establishment of direct facsimile communications between the National Centers. The equipment, security devices, and spare parts necessary for telecommunication links and the orderwire shall be provided by the United States side to the Soviet side in return for payment of costs thereof by the Soviet side.

Article 6

To ensure the exchange of information necessary for the operation and maintenance of the telecommunication system and equipment configuration.

Article 7

To take all possible measures to assure the continuous, secure and reliable operation of the equipment and communication link, including the orderwire, for which each Party is responsible in accordance with this Protocol.

Article 8

To determine, by mutual agreement between technical experts of the Parties, the distribution and calculation of expenses for putting into operation the communication link, its maintenance and further development.

Article 9

To convene meetings of technical experts of the Parties in order to consider initially questions pertaining to the practical implementation of the activities provided for in this Protocol and, thereafter, by mutual agreement and as necessary for the purpose of improving telecommunications and information technology in order to achieve the mutually agreed functions of the National Centers.

Article 10

This Protocol shall enter into force on the date of its signature and shall remain in force as long as the Agreement between the United States of America and the Union of Soviet Socialist Republics on the Establishment of Nuclear Risk Reduction Centers of September 15, 1987, remains in force.

APPENDIX B: EXCERPTS FROM JOINT U.S.-SOVIET SUMMIT DECLARATION

Following are excerpts from the joint United States – Soviet statement on the summit talks.[1]

I. Arms Control

Nuclear and Space Talks

The President and the General Secretary discussed the negotiations on reductions in strategic offensive arms. They noted the considerable progress which has been made toward conclusion of a treaty implementing the principle of 50-percent reductions. They agreed to instruct their negotiators in Geneva to work toward the completion of the Treaty on the Reduction and Limitation of Strategic Offensive Arms and all integral documents at the earliest possible date, preferably in time for signature of the treaty during the next meeting of leaders of state in the first half of 1988. Recognizing that areas of agreement and disagreement are recorded in detail in the Joint Draft Treaty Text, they agreed to instruct their negotiators to accelerate resolution of issues within the Joint Draft Treaty Text including early agreement on provisions for effective verification.

In so doing, the negotiators should build upon the agreements on 50-percent reductions achieved at Reykjavik as subsequently developed and now reflected in the agreed portions of the Joint Draft Start Treaty Text being developed in Geneva, including

– agreement on ceilings of no more than 1,600 strategic offensive delivery systems, 6,000 warheads, 1,540 warheads on 154 heavy missiles;

1 *New York Times*, December 12, 1987.

– the agreed rule of account for heavy bombers and their nuclear armament;

– an agreement that as a result of the reductions the aggregate throw-weight of the Soviet Union's ICBM's and SLBM's will be reduced to a level approximately 50 percent below the existing level, and this level will not be exceeded by either side. Such an agreement will be recorded in a mutually satisfactory manner.

As priority tasks, they should focus on the following issues:

(a) The additional steps necessary to insure that the reductions enhance strategic stability. This will include a ceiling of 4,900 on the aggregate number of ICBM plus SLBM warheads within the 6,000 total.

(b) The counting rules governing the number of long-range, nuclear-armed air-launched cruise missiles (ALCM's) to be attributed to each type of heavy bomber. The delegations shall define concrete rules in this area.

(c) The counting rules with respect to existing ballistic missiles. The sides proceed from the assumption that existing types of ballistic missiles are deployed with the following numbers of warheads. In the United States: Peacekeeper (MX): 10, Minuteman III: 3, Minuteman II: 1, Trident I: 8, Trident II: 8, Poseidon: 10. In the Soviet Union: SS-17: 4, SS-19: 6, SS-18: 10, SS-24: 10, SS-25: 1, SS-11: 1, SS-13: 1, SS-N-6: 1, SS-N-8: 1, SS-N-17: 1, SS-N-18: 7, SS-N-20: 10 and SS-N-23: 4.

Procedures will be developed that enable verification of the number of warheads on deployed ballistic missiles of each specific type. In the event either side changes the number of warheads declared for a type of deployed ballistic missile, the sides shall notify each other in advance. There shall also be agreement on how to account for warheads on future types of ballistic missiles covered by the Treaty on the Reduction and Limitation of Strategic Offensive Arms.

(d) The sides shall find a mutually acceptable solution to the question of limiting the deployment of long-range, nuclear-armed SLCM's. Such limitations will not involve counting long-range, nuclear-armed SLCM's within the 6,000 warhead and 1,600 strategic offensive delivery systems limits. The sides committed themselves to establish ceilings on such missiles, and to seek mutually acceptable and effective methods of verification of such limitations, which could include the employment of National Technical Means, co-operative measures and on-site inspection.

(e) Building upon the provisions of the Treaty on the Elimination of Their Intermediate-Range and Shorter-Range Missiles, the measures by which the provisions of the Treaty on the Reduction and Limitation of Strategic Offensive Arms, can be verified will, at a minimum, include:

1. Data exchanges, to include declarations by each side of the number and location of weapon systems limited by the Treaty and of facilities at which such systems are located and appropriate notifications. These facilities will include locations and facilities for production and final assembly, storage, testing and deployment of systems covered by this Treaty. Such declarations will be exchanged between the sides before the Treaty is signed and updated periodically after entry into force.

2. Baseline inspection to verify the accuracy of these declarations promptly after entry into force of the Treaty.

3. On-site observation of the elimination of strategic systems necessary to achieve the agreed limits.

4. Continuous on-site monitoring of the perimeter and portals of critical production and support facilities to confirm the output of these facilities.

5. Short-notice on-site inspection of:

(i) declared locations during the process of reducing to agreed limits;

(ii) locations where systems covered by this Treaty remain after achieving the agreed limits; and

(iii) locations where such systems have been located (formerly declared facilities).

6. The right to implement, in accordance with agreed-upon procedures, short-notice inspections at locations where either side considers covert deployment, production, storage or repair of strategic offensive arms could be occurring.

7. Provisions prohibiting the use of concealment or other activities which impede verification by national technical means. Such

provisions would include a ban on telemetry encryption and would allow for full access to all telemetric information broadcast during missile flight.

8. Measures designed to enhance observation of activities related to reduction and limitation of strategic offensive arms by National Technical Means. These would include open displays of treaty-limited items at missile bases, bomber bases, and submarine ports at locations and times chosen by the inspecting party.

Taking into account the prepraration of the Treaty on Strategic Offensive Arms, the leaders of the two countries also instructed their delegations in Geneva to work out an agreement that would commit the sides to observe the ABM Treaty, as signed in 1972, while conducting their research, development, and testing as required, which are permitted by the ABM Treaty, and not to withdraw from the ABM Treaty, for a specified period of time. Intensive discussions of strategic stability shall begin not later than three years before the end of the specified period, after which, in the event the sides have not agreed otherwise, each side will be free to decide its course of action. Such an agreement must have the same legal status as the Treaty on Strategic Offensive Arms, the ABM Treaty, and other similar, legally binding agreements. This agreement will be recorded in a mutually satisfactory manner. Therefore, they direct their delegations to address these issues on a priority basis.

The sides shall discuss ways to ensure predictability in the development of the U.S.-Soviet strategic relationship under conditions of strategic stability, to reduce the risk of nuclear war.

Chemical Weapons

The leaders expressed their commitment to negotiation of a verificable, comprehensive and effective international convention on the prohibition and destruction of chemical weapons. They wellcomed progress to date and reaffirmed the need for intensified negotiations toward conclusion of a truly global and verifiable convention encompassing all chemical weapons-capable states. The United States and Soviet Union are in favor of greater openness and intensified confidence-building with respect to chemical weapons both on a bilateral and a multilateral basis. They agreed to continue periodic discussions by experts on the growing problem of chemical weapons proliferation and use.

Conventional Forces

The President and the General Secretary discussed the importance of the task of reducing the level of military confrontation in Europe in the area of armed forces and conventional armaments. The two leaders spoke in favor of early completion of the work in Vienna on the mandate for negotiations on this issue, so that substantive negotiations may be started at the earliest time with a view to elaboration of concrete measures. They also noted that the implementation of the provisions of the Stockholm Conference on Confidence- and Security-Building Measures and Disarmament in Europe is an important factor in strengthening mutual understanding and enhancing stability, and spoke in favor of continuing and consolidating this process. The President and the General Secretary agreed to instruct their appropriate representatives to intensify efforts to achieve solutions to outstanding issues.

They also discussed the Vienna (Mutual and Balanced Force Reduction) negotiations.

Follow-Up Meeting of the Conference on Security and Cooperation in Europe

They expressed their determination, together with the other 33 participants in the Conference on Security and Cooperation in Europe, to bring the Vienna C.S.C.E. Follow-Up Conference to a successful conclusion, based on balanced progress in all principal areas of the Helsinki Final Act and Madrid Concluding Document.

II. Human Rights and Humanitarian Concerns

The leaders held a thorough and candid discussion of human rights and humanitarian questions and their place in the U.S.-Soviet dialogue.

III. Regional Issues

The President and the General Secretary engaged in a wide-ranging, frank and businesslike discussion of regional questions, including Afghanistan, the Iran-Iraq War, the Middle East, Cambodia, southern Africa, Central America and other issues. They acknowledged serious differences but agreed on the importance of their regular exchange of views. The two leaders noted the increasing importance of settling regional conflicts to reduce international tensions and to improve East-West relations. They agreed that the goal of the dialogue between the United States and the Soviet Union on these issues should be to help the parties to regional conflicts find peaceful solutions that advance their independence, freedom and securiceful solutions that emphasized the importance of enhancing the capacity of the United Nations and other international institutions to contribute to the resolution of regional conflicts.

It remains to be seen whether there can be such a thing as *Marxist-Leninist* game theory.

Thomas W. Robinson

APPENDIX C: GAME THEORY AND SOVIET NUCLEAR STRATEGY

Strategic thinkers in the West have been greatly influenced by their formulation of doctrine by game theory and its mathematical calculations. Game theorists base models on the belief that decisions are derived from utility-maximizing choices which are objectively neutral. A noted example is the "prisoner's dilemma." It stresses interdependent choice in many social and political situations. The basic story of the dilemma is told by Bruce Russet and Harvey Starr.[1]

Two people are arrested on suspicion after an armed robbery and murder have been committed. They are kept in separate cells with no chance to communicate with each other. Each person "is presented with a pair of unattractive options, as each is questioned separately and given this choice by the police official: 'I'm pretty sure that you two were responsible for the killing, but I don't have quite enough evidence to prove it. If you will confess first and testify against the other prisoner, I will see that you are set free without any penalty, though he will be sentenced to life imprisonment. On the other hand, I am making the same proposal to him, so if he confesses first you will be the one to spend life in prison and he will go free. If you both confess on the same day we will have a little mercy, but you still will be badly off because you both will then be sentenced to 20 years in prison for armed robbery. Should you

1 See Bruce Russet *et al.*, *World Politics: The Menu for Choice* (San Francisco: W.H. Freeman & Co., 1981), pp. 337-38.

both be stubborn, we cannot convict you for a major crime, and I can only punish you for a small crime in your past life, carrying a one-year prison term. If you want to take a chance that your fellow prisoner will keep quiet, therefore, go ahead. But if he doesn't – and you know what sort of criminal he is – you will do very badly. Think it over.'"

What will the prisoners do? On the face of things, it seems that it would serve the interests of both prisoners to remain silent. However, there is a great deal of uncertainty. One prisoner worries that the other might feel compelled to talk, since it would be to his advantage to do so. If under such conditions Prisoner A does not talk, A serves a full jail sentence. Prisoner B is, of course, contemplating similar thoughts about the possible actions of Prisoner A. Thus, both prisoners will talk and both will serve 20-years sentences, even though both would have been better off keeping quiet.

Importantly, according to game theory, both prisoners would be completely rational if they did talk. Both have to assume that the other prisoner will make his best move. Thus, each prisoner has to act in the way that would be best for himself *given the best move of the other prisoner*. This is the essence of game theory: Discover the best strategy for your adversary and act accordingly. While such a strategy may not obtain for you the maximum gain, it will prevent you from incurring the maximum loss.

The "prisoner's dilemma" turned out to be the perfect intellectual rationale for the "cold war." For instance, it was possible to apply the dilemma to the Soviet-American arms race. One only had to substitute "build more" for "talk" and "stop building" for "silence." It made sense for both sides to stop building, but neither superpower could have the confidence to agree to a treaty to stop building arms because it suspected that the other might cheat, build more and go on to victory. In this way, distrust and the fostering of international tensions could be elevated to the status of an intellectual exercise, a mathematical axiom.

One of the main problems with deterrent strategies based on such game-theoretical assumptions is that they presume simultaneous choice. Thus, game theory fails to capture the dynamic nature of international relations. World events do not simply occur in a historical vacuum. Rather, they take place in a highly complex context of action and reaction, much of which is difficult to explain without fuller information than often is initially the case.[2]

In this context, it may be useful to recall the warning offered by William H. Riker and Peter C. Ordeshook:[3]

Political scientists too often take examples (as well as the theorems of game theory) as fully operating models of real political processes. Thus, we read such sentences as "let China be the first decision maker with strategies a_1 *and* a_2*, and let ..." But it is absurd to believe that any complex process can be so simply modeled, just as it is absurd to suppose that the design of an efficient gas turbine resides somewhere as a deduction from the basic laws of thermodynamics.*

This warning should not be misunderstood as a bar to inquiry based on mathematical theory. But one can not afford to overlook the very real and serious limitations of this theory when applied to real-life situations in international politics, particularly the crucial matter of nuclear deterrence.

There are many problems with applying game theoretical models to Soviet-American relations, but no doubt the greatest problems with this analysis is the growing body of literature which suggests that the Soviets are extremely skeptical of this approach. Perhaps one of the best studies on the Soviet views on the application of game-theoretical propositions to international relations is the investigation undertaken in the late 1960s by Thomas W. Robinson.[4]

Robinson notes in his essay that the Soviets in 1966 published

2 Many deterrence theorists maintain that the exact relationship between game theory and deterrence theory is frequently misunderstood. Albert Wohlstetter, for instance, has managed at one and the same time to insist both that deterrence theorists have not, as charged, made much use of game theory, and that it has been very useful to them. His argument reminds one critic of the apocryphal defense attorney's opening address to the jury: "Ladies and Gentlemen of the jury, the defense will prove that my client never saw this woman before; that in any event he did not attack her but she consented; and that furthermore he was temporarily deranged while under the influence of alcohol and thus unable to tell right from wrong or know the nature and consequences of his acts." Phillip Greene, *Deadly Logic: The Theory of Nuclear Deterrence* (Columbus: Ohio State University, 1966), p. 93. Greene argues that misunderstanding has often been the fault of deterrence theorists rather than of their critics and the general public.

3 William H. Riker and Peter C. Ordeshook, *An Introduction to Positive Theory* (Englewood Cliffs, N.J.: Prentice-Hall, 1973), p. 239.

4 Thomas Robinson, "Game Theory and Politics: Recent Soviet Views," *Studies in Soviet Thought*, Vol. 10 (1970), p. 291-315.

two articles, which for the first time, outlined Soviet views on the subject in Soviet periodicals.[5] The fact that the Soviets waited so long to address this important topic – more than a decade after the first American publication on game theory and international relations – raises serious questions about the Soviet attitude toward the use of game theory in international politics.

Generally, the Soviets view game theory with suspicion because of its Western origins. Thus, they spend much of their time criticizing what they tend to regard as its inherent defects. Furthermore, they seem reluctant to study the subject in depth out of fear that the objective features of game theory might lead them to unpalatable ideological conclusions – in both theory and application.

One Soviet author, G. Gerasimov, tries to show how "the American militarists and their civilian hangers-on" have turned game theory, a mathematically precise method of determining rational strategies in the face of critical uncertainties, into a tool for their own selfish political purpose.[6] Gerasimov labels as pernicious the kind of "zero-sum thinking" (i.e., whatever I gain, you must lose) that is taken from game theory and applied to international politics. According to this writer, the American militarists have eagerly latched onto the zero-sum model as scientific proof to support their arguments about the Cold War. Gerasimov, in his attacks on Thomas Schelling, the leading American game theorist in international relations, is careful to point out that many aspects of international politics are better seen as *non*-zero-sum games, which involve a mixture of competition and tacit cooperation (e.g., international law and peaceful coexistence).

Gerasimov offers this advice to his Soviet readers. Despite its abuse by American strategic thinkers, game theory still can be used

5 One should not conclude from this statement that the Soviets had never before studied game theory. For a number of years before 1966 they were actively engaged in translating Western-language classics in the field. At the same time they even contributed to the theoretical literature. For an example of the former see the three volumes edited by N.N. Vorob'ev *et al.*, *Matrix Games, Infinite Antagonistic Games and Positional Games* (Moscow: Physics-Mathematics Publishing House, 1961, 1963 and 1967). For an example of Russian game theory, see Kiyoshi Takeuchi *et al.* (transl.) *Selected Russian Papers on Game Theory, 1959-1965* (Princeton: Princeton University Econometric Research Program, 1968).

6 G. Gerasimov, "Theory of Games and International Relations," *Mirovaja ekonomika i mezdunarodyne otnosenija,* No. 7 (1966), pp.101-108.

in analyzing international affairs. But it must be placed in the safer hands of the Russians themselves. In this connection, he warns: do not be overenamored with the simplicity of the zero-sum approach. Do not try to apply game theory to all aspects of international politics. Do not waste much time with the two-person model; instead investigate several-person games. Be aware of the problems of defining the value of the game in international affairs. Finally, and most importantly, be sure to understand that models, while necessary, are merely abstractions which may not accurately reflect international realities.

In another article, Gerasimov advises his Soviet readers to avoid two basic temptations in applying game theory to politics. One is the belief that proper game theory requires a pay-off matrix (i.e., quantitative valuations must be attached to utility preferences of the players). In international politics, he points out, either such values are impossible to obtain, as in nuclear war, or they lie outside the framework of the theory of games. Thus, game theory cannot be used for nuclear war calculations. Such analogies as "nuclear chicken" have no place in international politics.[7]

Another Soviet writer emphasizes some of the methodological problems connected with the theory of games.[8] N.N. Vorob'ev warns that social reality is much too complex to be represented with complete accuracy by games. For instance, even such a seemingly simple task as identifying the players frequently presents a difficult obstacle in applying game theory. This is certainly not the case for traditional Marxist theorists who have little trouble with the identification of antagonistic classes: one has only to look at who possesses the means of production.

Vorob'ev has great difficulty with the "randomness" of game theory. For randomness is hardly an acceptable quality to Marxist-Leninists, particularly in helping them to make correct political-social decisions. It is intolerable for Marxist-Leninists to accept, as game theory does, that one's own strategy and objectives are as dependent upon the goals and strategies of the adversary as they are on one's own.

7 G.I. Gerasimov, "Game Theory in the Service of American Militarist," *Problemy vojny i mira,* June 25, 1967, pp.244-61.

8 See N.N. Vorob'ev, "Some Methodological Problems of the Theory of Games," *Voprosy filosofii,* No. 1 (1966), pp.93-103.

Another Soviet writer, L.A. Petrovskaja, attempts to come to grips with Thomas Schelling's classic work, *The Strategy of Conflict.*[9] Although this article is more positive in tone, it still represents a critical view of some of Schelling's key ideas. The Soviet author, for instance, asserts that Schelling stresses too heavily the role of nuclear blackmail, policies of strength, the virtue of unanswerable threats and the political uses of new weapons systems. Interestingly, Petrovskaja argues that Schelling is not so much to blame for these errors as his "bourgeois masters." In order to attract their attention, he must make "incorrect use of a theory which itself is correct."

Other Soviet writers tend to take more of a negative view of the theory of games as applied to international politics. They allege that game theory does not distinguish between the tactical and strategic thoughts of the players. Moreover, it improperly presumes complete knowledge on the part of the players. Finally, game theorists define the utility function either *a priori* or without knowledge that it exists in real life.

In short, U.S. nuclear deterrent strategies that rest on game theoretical assumptions are not accepted in the same way (if at all) by the Soviets whom American officials hope to influence. Most Soviet writers on the subject, with their Marxist-Leninist background, have trouble accepting the claim by Western strategic thinkers that game theory is "ideologically neutral." As Thomas W. Robinson observes in his perceptive study of Soviet views on the subject: "It remains to be seen whether there can be such a thing as *Marxist-Leninist* game theory."

9 L.A. Petrovskaja, "On a Militaristic Conception of International Conflict," *Naucnye doklady vyssej skoly filosofskie nauki,* No. 3 (1968), pp. 94-103.

APPENDIX D: A NEW SOVIET MILITARY DOCTRINE?[1]

The excerpts below are from "Our Military Doctrine in the Light of New Political Thinking," an article by Rear Admiral G. Kostev, published in *Kommunist Vooruzhennykh Sil* (Communist of the Armed Forces), No. 17, September 1987.

Kostev spells out the principles said to underlie the new military doctrine adopted by the Warsaw Pact in May 1987.

"At the meeting of the Political Consultative Committee held in Berlin on May 29, 1987, the member states of the Warsaw Pact adopted a military doctrine. It attracted a great deal of attention on the part of the world's public ... The document signed in Berlin is an example of the expression of new political thinking in the nuclear-missile age – it reflects a recognition of the fatal consequences of further increases in nuclear arsenals, the buildup of opposing military forces, the intensification of international tension and hostility, and the need to overcome suspicion and distrust. Comrade M.S. Gorbachev emphasizes that 'the members of the Warsaw Pact have clearly spelled out their military doctrine, whose aim is to prevent war – be it nuclear or conventional – and is oriented on maintaining reasonable sufficiency in the size and character of armaments and armed forces intended solely for defensive purposes.

"The public spelling out of the military doctrine by the socialist countries reflects the defensive nature of socialism's military strategy ... In the interest of strengthening mutual trust and deepening the understanding of the aims and intentions of the opposing military-political alliances, they (the Warsaw Pact states) call for a meeting of military experts of the Warsaw Pact and NATO in order to examine

1 Translation prepared by Leon Goure in *The Strategic Review*, (Fall, 1987), pp.85-87.

objectively and without prejudice and elucidate for each other the content and purposes of their military doctrines, to compare them and to jointly clarify their concepts ...

"In response to the initiative of the USSR to liquidate nuclear weapons and to the proposal of the Warsaw Pact to the effect that the military concepts and doctrines of the military blocs and their members be based on defensive principles, the aggressive circles in the United States and other NATO countries continue their preparations for war. The United States intends to place nuclear weapons in outer space, to greatly increase its strategic offensive potential by the early 1990s.

"As long as international reaction whips up the arms race, as long as it (the United States) has not given up its policy of social "revanche" and "crusade" against socialism the CPSU and the fraternal parties will do everything that is necessary to maintain the defense might of our country and of the socialist fraternity at the appropriate level. The Party and the people objectively assess the true state of affairs, and consider the defense of the socialist fatherland and the insurance of its security to be some of the most important functions of the Soviet state ... The defensive character of our military doctrine is reflected in the following fundamental principles:

- "The Soviet Union will never, under any circumstances, initiate military actions against any state or alliance of states if it does not itself become the target of armed aggression ...
- "The Soviet Union has no territorial claims against any state in or outside Europe; it has no need to expand its state borders. But in the event that it is subjected to attack, the aggressor will receive a devastating rebuff. Our people will defend themselves with utter determination.
- "The Soviet Union will equally defend itself and any socialist state member of the Pact ...

"In view of the fact that the Soviet Union and other states of the Warsaw Pact are forced to maintain armed forces capable of rebuffing any attack from outside, the military side of our doctrine includes questions of perfecting the Army and Navy, and of maintaining their combat readiness at such a level as to prevent our being caught unawares. The most important of these question are: the main direction of preparations by the Soviet Army and Navy, their technical equipment and organizational structure, the preparation for them of highly qualified cadres, demands for (high) combat skill on the part of the troops, and the instilling in the personnel of a spirit of high vigilance and constant readiness to repel aggression.

"The defensive direction of our military doctrine ... in no way signifies that our actions will be of a passive character ...

"The present state of development of Soviet military doctrine has come about in the 1980s. By that time, the two leading nuclear powers – the USSR and the United States – had accumulated an enormous nuclear might. In addition, several other states have created stocks of nuclear weapons and were perfecting them. This is the principal peculiarity of the present epoch, which gives rise to new views in the socialist countries about the character of a future war and which differs fundamentally from those held in the 1940s and 1950s ...

... The organic interconnection of the struggle for the survival of mankind and of measures to strengthen national security, as well as the increased role of the military-technological aspects in war, persistently dictate the necessity for new political thinking.

Military doctrine shapes the development of military science. Consequently, the changes introduced into our doctrine, in conjunction with new political thinking, objectively require clarification of the theory of military art which has presently been enriched by a number of new principles.

"First, the Soviet Union will not be the first to employ nuclear weapons and will never use them against countries which do not have them on their territory ...

The commitment not to be the first to use nuclear weapons is not simply an empty declaration, but an immutable demand placed on our military construction. It is put into practice in the training of commanders, staffs and troops, in the organization of the strictest control which ensures that there will be no unsanctioned use of nuclear weapons, in the raising of the combat readiness of the troops to rebuff aggression, of command, control and communications, and in the raising of the political-moral attitude of the service personnel.

"Second, at the foundation of our program of construction of the Armed Forces lies the principle of sufficiency for defense. It means that the composition of the troops and fleets and the quantity and quality of the means of armed struggle are strictly commensurate with the level of the military threat, the character and intensity of imperialism's military preparations ... Reasonable sufficiency for defense is determined by the need to insure that a nuclear attack in any, even the most unfavorable conditions, will not remain unpunished, and also by the existing military-strategic parity, which remains the decisive factor for the prevention of war ...

"Third, the content of the Soviet military doctrine has changed the following principle: if (war) is unleashed by the imperalists, (it) will inevitably have the character of a nuclear-missile war – that is, a war in which the main means of destruction will be nuclear weapons and the main means of delivery to their targets will be missiles. Today, this principle is not appropriate for the real situation. The extraordinary danger of nuclear war is understood by the United States and NATO to a certain degree. Consequently, while not giving up the "from a position of strength" policy, in their "flexible response" strategy they make active preparations to conduct not only nuclear but also a protracted conventional war. In so doing, (conventional) weapons are being created which in their characteristics (i.e., effectiveness) are almost indistinguishable from small-yield nuclear weapons. From this there follows the need for all-around preparation of our country for armed defense with the use not only of nuclear, but also highly effective conventional weapons. The task is to ensure that we will not find ourselves weaker than the probable enemy.

"Fourth, ... of extreme importance is the maintenance of military-strategic parity by means of strengthening the Soviet Armed Forces, which devalues attempts by imperialism to disrupt the balance of forces. In this connection, of great significance is the preparation of the Army and Navy for war amid conditions where the enemy possesses weapons of gigantic power. This concerns not only the perfecting of weapons and combat equipment, but also the activization of the human factor, the decisive raising of command skills of the officers and the special training of the personnel."

List of Abbreviations

ABM	Antiballistic Missile
ALCM	Air Launched Cruise Missile
ASAT	Antisatellite Weapons System
BMD	Ballistic Missile Defense
C^3I	Command, Control, Communications and Intelligence
CD	Civil Defense
CEP	Circular Error Probable
CIA	Central Intelligence Agency
DIA	Defense Intelligence Agency
DOD	Department of Defense
EMP	Electromagnetic Pulse
FBS	Forward Based Systems
GAO	Government Accounting Office
GKO	State Committee of Defense
GNP	Gross National Product
GLCM	Ground Launched Cruise Missile
ICBM	Intercontinental Ballistic Missile
IRBM	Intermediate Range Ballistic Missile
KGB	Committee on State Security
LOW	Launch on Warning
LPARS	Large Phased-Array Radars
LRINF	Long Range Intermediate Range Nuclear Forces

MAD	Mutual Assured Destruction
MARV	Maneuverable Re-Entry Vehicle
MBFR	Mutual and Balanced Forces Reduction
MIRV	Multiple Independently Targeted Re-Entry Vehicle
MOD	Ministry of Defense
MX	Missile Experimental
NATO	North Atlantic Treaty Organization
NCA	National Command Authority
PVO	Air Defense Forces
SAC	Strategic Air Command
SALT	Strategic Arms Limitation Talks
SAM	Surface to Air Missile
SDI	Strategic Defense Initiative
SDIO	Strategic Defense Initiative Organization
SRF	Strategic Rocket Forces
Stavka	General Headquarters of the Supreme High Command
TVD	Theater of Military Operations
UN	United Nations
VGK	Supreme High Command

SELECT BIBLIOGRAPHY

Official Publications

Director of Central Intelligence. *Soviet Civil Defense.* Washington, D.C.: CIA, 1978.

U.S. Arms Control and Disarmament Agency. *Arms Control and Disarmament Agreements.* Washington, D.C.: Government Printing Office, 1982.

U.S. Arms Control and Disarmament Agency. *Fiscal Year 1980 Arms Control Impact Statements.* Washington, D.C.: Government Printing Office, 1979.

U.S. Arms Control and Disarmament Agency. *Fiscal Year 1986 Arms Control Impact Statements.* Washington, D.C.: Government Printing Office, 1985.

U.S. Congress. *Allocation of Resources in the Soviet Union and China – 1978.* Hearings before the Subcommittee on Priorities and Economy in Government of the Joint Economic Committee, 95th Congress, 2nd Session. Washington, D.C.: Government Printing Office, 1978.

U.S. Congress. *Allocation of Resources in the Soviet Union and China – 1983.* Hearings before the Subcommittee on International Trade, Finance and Security Economics of the Joint Economic Committee, 98th Congress, 1st Session. Washington, D.C.: Government Printing Office, 1984.

U.S. Congress. *Fiscal Year 1972 Authorization for Military Procurement, Research and Development, Construction and Real Estate Acquisition for the Safeguard ABM, and Reserve Strengths.* Hearings before the Senate Armed Services Committee, 92nd Congress, 1st Session. Washington, D.C.: Government Printing Office, 1971.

U.S. Congress. *Hearings on the Scope, Magnitude, and Implications of the United States Antiballistic Missile Program, November 6 and 7, 1967.* Subcommittee on Military Applications, Joint Committee on Atomic Energy. Washington, D.C.: Government Printing Office, 1968.

U.S. Congress. *Hearings before the Subcommittee on Strategic Arms Limitations Talks.* U.S. Senate, Armed Services Committee. Washington, D.C.: Government Printing Office, 1970.

U.S. Congress. *Military Implications of the Treaty on the Limitation of Strategic Offensive Arms and Protocol Thereto.* Hearings before the Committee on Armed Services, 96th Congress, 1st Session. Washington, D.C.: Government Printing Office, 1979.

U.S. Defense Intelligence Agency, *Handbook on Soviet Armed Forces.* DIA, 1978.

U.S. Department of Defense. *Annual Report, Fiscal Year 1981.* Washington, D.C.: Government Printing Office, 1980.

U.S. Department of Defense. *Annual Report, Fiscal Year 1982.* Washington, D.C.: Government Printing Office, 1982.

U.S. Department of Defense. *Annual Report to Congress, FY 1984.* Washington, D.C.: Government Printing Office, 1983.

U.S. Department of Defense. *Soviet Military Power.* Washington, D.C.: Government Printing Office, 1985.

U.S. Department of Defense. *Soviet Military Power.* Washington, D.C.: Government Printing Office, 1986.

U.S. Department of Defense. *Soviet Strategic Defense Programs.* Washington, D.C.: Government Printing Office, 1985.

U.S. Department of Defense. *United States Military Posture for FY 1979.* Washington, D.C.: Office of the Joint Chiefs of Staff, 1978.

U.S. Department of State. *Foreign Relations of the United States, 1950; National Security Affairs; Foreign Economic Policy.* Vol. I. 82nd Congress, 1st Session. Washington, D.C.: Government Printing Office, 1977.

U.S.S.R. Ministry of Defense. *Whence the Threat to Peace.* Moscow: Voyenizdat, 1982.

U.S. Office of Technology Assessment. *The Effects of the Nuclear War.* Washington, D.C.: Government Printing Office, 1979.

U.S. Senate. *Department of Defense Appropriations Fiscal Year 1980.* Washington, D.C.: Government Printing Office, 1981.

Encyclopedias and Dictionaries

Sovyetskaya Voennaya Entsiklopedia. Vol. 3. Moscow: Voenizdat, 1977.

Slovar' Osnovnykh Voyennykh Terminov. Moscow: Voenizdat, 1965.

Articles

Ackley, Richard T. "What's Left of SALT?" *Naval War College Review* (May-June, 1974).

Akhromeyev, Sergei F. "Dangerous US Aspirations to Nuclear Supremacy," *Horizont,* No. 3 (January, 1980).

Alexander, Arthur. "Decisionmaking in Soviet Weapons Procurement," *Adelphi Papers Nos. 147-48* (London: International Institute for Strategic Studies, 1978).

Arbatov, G.A. "The Impasses of the Policy of Force," *Problemy Mira i Sotsializma,* No. 2 (February, 1974).

Arkin, William M. *et al.* "The Soviet Nuclear Stockpile," *Arms Control Today* (June, 1984).

Arnett, Robert L. "Soviet Attitudes Towards Nuclear War: Do They Really Think They Can Win?," *Journal of Strategic Studies,* Vol. 2, No. 2 (1979).

Ball, Desmond. "Research Note: Soviet ICBM Deployment," *Survival* (July-August, 1980).

Ball, Desmond. "Soviet Strategic Planning and the Control of Nuclear War," in Roman Kolkowitz *et al.* (eds.), *The Soviet Calculus of Nuclear War* (Massachusetts: Lexington Books, 1986).

Bellany, Ian. "Sea Power and the Soviet Submarine Forces," *Survival,* Vol. 24, Nos. 1-2 (January-April, 1982).

Bellany, Ian. "Strategic Arms Competition and the Logistic Curve," *Survival* (September-October, 1974).

Block, Herbert. "Value and Burden of Soviet Defense," in Joint Economic Committee (eds.), *Soviet Economic Prospects for the Seventies* (Washington, D.C.: Government Printing Office, 1973).

Bochkarev, L. "The Question of the Sociological Aspect of the Struggle Against the Forces of Aggression and War," *Voyennaya Mysl',* No. 9 (September, 1968).

Brennan, Donald G. "Commentary," *International Security* (Winter, 1978), pp. 193-98.

Chuikov, V.I. "The Defense of the Population is the Main Task of Civil Defense," *Military Knowledge,* No. 1 (January, 1964).

Cousins, Norman. "Notes on a 1963 visit with Khrushchev," *Saturday Review* (November 7, 1964).

Deane, Michael J. "The Soviet Assessment of the 'Correlation of World Forces': Implications for American Foreign Policy," *Orbis* (Fall, 1976), pp. 625-36.

Douglass, Joseph C., Jr. "Soviet Nuclear Strategy in Europe: A Selective Targeting Doctrine?," *Strategic Review,* No. 5 (Fall, 1977).

Erickson, John. "The Chimera of Mutual Deterrence," *Strategic Review* (Spring, 1978).

Erickson, John. "The Soviet View of Deterrence: A General Survey," *Survival,* Vol. 24, No. 6 (November-December, 1982).

Erickson, John. "The Warsaw Pact: From Here to Eternity," *Current History,* Vol. 184, No. 505 (November, 1985).

Ermarth, Fritz W. "Contrasts in American and Soviet Strategic Thought," *International Security,* Vol. 3, No. 2 (Fall, 1978).

Fletcher, James C. "The Technologies for Ballistic Missile Defense," *Issues in Science and Technology* (Fall, 1984).

Frye, Alton. "Strategic Synthesis," *Foreign Policy,* No. 58 (Spring, 1985).

Gallagher, Matthew P. "The Military Role in Soviet Decision-Making," in M. MccGwire *et al.* (eds.), *Soviet Naval Policy: Objectives and Constraints* (New York: Praeger, 1975).

Garthoff, Raymond L. "BMD and East-West Relations," in Ashton B. Carter *et al.* (eds.), *Ballistic Missile Defense* (Washington, D.C.: The Brookings Institution, 1984).

Garthoff, Raymond L. "Khrushchev and the Military," in Alexander Dallin *et al.* (eds.), *Politics in the Soviet Union* (New York: Harcourt, Brace and World, 1966).

Garthoff, Raymond L. "Mutual Deterrence and Strategic Arms Limitation in Soviet Policy," *International Security,* Vol. 3 (Summer, 1978).

Garthoff, Raymond L. "Negotiating with the Russians: Some Lessons from SALT," *International Security* (Spring, 1977).

Garthoff, Raymond L. "On Estimating and Imputing Intentions," *International Security* (Winter, 1978), pp.22-32.

Garthoff, Raymond L. "SALT I: An Evaluation," *World Politics* (October, 1978).

Garthoff, Raymond L. "SALT and the Soviet Military," *Problems of Communism* (January-February, 1975).

Gerasimov, G. "The First-Strike Theory," *International Affairs,* No. 3 (March, 1965), pp.39-45.

Gerasimov, G. "Game Theory in the Service of American Militarist," *Problemy vojny i mira,* June 25, 1967, pp.244-61.

Gerasimov, G. "Theory of Games and International Relations," *Mirovaja ekonomika i mezdunarodnye otnosenija,* No. 7 (1966), pp.101-108.

Gordon, Michael. "CIA is Skeptical That New Radar is Part of an ABM Defense System," *National Journal* (March 9, 1985), pp.523-24.

Gottemoeller, Rose E. "Soviet Arms Control Decision Making since Brezhnev," in Roman Kolkowicz *et al.* (eds.), *The Soviet Calculus of Nuclear War* (Massachusetts: Lexington Books, 1986).

Goure, Leon *et al.* "The Soviet Strategic View," *Strategic Review* (Winter, 1980).

Grechko, A.A. "V.D. Lenin and the Building of the Soviet Armed Forces," *Kommunist,* No. 3 (February, 1969).

Halperin, Morton H. "The Decision to Deploy the ABM: Bureaucratic and Domestic Politics in the Johnson Administration," *World Politics,* Vol. 24 (October, 1972), pp.62-95.

Hoffman, Hubertus G. "A Missile Defense for Europe?," *Strategic Review* (Summer, 1984).

Holloway, David. "Military Power and Political Purpose in Soviet Policy," *Daedalus* (Fall, 1980).

Holloway, David. "Research Note: Soviet Thermonuclear Development," *International Security* (Winter, 1979-80), pp.192-197.

Horelick, A. "The Cuban Missile Crisis: An Analysis of Soviet Calculations and Behavior," *World Politics,* No. 3 (April, 1964).

Hough, Jerry E. "Gorbachev's Strategy," *Foreign Affairs* (Fall, 1985).

Hyland, William G. "The USSR and Nuclear War," in Barry M. Blechman (ed.), *Rethinking the U.S. Strategic Posture* (Cambridge: Ballinger Publishing Co., 1982), pp.47-75.

Ivanov, S.P. "Soviet Military Doctrine and Strategy," *Voyennaya mysl',* No. 5 (May, 1969).

Jackson, William D. "The Soviets and Strategic Arms: Toward an Evaluation of the Record," *Political Science Quarterly,* Vol. 94, No. 2 (Summer, 1979).

Jones, Ellen. "Soviet Military Manpower: Prospects in the 1980s," *Strategic Studies* (Fall, 1981).

Joubert, P. "Long Range Air Attack," in A. Lee (ed.), *The Soviet Air and Rocket Forces* (New York: Praeger, 1959).

Kaplan, Fred. "The Soviet Civil Defense Myth," *The Bulletin of Atomic Scientists.* Vol. 34, Nos. 3 & 4 (March-April, 1978).

Kaufman, Richard F. "Causes of the Slowdown in Soviet Defense," *Soviet Economy,* Vol. 1 (January-March, 1985), pp.9-41.

Kolkowicz, Roman. "Strategic Elites and Politics of Superpowers," *Journal of International Affairs,* Vol. 26, No. 1 (1972).

Kolkowicz, Roman. "Strategic Parity and Beyond: Soviet Perspectives," *World Politics* (April, 1971).

Kolkowicz, Roman. "U.S. and Soviet Approaches to Military Strategy: Theory vs. Experience," *Orbis* (Summer, 1981).

Korotkov, I. "The Development of Soviet Military Theory in the Postwar Years," *Voenno-istoricheskii Zhurnal,* No. 4 (April, 1964).

Krepon, Michael. "Dormant Threat to the ABM Treaty," *Bulletin of the Atomic Scientists* (January, 1986), pp.31-33.

Krylov, Marshal N.I. "The Nuclear Shield of the Soviet State," *Voyennaya mysl',* No. 11 (November, 1967).

Lambeth, Benjamin S. "The Political Potential of Soviet Equivalence," *International Security* (Fall, 1979).

Lee, William T. "Soviet Targeting Strategy and SALT," *Air Force Magazine* (September, 1978).

Lerner, Eric J. "Electromagnetic Pulse: Potential Crippler," *IEEE Spectrum* (May, 1981).

McNamara, Robert. "The Military Role of Nuclear Weapons: Perceptions and Misperceptions," *Foreign Affairs,* Vol. 62, No. 1 (Fall, 1983).

Meyer, Stephen M. "Civilian and Military Influence in Managing the Arms Race in the U.S.S.R.," in Robert J. Art *et al., Reorganizing America's Defense* (New York: Pergamon-Brassey's, 1985).

Meyer, Stephen M. "Soviet Theatre Nuclear Forces, Part I: Development of Doctrine and Objectives." *Adelphi Paper No. 188* (London: *The International Institute for Strategic Studies,* 1984).

Meyer, Stephen M. "Soviet Theatre Nuclear Forces: Part II: Capabilities and Implications," *Adelphi Paper No. 187* (London: *The International Institute for Strategic Studies,* 1984).

Moffit, Robert E. "The Cruise Missile and SALT II," *International Security Review,* Vol. 4 (Fall, 1979).

Ogarkov, N.V. "In the Interests of Raising Combat Readiness," *Kommunist vooruzhennykh sil,* No. 14 (July, 1980).

Peterson, Philip A. "'Flexibility': A Driving Force in Soviet Strategy," *Air Force Magazine* (March, 1980).

Peterson, Philip A. *et al.,* "The Conventional Offensive in Soviet Theater Strategy," *Orbis* (Fall, 1983).

Petrovskaja, L.A. "On a Militaristic Conception of International Conflict," *Naucnye doklady vyssej skoly filosofskie nauki,* No. 3 (1968), pp.94-103.

Pipes, Richard. "Why the Soviet Union Thinks it Could Fight and Win a Nuclear War," *Commentary,* Vol. 64 (July, 1977).

Popov, N.G. *et al.* "Basic and Applied Military Science Research," *Voyennaya mysl',* No. 9 (September, 1977).

Proektor, D. "Two Approaches to Military Policy," *Novoye vremya,* No. 48 (November, 1978).

Raloff, Janet. "EMP: A Sleeping Electronic Dragon," *Science News* (May 9, 1981).

Reitz, James T. "Underrating Soviet Might," *Problems of Communism* (November-December, 1983).

Rivkin, David B., Jr. "What Does Moscow Think?," *Foreign Policy,* No. 59 (Summer, 1985).

Robinson, Clarence A., Jr. "Soviets Push for a Beam Weapon," *Aviation Week and Space Technology* (May 2, 1977), pp.16-61.

Robinson, Thomas. "Game Theory and Politics: Recent Soviet Views," *Studies in Soviet Thought,* Vol. 10 (1970), pp.291-315.

Ross, Dennis. "Rethinking Soviet Strategic Policy: Inputs and Implications," in John Batlsis *et al., Soviet Strategy* (London: Croom Helm, 1981).

Schear, James A. "Arms Control Treaty Compliance," *International Security,* Vol. 10, No. 2 (Fall, 1985).

Schwartz, Morton. "The Cuban Missile Venture," in James B. Christoph *et al., Cases in Comparative Politics,* 3rd ed. (Boston: Little, Brown & Co., 1976).

Scott, William F. "Troops of National Air Defense," *Air Force Magazine* (March, 1978).

Sheer, Alan B. "The Language of Arms Control," *Bulletin of the Atomic Scientists* (November, 1985), pp.23-29.

Shenfield, Stephen. "Soviets may not imitate Star Wars," *Bulletin of the Atomic Scientists* (June-July, 1985).

Shirokov, M. "Military Geography at the Present Stage," *Voennaia Mysl',* No. 11 (1966).

Smith, Hedrick. "Geneva: A Test of Two Wills," *The New York Times Magazine* (November 17, 1985).

Soll, Richard S. "The Soviet Union and Protracted Nuclear War," *Strategic Review* (Fall, 1980), pp.15-28.

Steinbrunner, John. "Nuclear Decapitation," *Foreign Policy* (Winter, 1981-82).

Steinbrunner, John. "Strategic Command and Control Vulnerabilities: Dangers and Remedies," *Orbis,* Vol. 26, No. 4 (Winter, 1983).

Stevens, Sayre. "The Soviet BMD Program," in Ashton B. Carter *et al.* (eds.) *Ballistic Missile Defense* (Washington, D.C.: The Brookings Institution, 1984).

Strode, Rebecca V. "Space-Based Lasers for Ballistic Missile Defense: Soviet Policy Options," in Keith B. Payne (ed.), *Laser Weapons in Space: Policy and Doctrine* (Boulder, Colo.: Westview Press, 1983).

Tabunov, N. "New Weapons and the Moral Factor," *Kommunist vooruzhennykh sil,* No. 2 (January, 1969), pp.25-32.

Thorpe, Claude R. "Mission Priorities of the Soviet Navy," in Paul J. Murphy (ed.), *Naval Power in Soviet Policy* (Washington, D.C.: U.S. Government Printing Office, 1978).

Trofimenko, Henry A. "Counterforce: Illusion of a Panacea," *International Security,* Vol. 5 (Spring, 1981), pp.28-49.

Vagts, Alfred. "Land and Sea Power in the Second German Reich," *Journal of the American Military Institute,* Vol. 3 (Winter, 1939).

Valenta, Juri. "Soviet Use of Surprise and Deception," *Survival,* Vol. 24, No. 2 (January-April, 1982), pp.50-59.

Vick, Alan J. "Post-Attack Strategic Command and Control Survival: Options for the Future," *Orbis,* Vol. 29, No. 1 (Spring, 1985), pp.95-117.

Vorob'ev, N.N. "Some Methodological Problems of the Theory of Games," *Voprosy filosofii,* No. 1 (1966), pp. 93-103.

Waltz, Kenneth N. "International Structure, National Force, and the Balance of World Power," *Journal of World Affairs,* Vol. 21, No. 2 (1967), pp.215-231.

Warner, Edward L. "Defense Policymaking in the Soviet Union," in Robert J. Art *et al., Reorganizing America's Defense* (New York: Pergamon-Brassey's, 1985).

Warner, Edward L.: "The Soviet Military," *Problems of Communism,* Vol. 23 (March-April, 1974).

Wessel, Nils H. "Soviet-American Arms Control Negotiations," *Current History* (May, 1983).

Wit, Joel S. "Advances in Antisubmarine Warfare," *Scientific American,* Vol. 244, No. 2 (February, 1981).

Wit, Joel S. "American SLBM: Counterforce Options and Strategic Implications," *Survival,* Vol. 24, Nos. 4-5 (July-October, 1982), pp.163-174.

Wohlstetter, Albert. "The Delicate Balance of Terror," *Foreign Affairs,* Vol. 37, No. 2 (January, 1959).

Yost, David S. "Soviet Ballistic Missile Defense and NATO," *Orbis,* Vol. 29, No. 3 (Summer, 1985).

Zav'yalov, I. "Evolution in the Correlation of Strategy, Operational Art and Tactics," *Military Thought,* No. 2 (1971).

Books

Alexander, Arthur J. *Decision-Making in Soviet Weapons Procurement.* London: International Institute for Strategic Studies, 1978-79.

Allison, Graham T. *Essence of Decision: Explaining the Cuban Missile Crisis.* Boston: Little, Brown & Co., 1971.

Arkin, William M. *et al. Nuclear Battlefields: Global Links in the Arms Race.* Cambridge: Ballinger Publishing Co., 1985.

Art, Robert J. *et al. Reorganizing America's Defense.* New York: Pergamon-Brassey's, 1985.

Astashenkov, P. *Kurchatov.* Moscow: 1968.

Ball, Desmond, *Can Nuclear War be Controlled?* London: International Institute for Strategic Studies, 1981.

Ball, Desmond. *Politics and Force Levels: The Strategic Missile Program of the Kennedy Administration.* Berkeley: University of California Press, 1980.

Barber, Noel. *The Week France Fell.* New York: Stein & Day, 1976.

Barnett, Richard J. *Real Security: Restoring American Power in a Dangerous Decade.* New York: Touchstone Books, 1981.

Barron, John. *MIG Pilot: The Final Escape of Lt. Belenko.* New York: Avon Books, 1980.

Berman, Robert P. *Soviet Air Power in Transition.* Washington, D.C.: The Brookings Institution, 1978.

Berman, Robert P. and Baker, John C. *Soviet Strategic Forces: Requirements and Responses.* Washington, D.C.: The Brookings Institution, 1982.

Betts, Richard K. (ed.) *Cruise Missiles: Technology, Strategy, Politics.* Washington, D.C.: The Brookings Institution, 1981.

Blechman, Harry M. (ed.). *Rethinking the U.S. Strategic Posture.* Cambridge: Ballinger Publishing Co., 1982.

Bloomfield, L. *et al. Khrushchev and the Arms Race.* Cambridge: MIT Press, 1966.

Bracken, Paul. *The Command and Control of Nuclear Forces.* New Haven: Yale University Press, 1983.

Byrnes, Robert F. (ed.). *After Brezhnev.* Bloomington: Indiana University Press, 1983.

Carnesdale, Arthur. *et al. Living with Nuclear Weapons.* New York: Bantam Books, 1983.

Carter, Ashton B. *et al.* (eds.). *Ballistic Missile Defense.* Washington, D.C.: The Brookings Institution, 1984.

Cockburn, Andrew. *The Threat: Inside the Soviet Military Machine.* New York: Random House, 1983.

Colton, Timothy. *Commissars, Commanders and Civilian Authority: The Structure of Soviet Military Politics.* Cambridge: Harvard University Press, 1979.

Cunningham, Ann M. *et al. Future Fire.* New York: Warner Books, 1983.

Dallin, Alexander (ed.). *Politics in the Soviet Union.* New York: Brace and World, 1966.

Dinerstein, Herbert S. *The Making of a Missile Crisis. October 1962.* Baltimore: Johns Hopkins University Press, 1976.

Dinerstein, Herbert S. *War and the Soviet Union: Nuclear Weapons and the Revolution in Soviet Military and Political Thinking.* New York: Praeger, 1959.

Douglass, Joseph D., Jr. *et al. Conventional War and Escalation: The Soviet View.* New York: Crane, Russak & Co., 1981.

Douglass, Joseph D., Jr. *Soviet Strategy for Nuclear War.* Stanford: Hoover Institution Press, 1979.

Douglass, Joseph D., Jr. *The Soviet Theater Nuclear Offensive.* Washington, D.C.: U.S. Government Printing Office, 1976.

Dunnigan, James F. *How to Make War.* New York: Quill, 1983.

Dziak, John J. *Soviet Perceptions of Military Power: The Interaction of Theory and Practice.* New York: Crane, Russak & Co., 1981.

Erickson, John. *Soviet Military Power.* London: Royal United Services Institute for Defense Studies, 1972.

Erickson, John (ed.). *The Military-Technical Revolution.* New York: Praeger, 1966.

Erickson, John *et al. Soviet Military Power and Performance.* Hamden, Ct.: The Shoestring Press.

Fedorov, G. *et al. Marxism-Leninism on War and Army.* 5th ed. Moscow: Progress Publishers, 1972.

Freedman, Lawrence. *The Evolution of Nuclear Strategy.* New York: St. Martin's Press, 1983.

Freedman, Lawrence. *U.S. Intelligence and the Soviet Strategic Threat.* Boulder, Colo.: Westview Press, 1977.

Frunze, M.V. *Izbranneye proizvedeniia.* Moscow: Voenizdat, 1965.

Gaddis, John. *The United States and the Origins of the Cold War 1941-1947.* New York: Columbia University Press, 1972.

Gallagher, M.P. *et al. Soviet Decision-Making for Defense: A Critique of U.S. Perspectives on the Arms Race.* New York: Praeger, 1972.

Garthoff, Raymond. *Detente and Confrontation: Soviet-American Relations from Nixon to Reagan.* Washington, D.C.: The Brookings Institution, 1985.

Garthoff, Raymond. *Soviet Strategy in the Nuclear Age.* New York: Praeger Press, 1958.

George, Alexander *et al. Deterrence in American Foreign Policy.* New York: Columbia University Press, 1974.

Goldman, Harry. *The Brezhnev Politburo and the Decline of Detente.* Ithaca: Cornell University Press, 1984.

Goure, Leon. *War Survival in Soviet Strategy: Soviet Civil Defense.* Coral Gables, Fla.: Center for Advanced International Studies, University of Miami, 1976.

Goure, Leon *et al. The Role of Nuclear Forces in Current Soviet Strategy.* Coral Gables, Fla.: Center for Advanced International Studies, University of Miami, 1974.

Graham, Daniel L. *Shall America be Defended.* Arlington House, 1979.

Grechko, A.A. *The Armed Forces of the Soviet Union.* Moscow: Progress Publishers, 1977.

Grechko, A.A. *Na Strazhe mira i stroitel'stva Kommunizma.* Moscow: 1971.

Grechko, A.A. *Vooruzhenny Sily Sovetsskogo Gosudarstva.* 2nd ed. Moscow: Voyenizdat, 1975.

Green, Philip. *Deadly Logic: The Theory of Nuclear Deterrence.* Columbus: Ohio State University, 1966.

Holloway, David. *The Soviet Union and the Arms Race.* 2nd ed. New Haven: Yale University Press, 1984.

Holst, John J. *Comparative U.S. and Soviet Deployments, Doctrines and Arms Limitation.* Chicago: University of Chicago, 1970.

Horelick, A.L. and Rush, M. *Strategic Power and Soviet Foreign Policy.* Chicago: University of Chicago Press, 1965.

Huntington, Samuel P. *The Soldier and the State: The Theory and Politics of Civil-Military Relations.* Harvard University Press, 1981.

Isby, David C. *Weapons and Tactics of the Soviet Army.* New York: Jares, 1981.

Ivanov, S.P. (ed.). *Nachal'nyy period voyny.* Moscow: 1974.

Jones, D.R. (ed.). *Soviet Armed Forces Review Annual.* Gulf Breeze, Fla.: Academic International, 1980.

Kaplan, Fred. *The Wizards of Armageddon.* New York: Simon & Schuster, 1983.

Khrushchev, Nikita. *Khrushchev Remembers.* Boston: Little, Brown, 1970.

Khrushchev, Nikita. *Khrushchev Remembers: The Last Testament.* New York: Bantam Books, 1976.

Kolkowicz, Roman. *The Dilemma of Superpower: Soviet Policy and Strategy in Transition.* Washington, D.C.: Institute for Defense Analysis, 1967.
Kolkowicz, Roman. *The Soviet Military and the Communist Party.* Princeton: Princeton University Press, 1967.
Kolkowicz, Roman *et al. The Soviet Calculus of Nuclear War.* Massachusetts: Lexington Books, 1986.
Kramish, Arnold. *Atomic Energy in the Soviet Union.* Stanford University Press, 1959.
Kruger, C.H. *et al. Causes and Effects of Stratospheric Ozone Reduction: An Update.* Washington, D.C.: National Academy of Sciences, 1982.
Kulish, V.M. *Military Forces and International Relations.* Moscow: Izdatel'stvo Mezhdunarodyne Otnosheniia, 1972.

Laird, Robbin F. *et al. The Soviet Union and Strategic Arms.* Boulder, Colo.: Westview Press, 1984.
Lambeth, Benjamin S. *The Politics of the Soviet Military under Brezhnev and Kosygin.* Washington, D.C.: Georgetown University Press, 1968.
Lambeth, Benjamin S. *Selective Nuclear Options in American and Soviet Strategic Policy.* Santa Monica: The RAND Corporation, 1976.
Lambeth, Benjamin S. *The State of Western Research on Soviet Military Strategy and Policy.* Santa Monica: The RAND Corporation, 1984.
Lee, A. (ed.). *The Soviet Air and Rocket Forces.* New York: Praeger, 1959.
Lee, William T. *Military Decision-Making in the USSR: An Approach to the Problems.* Unpublished manuscript, 1977.
Leebert, Derek (ed.). *Soviet Military Thinking.* London: Allen & Unwin, 1981.
Legge, J. Michael. *Theater Nuclear Weapons and the NATO Strategy of Flexible Response.* Santa Monica: Rand Corporation, 1983.
Leites, Nathan. *Soviet Style in War.* New York: Crane, Russak, 1982.
Lifton, Robert J. *et al. Indefensible Weapons: The Political and Psychological Case Against Nuclearism.* New York: Basic Books, 1982.
Linden, Carl A. *Khrushchev and the Soviet Leadership. 1957-1964.* Baltimore: Johns Hopkins Press, 1966.
Linz, Susan J. *The Impact of World War II on the Soviet Union.* Totowa, N.J.: Rowman & Allanheld, 1985.
Lockwood, Jonathan S. *The Soviet View of U.S. Strategic Doctrine.* New Brunswick, N.J.: Transaction Books, 1983.

MccGwire, M. *et al.* (eds.). *Soviet Naval Policy: Objectives and Constraints.* New York: Praeger, 1975.
Miller, Mark. *Soviet Strategic Power and Doctrine: The Quest for Superiority.* Washington, D.C.: Advanced International Studies Institute, 1982.

Newhouse, John. *Cold Dawn: The Story of SALT.* New York: Holt, Rinehart & Winston, 1973.
Nicholson, Arthur D., Jr. *The Soviet Union and Strategic Nuclear War.* Monterey: Naval Postgraduate School, 1980.
Nikolayev, M.N. *Snaryad protiv snaryada.* Moscow: Voyenizdat, 1960.
Nye, Joseph S., Jr. *The Making of America's Soviet Policy.* New Haven: Yale University Press, 1985.

The Penkovskiy Papers. New York: Doubleday, 1965.
Pierre, Andrew J. (ed.). *Nuclear Weapons in Europe.* New York: New York University Press, 1985.
Pipes, Richard. *Soviet Strategy in Europe.* New York: Crane, Russak, 1976.
Polmar, Norman. *Strategic Weapons.* New York: Crane, Russak, 1982.
Power, Thomas S. *Design for Survival.* New York: Coward-McCann, 1964.
Prados, John. *The Soviet Estimate: U.S. Intelligence Analysis and Russian Military Strength.* New York: Dial, 1982.

Riker, William H. *et al. An Introduction to Positive Theory.* Englewood Cliffs, N.J.: Prentice-Hall, 1973.
Romanov, P.I. *et al. Konstitutsiia SSSR i zashchita otchestva.* Moscow: Voenizdat, 1983.
Russet, Bruce *et al. World Politics: The Menu for Choice.* San Francisco: W.H. Freeman & Co., 1981.

Schauer, William H. *The Politics of Space: A Comparison of the Soviet and American Space Programs.* New York: Holmes & Meiers, 1976.
Scheer, Robert. *With Enough Shovels: Reagan, Bush and Nuclear War.* New York: Random House, 1982.
Schwartz, Morton. *Soviet Perceptions of the United States.* Los Angeles: University of California Press, 1978.
Scott, Harriet F. *Soviet Military Doctrine: Its Continuity 1960-1970.* Stanford: Stanford University Research Institute, 1971.
Scott, Harriet F. *et al. The Soviet Art of War.* Boulder, Colo.: Westview Press, 1982.
Scott, Harriet F. *The Soviet Control Structure and Capabilities for Wartime Survival.* New York: Crane, Russak & Co., 1983.
Seaborg, Glenn T. *Kennedy, Khrushchev and the Test Ban.* Berkeley: University of California Press, 1981.
Shtemenko, S.M. *General'nyi shtab v gody voiny.* Moscow: Voenizdat, 1973.
Skirdo, M.P. *Narod armiya polkovodets.* Moscow: Voenizdat, 1970.
Smith, Gerard. *Doubletalk: The Story of the First Strategic Arms Limitations Talks.* New York: Doubleday, 1980.

Smoke, Richard. *National Security and the Nuclear Dilemma: An Introduction to the American Experience*. Mass.: Addison-Wesley Publishing Co., 1984.

Snyder, Glenn. *Deterrence and Defense*. Princeton: Princeton University Press, 1961.

Snyder, Jack L. *The Soviet Strategic Culture: Implications for Limited Nuclear Operations*. Santa Monica: RAND Corporation, 1977.

Sokolovsky, Marshal V.D. (ed.). *Military Strategy: Soviet Doctrine and Concepts*. New York: Praeger, 1967.

Sorensen, Theodore C. *Kennedy*. New York: Bantam Books, 1966.

Spanier, John. *American Foreign Policy Since World War II*. 9th ed. New York: Holt, Rinehart & Winston, 1983.

Spanier, John. *Games Nations Play*. 4th ed. New York: Holt, Rinehart & Winston, 1983.

Spielmann, Karl F. *Analyzing Soviet Strategic Decisions*. Boulder, Colo.: Westview Press, 1979.

Stalin, J.V. *Works*. Stanford, 1967.

Stoiko, Michael. *Soviet Rocketry: Past, Present and Future*. New York: Holt, Rinehart and Winston, 1970.

Takeuchi, Kiyoshi *et al*. *Selected Russian Papers on Game Theory, 1959-1965*. Princeton: Princeton University Econometric Research Program, 1968.

Talbott, Strobe. *Deadly Gambits: The Reagan Administration and the Stalemate in Nuclear Arms Control*. New York: Knopf, 1984.

Talbott, Strobe. *Endgame: The Inside Story of SALT II*. New York: Harper Colophon Books, 1980.

Tatu, Michael. *Power in the Kremlin*. New York: Viking Press, 1969.

Tokaev, G.A. *Stalin Means War*. London: George Weidenfeld & Nicolson, Ltd., 1951.

Tolubko, V. *Nedelin*. Moscow: 1979.

Trofimenko, Henry. *Changing Attitudes Toward Deterrence*. Los Angeles: UCLA Center for International and Strategic Affairs, 1980.

Tucker, Robert C. *The Soviet Political Mind: Studies in Stalinism and Post Stalin Change*. New York: W.W. Norton & Co., 1971.

Valenta, Jiri. *et al*. *Soviet Decision-Making for National Security*. London: George Allen & Unwin, 1984.

Vorob'ev, N.N. *et al*. *Matrix Games, Infinite Antagonistic Games and Positional Games*. Moscow: Physics-Mathematics Publishing House, 1961.

Warner, Edward L. *The Military in Contemporary Soviet Politics*. New York: Praeger, 1977.

Werth, Alexander. *Russia at War.* New York: Avon Books, 1965.
Weston, Burns H. (ed.). *Toward Nuclear Disarmament and Global Security: A Search for Alternatives.* Boulder, Colo.: Westview Press, 1984.
Whetten, Lawrence L. (ed.). *The Future of Soviet Military Power.* New York: Crane, Russak & Co., 1976.
Wolfe, Thomas W. *Soviet Power and Europe 1945-1970.* Baltimore: The Johns Hopkins University Press, 1970.
Wolfe, Thomas W. *The Soviet Union and the Sino-Soviet Dispute.* Calif.: The RAND Corporation, 1965.

Zhukov, G.K. *Vospominanie i razmyshlenie.* Moscow: Novosti Press Agency, 1969.
Zimmerman, William. *Soviet Perspectives on International Relations, 1956-1967.* Princeton: Princeton University Press, 1969.

INDEX